I received a lot of chocolate again on Valentine's Day this year. I hear that every year around this time the *Jump* editorial office can't wait to find out what record-setting number of chocolates *The Prince of Tennis* receives will be. I hope it fills the office up to the ceiling. Thanks, everyone*!!*

— Takeshi Konomi, 2004

About Takeshi Konomi

Takeshi Konomi exploded onto the manga scene with the incredible **THE PRINCE OF TENNIS**. His refined art style and sleek character designs proved popular with **Weekly Shonen Jump** readers, and **THE PRINCE OF TENNIS** became the number one sports manga in Japan almost overnight. Its cast of fascinating male tennis players attracted legions of female readers even though it was originally intended to be a boys' comic. The manga continues to be a success in Japan and has inspired a hit anime series, as well as several video games and mountains of merchandise.

D0150123

THE PRINCE OF TENNIS
VOL. 23
The SHONEN JUMP Manga Edition

STORY AND ART BY
TAKESHI KONOMI

Translation/Joe Yamazaki
Consultant/Michelle Pangilinan
Touch-up Art & Lettering/Vanessa Satone
Design/Sam Elzway
Editor/Leyla Aker

Editor in Chief, Books/Alvin Lu
Editor in Chief, Magazines/Marc Weidenbaum
VP of Publishing Licensing/Rika Inouye
VP of Sales/Gonzalo Ferreyra
Sr. VP of Marketing/Liza Coppola
Publisher/Hyoe Narita

THE PRINCE OF TENNIS © 1999 by Takeshi Konomi. All rights reserved. First published in Japan in 1999 by SHUEISHA Inc., Tokyo. English translation rights in the United States of America, Canada and the United Kingdom arranged by SHUEISHA Inc. The stories, characters and incidents mentioned in this publication are entirely fictional.

No portion of this book may be reproduced or transmitted in any form or by any means without written permission from the copyright holders.

The rights of the author(s) of the work(s) in this publication to be so identified have been asserted in accordance with the Copyright, Designs and Patents Act 1988. A CIP catalogue record for this book is available from the British Library.

Printed in the U.S.A.

Published by VIZ Media, LLC
P.O. Box 77010
San Francisco, CA 94107

SHONEN JUMP Manga Edition
10 9 8 7 6 5 4 3 2 1
First printing, January 2008

PARENTAL ADVISORY
THE PRINCE OF TENNIS is rated A and is suitable for readers of all ages.
ratings.viz.com

www.viz.com

THE WORLD'S MOST POPULAR MANGA

www.shonenjump.com

テニスの王子

THE PRINCE OF TENNIS

VOL. 23
Rikkai's Law

Story & Art by
Takeshi Konomi

ENNIS CLUB

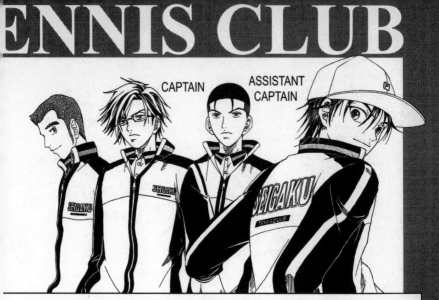

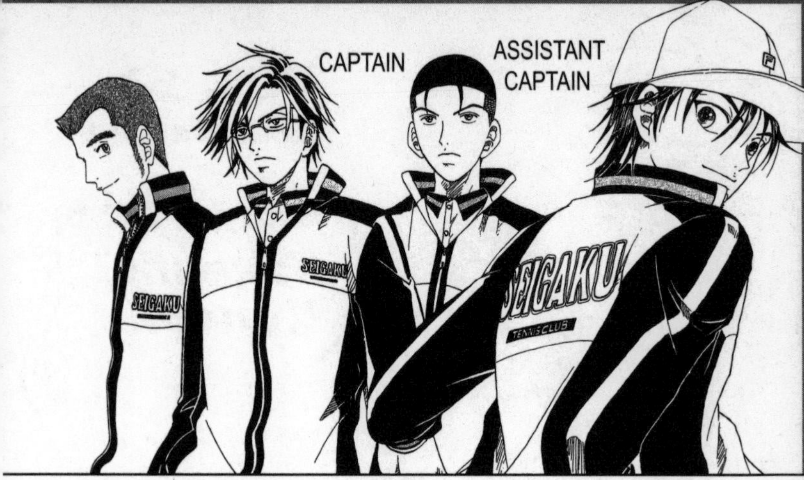
CAPTAIN
ASSISTANT CAPTAIN

●TAKASHI KAWAMURA ●KUNIMITSU TEZUKA ● SHUICHIRO OISHI ● RYOMA ECHIZEN ●

STORY & HARACTERS

Seishun Academy student Ryoma Echizen is a tennis prodigy with wins in four consecutive U.S. Junior tournaments under his belt. Then he became a starter as a 7th grader and led his team to the District Preliminaries! Despite a few mishaps, Seishun won the District Prelims and City Tournament, and even earned a ticket to the Kanto Tournament.

Seishun emerges victorious from the first round of the tournament but loses captain Kunimitsu and assistant captain Shuichiro to injury. However, the team members strengthen their unity and defeat Midoriyama and Rokkaku to reach the finals, where their opponent will be the reigning champions, Rikkai. After a fearsome impromptu match between Ryoma and Akaya Kirihara, the players on both teams prepare feverishly for their showdown. First up: Kaoru and Momo versus Bunta Marui and Jackal Kuwahara.

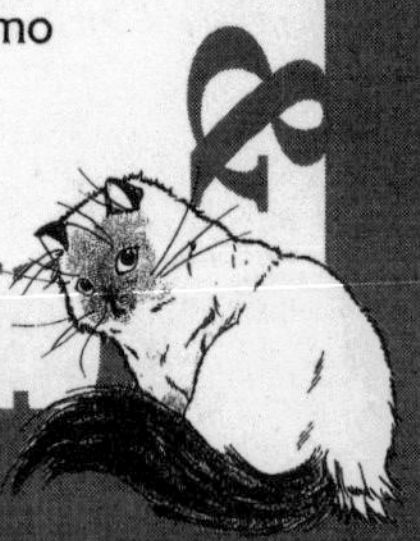

SEIGAKU T

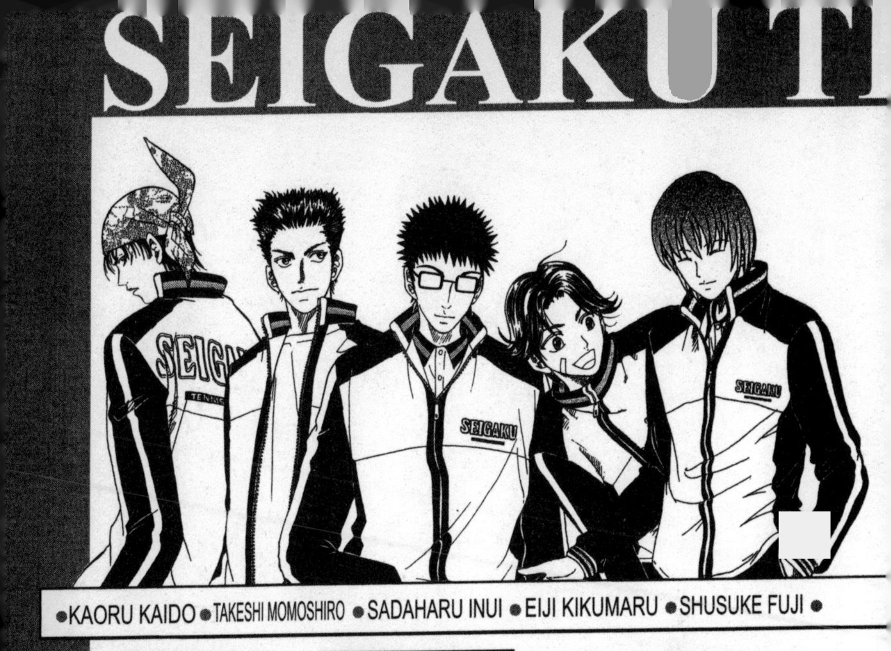

●KAORU KAIDO ●TAKESHI MOMOSHIRO ●SADAHARU INUI ●EIJI KIKUMARU ●SHUSUKE FUJI ●

THE PRINCE OF TENNIS

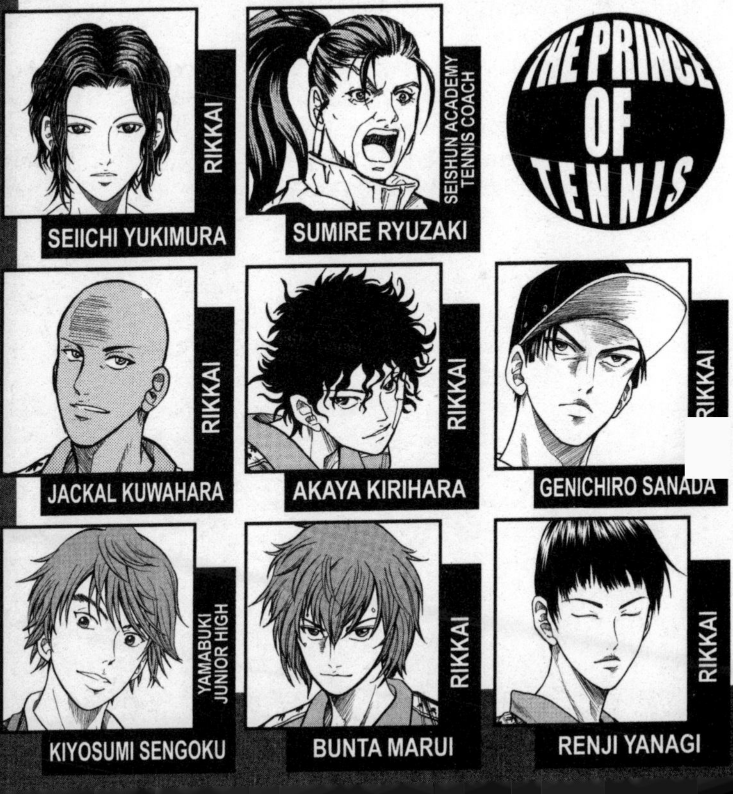
RIKKAI
SEIICHI YUKIMURA
SEISHUN ACADEMY TENNIS COACH
SUMIRE RYUZAKI
RIKKAI
JACKAL KUWAHARA
RIKKAI
AKAYA KIRIHARA
RIKKAI
GENICHIRO SANADA
YAMABUKI JUNIOR HIGH
KIYOSUMI SENGOKU
RIKKAI
BUNTA MARUI
RIKKAI
RENJI YANAGI

CONTENTS

Vol. 23
Rikkai's Law

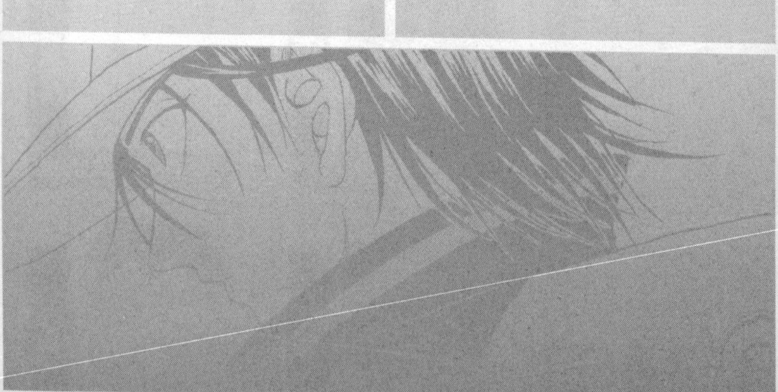

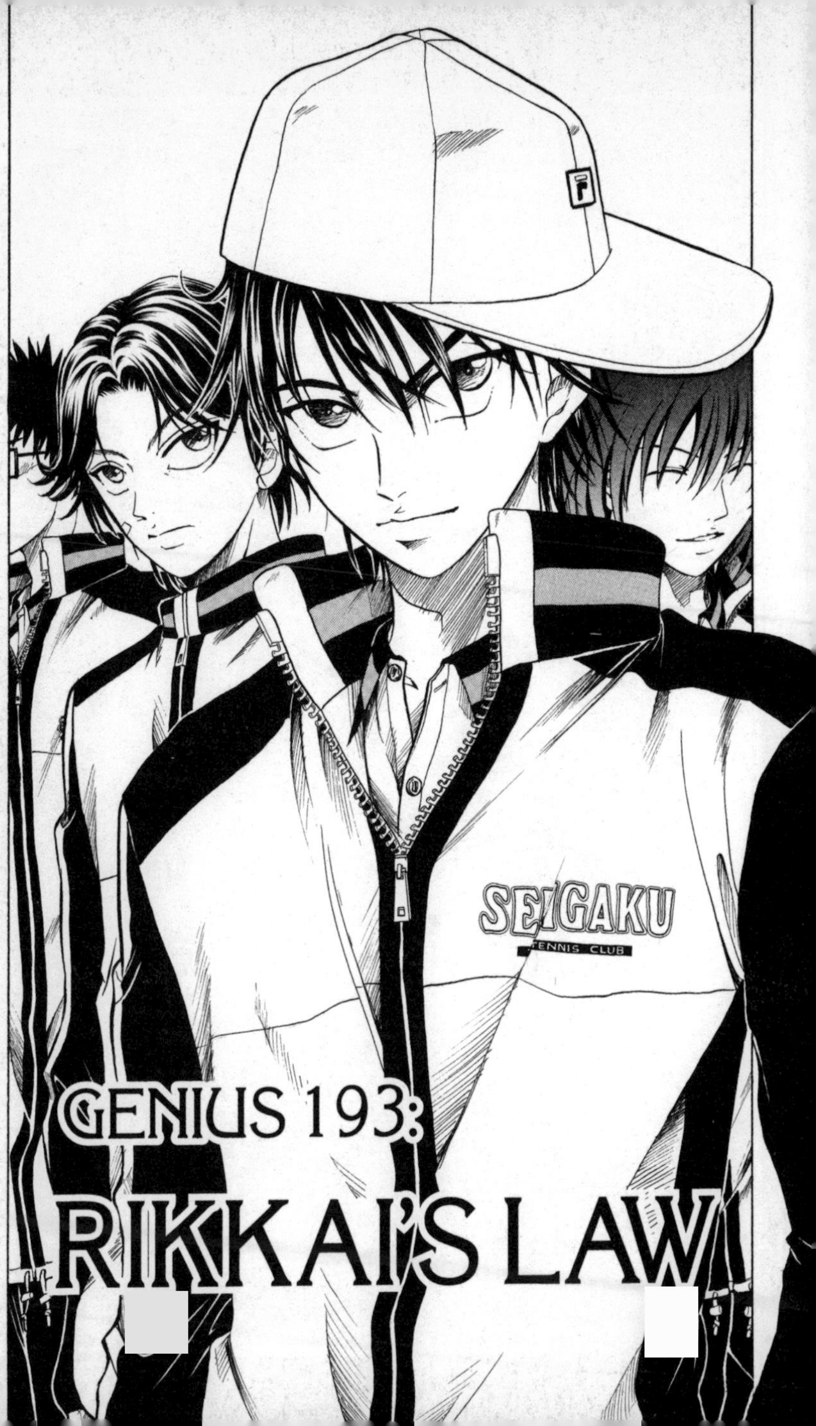
SEIGAKU
TENNIS CLUB
GENIUS 193:
RIKKAI'S LAW

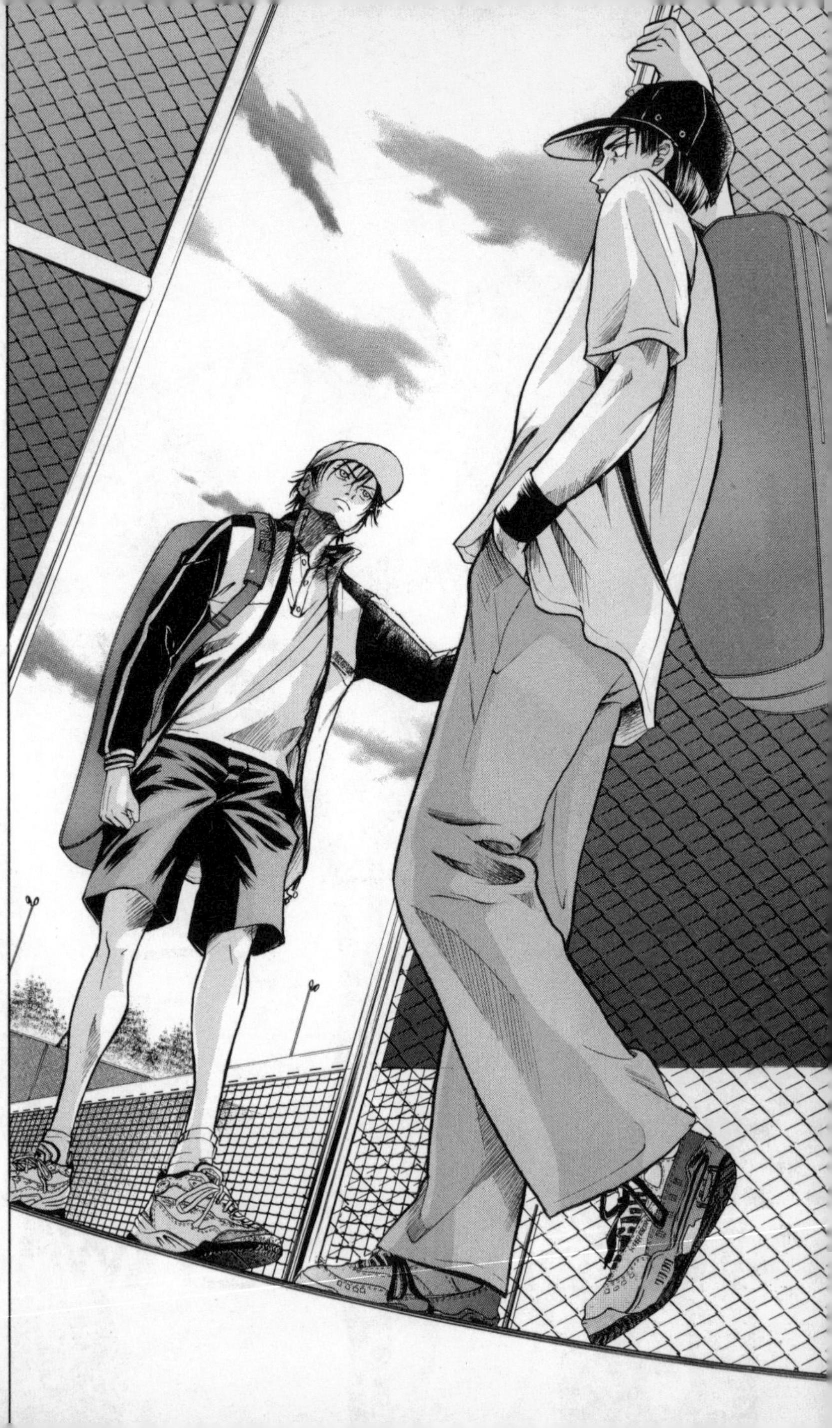

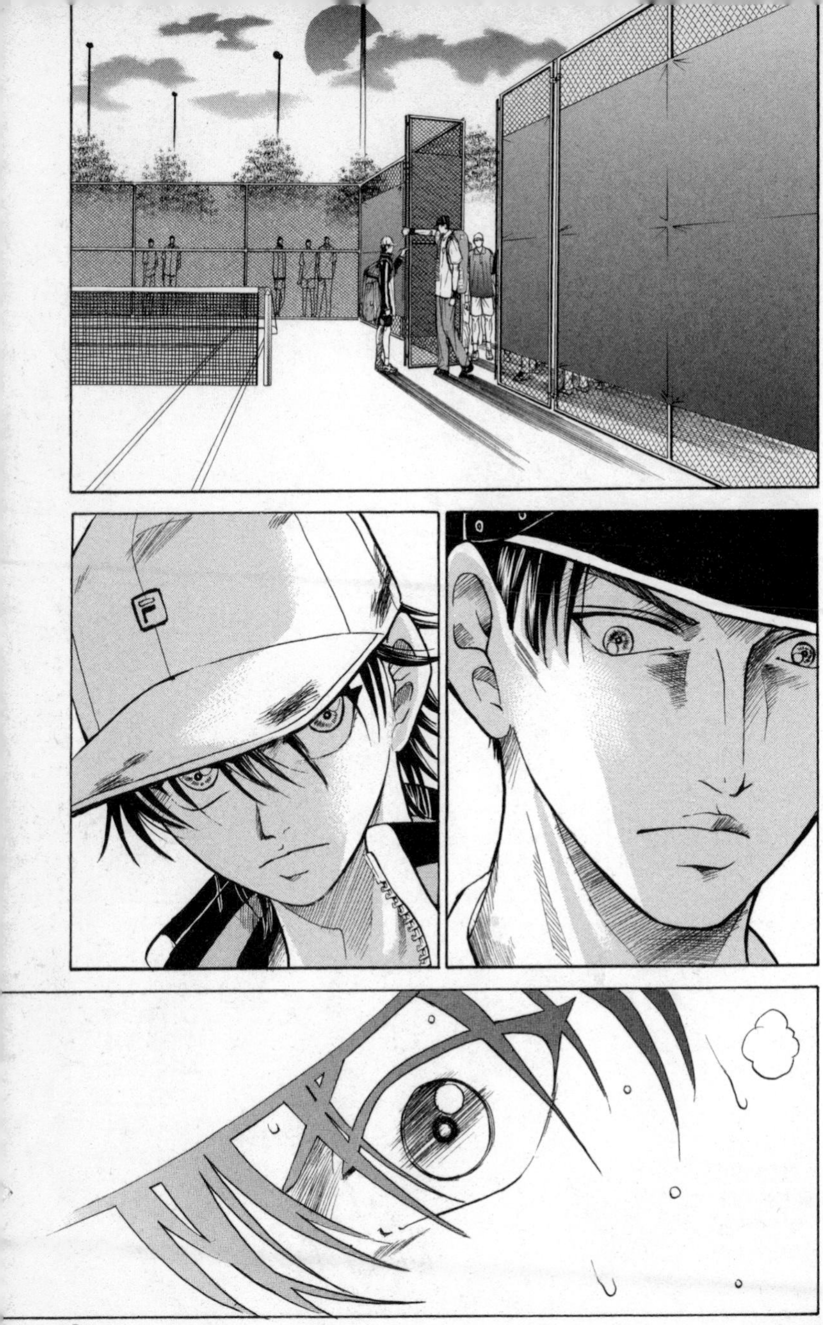

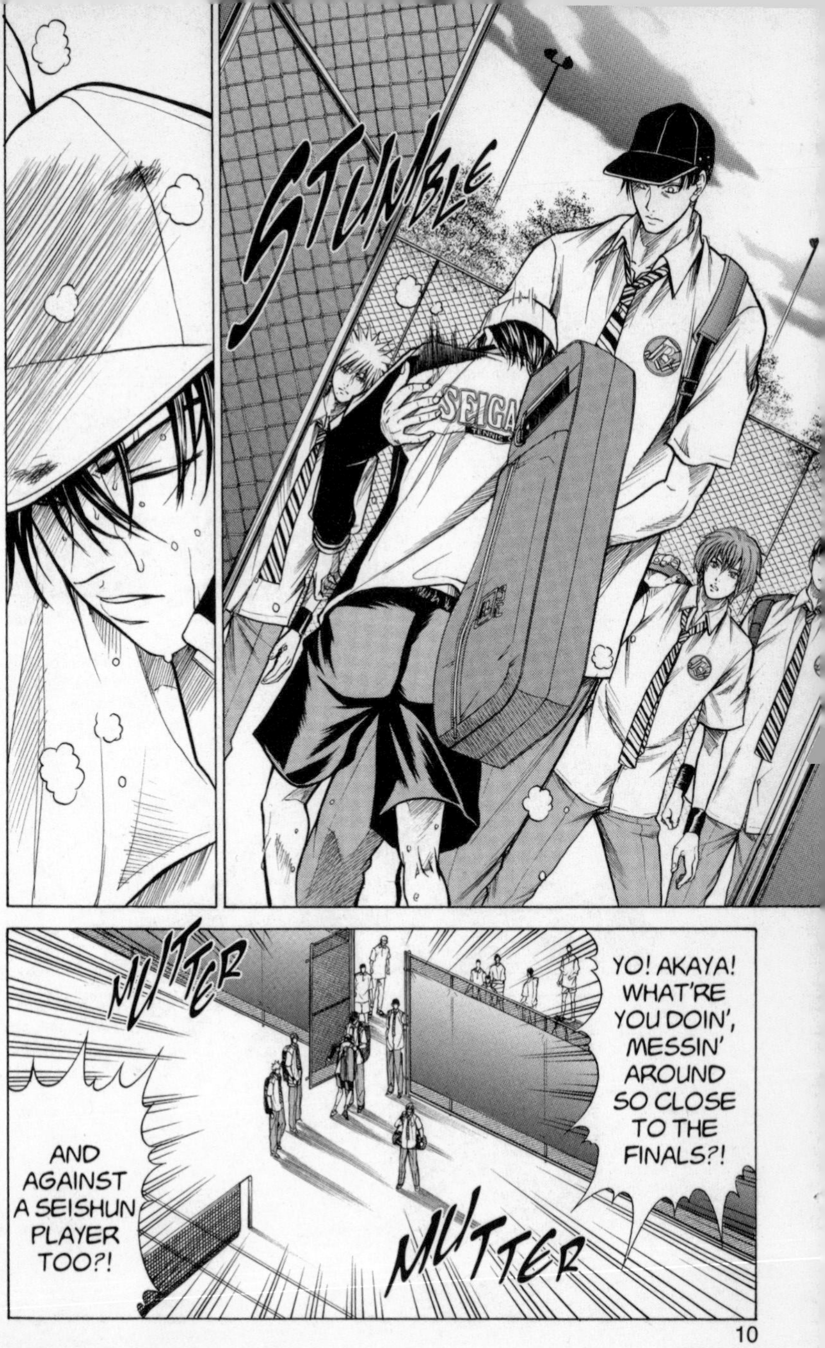
STUMBLE
YO! AKAYA! WHAT'RE YOU DOIN', MESSIN' AROUND SO CLOSE TO THE FINALS?!
MUTTER
AND AGAINST A SEISHUN PLAYER TOO?!
MUTTER

READ THIS WAY

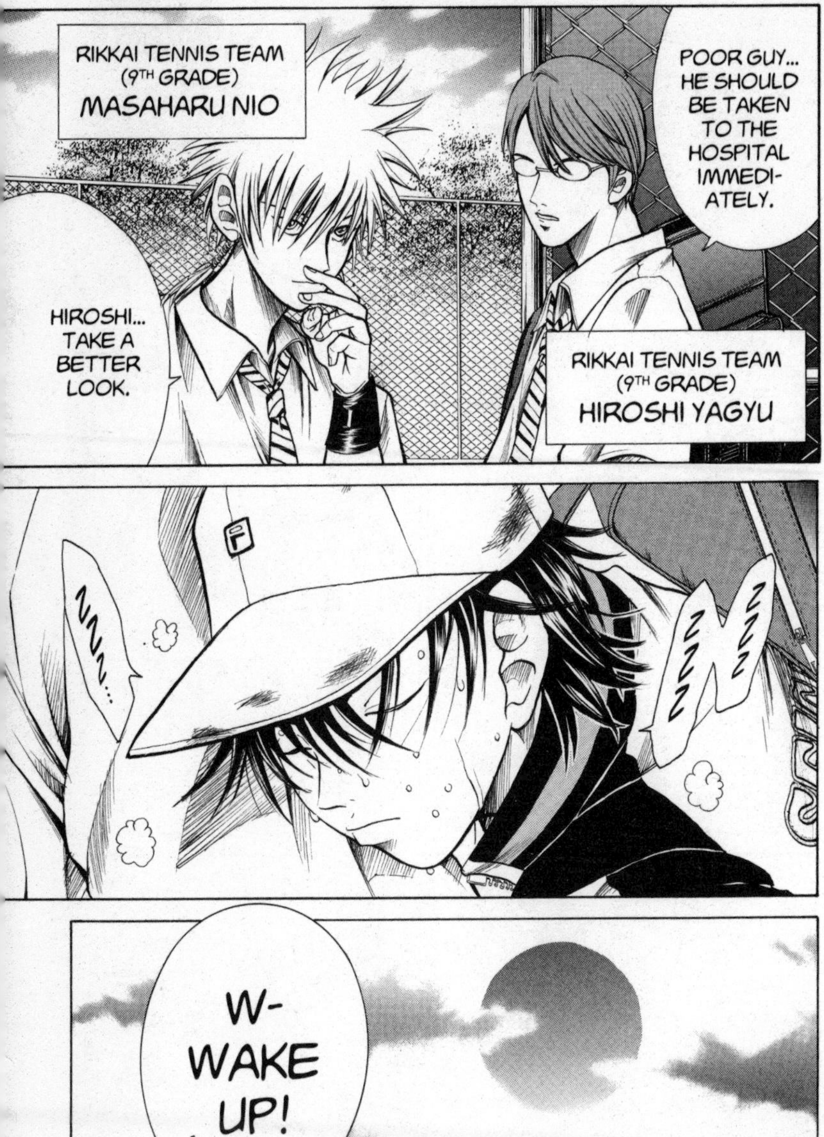
POOR GUY... HE SHOULD BE TAKEN TO THE HOSPITAL IMMEDI-ATELY.
RIKKAI TENNIS TEAM (9TH GRADE) MASAHARU NIO
RIKKAI TENNIS TEAM (9TH GRADE) HIROSHI YAGYU
HIROSHI... TAKE A BETTER LOOK.
ZZZ ZZZZ
ZZZ...
W-WAKE UP!

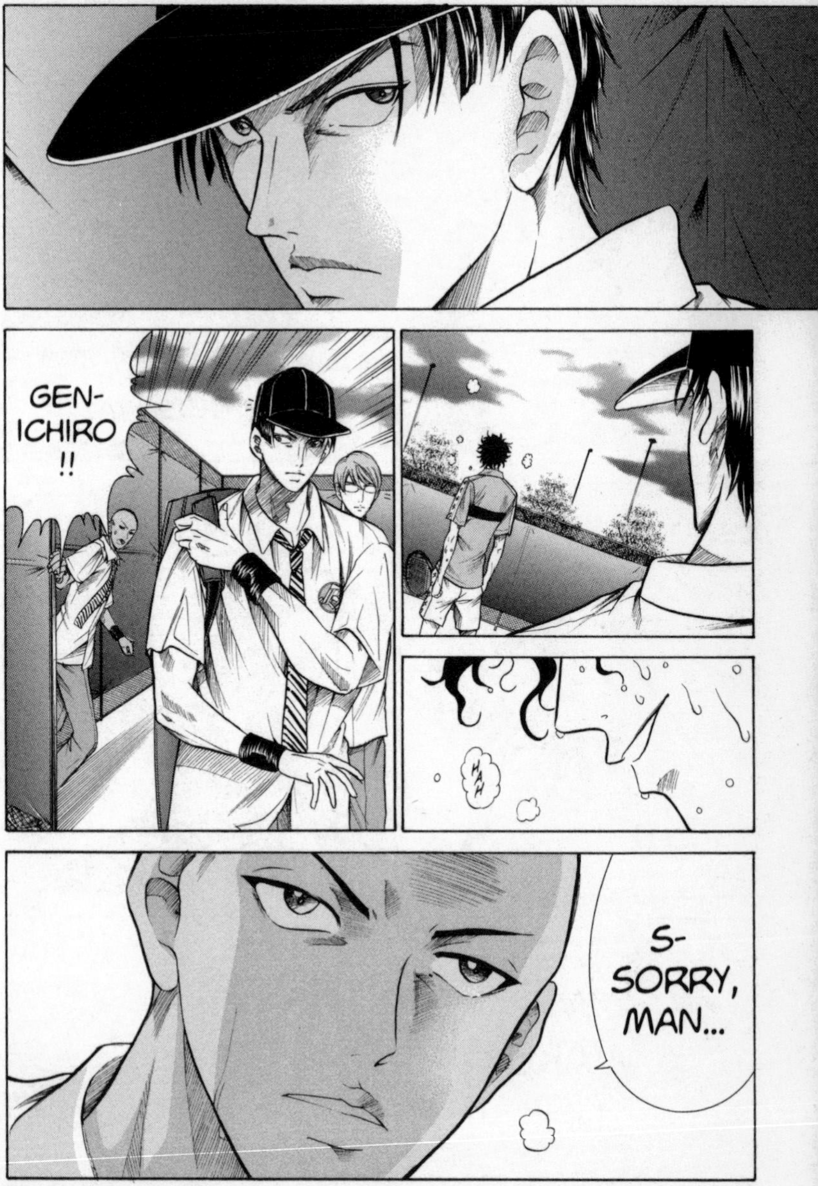
HAH
GEN-ICHIRO!!
S-SORRY, MAN...

READ THIS WAY

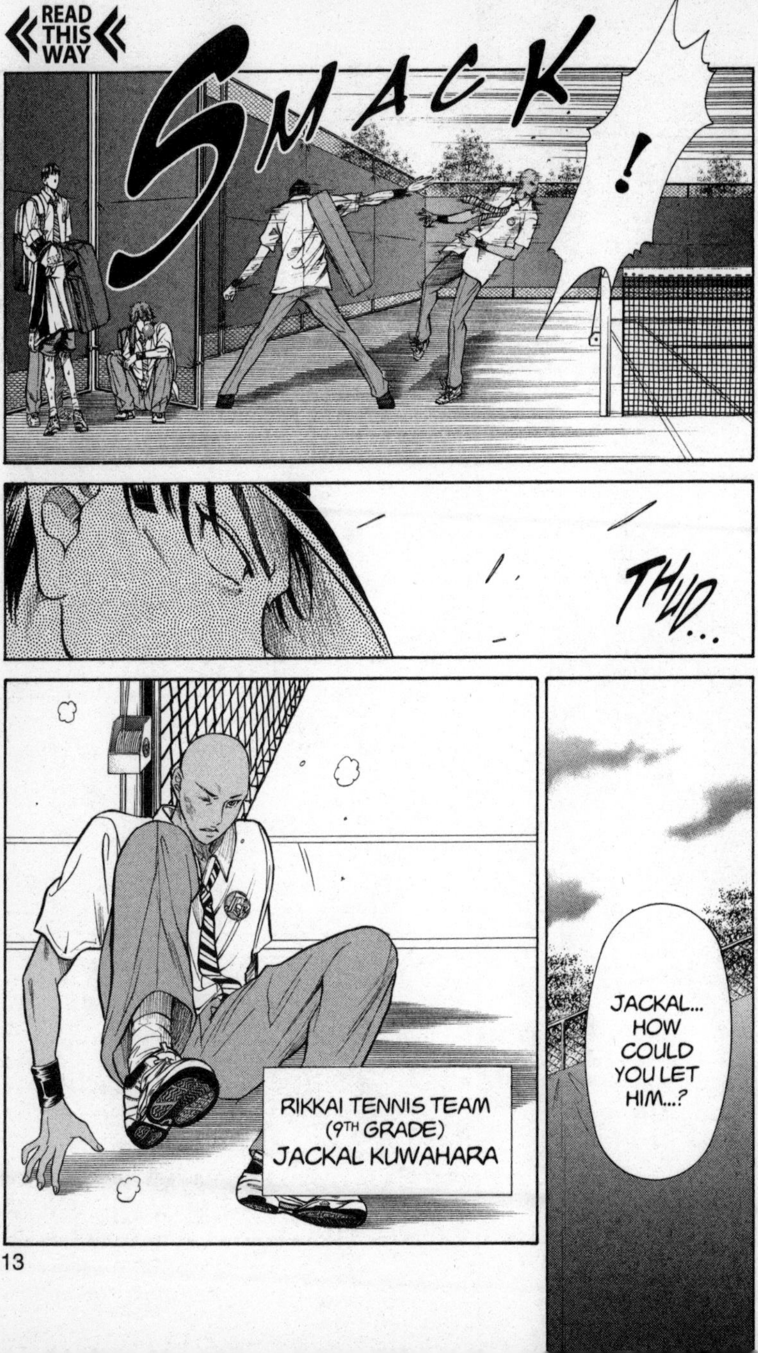
SMACK!
THUD...
JACKAL... HOW COULD YOU LET HIM...?
RIKKAI TENNIS TEAM (9TH GRADE) JACKAL KUWAHARA

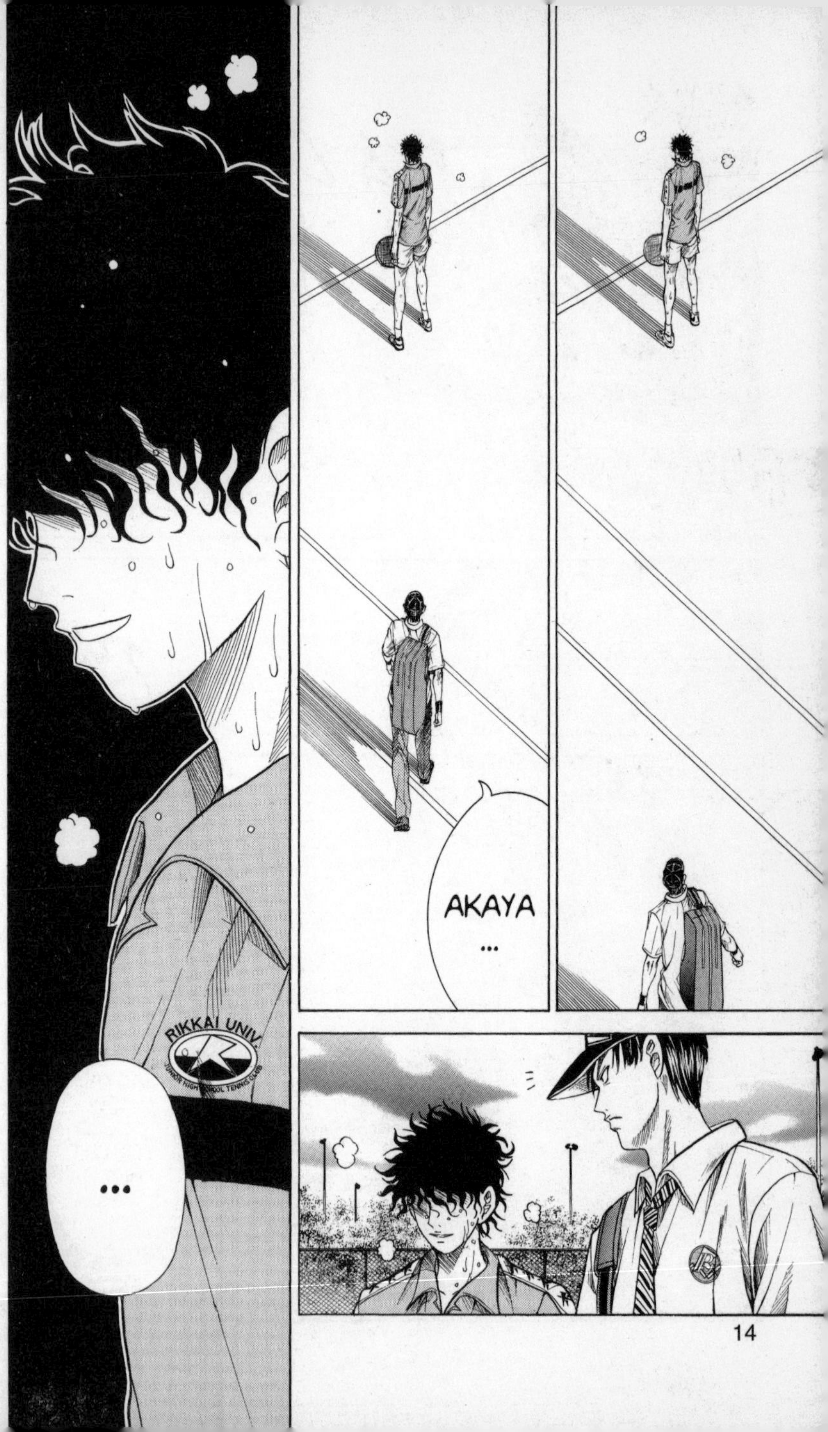
AKAYA ...
RIKKAI UNIV.
JUNIOR HIGH SCHOOL TENNIS CLUB
...

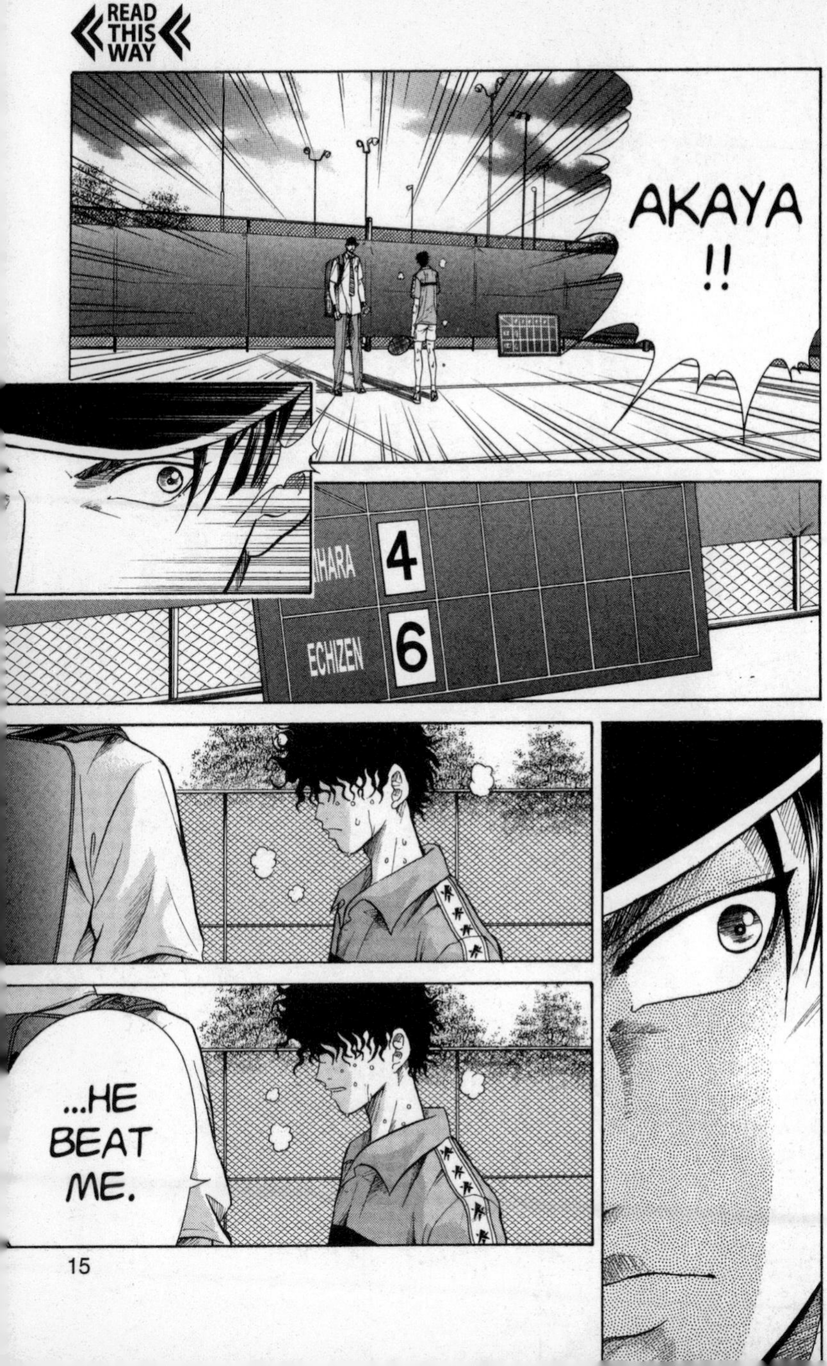
READ THIS WAY
AKAYA !!
KIHARA
4
ECHIZEN
6
...HE BEAT ME.

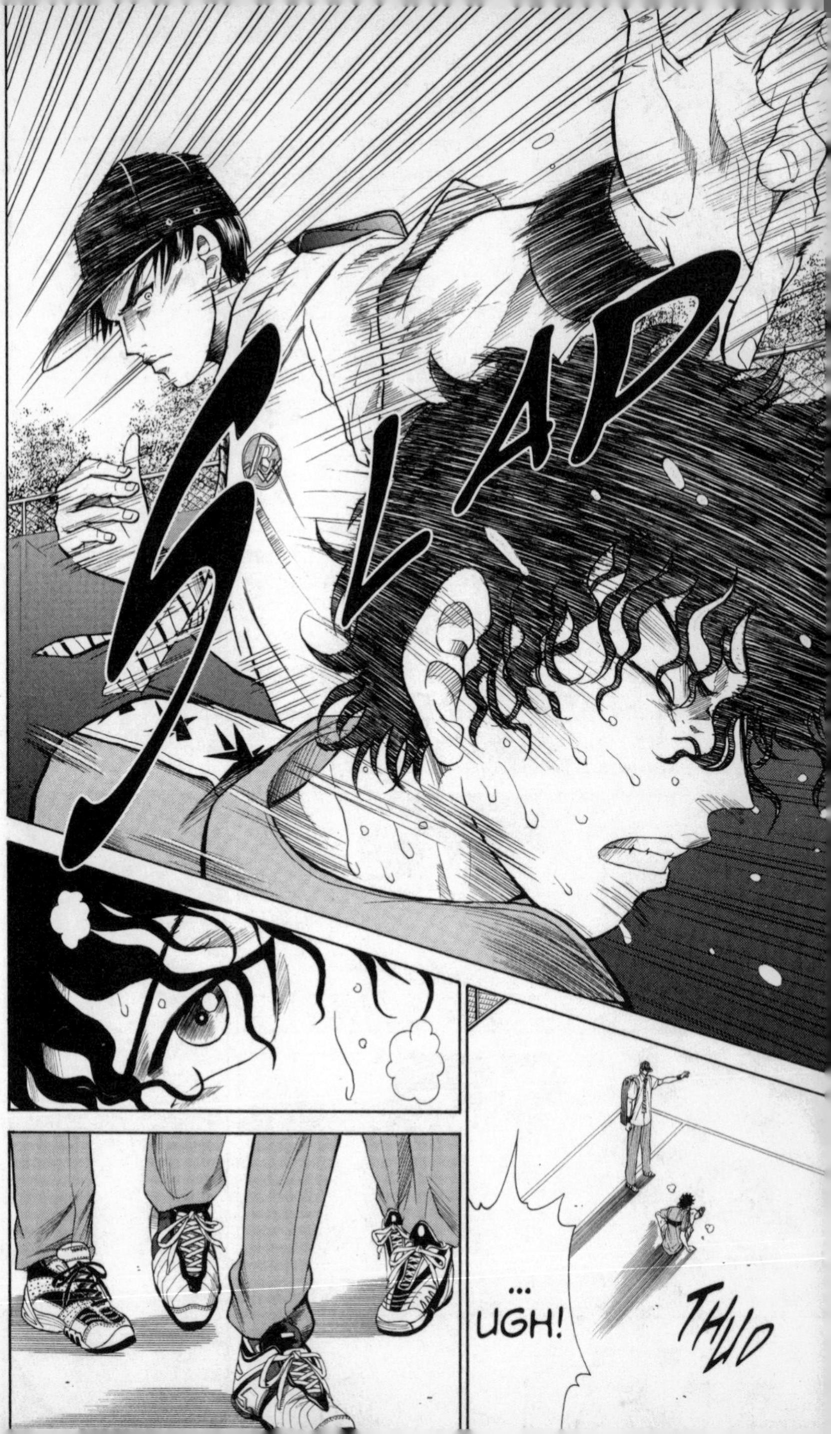
SLAP
THUD
...UGH!

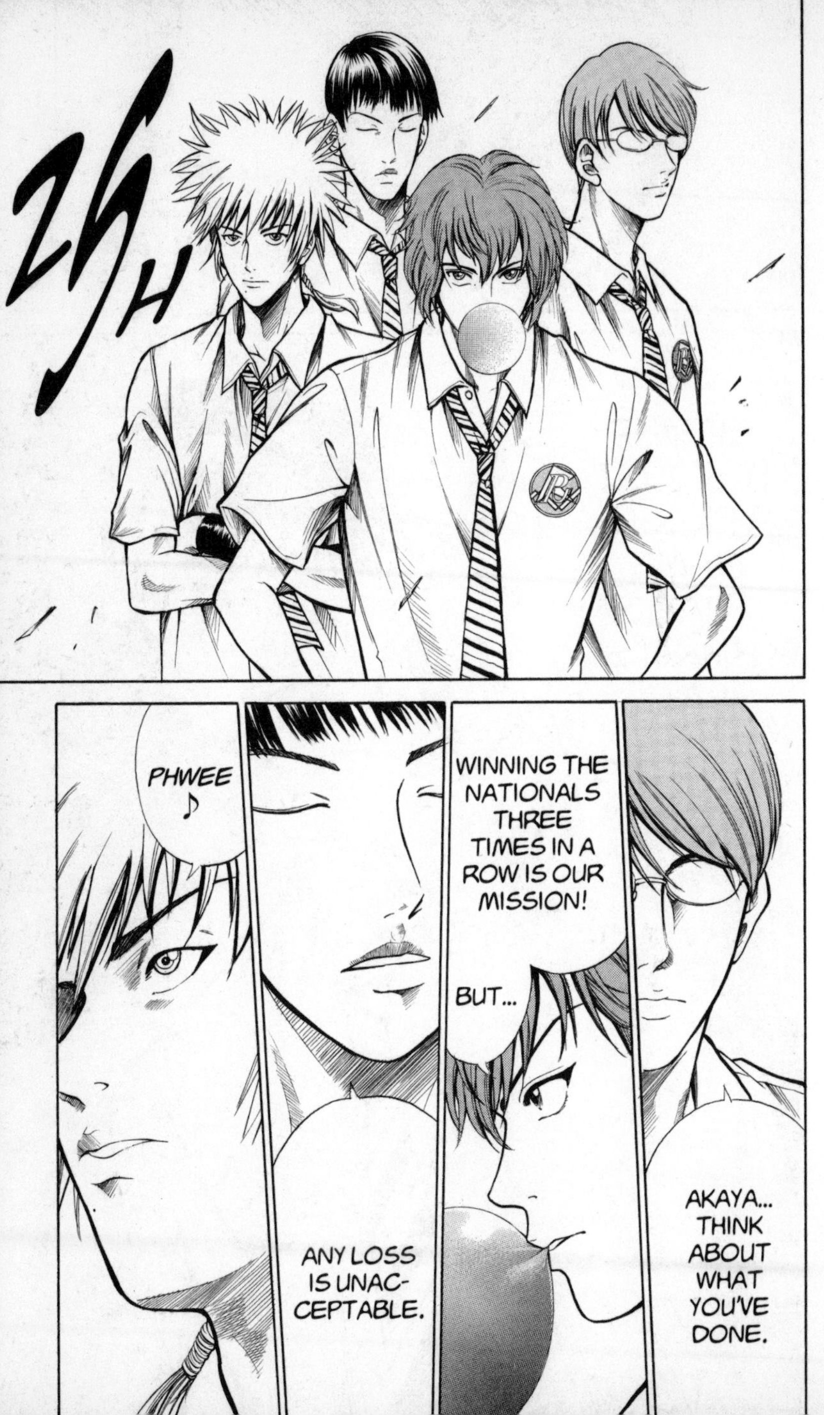
AKAYA... THINK ABOUT WHAT YOU'VE DONE.
WINNING THE NATIONALS THREE TIMES IN A ROW IS OUR MISSION!
BUT...
ANY LOSS IS UNAC-CEPTABLE.
PHWEE ♪

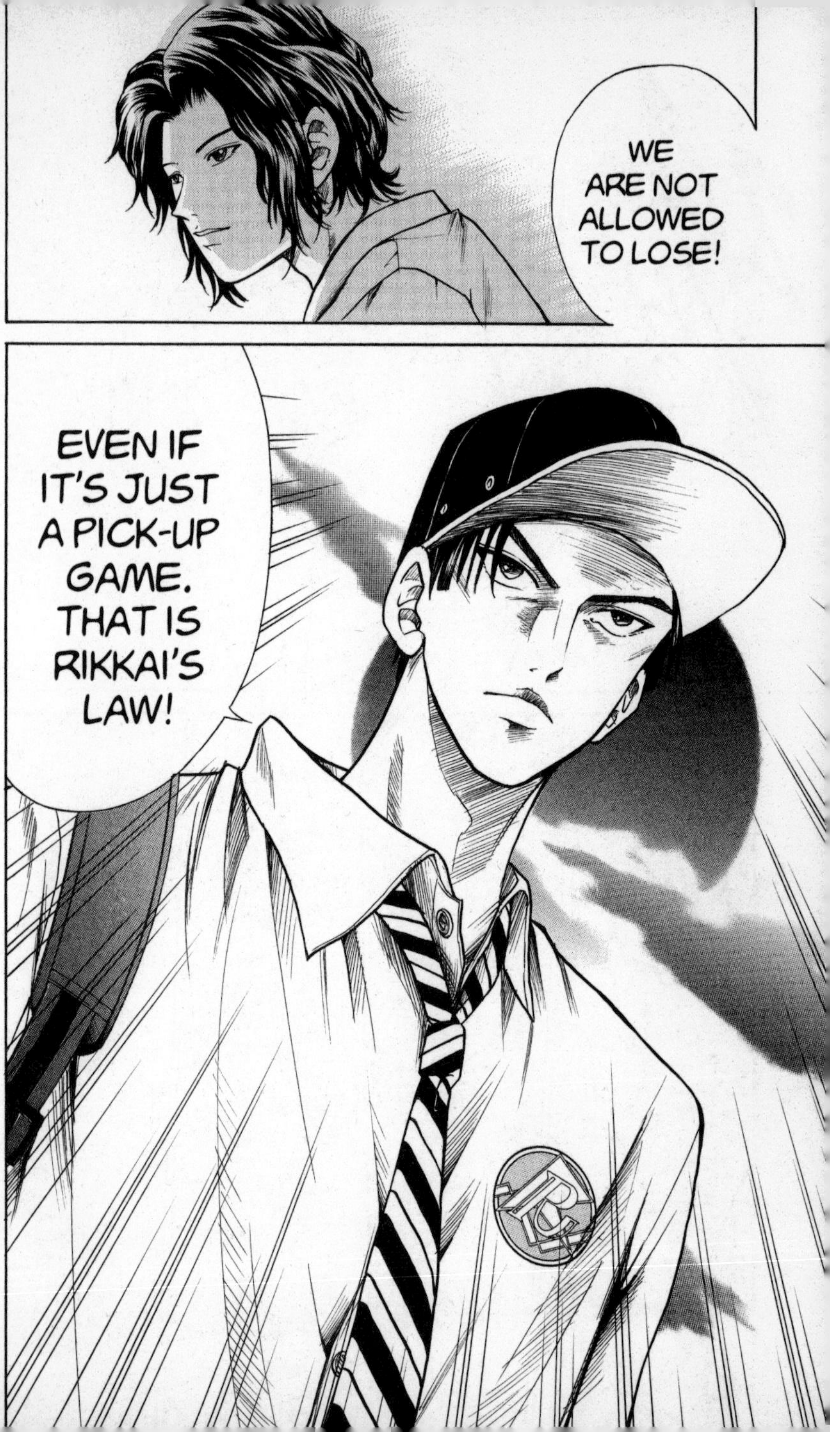
WE ARE NOT ALLOWED TO LOSE!
EVEN IF IT'S JUST A PICK-UP GAME. THAT IS RIKKAI'S LAW!

READ THIS WAY

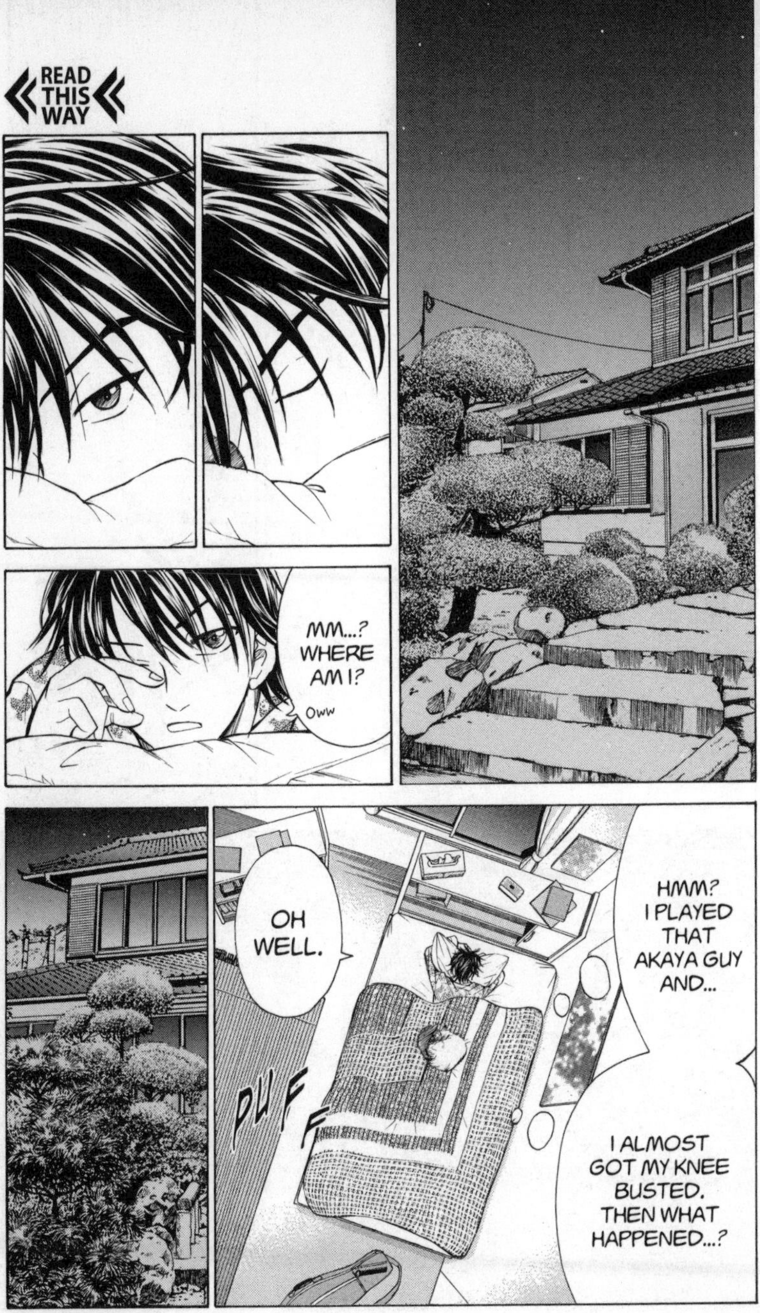
MM...? WHERE AM I?
Oww
HMM? I PLAYED THAT AKAYA GUY AND...
I ALMOST GOT MY KNEE BUSTED. THEN WHAT HAPPENED...?
OH WELL.
PUFF

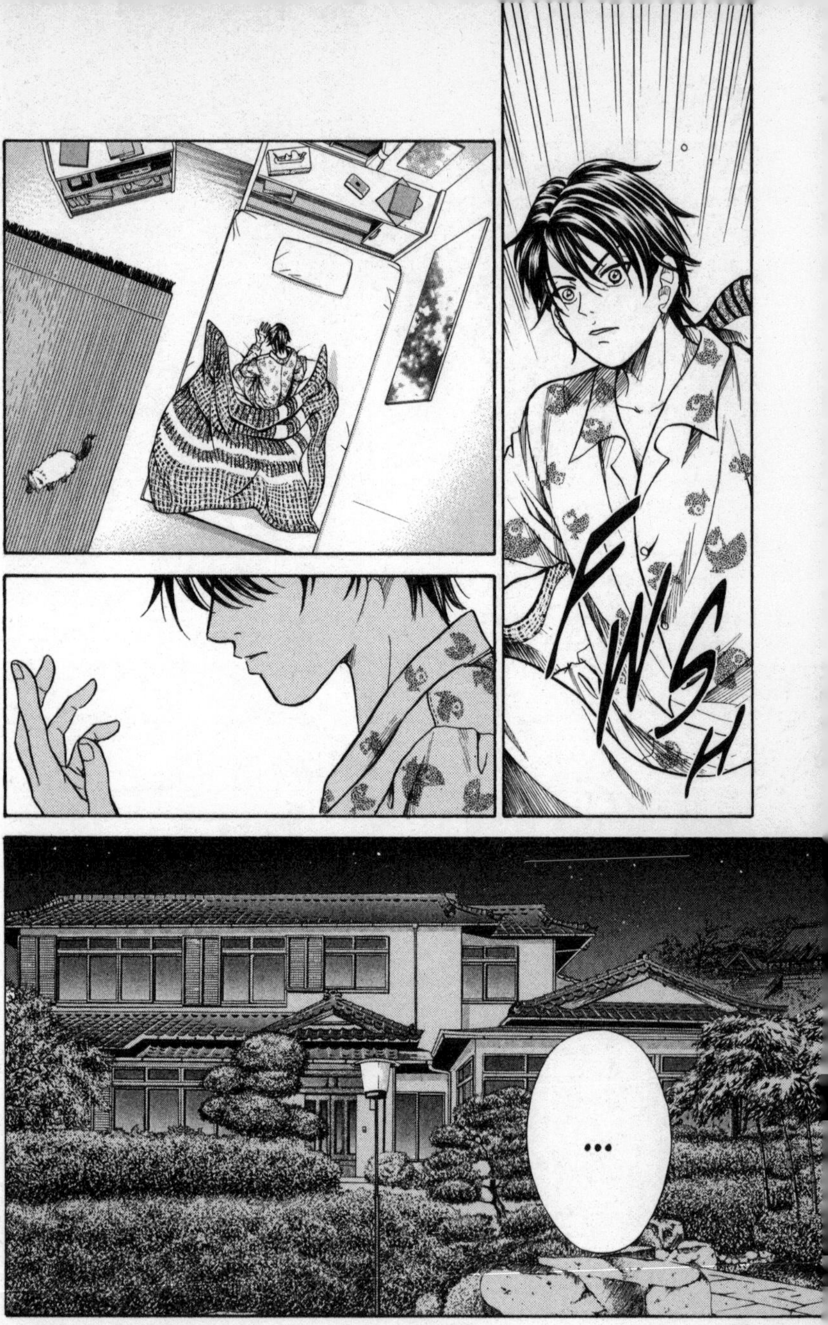
FWISH
...

READ THIS WAY

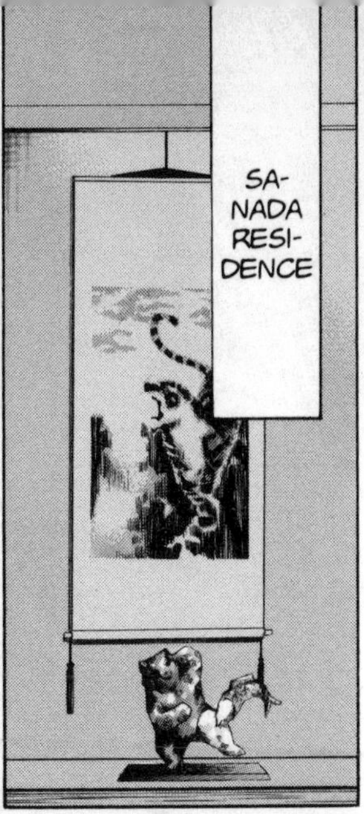
SA-NADA RESI-DENCE

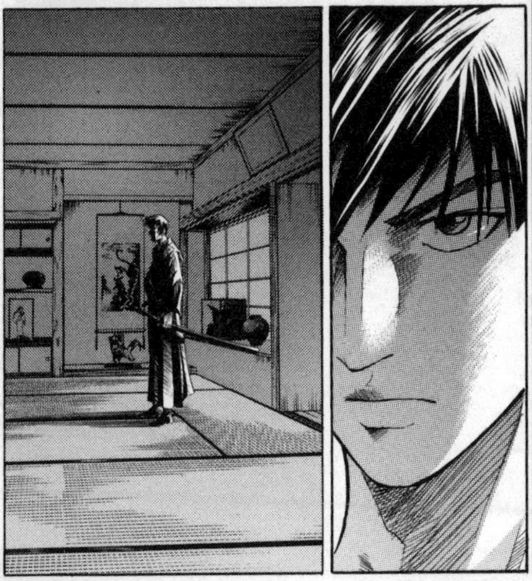

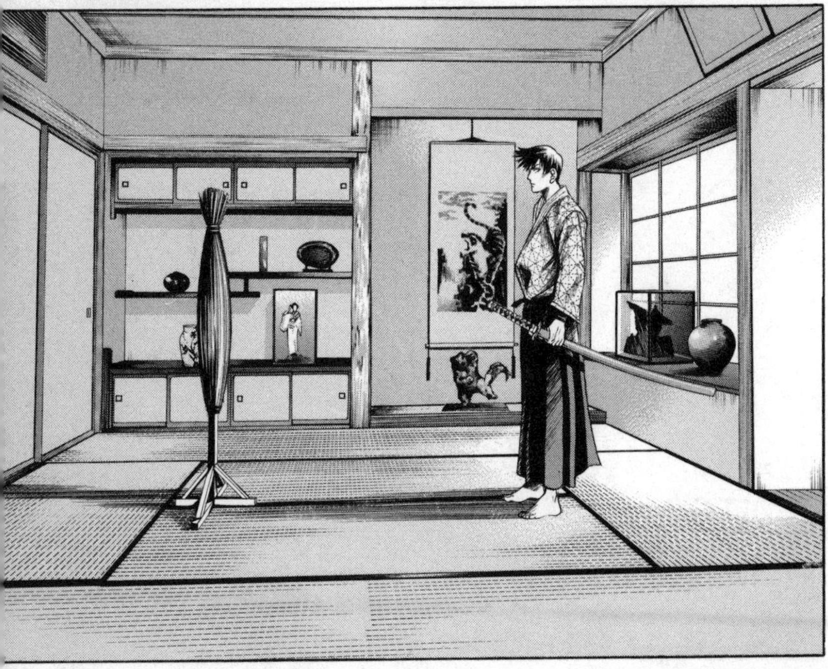

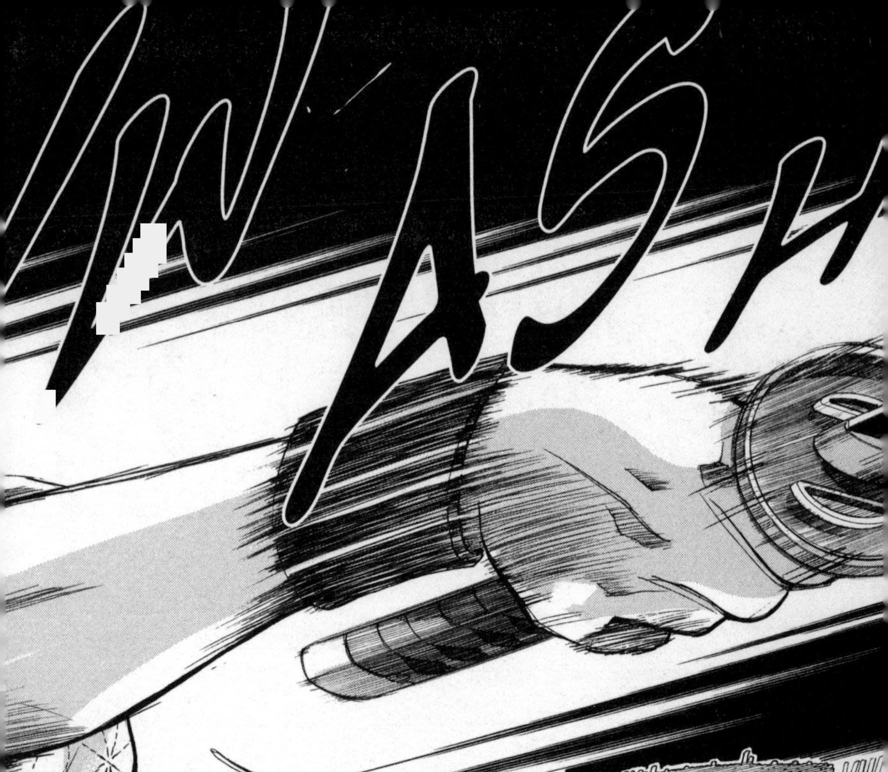
WASH
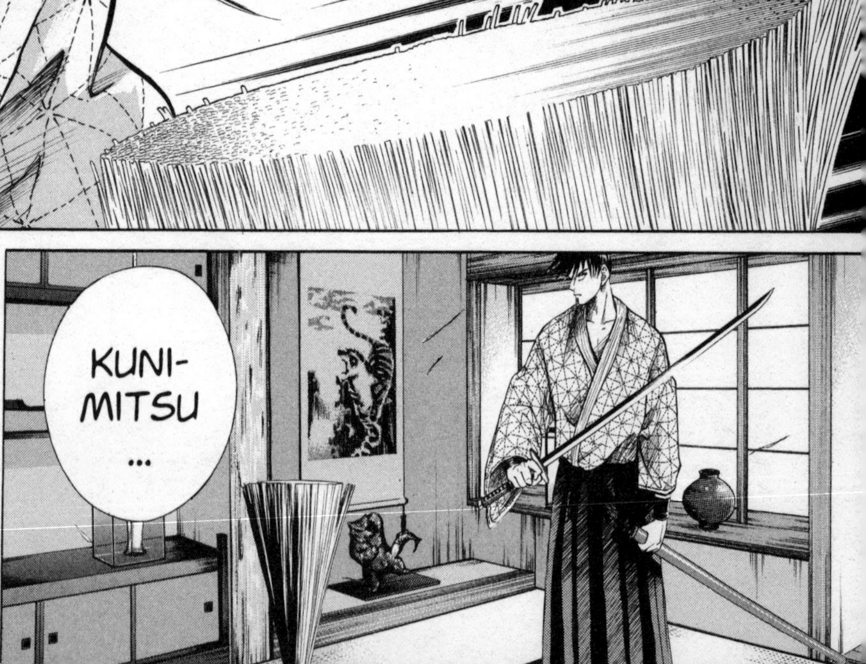
KUNI-
MITSU
...

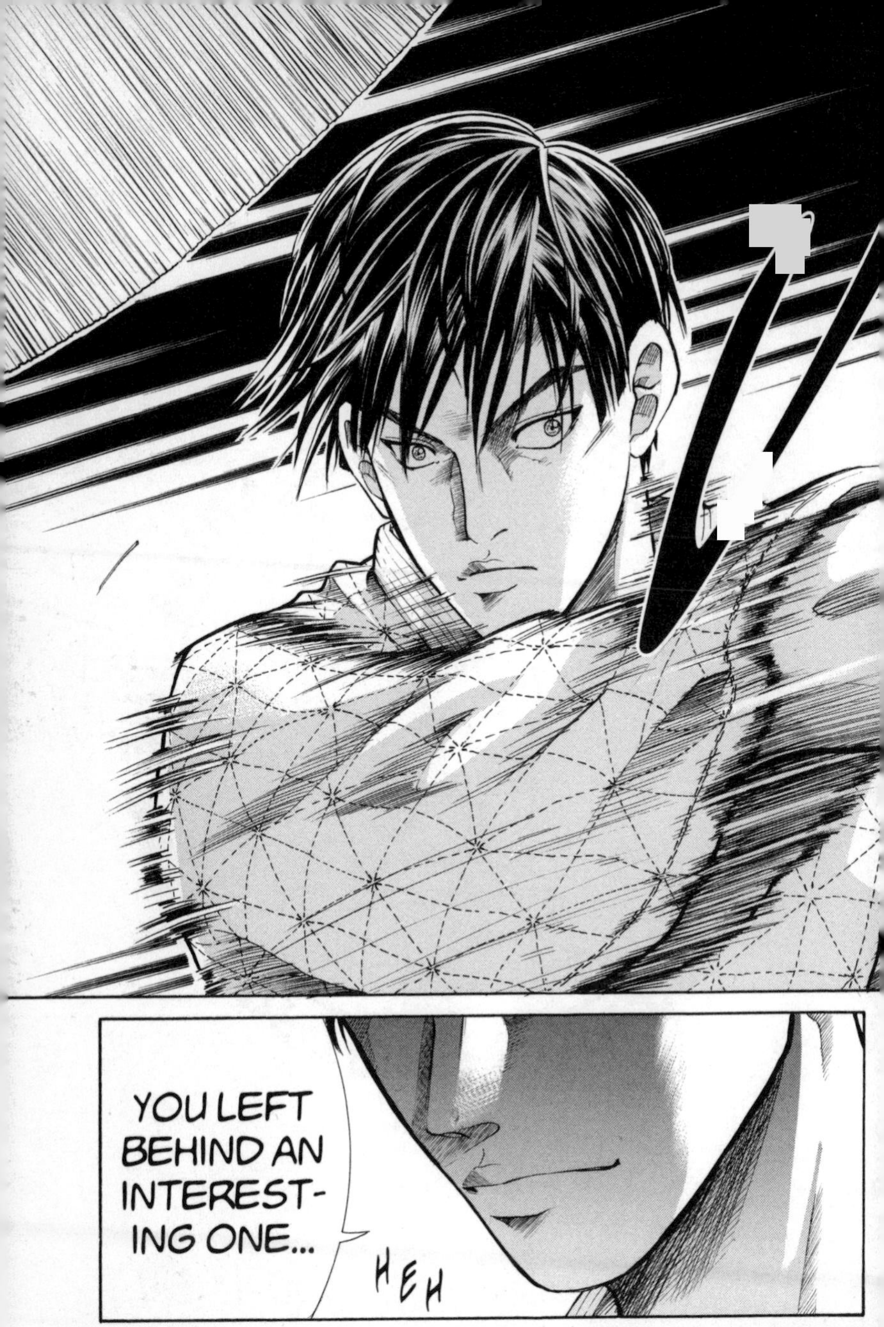
YOU LEFT BEHIND AN INTERESTING ONE...
HEH

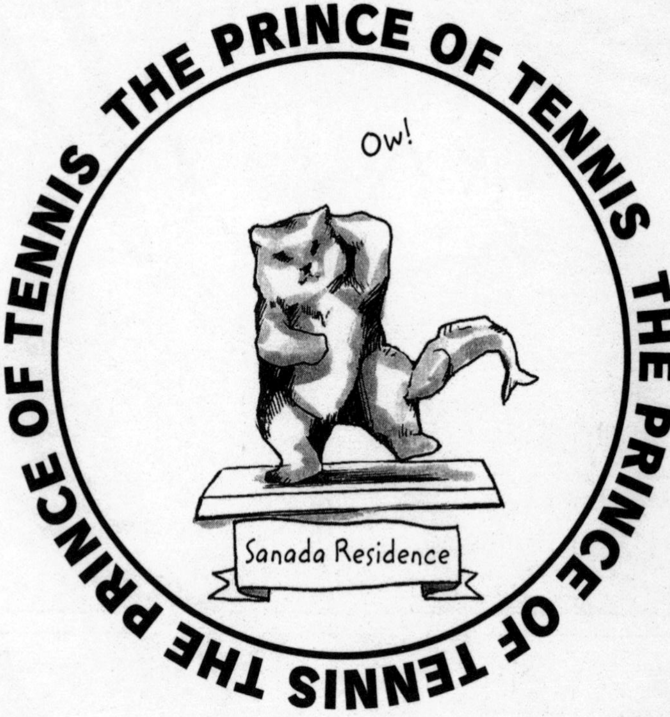
THE PRINCE OF TENNIS THE PRINCE OF TENNIS THE PRINCE OF TENNIS
Ow!
Sanada Residence

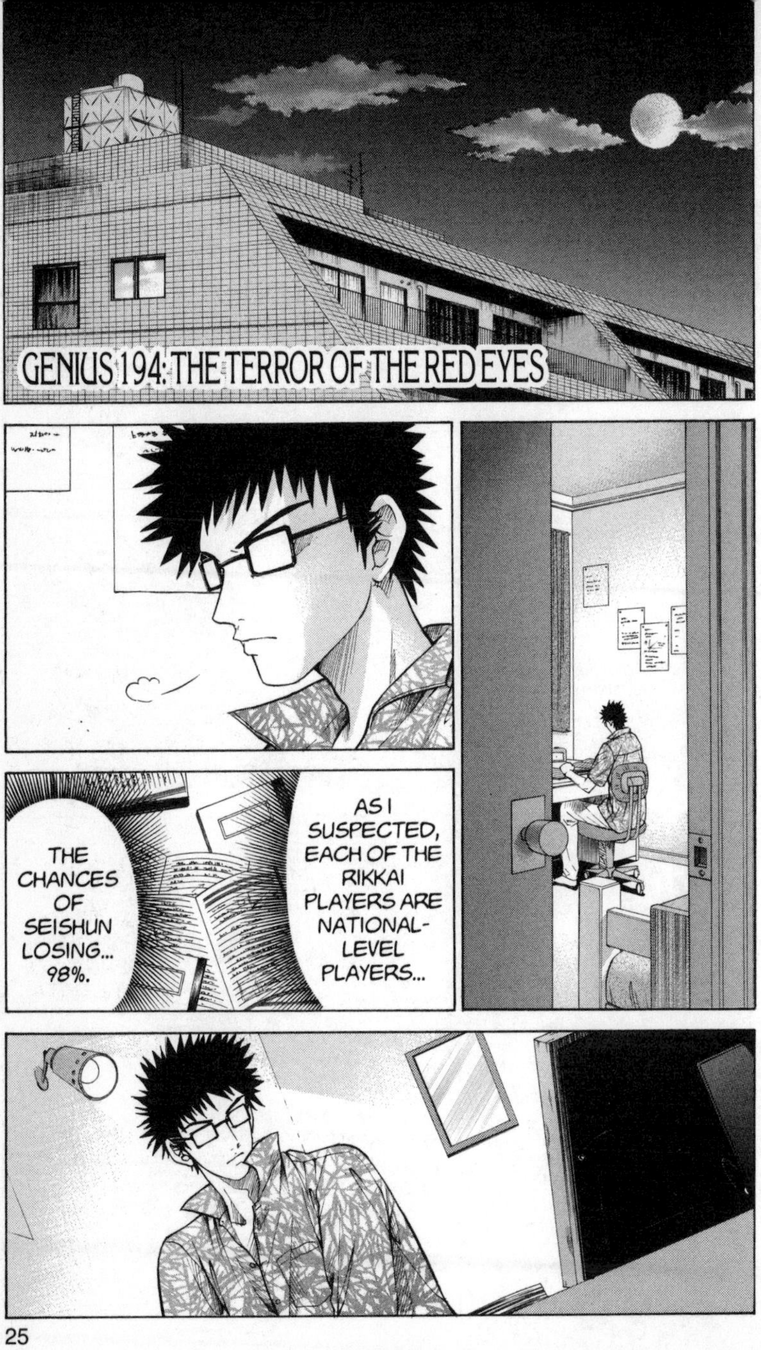
GENIUS 194: THE TERROR OF THE RED EYES
AS I SUSPECTED, EACH OF THE RIKKAI PLAYERS ARE NATIONAL-LEVEL PLAYERS...
THE CHANCES OF SEISHUN LOSING... 98%.

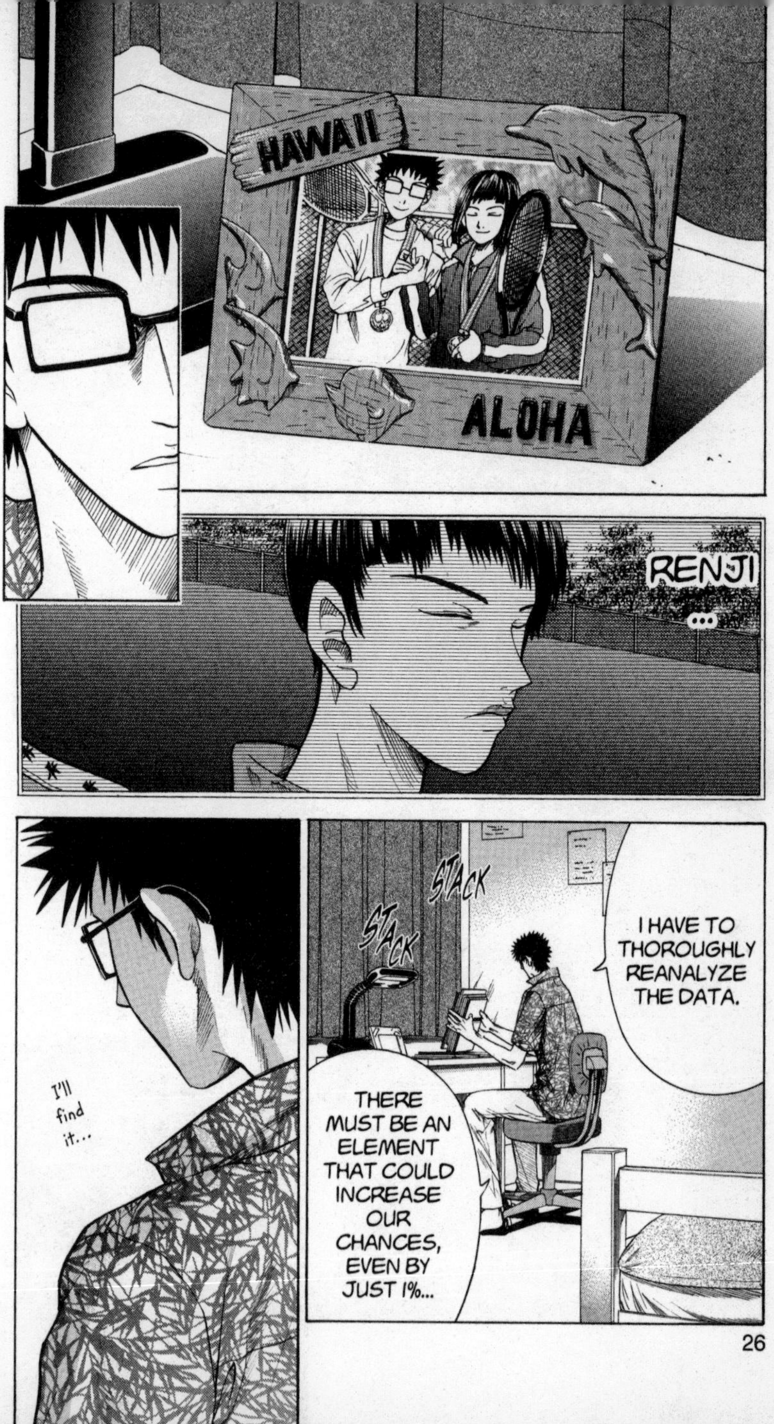
HAWAII
ALOHA
RENJI ...
I HAVE TO THOROUGHLY REANALYZE THE DATA.
STACK
STACK
THERE MUST BE AN ELEMENT THAT COULD INCREASE OUR CHANCES, EVEN BY JUST 1%...
I'll find it...

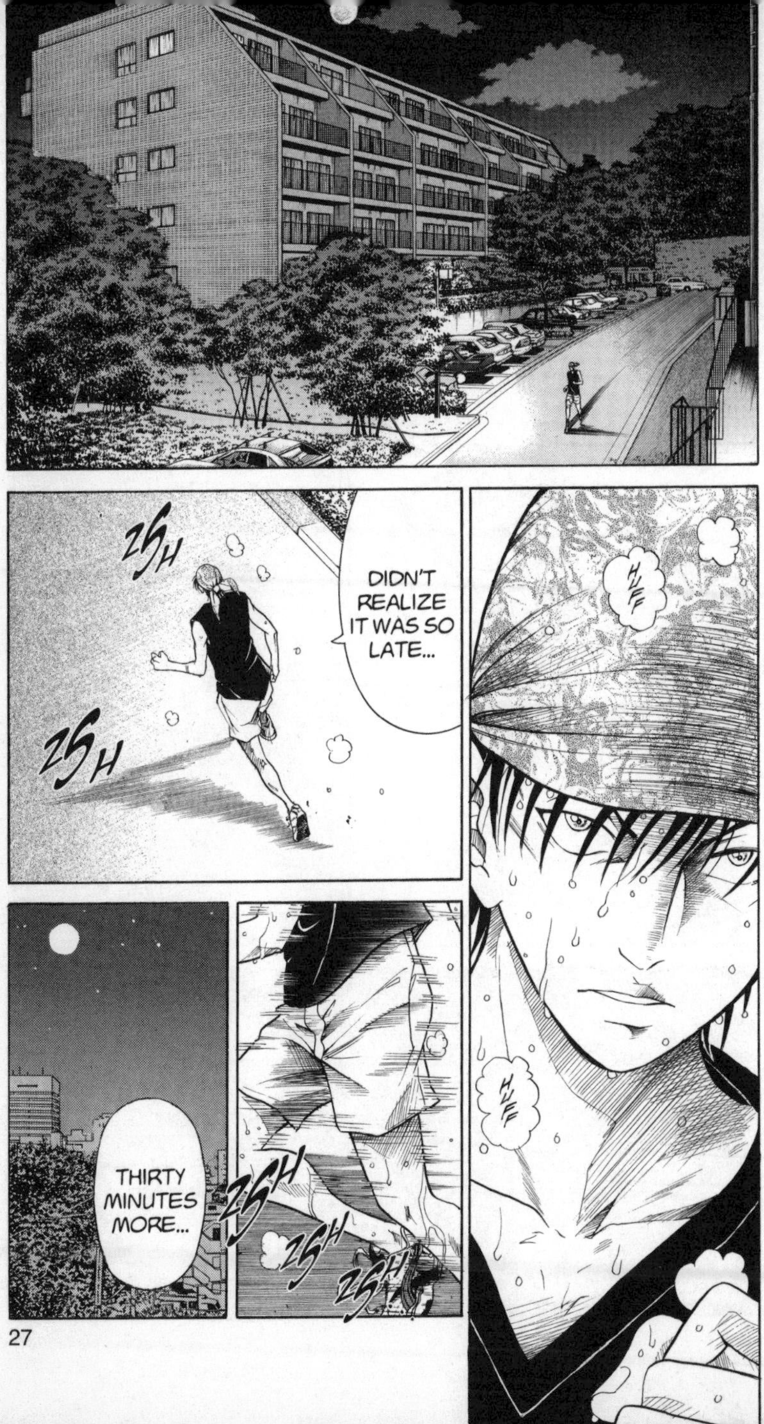
HUFF
HUFF
DIDN'T REALIZE IT WAS SO LATE...
ZSH
ZSH
ZSH
ZSH
ZSH
THIRTY MINUTES MORE...

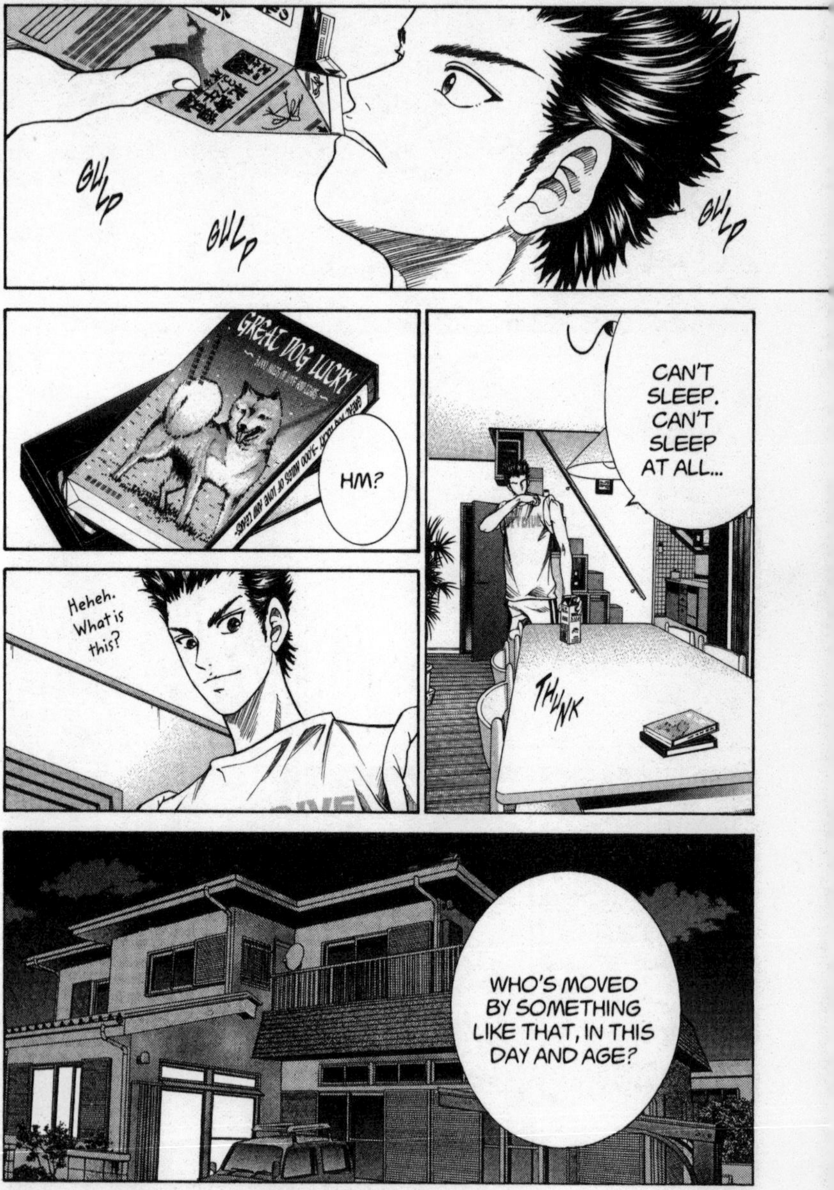
GULP
GULP
GULP
CAN'T SLEEP. CAN'T SLEEP AT ALL...
THUNK
GREAT DOG LUCKY
HM?
Heheh. What is this?
WHO'S MOVED BY SOMETHING LIKE THAT, IN THIS DAY AND AGE?

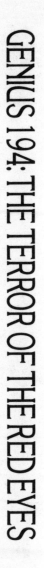

GENIUS 194: THE TERROR OF THE RED EYES

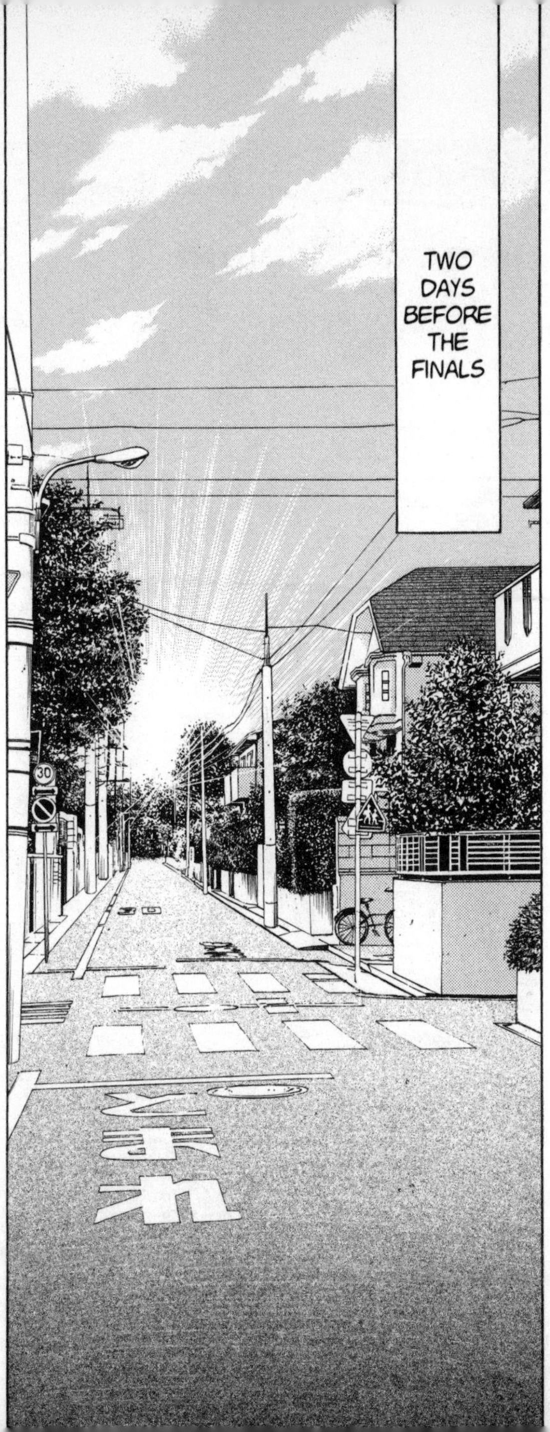
TWO DAYS BEFORE THE FINALS

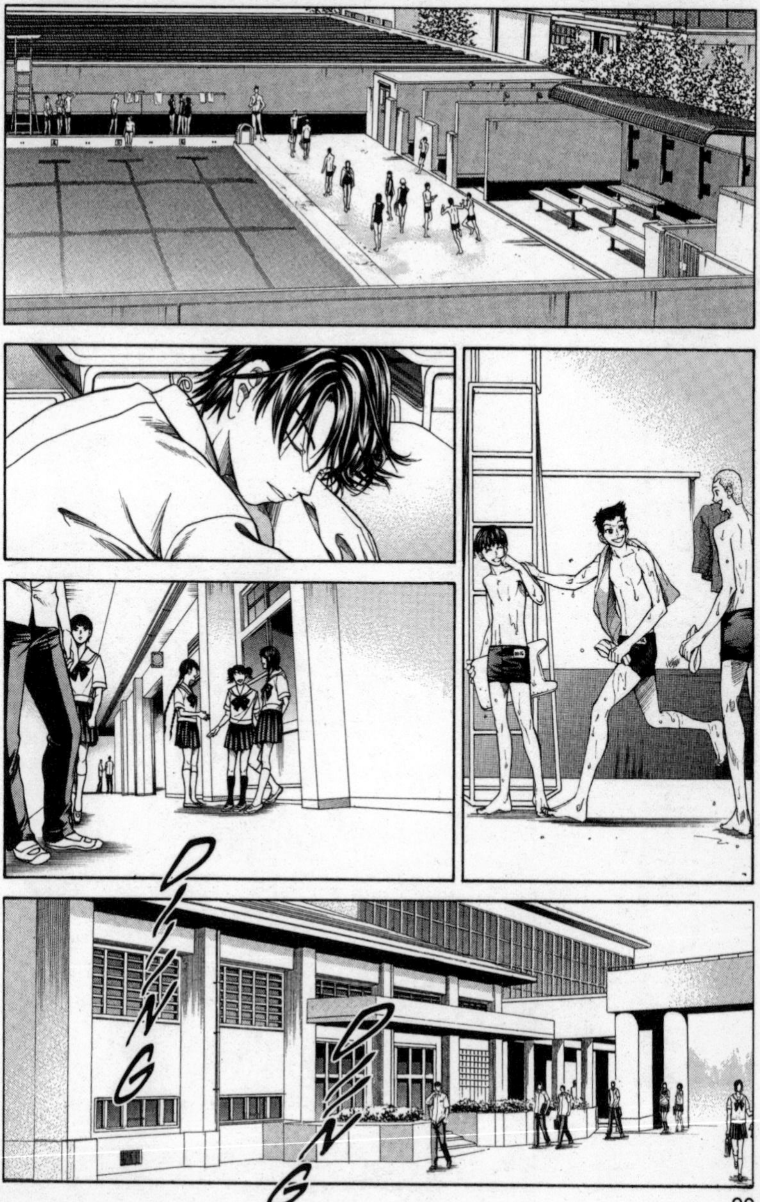
DIIING
DIING

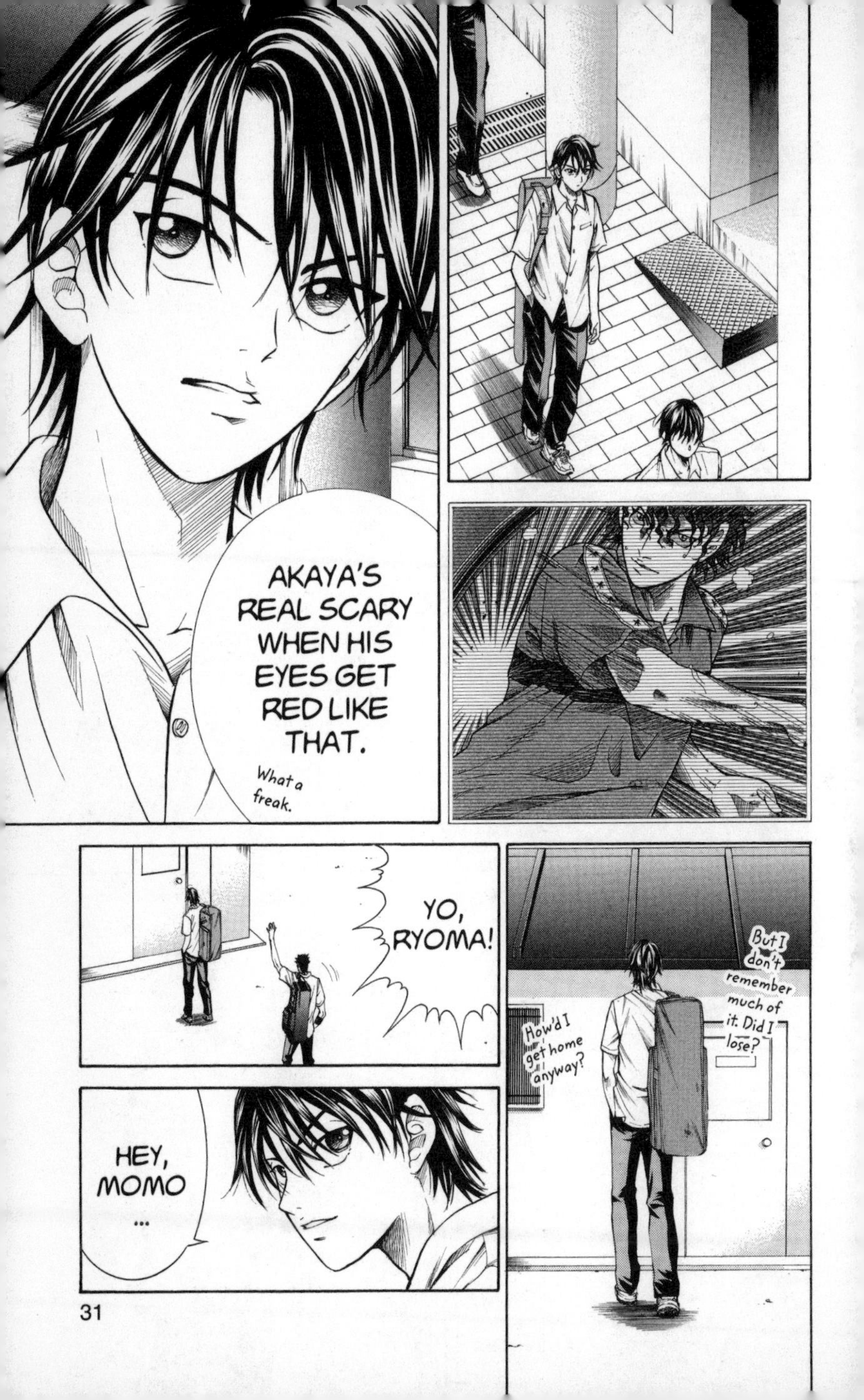
AKAYA'S REAL SCARY WHEN HIS EYES GET RED LIKE THAT.
What a freak.
But I don't remember much of it. Did I lose?
How'd I get home anyway?
YO, RYOMA!
HEY, MOMO ...

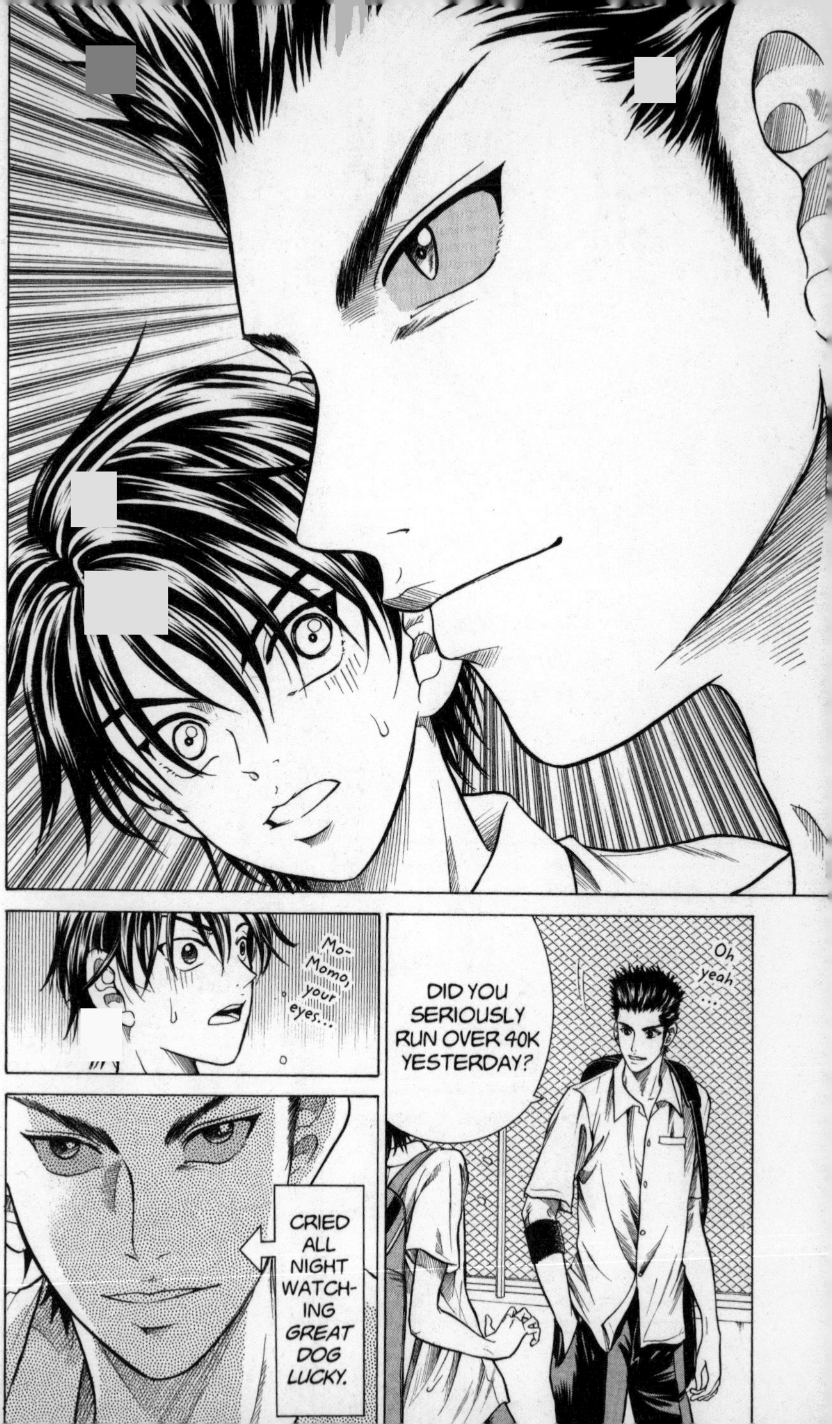
DID YOU SERIOUSLY RUN OVER 40K YESTERDAY?
Oh yeah...
Mo-Momo, your eyes...
CRIED ALL NIGHT WATCHING GREAT DOG LUCKY.

READ THIS WAY

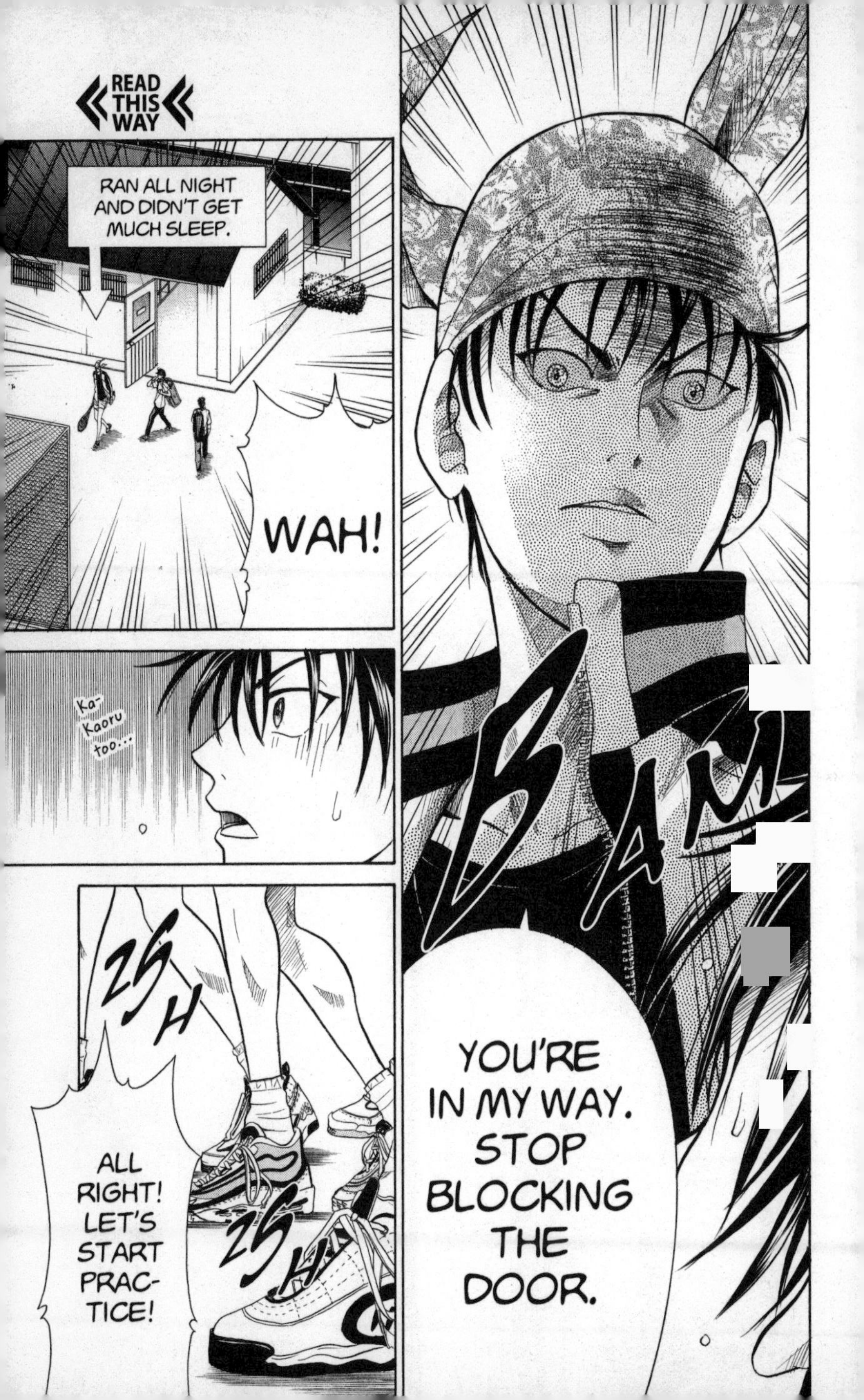
BAM
YOU'RE IN MY WAY. STOP BLOCKING THE DOOR.
RAN ALL NIGHT AND DIDN'T GET MUCH SLEEP.
WAH!
Ka-Kaoru too...
ZSH
ALL RIGHT! LET'S START PRAC-TICE!
ZSH

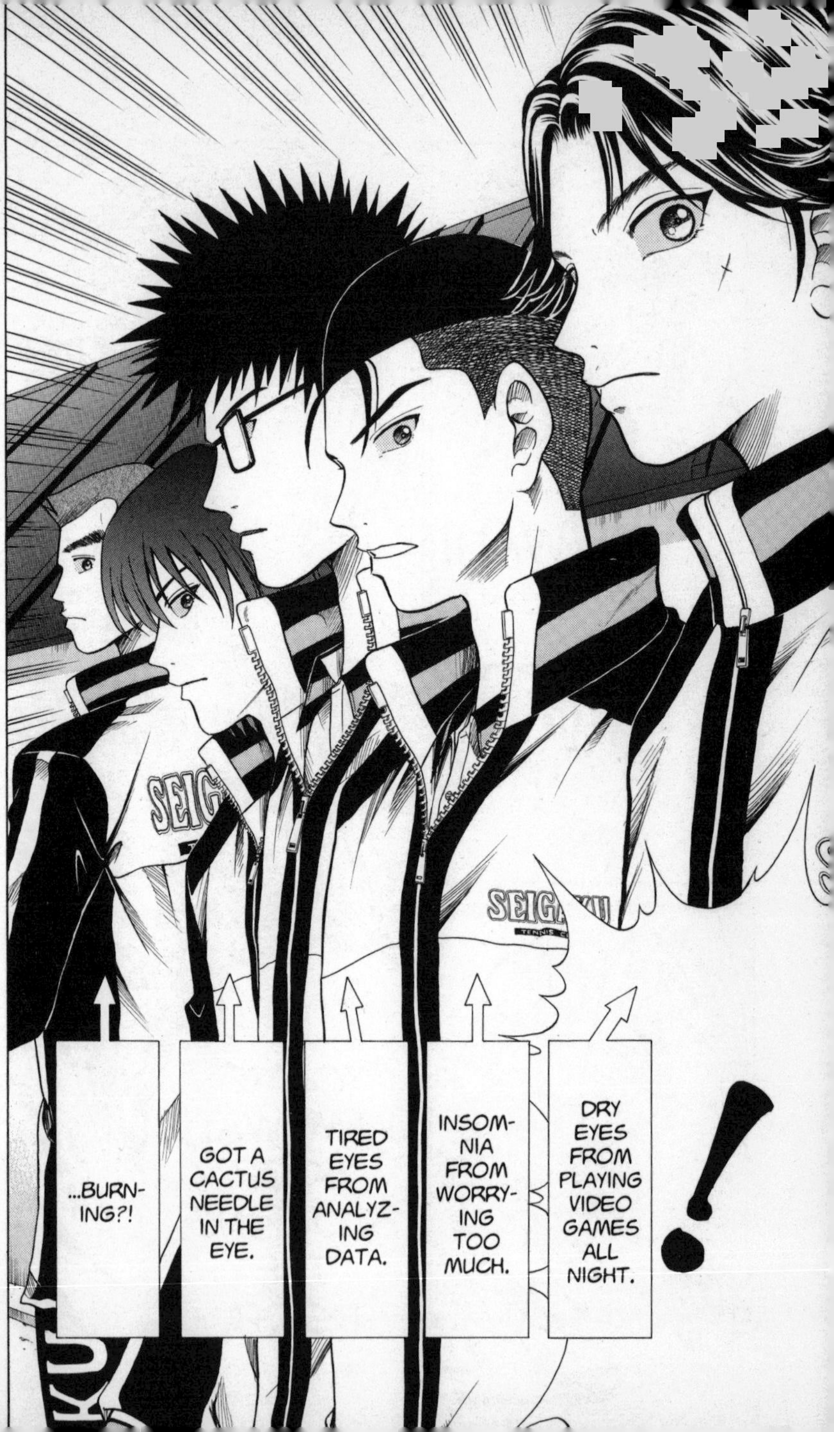

DRY EYES FROM PLAYING VIDEO GAMES ALL NIGHT.
INSOM-NIA FROM WORRY-ING TOO MUCH.
TIRED EYES FROM ANALYZ-ING DATA.
GOT A CACTUS NEEDLE IN THE EYE.
...BURN-ING?!
!

READ THIS WAY

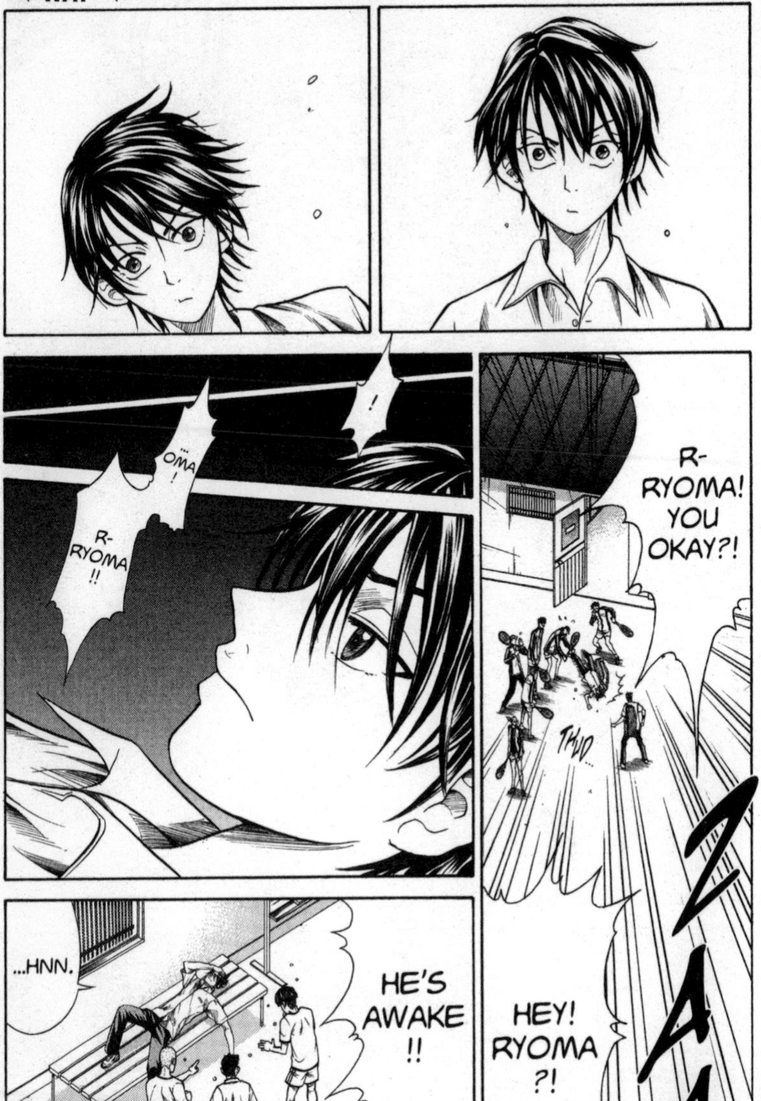

R-RYOMA! YOU OKAY?!
THUD...
ZAAA
HEY! RYOMA?!
!
...OMA!
R-RYOMA!!
HE'S AWAKE!!
...HNN.

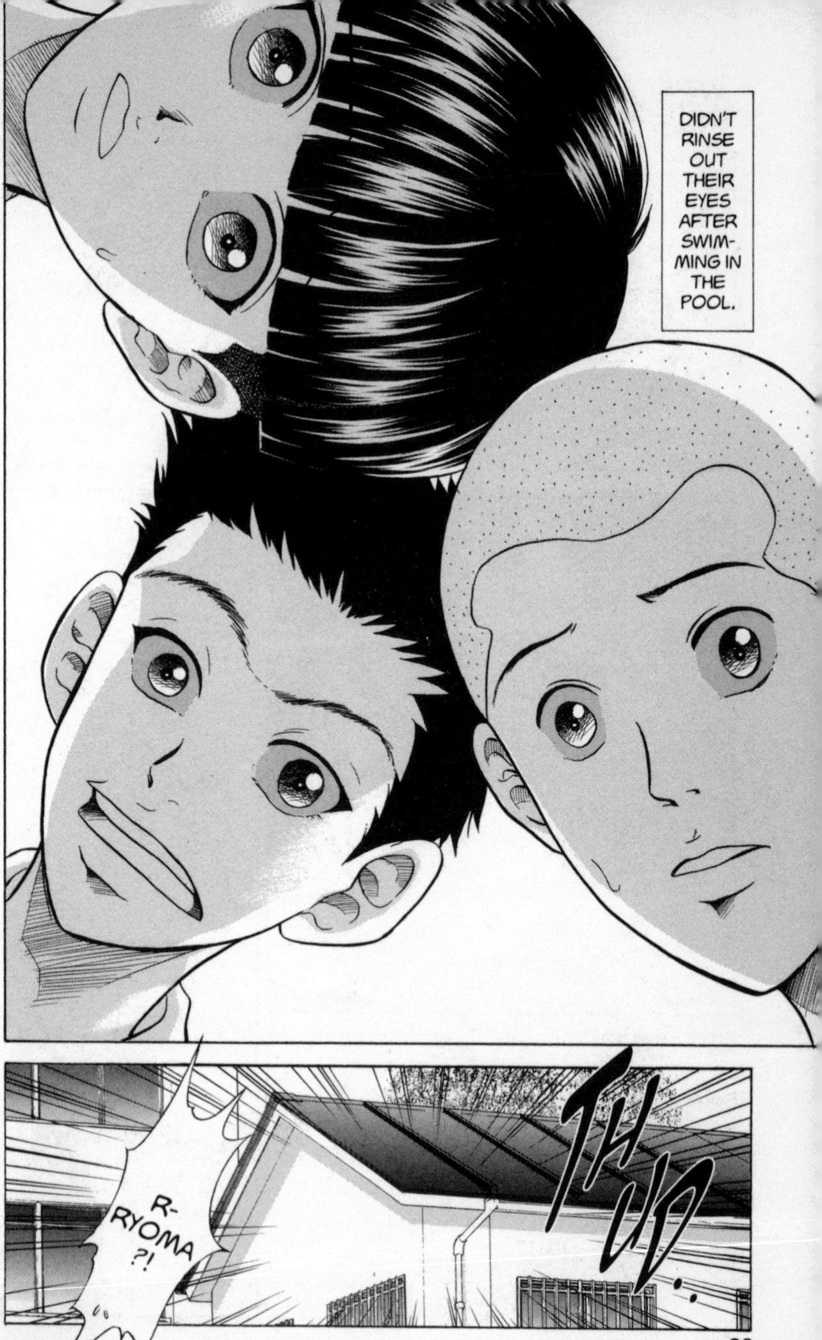
DIDN'T RINSE OUT THEIR EYES AFTER SWIMMING IN THE POOL.
THUD...
R-RYOMA?!

READ THIS WAY

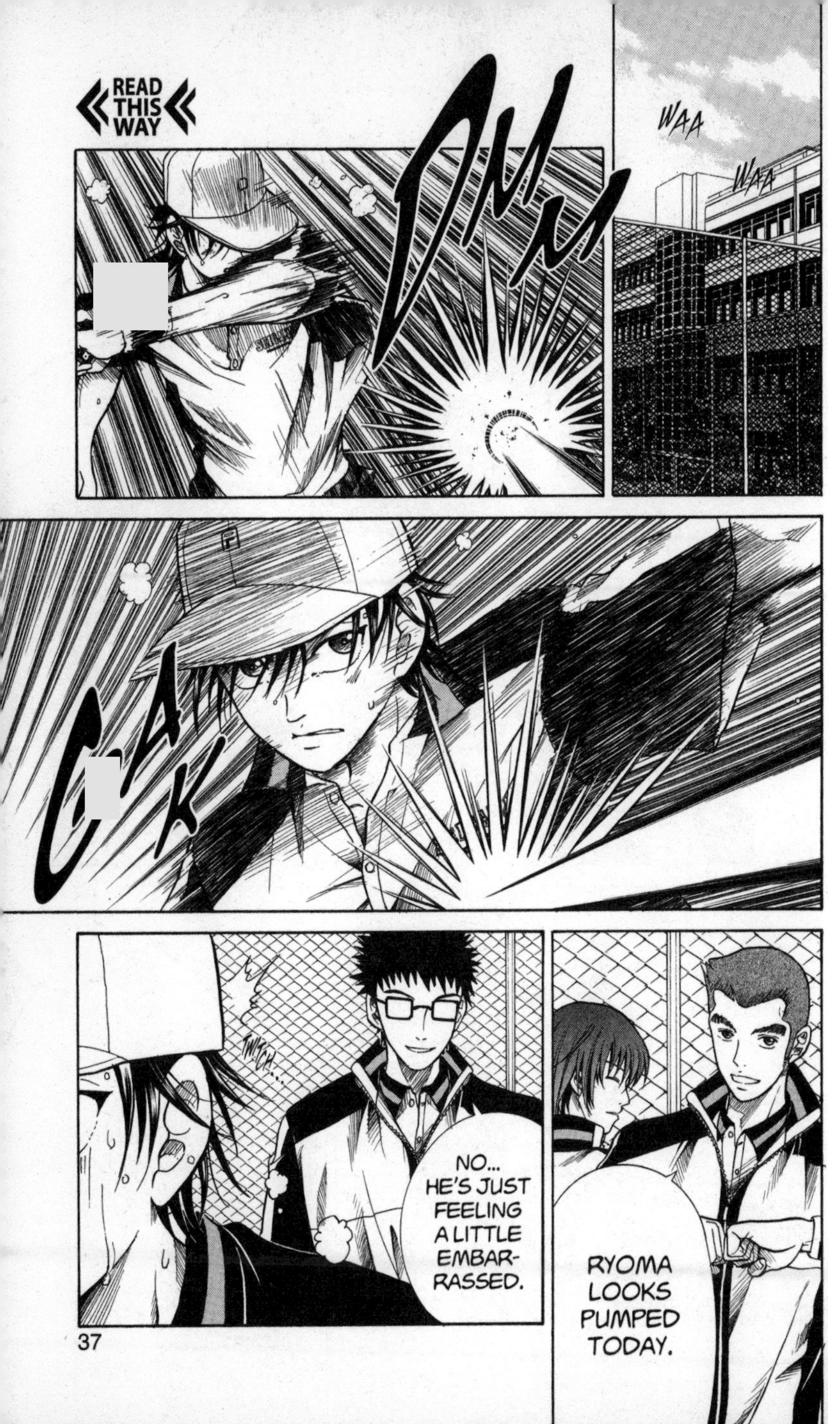

WAA
WAA
RYOMA LOOKS PUMPED TODAY.
NO... HE'S JUST FEELING A LITTLE EMBARRASSED.
TWITCH...

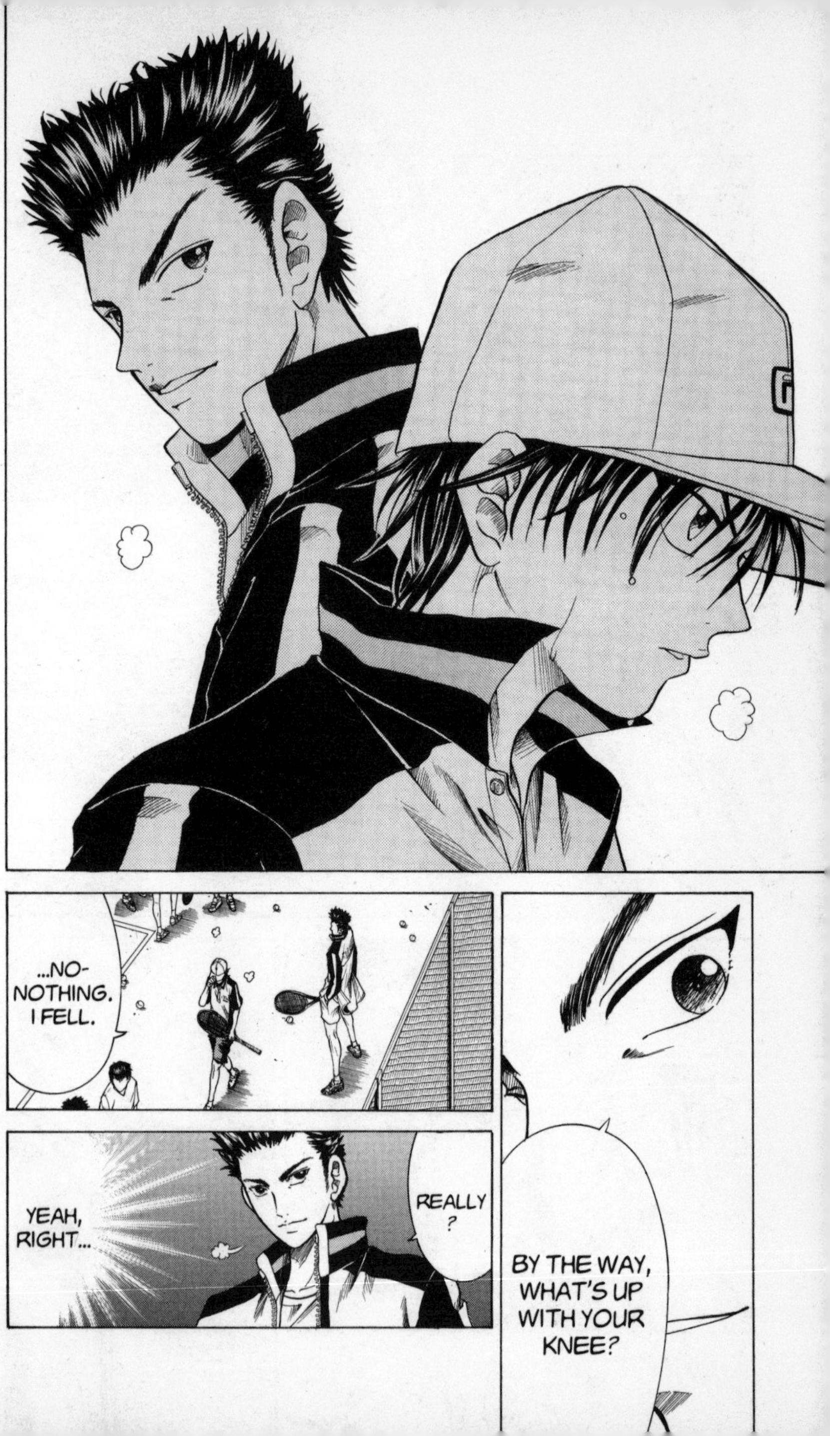
BY THE WAY, WHAT'S UP WITH YOUR KNEE?
...NO- NOTHING. I FELL.
REALLY ?
YEAH, RIGHT...

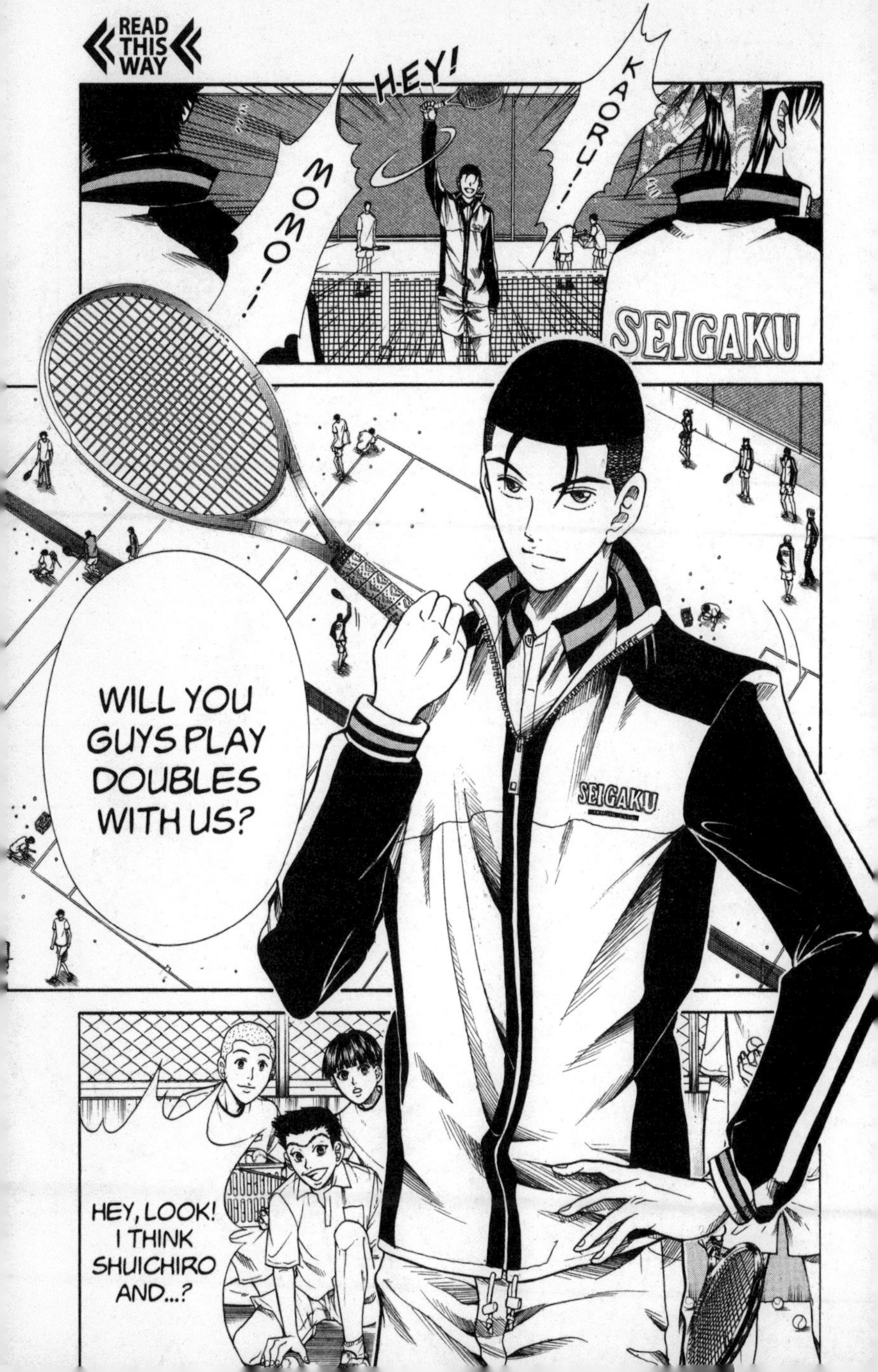
READ THIS WAY
KAORU...!
HEY!
MOMO...!
SEIGAKU
WILL YOU GUYS PLAY DOUBLES WITH US?
SEIGAKU
HEY, LOOK! I THINK SHUICHIRO AND...?

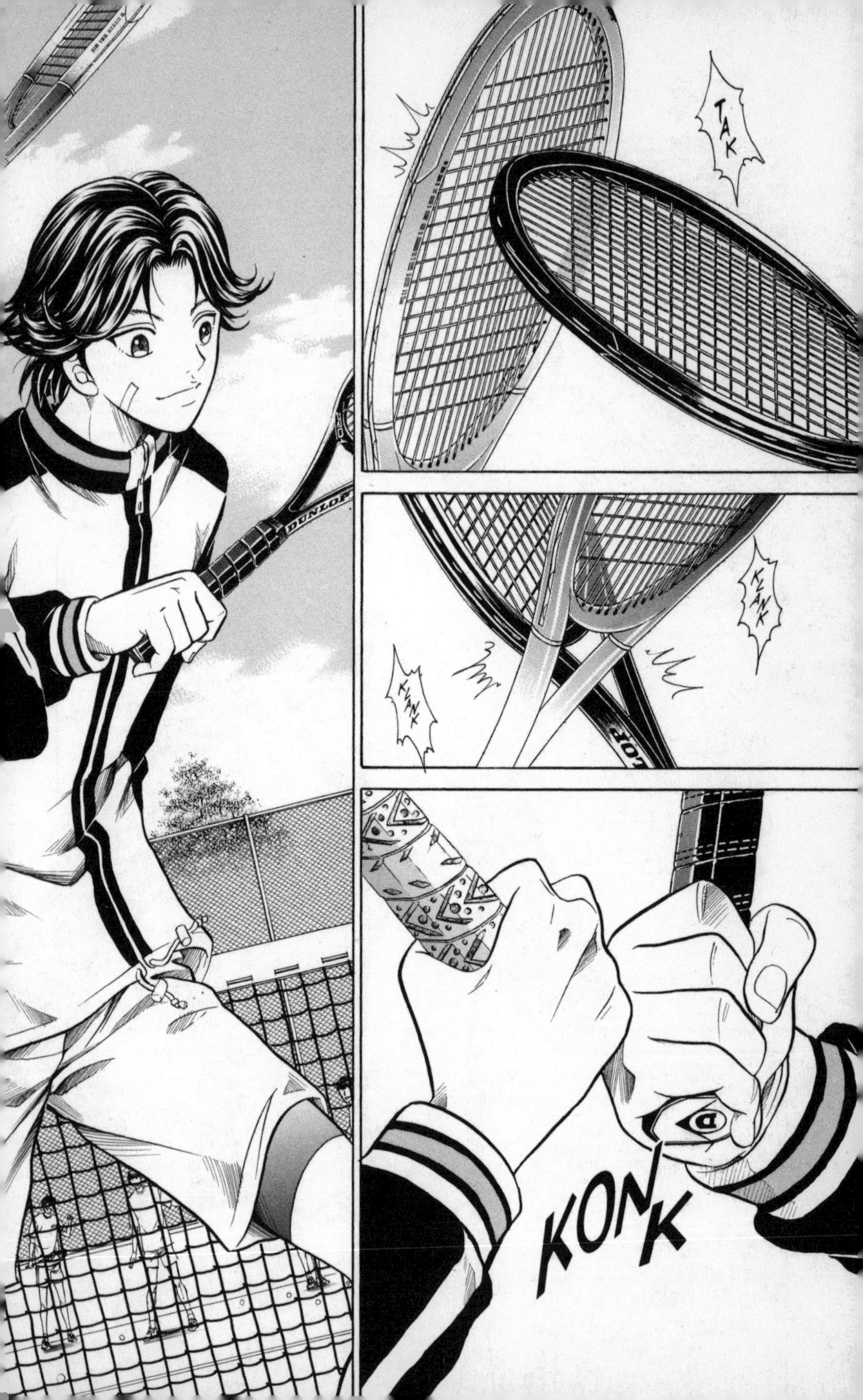
TAK
KLANK
KLANK
KONK
DUNLOP

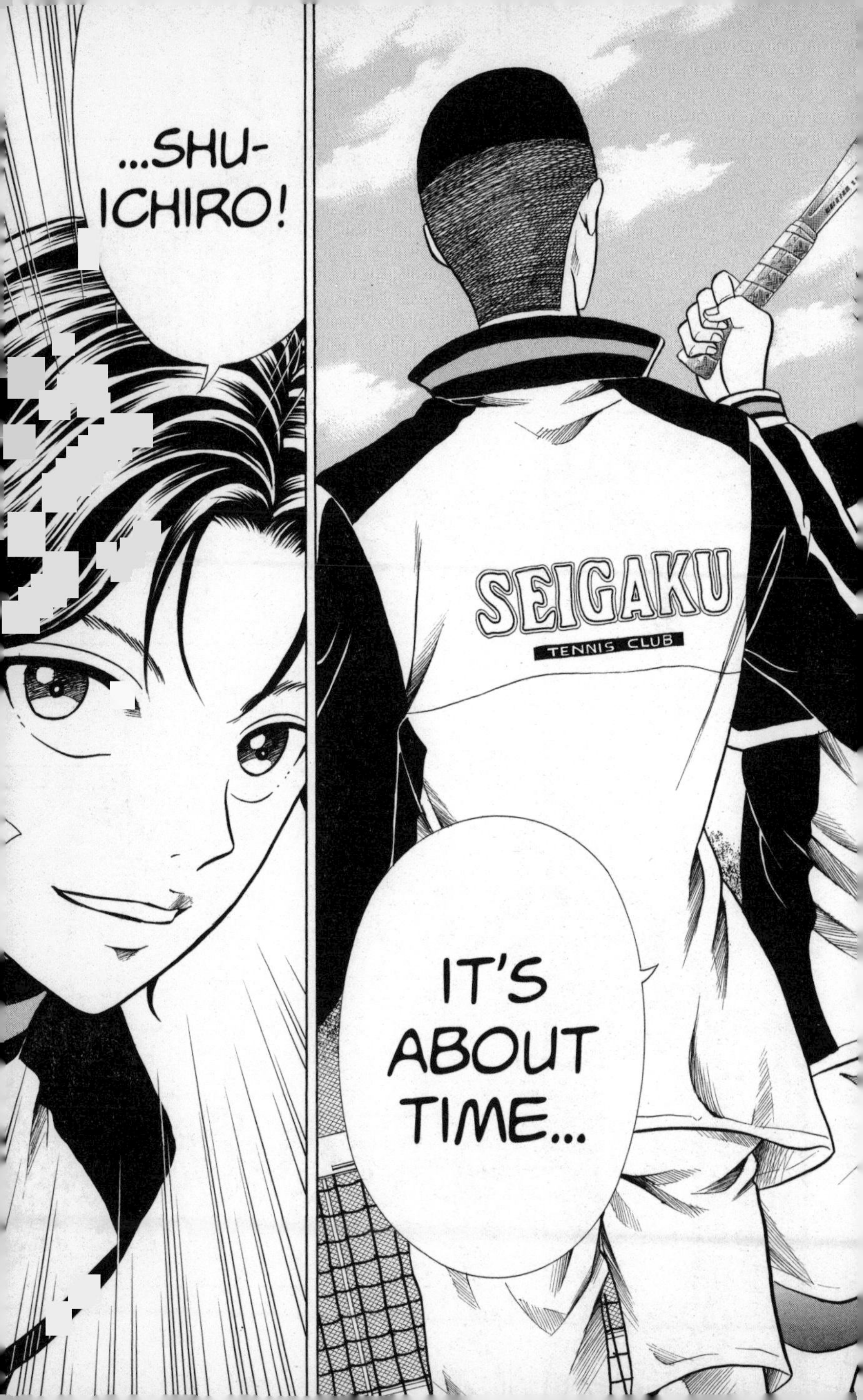
SEIGAKU
TENNIS CLUB
IT'S ABOUT TIME...
...SHU-ICHIRO!

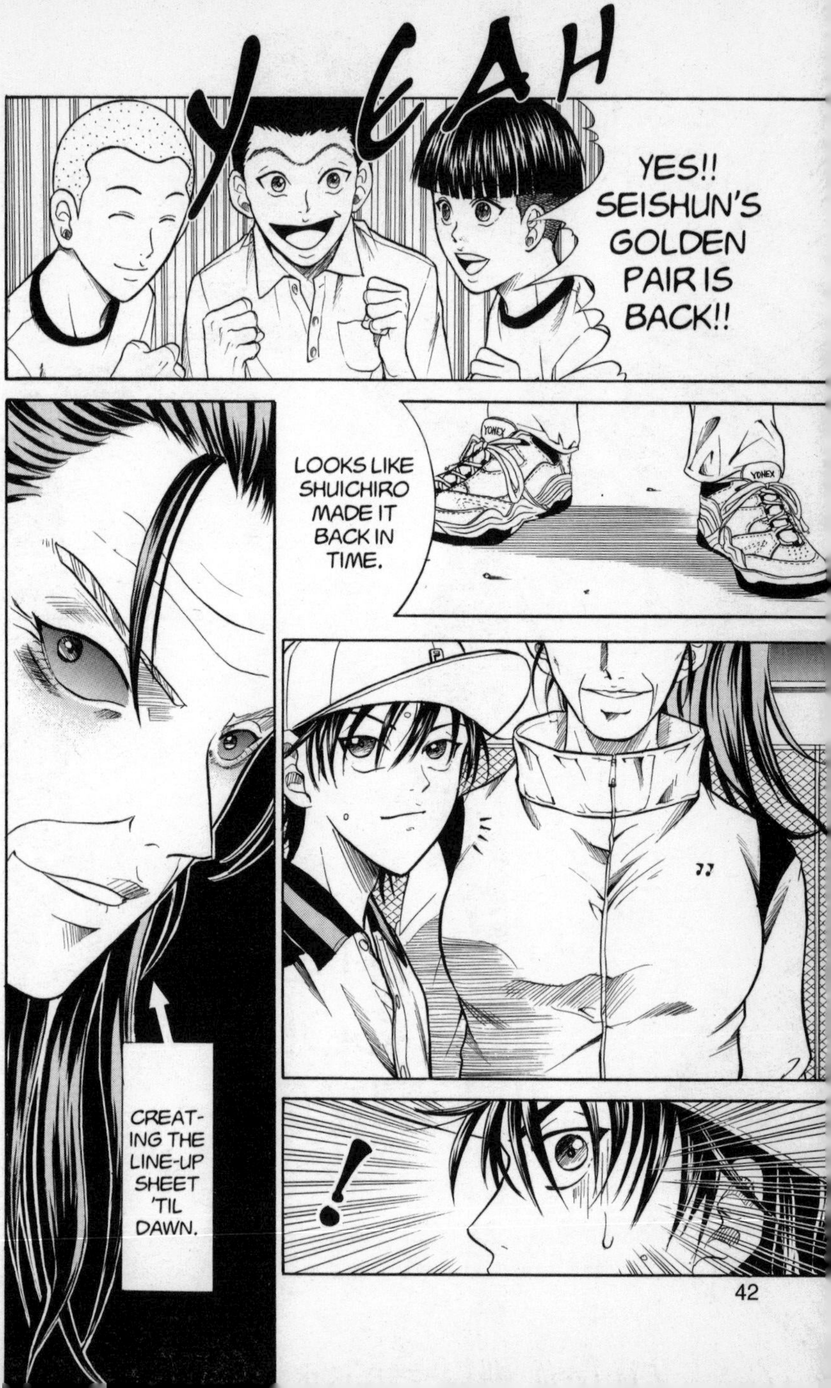
YEAH
YES!! SEISHUN'S GOLDEN PAIR IS BACK!!
LOOKS LIKE SHUICHIRO MADE IT BACK IN TIME.
!
CREAT-ING THE LINE-UP SHEET 'TIL DAWN.

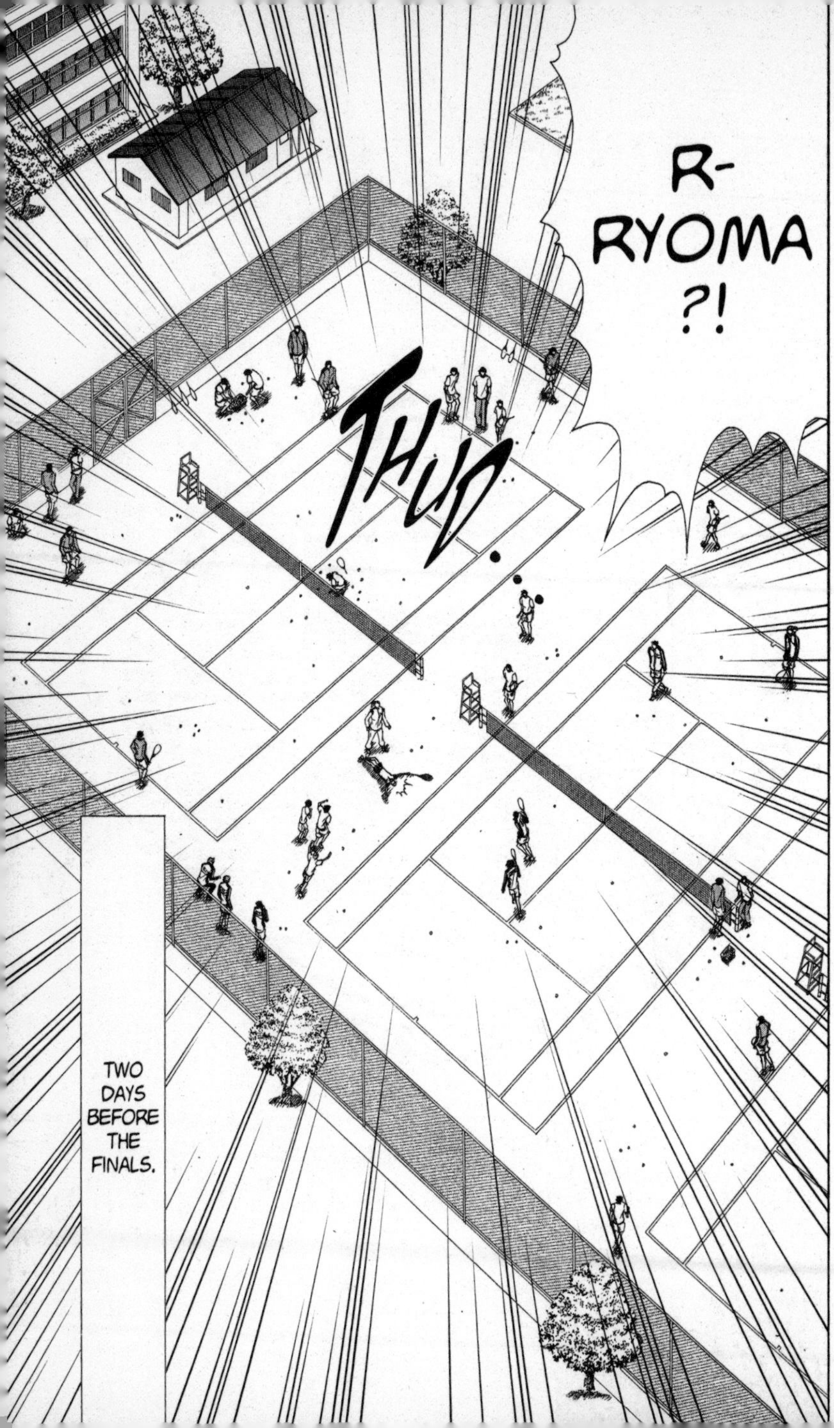
R-RYOMA?!
THUD
TWO DAYS BEFORE THE FINALS.

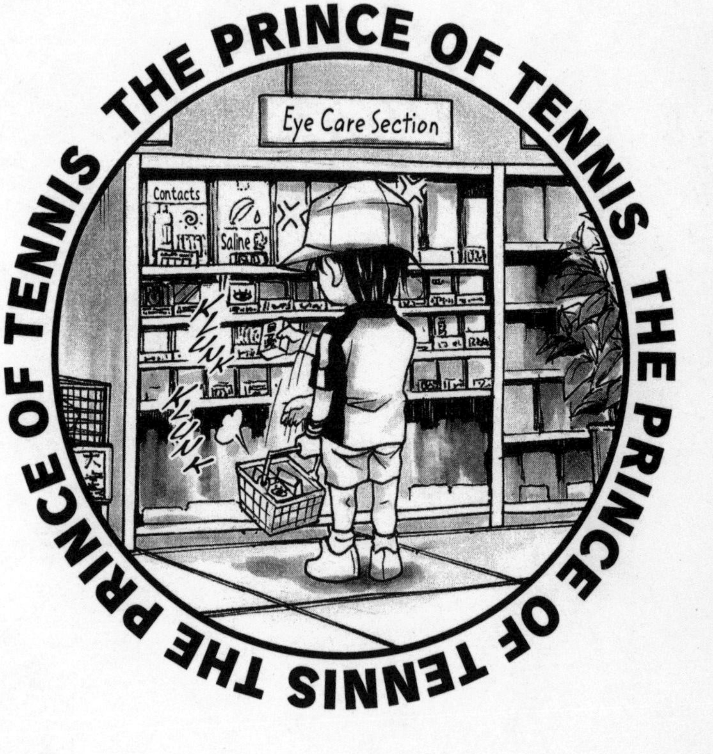
THE PRINCE OF TENNIS THE PRINCE OF TENNIS THE PRINCE OF TENNIS
Eye Care Section
Contacts
Saline
KVUNK
KVUNK

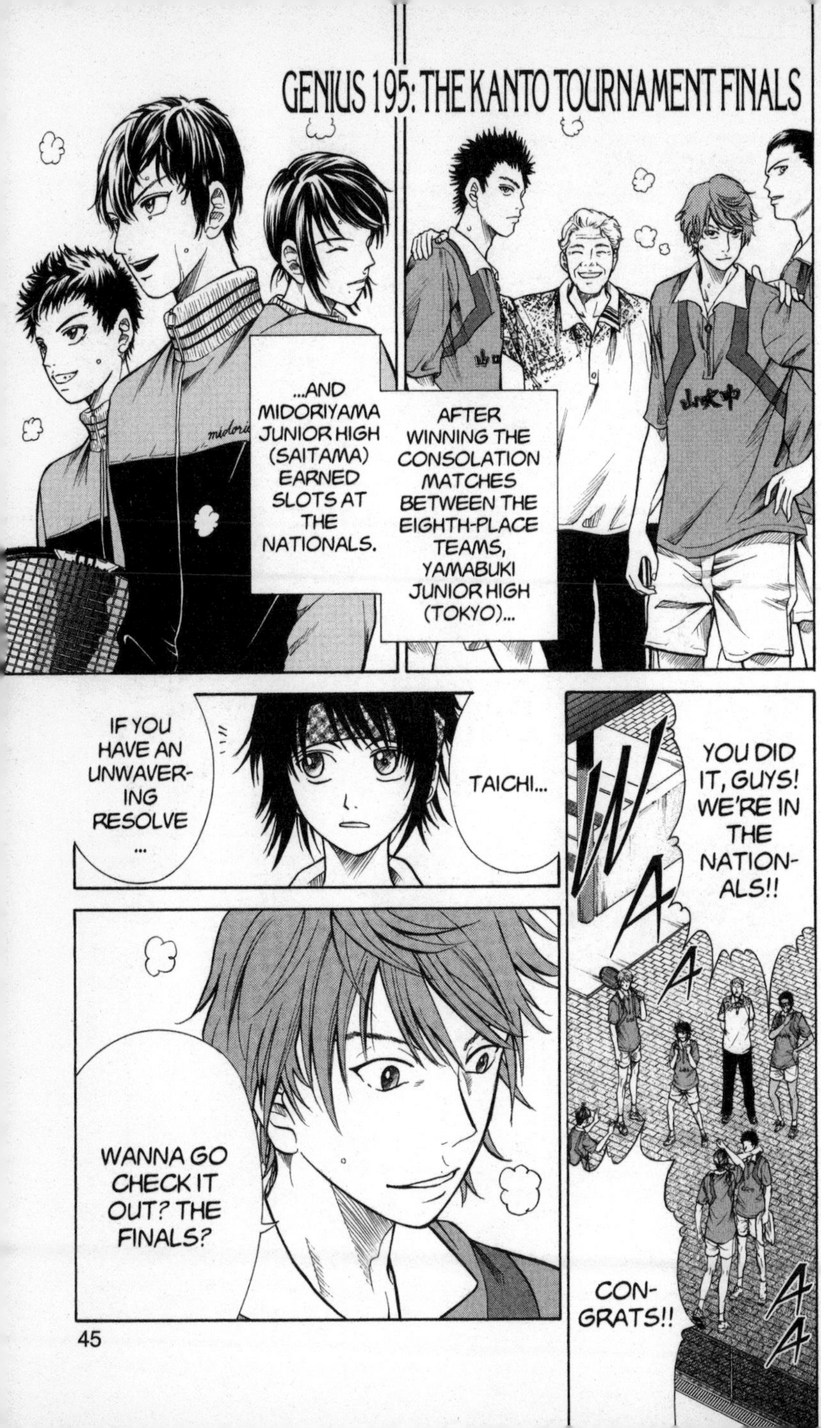
GENIUS 195: THE KANTO TOURNAMENT FINALS
AFTER WINNING THE CONSOLATION MATCHES BETWEEN THE EIGHTH-PLACE TEAMS, YAMABUKI JUNIOR HIGH (TOKYO)...
...AND MIDORIYAMA JUNIOR HIGH (SAITAMA) EARNED SLOTS AT THE NATIONALS.
WAAAA
YOU DID IT, GUYS! WE'RE IN THE NATIONALS!!
CONGRATS!!
TAICHI...
IF YOU HAVE AN UNWAVERING RESOLVE...
WANNA GO CHECK IT OUT? THE FINALS?

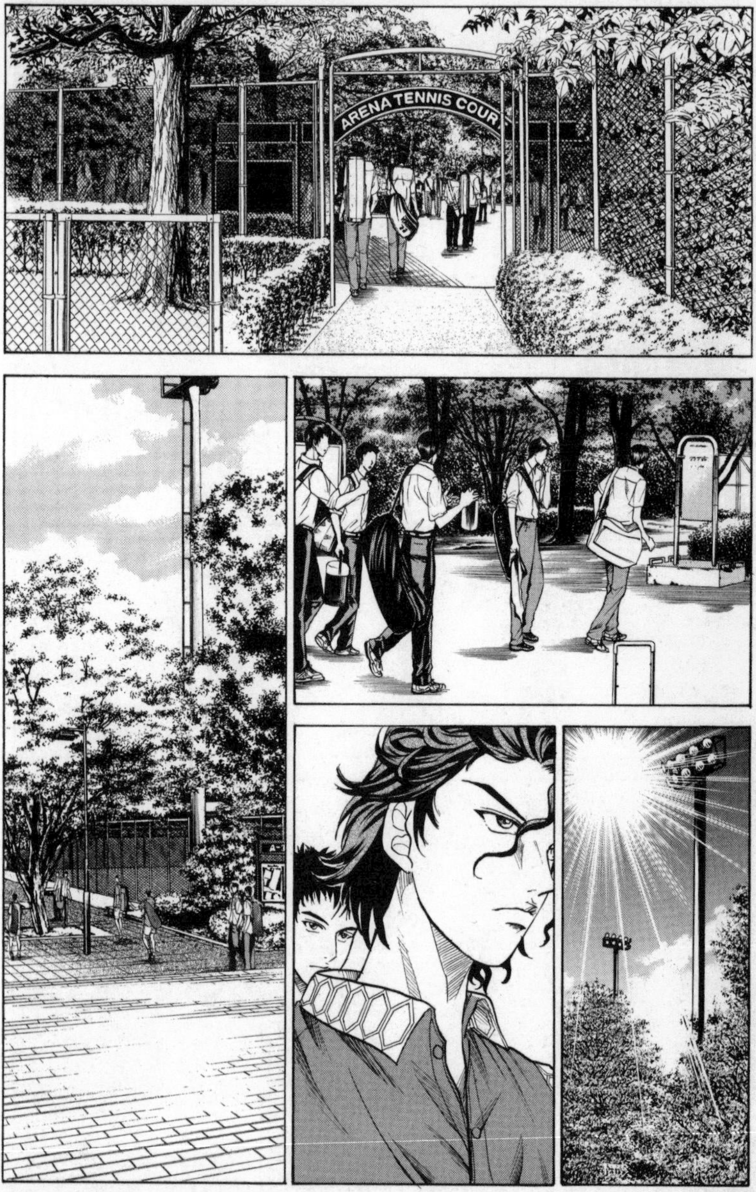
ARENA TENNIS COURT

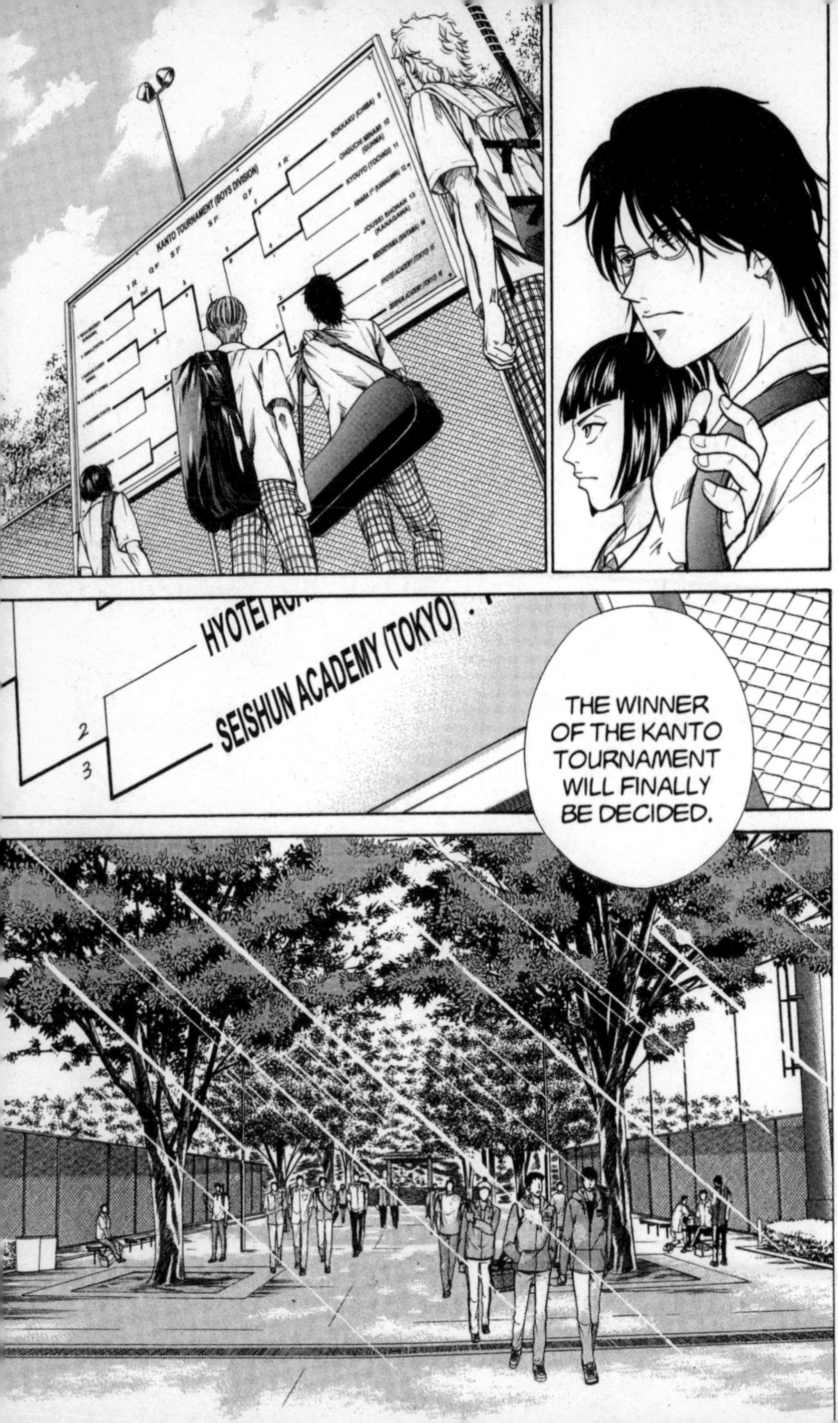
KANTO TOURNAMENT (BOYS DIVISION)
SEISHUN ACADEMY (TOKYO)
2
3
THE WINNER OF THE KANTO TOURNAMENT WILL FINALLY BE DECIDED.

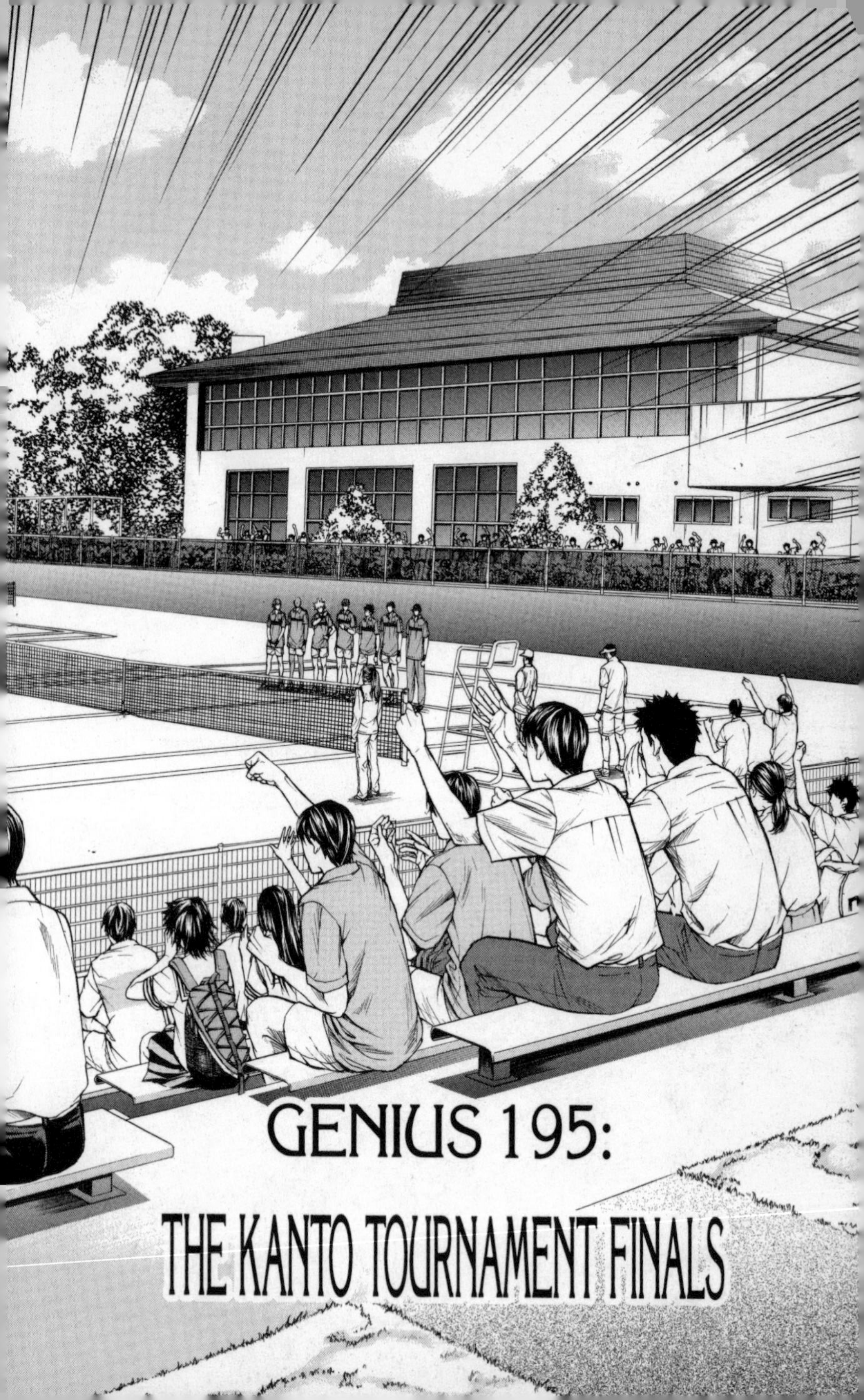
GENIUS 195:
THE KANTO TOURNAMENT FINALS

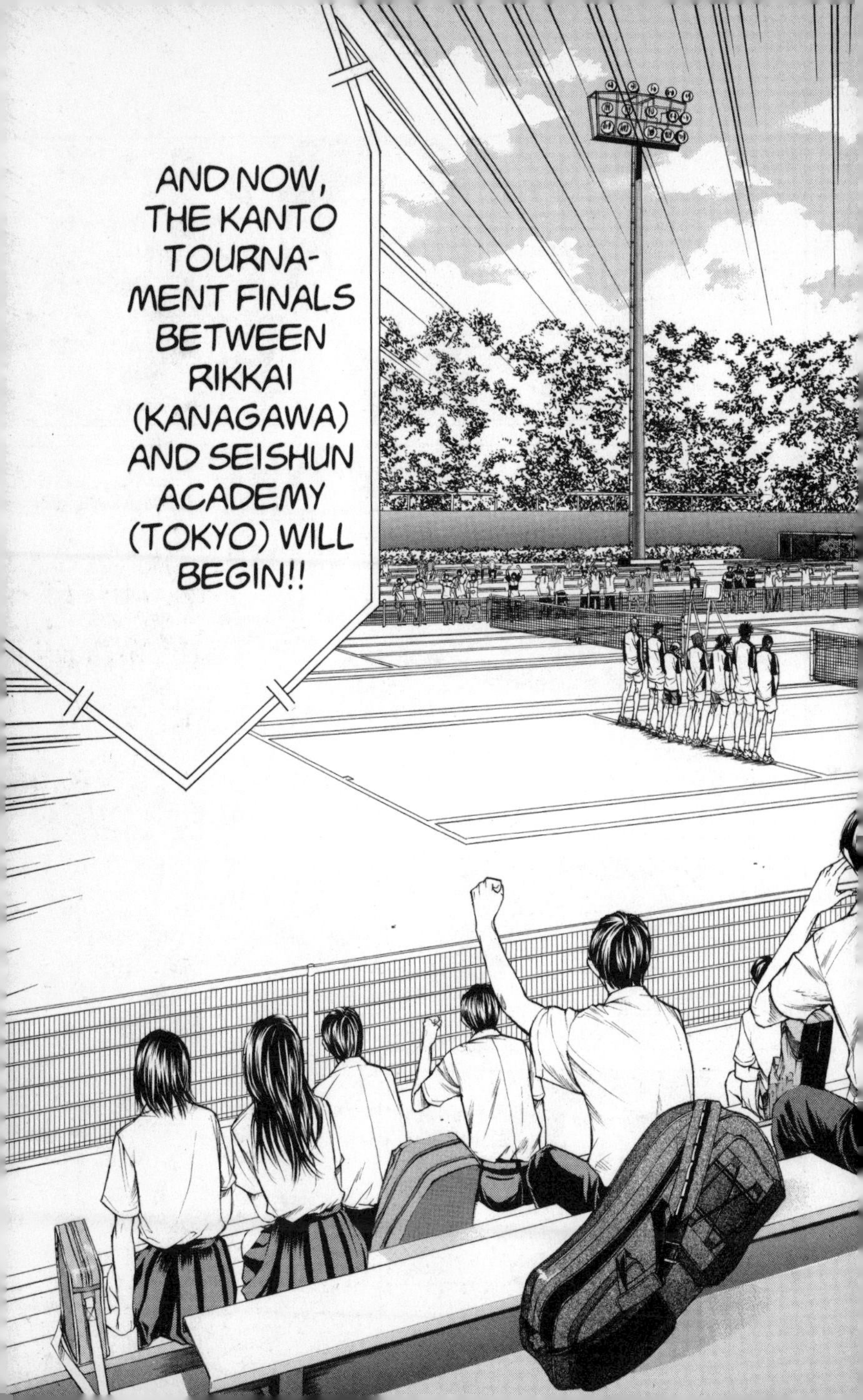
AND NOW, THE KANTO TOURNAMENT FINALS BETWEEN RIKKAI (KANAGAWA) AND SEISHUN ACADEMY (TOKYO) WILL BEGIN!!

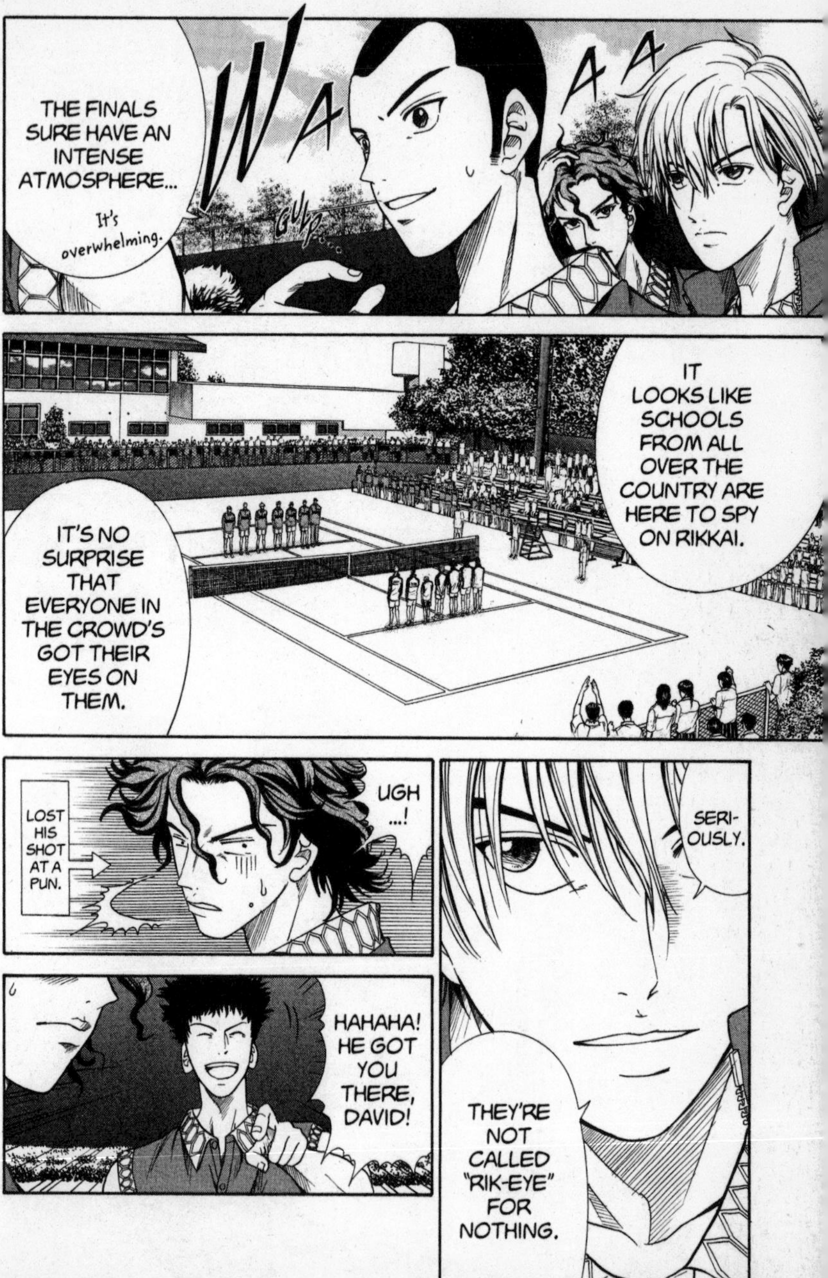
WAAAA
THE FINALS SURE HAVE AN INTENSE ATMOSPHERE...
It's overwhelming.
GULP
IT LOOKS LIKE SCHOOLS FROM ALL OVER THE COUNTRY ARE HERE TO SPY ON RIKKAI.
IT'S NO SURPRISE THAT EVERYONE IN THE CROWD'S GOT THEIR EYES ON THEM.
SERIOUSLY.
THEY'RE NOT CALLED "RIK-EYE" FOR NOTHING.
UGH ...!
LOST HIS SHOT AT A PUN.
HAHAHA! HE GOT YOU THERE, DAVID!

READ THIS WAY

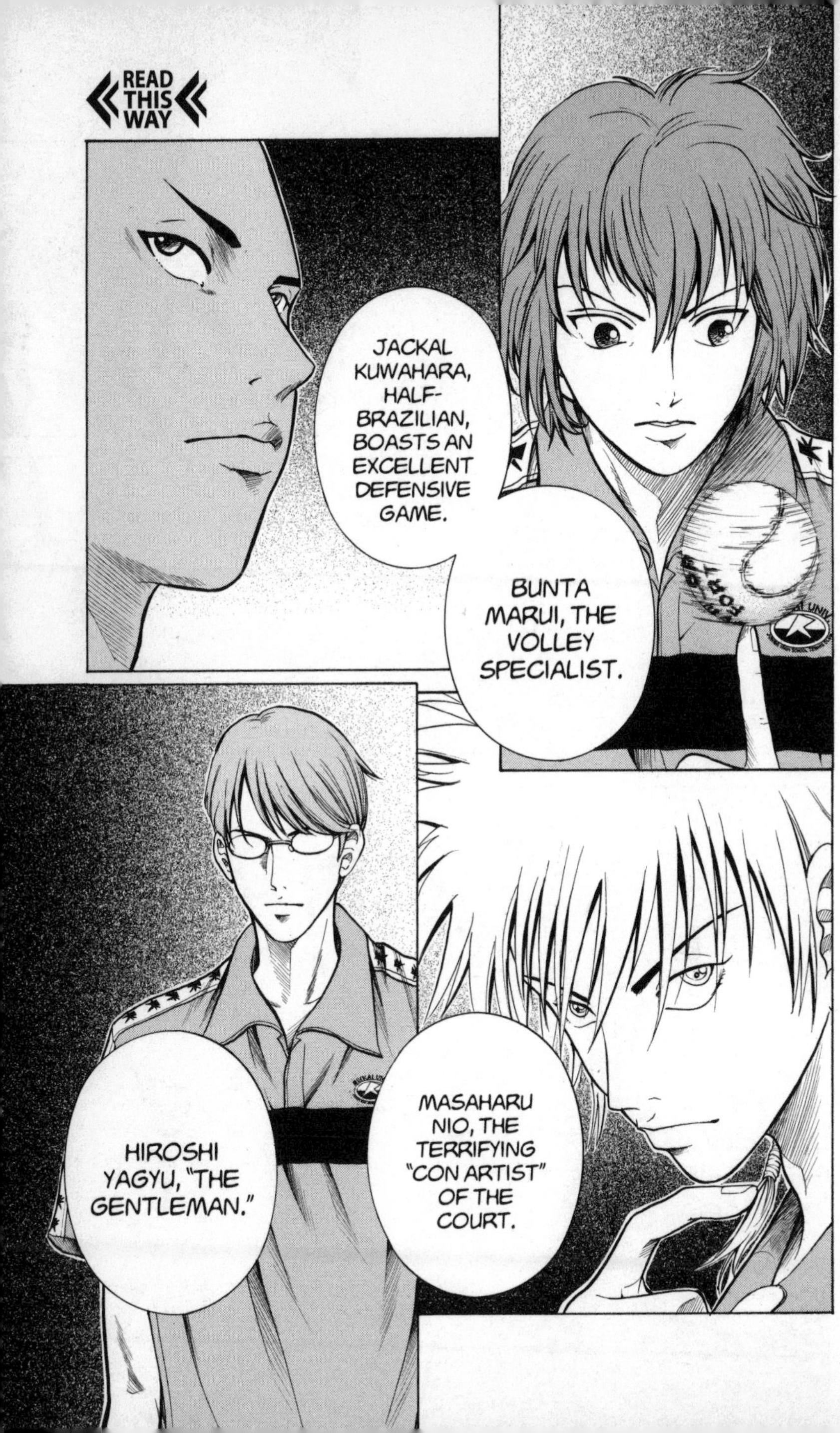
JACKAL KUWAHARA, HALF-BRAZILIAN, BOASTS AN EXCELLENT DEFENSIVE GAME.
BUNTA MARUI, THE VOLLEY SPECIALIST.
MASAHARU NIO, THE TERRIFYING "CON ARTIST" OF THE COURT.
HIROSHI YAGYU, "THE GENTLEMAN."

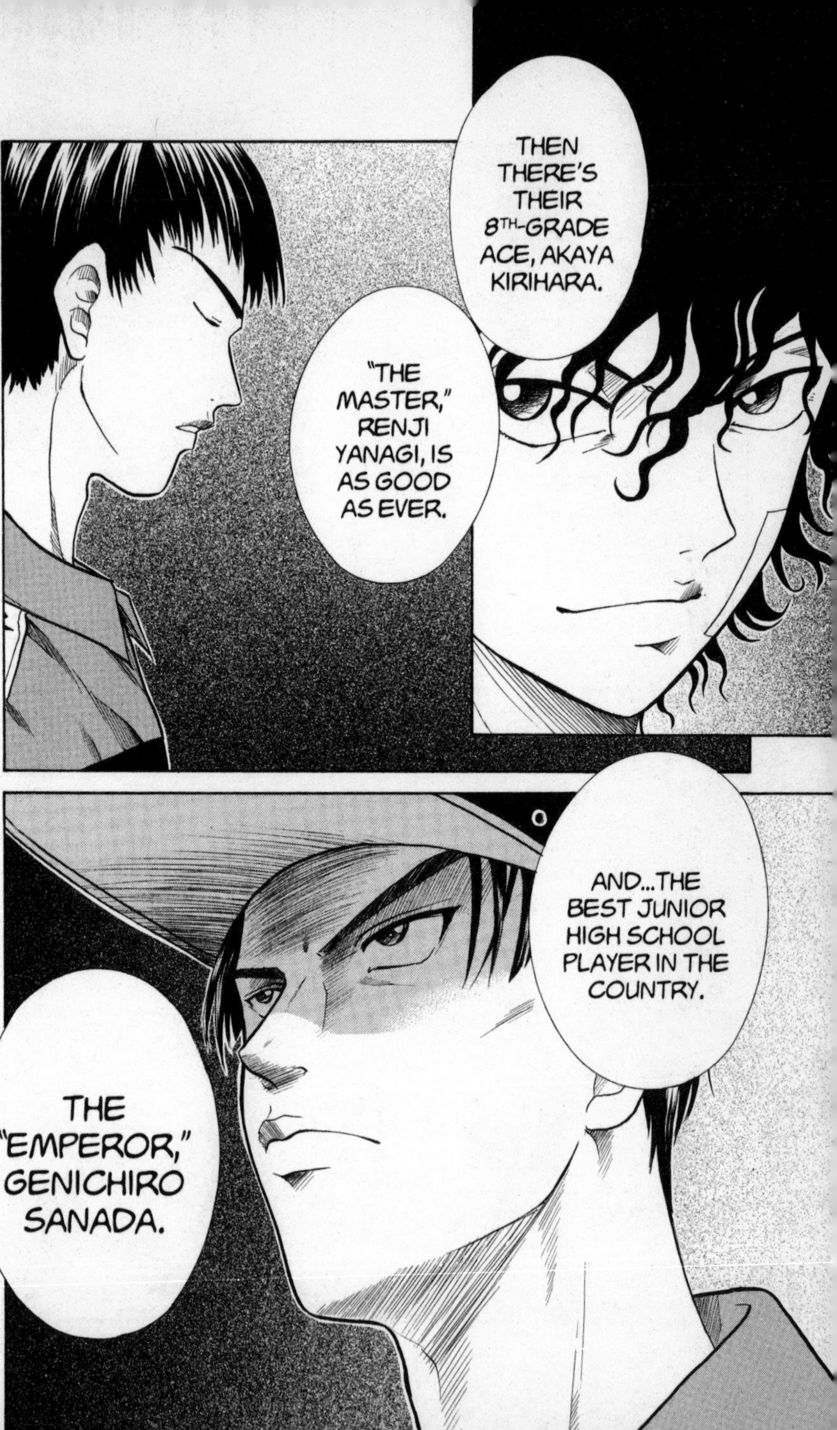
THEN THERE'S THEIR 8TH-GRADE ACE, AKAYA KIRIHARA.
"THE MASTER," RENJI YANAGI, IS AS GOOD AS EVER.
AND...THE BEST JUNIOR HIGH SCHOOL PLAYER IN THE COUNTRY.
THE "EMPEROR," GENICHIRO SANADA.

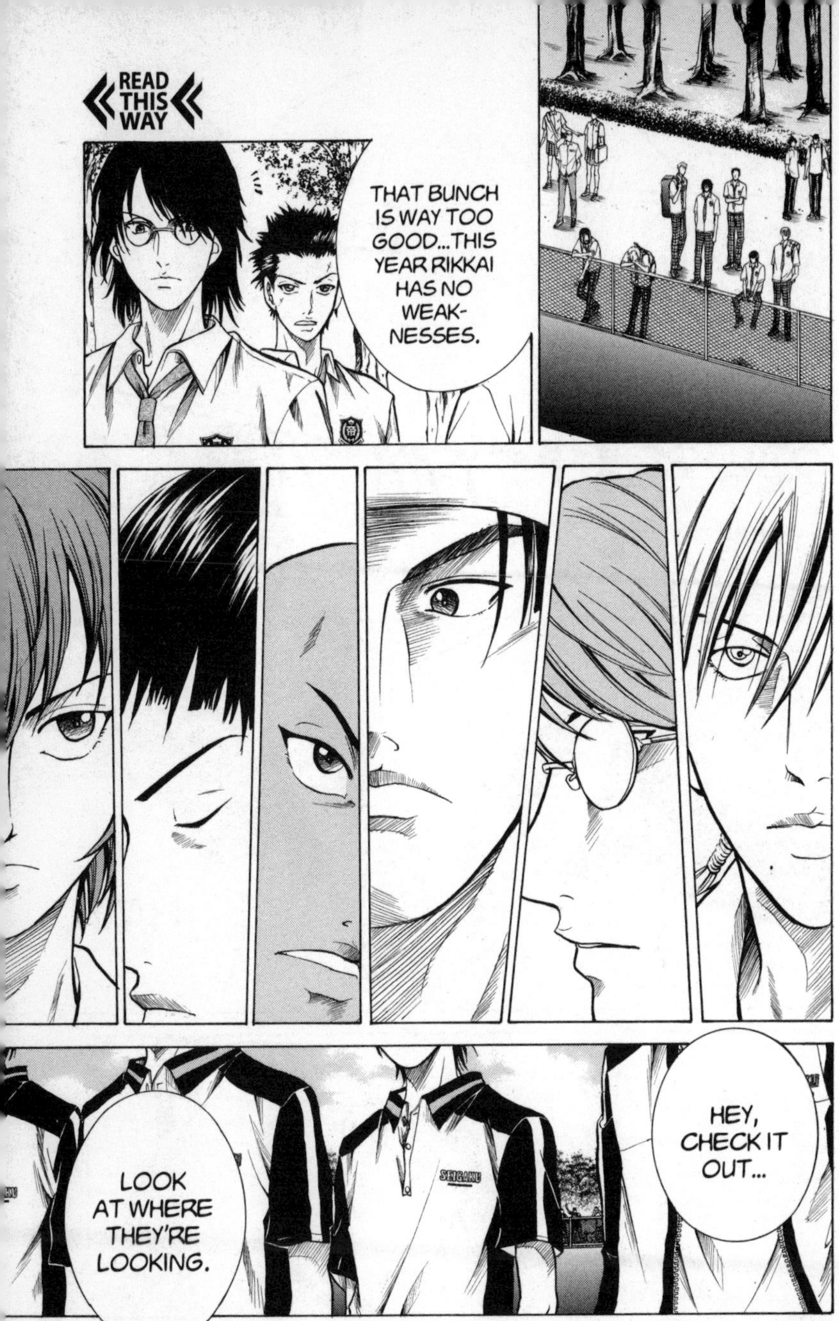
READ THIS WAY
THAT BUNCH IS WAY TOO GOOD...THIS YEAR RIKKAI HAS NO WEAK-NESSES.
HEY, CHECK IT OUT...
LOOK AT WHERE THEY'RE LOOKING.

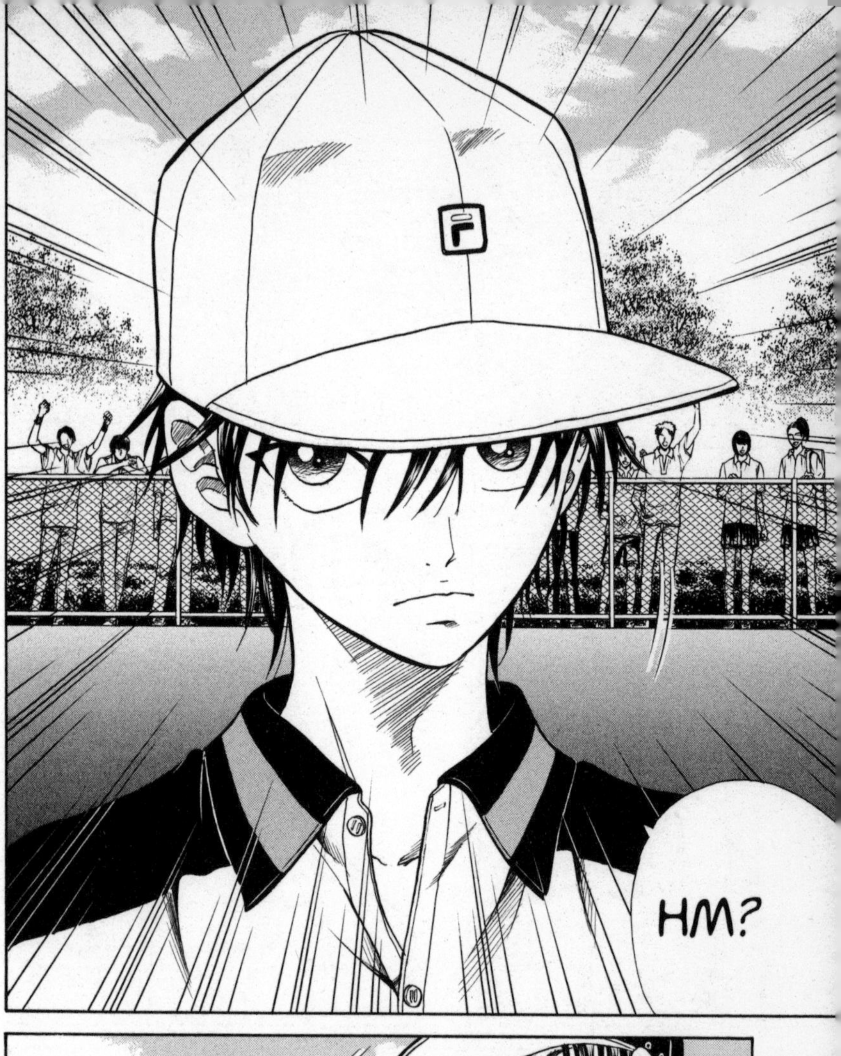
HM?
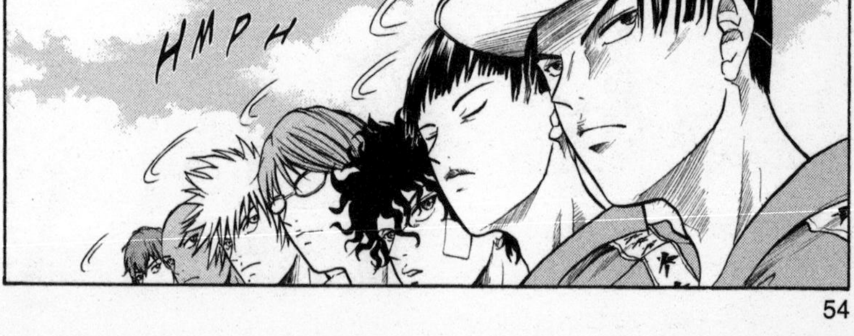
HMPH

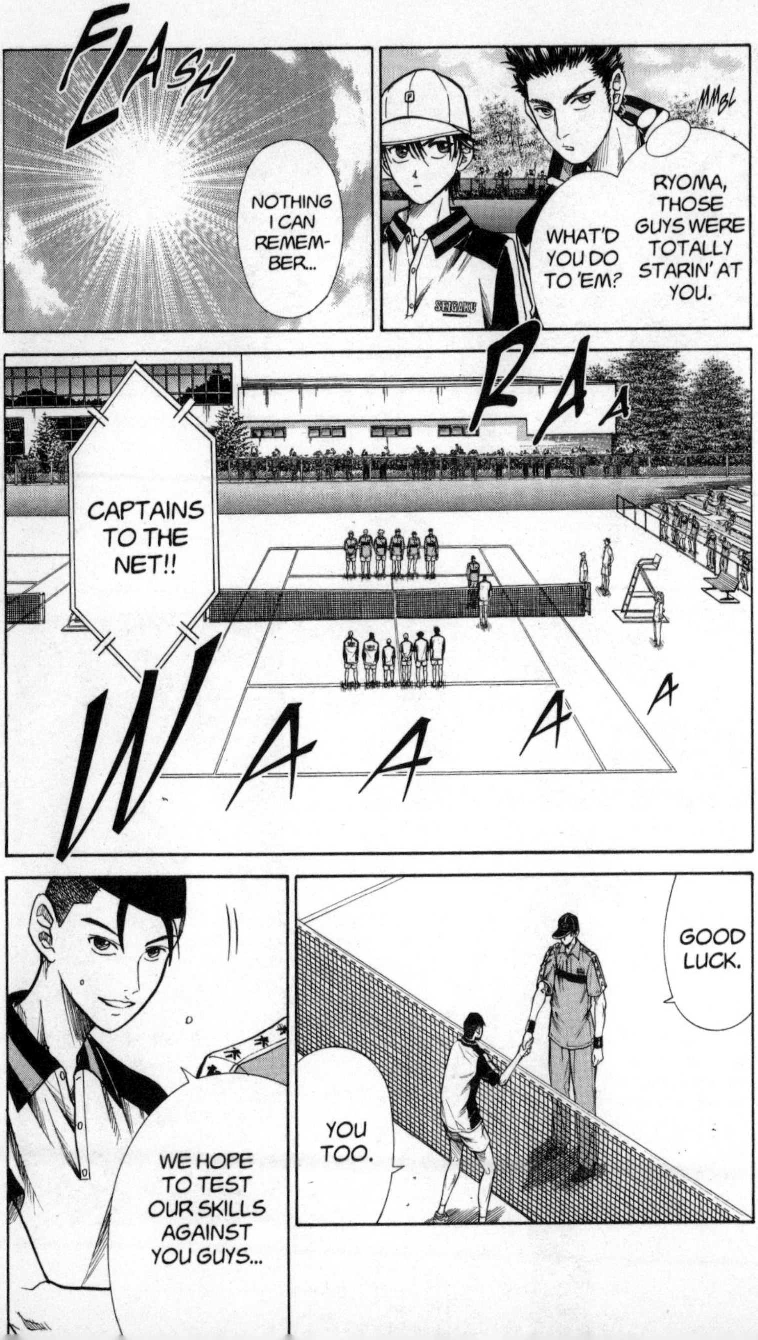
MMBL
RYOMA, THOSE GUYS WERE TOTALLY STARIN' AT YOU.
WHAT'D YOU DO TO 'EM?
FLASH
NOTHING I CAN REMEMBER...
RAAA
CAPTAINS TO THE NET!!
WAAAA
GOOD LUCK.
YOU TOO.
WE HOPE TO TEST OUR SKILLS AGAINST YOU GUYS...

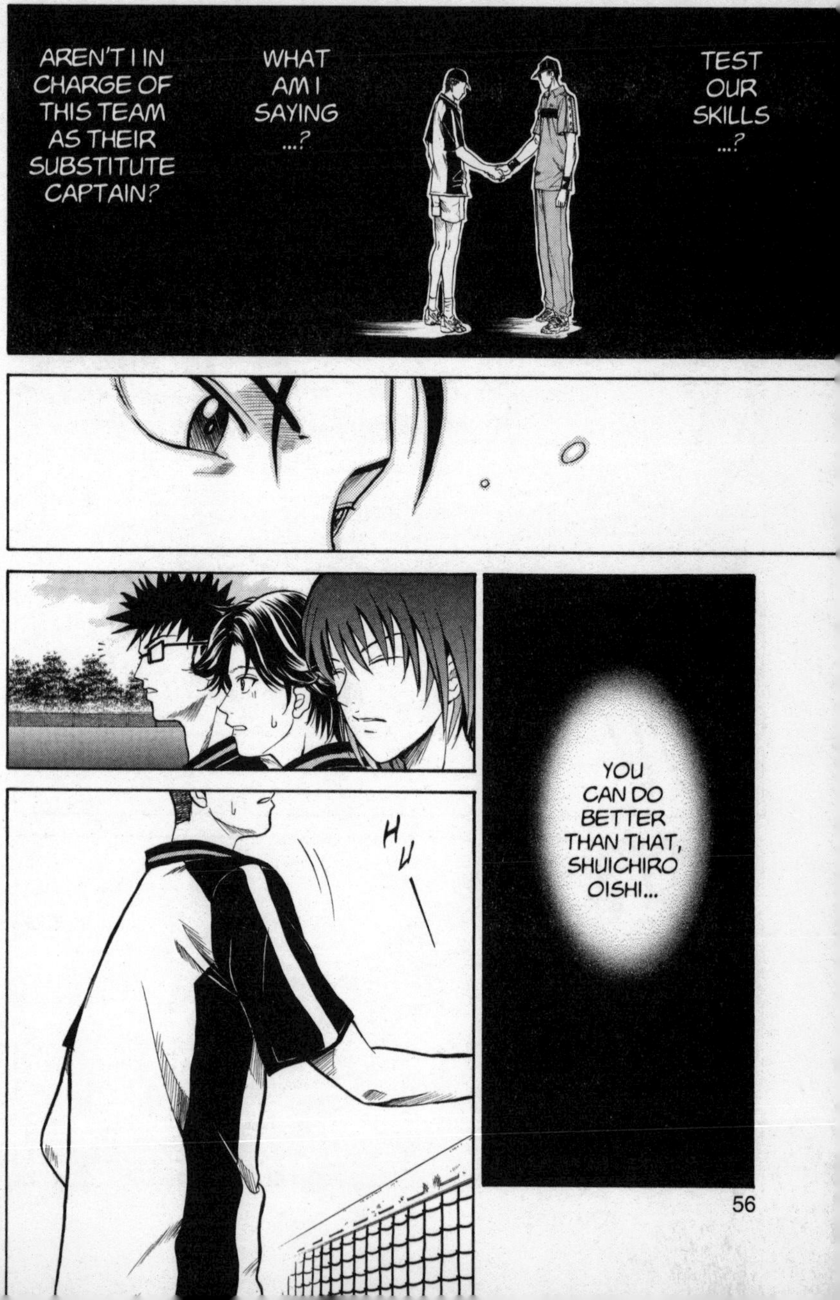
TEST OUR SKILLS ...?
WHAT AM I SAYING ...?
AREN'T I IN CHARGE OF THIS TEAM AS THEIR SUBSTITUTE CAPTAIN?
YOU CAN DO BETTER THAN THAT, SHUICHIRO OISHI...
HU

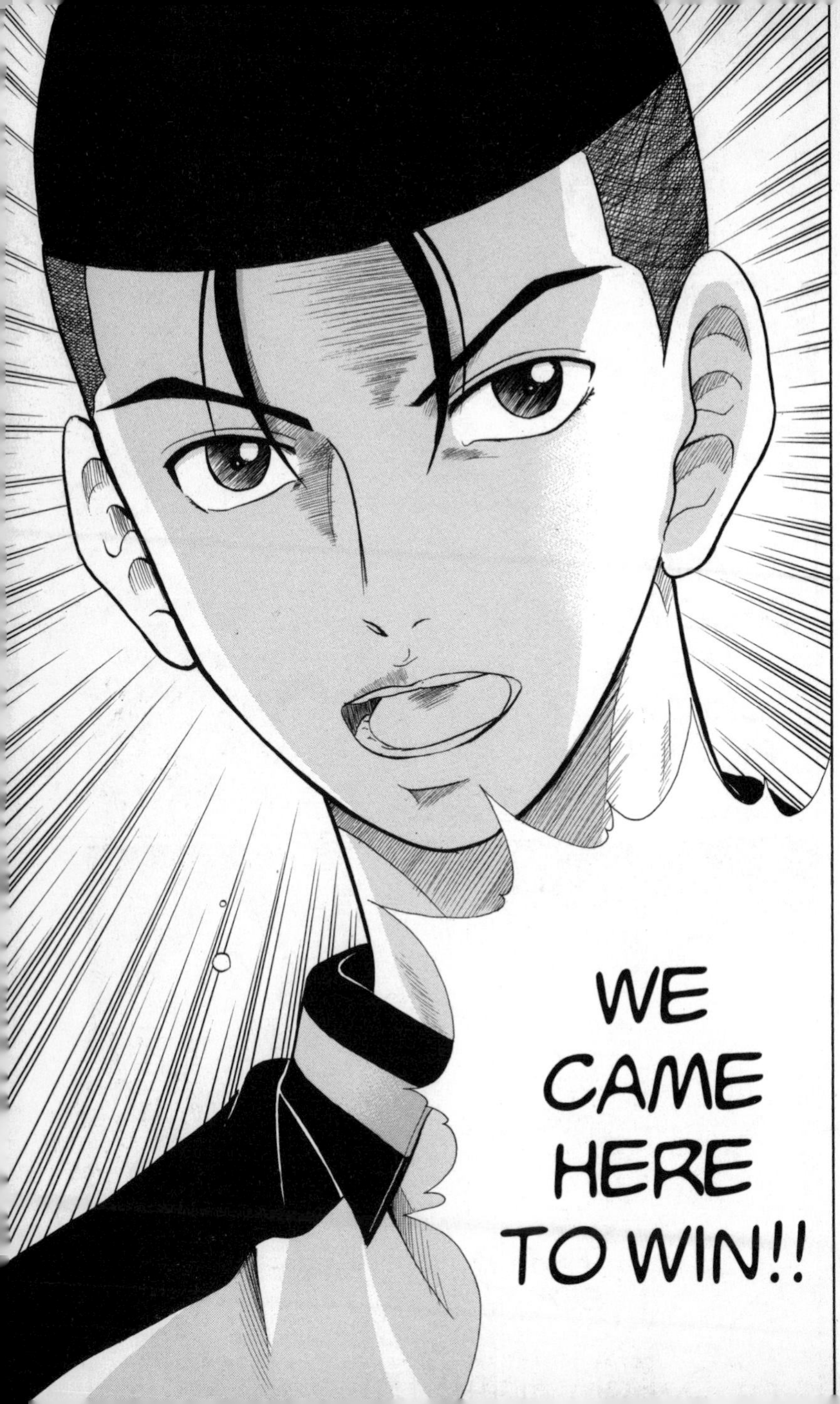
WE CAME HERE TO WIN!!

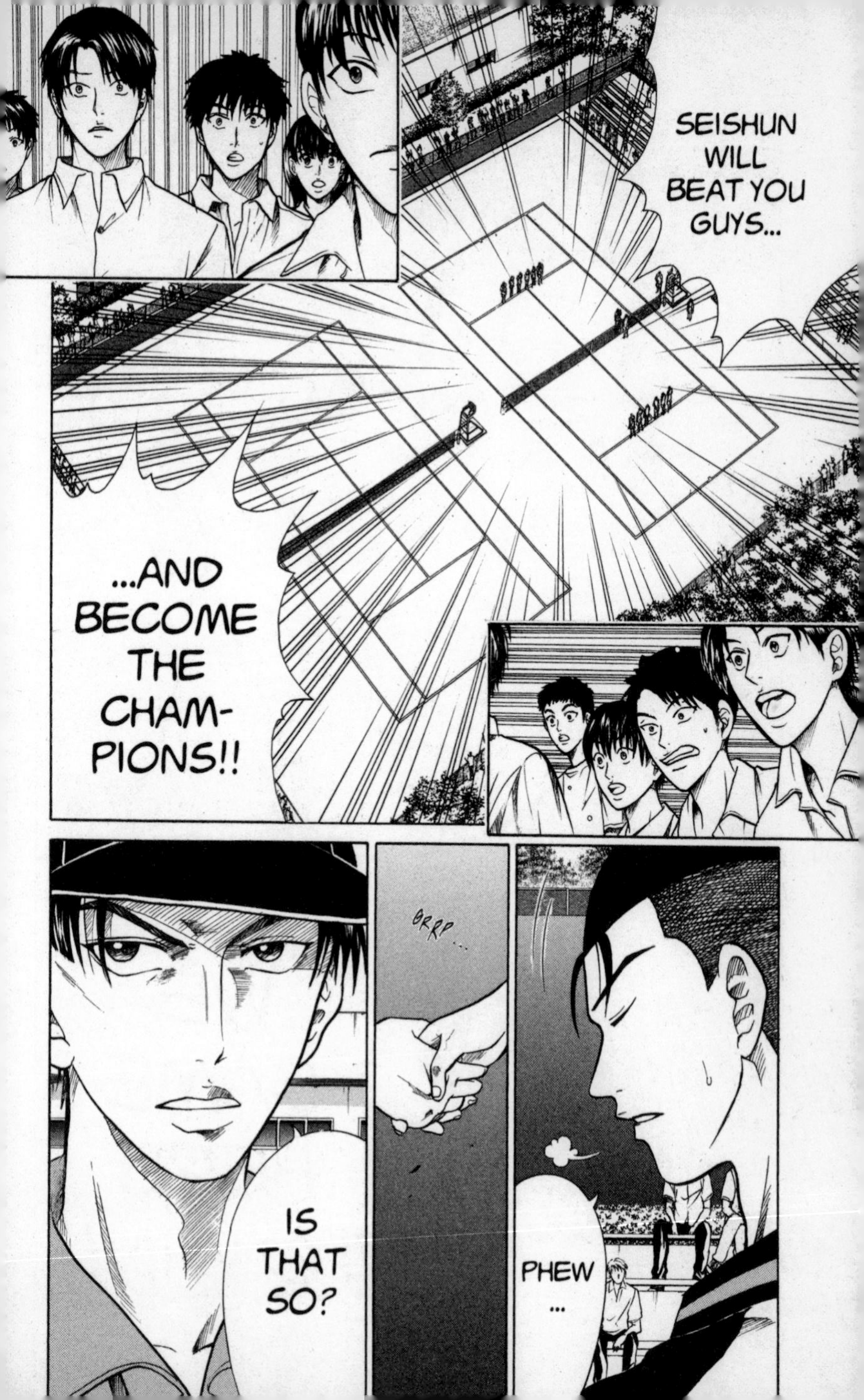
SEISHUN WILL BEAT YOU GUYS...
...AND BECOME THE CHAMPIONS!!
PHEW ...
GRRP...
IS THAT SO?

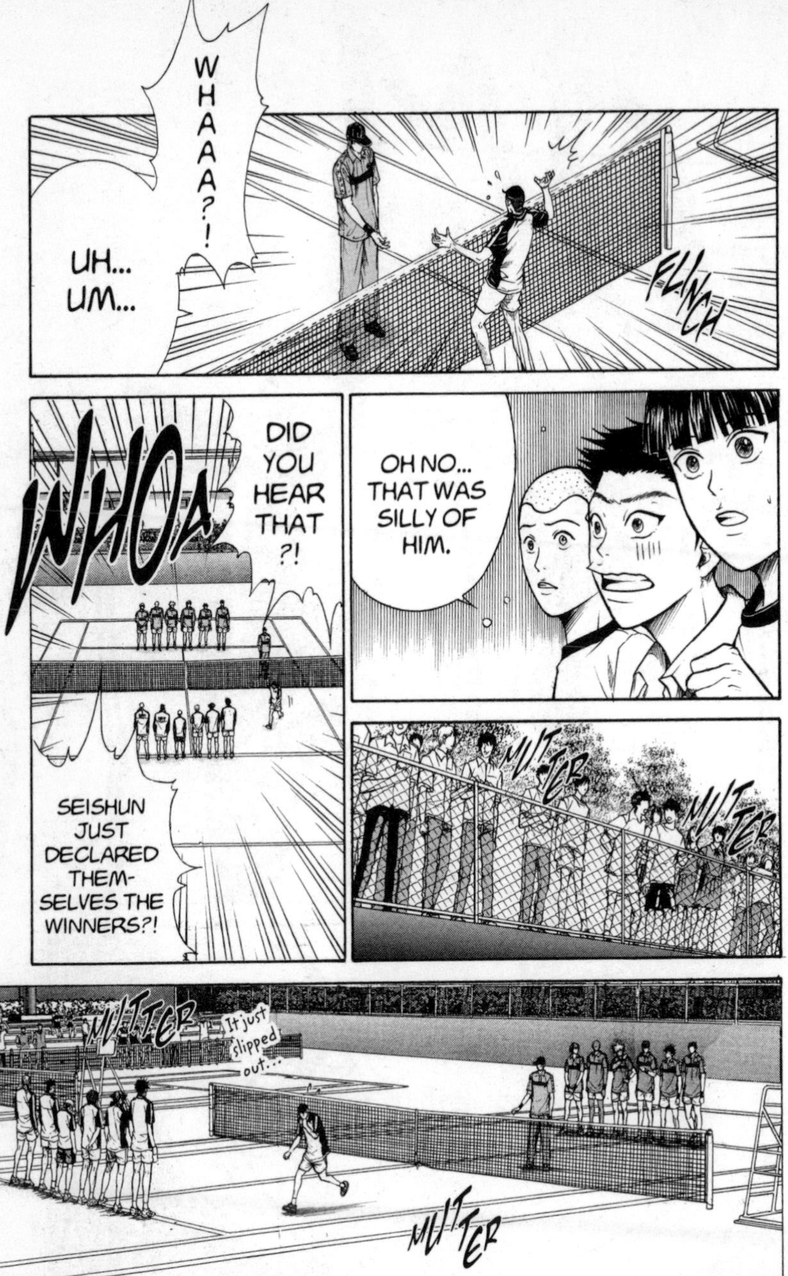
WHAAAA?!
FLINCH
UH... UM...
OH NO... THAT WAS SILLY OF HIM.
MUTTER
MUTTER
DID YOU HEAR THAT?!
WHOA
SEISHUN JUST DECLARED THEMSELVES THE WINNERS?!
It just slipped out...
MUTTER
MUTTER

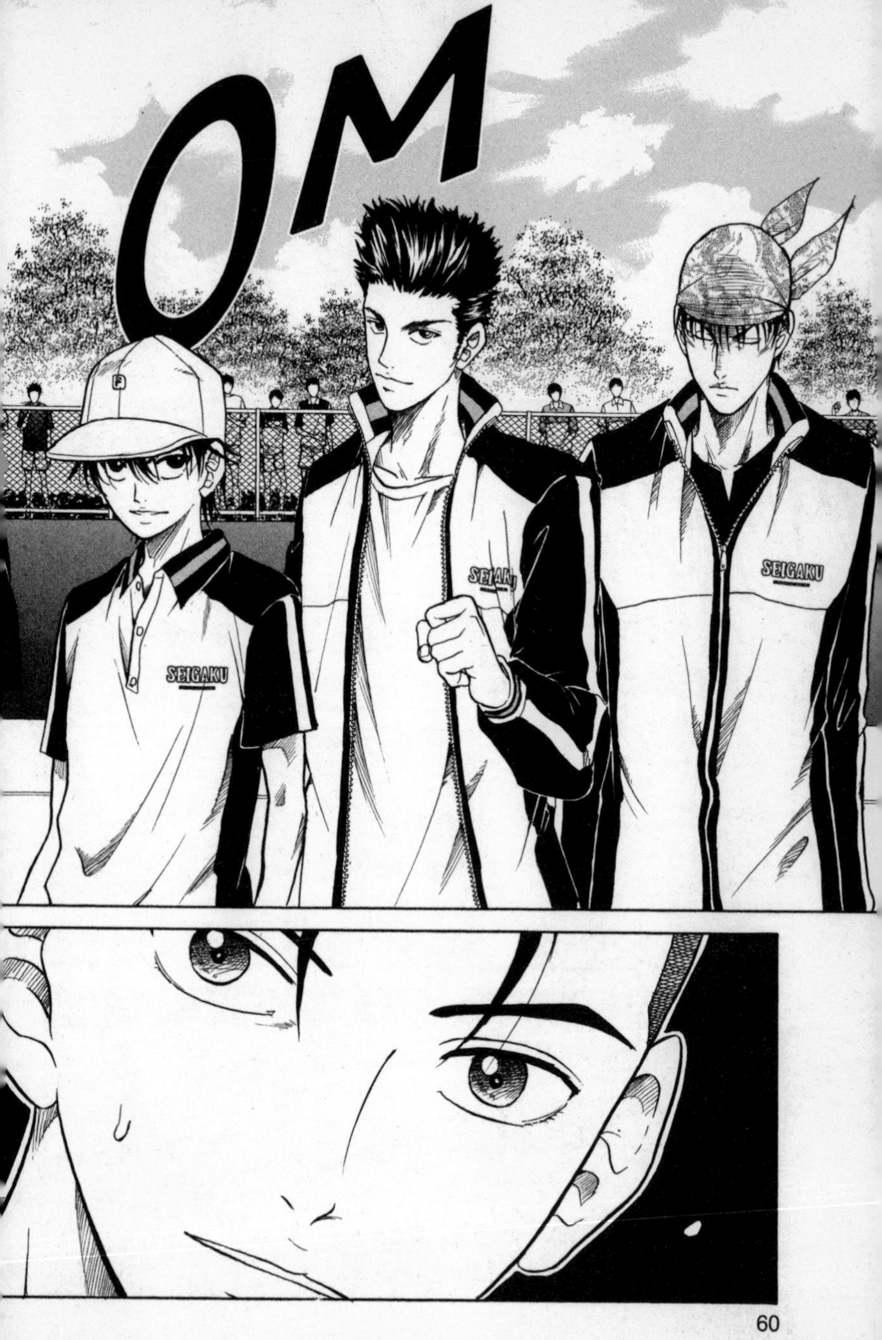
OM
SEIGAKU
SEIGAKU
SEIGAKU

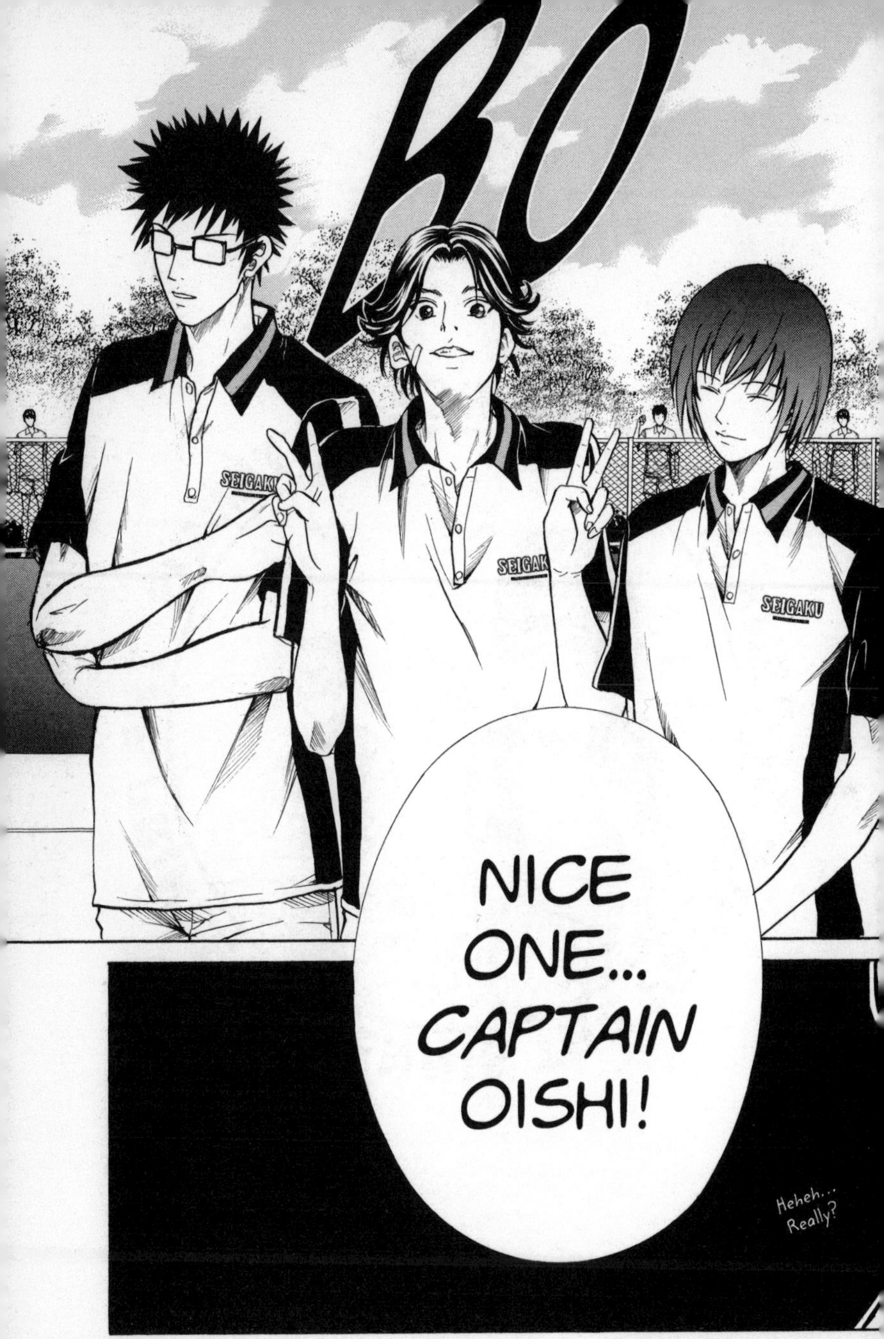
BO
NICE ONE... CAPTAIN OISHI!
Heheh... Really?

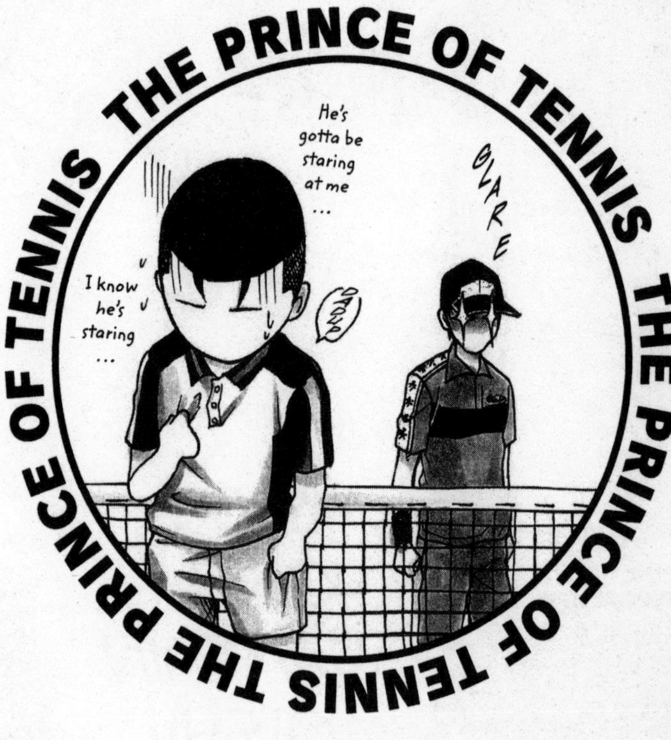
THE PRINCE OF TENNIS THE PRINCE OF TENNIS THE PRINCE OF TENNIS
GLARE
He's gotta be staring at me ...
I know he's staring ...

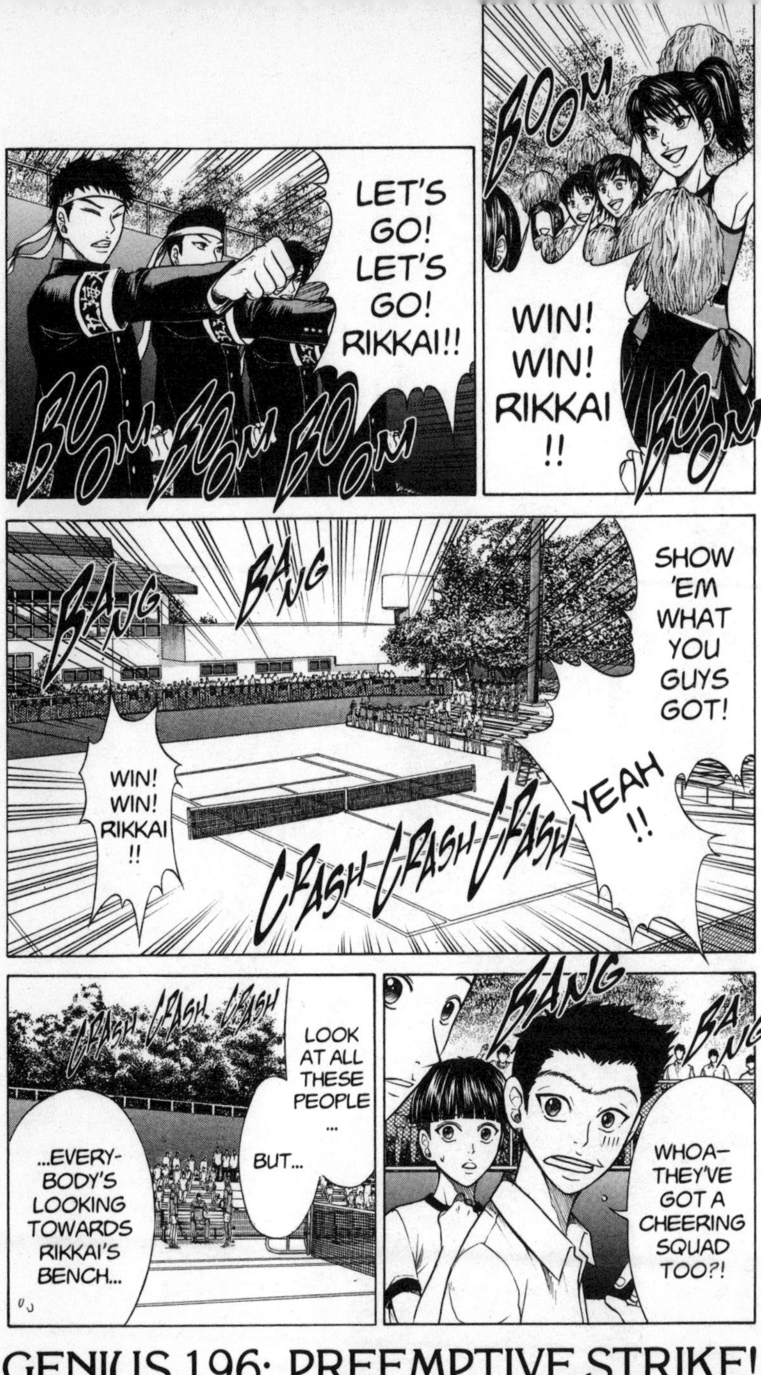
BOOM
WIN! WIN! RIKKAI!!
BOOM
LET'S GO! LET'S GO! RIKKAI!!
BOOM BOOM BOOM
SHOW 'EM WHAT YOU GUYS GOT!
BANG BANG
YEAH!!
CRASH CRASH CRASH
WIN! WIN! RIKKAI!!
BANG
BANG
WHOA—THEY'VE GOT A CHEERING SQUAD TOO?!
CRASH CRASH CRASH
LOOK AT ALL THESE PEOPLE...
BUT...
...EVERYBODY'S LOOKING TOWARDS RIKKAI'S BENCH...

GENIUS 196: PREEMPTIVE STRIKE!

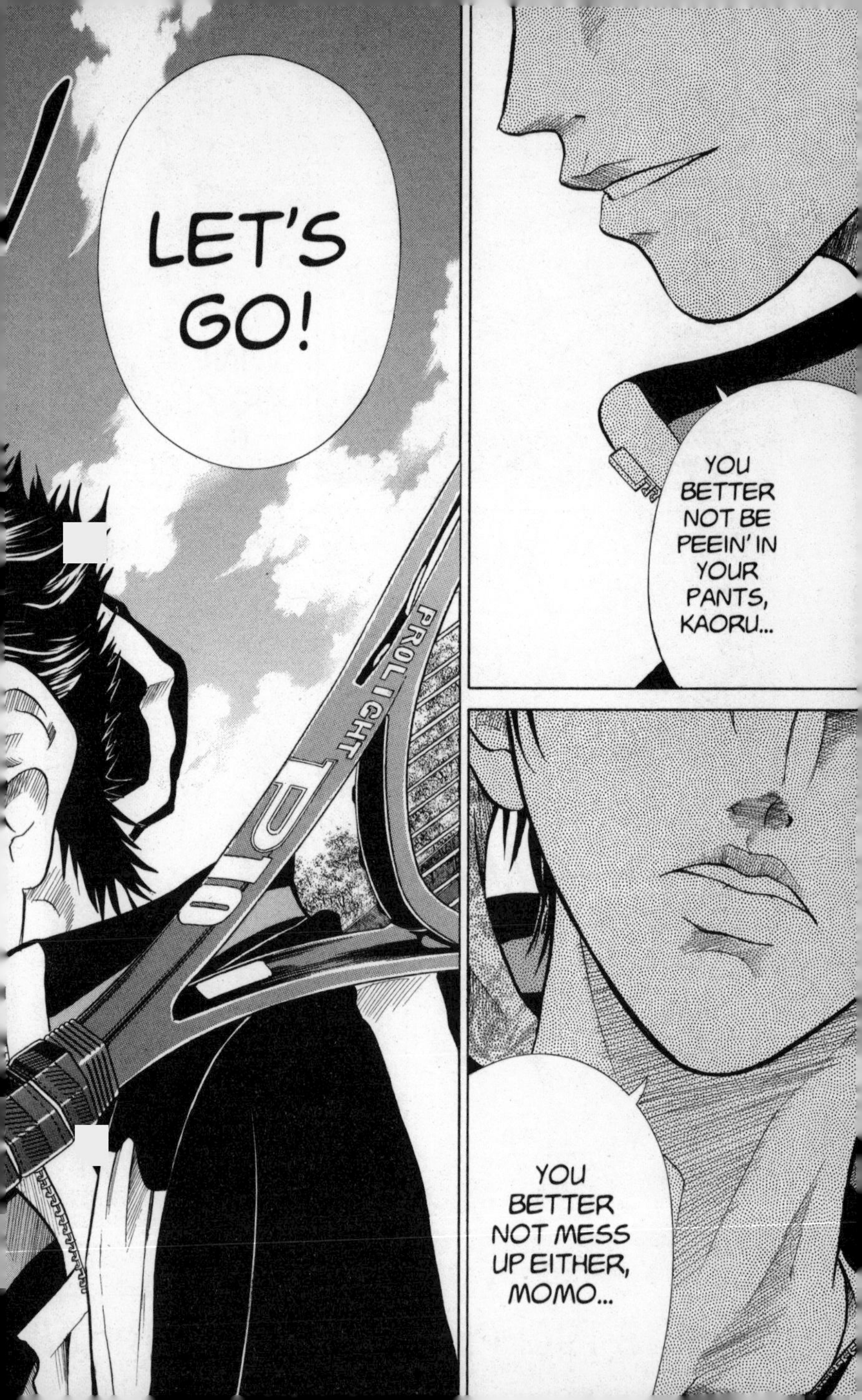
YOU BETTER NOT BE PEEIN' IN YOUR PANTS, KAORU...
YOU BETTER NOT MESS UP EITHER, MOMO...
LET'S GO!
PROLIGHT

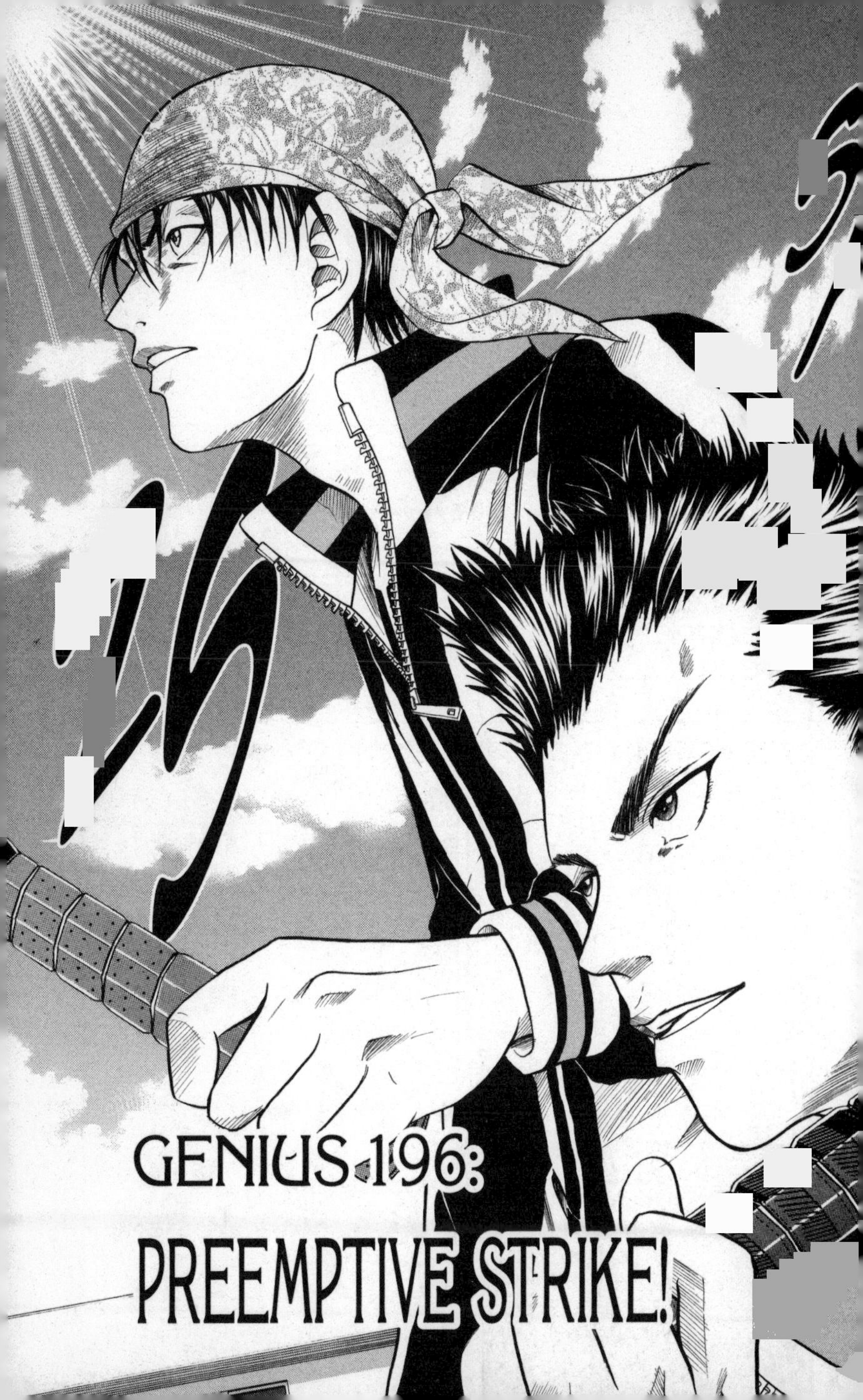
GENIUS 196:
PREEMPTIVE STRIKE!

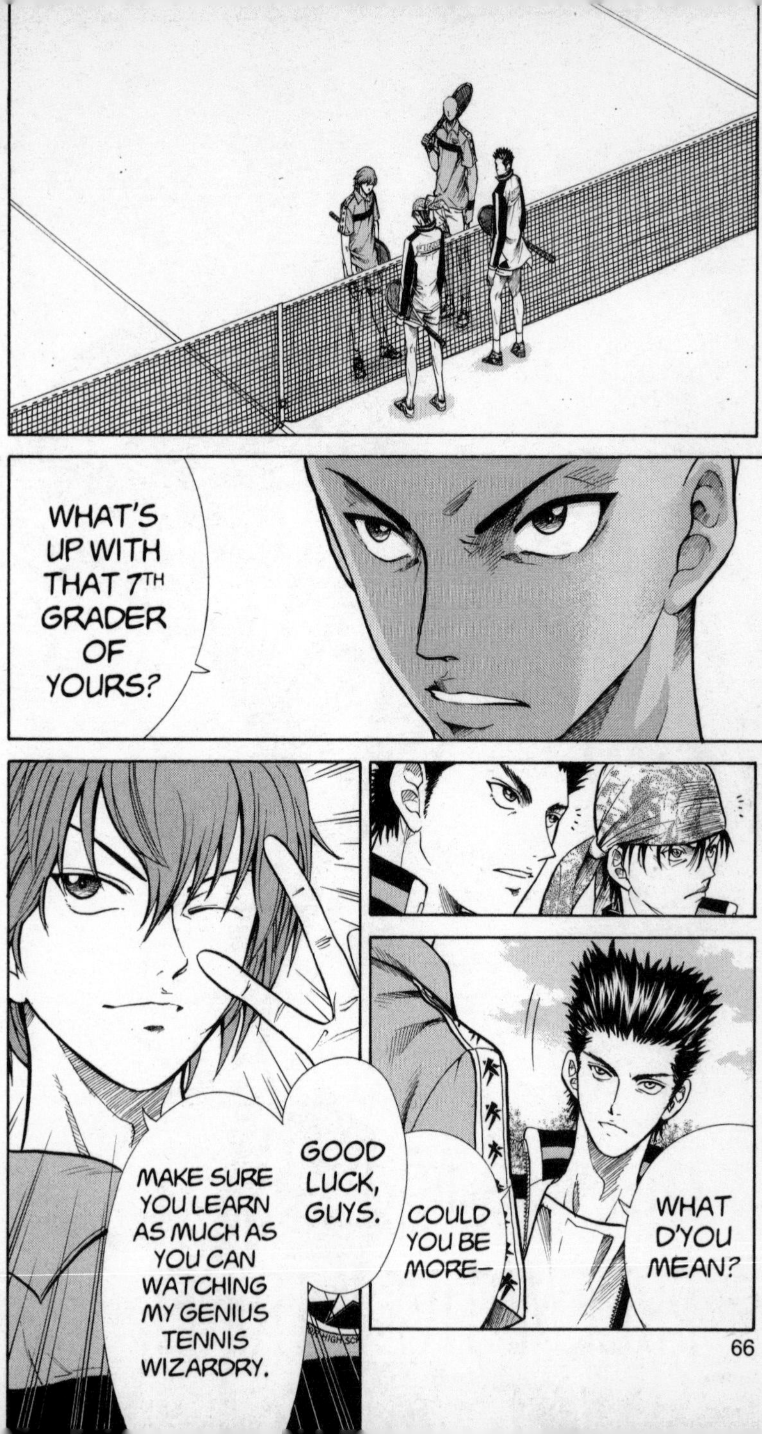
WHAT'S UP WITH THAT 7TH GRADER OF YOURS?
WHAT D'YOU MEAN?
COULD YOU BE MORE–
GOOD LUCK, GUYS.
MAKE SURE YOU LEARN AS MUCH AS YOU CAN WATCHING MY GENIUS TENNIS WIZARDRY.

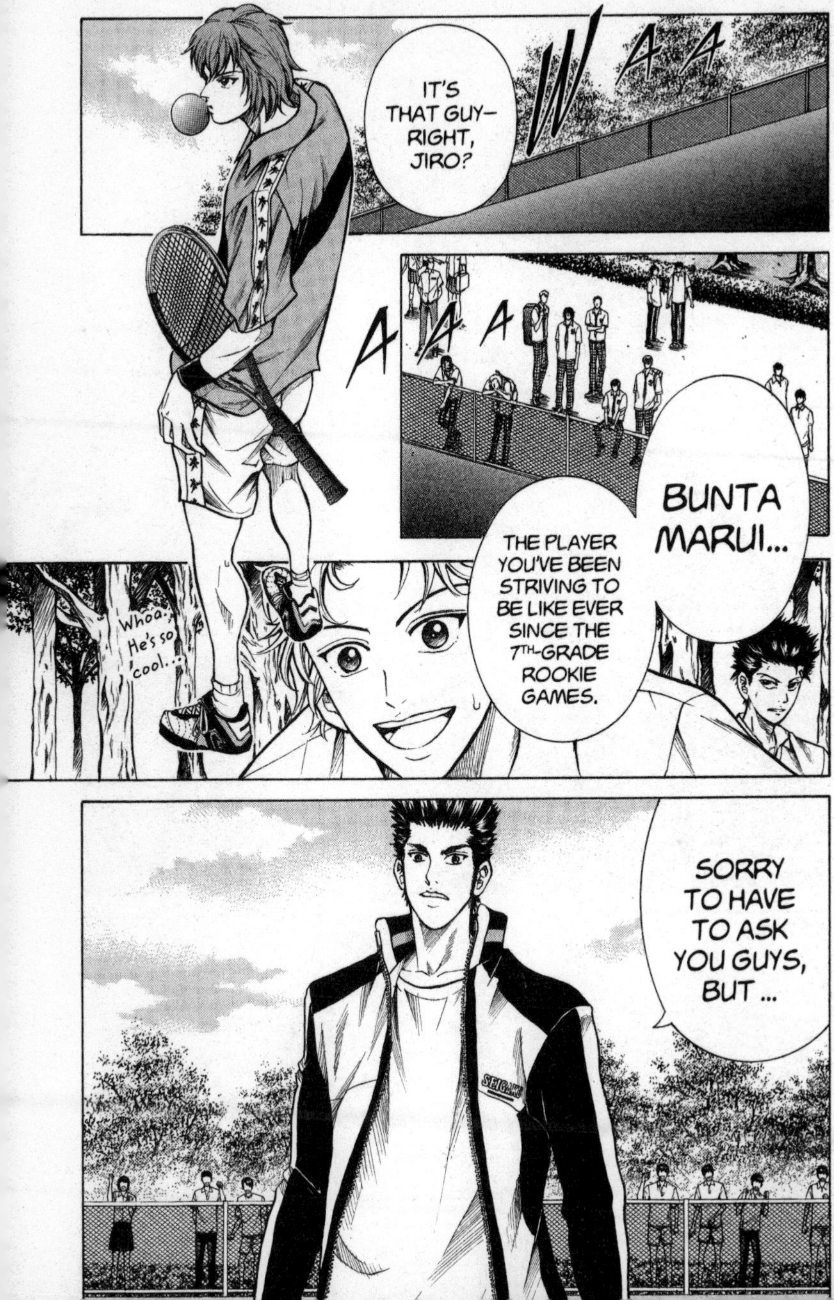
WAA
IT'S THAT GUY—RIGHT, JIRO?
AAA
BUNTA MARUI...
THE PLAYER YOU'VE BEEN STRIVING TO BE LIKE EVER SINCE THE 7TH-GRADE ROOKIE GAMES.
Whoa. He's so cool...
SORRY TO HAVE TO ASK YOU GUYS, BUT ...

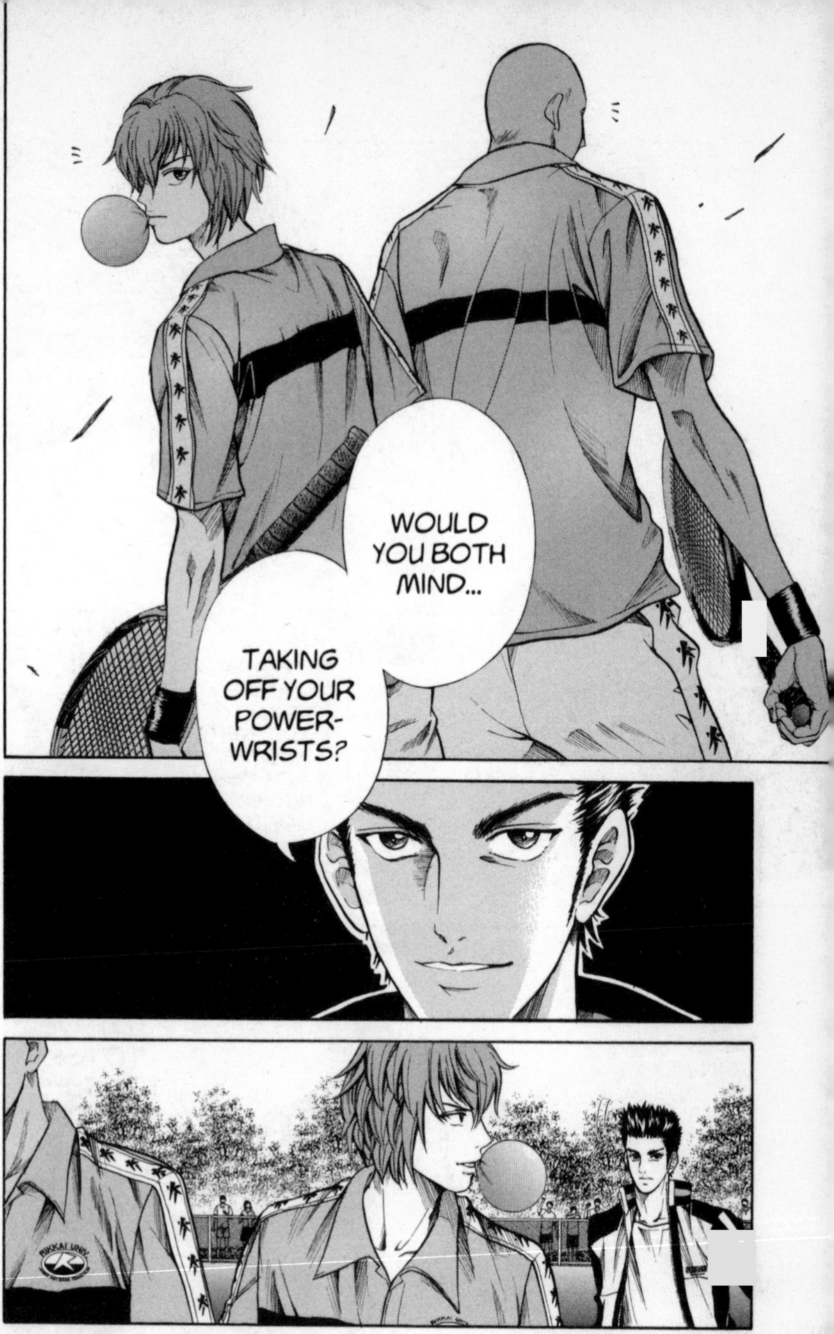
WOULD YOU BOTH MIND...
TAKING OFF YOUR POWER-WRISTS?

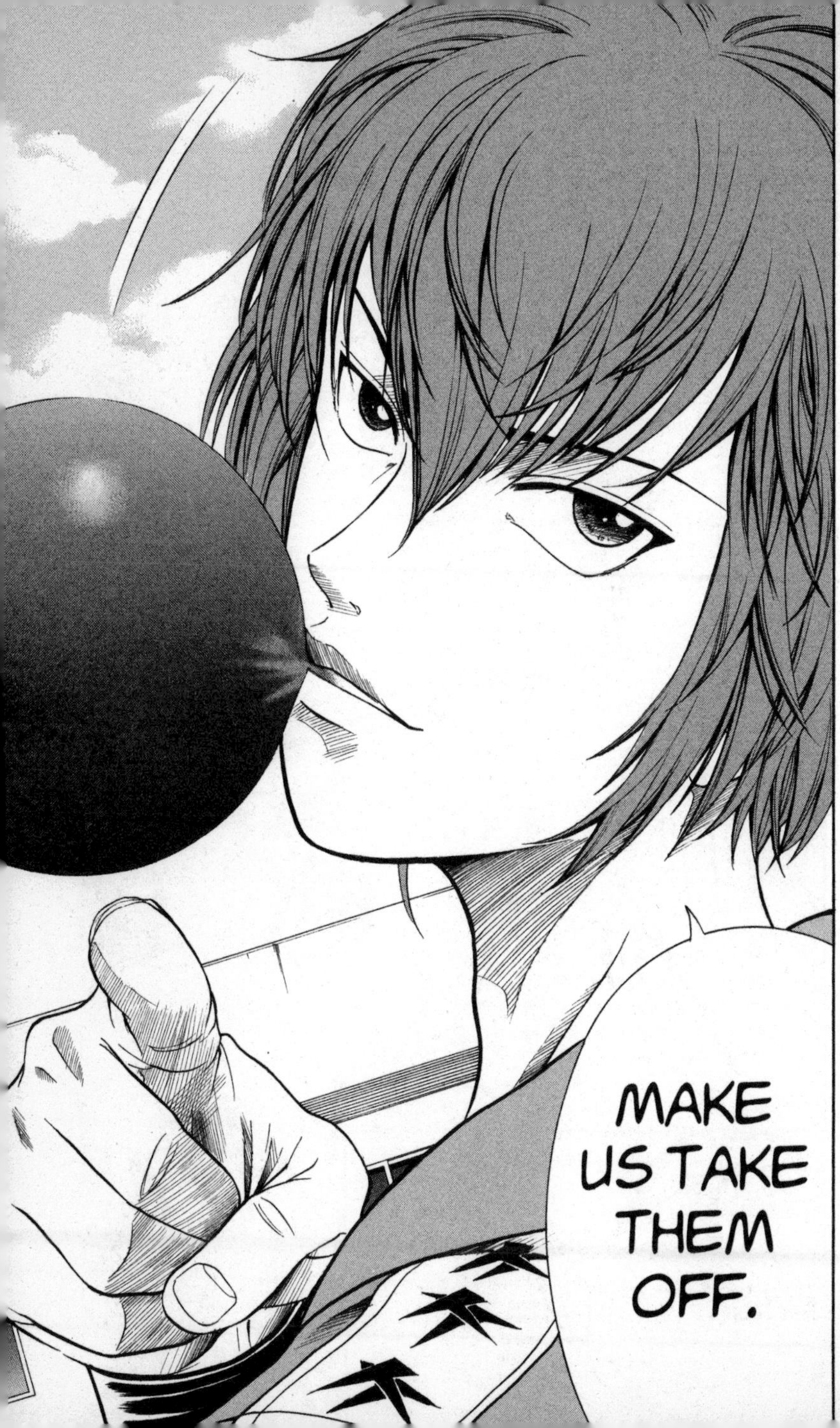
MAKE US TAKE THEM OFF.

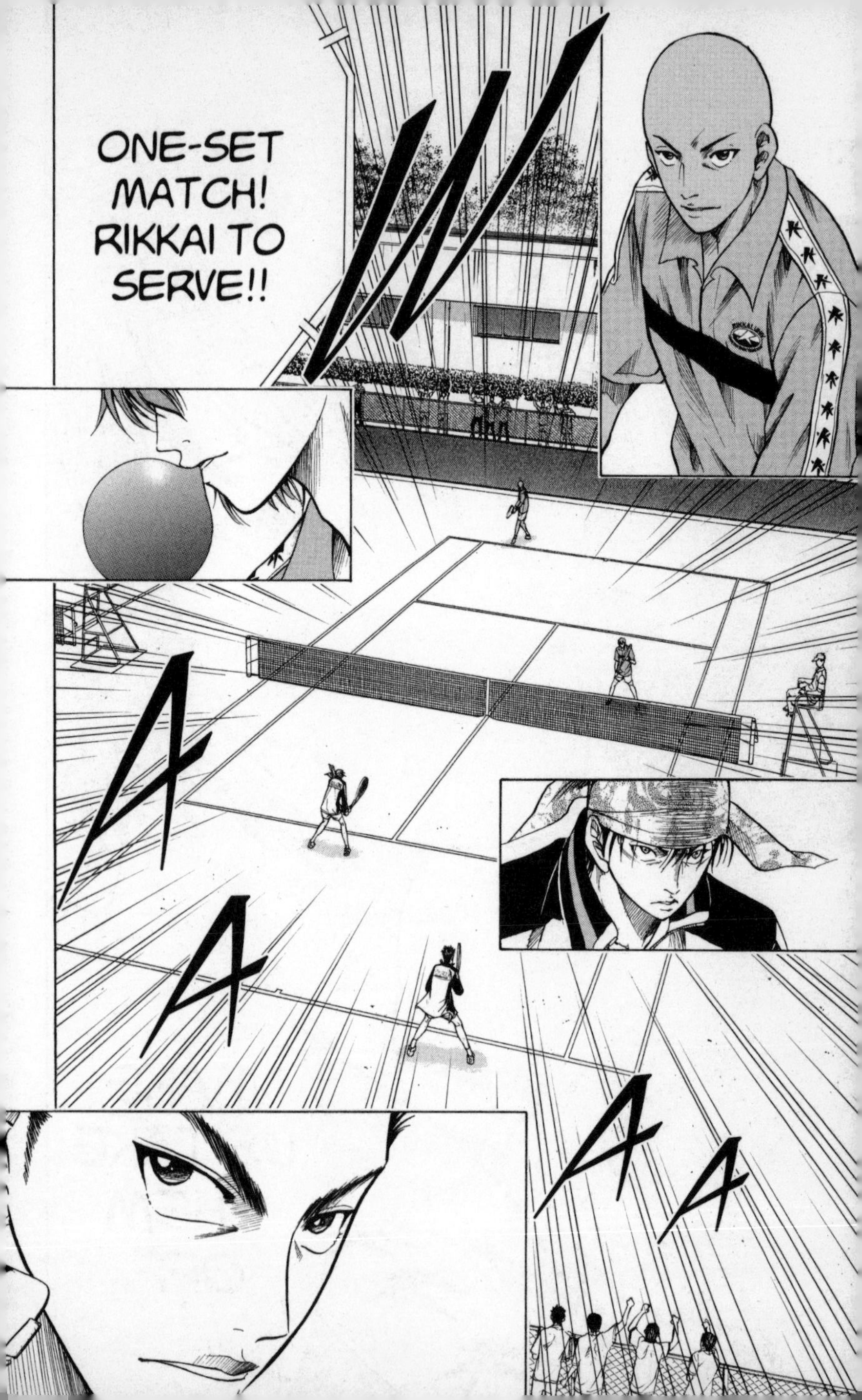
ONE-SET MATCH! RIKKAI TO SERVE!!
WAAAA

READ THIS WAY

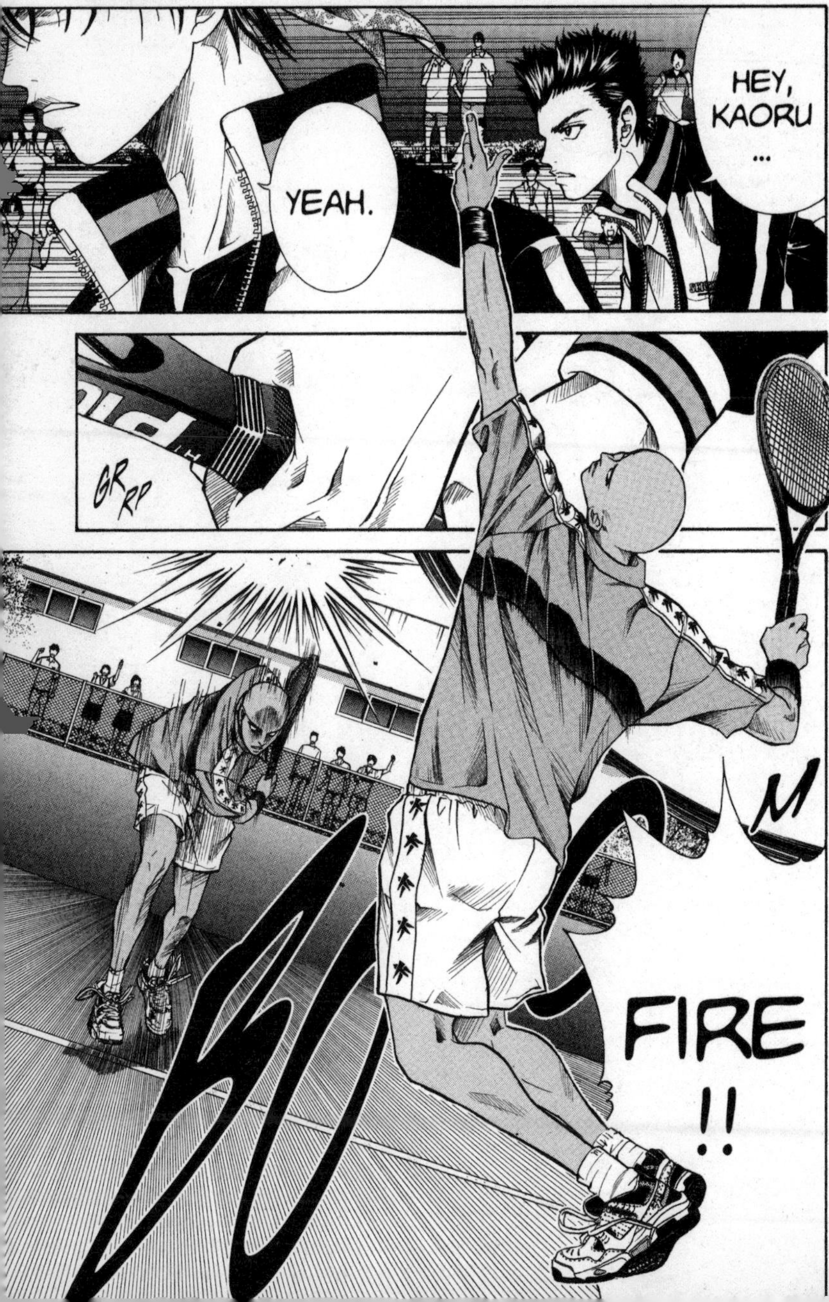
HEY, KAORU ...
YEAH.
GRRP
M
FIRE !!

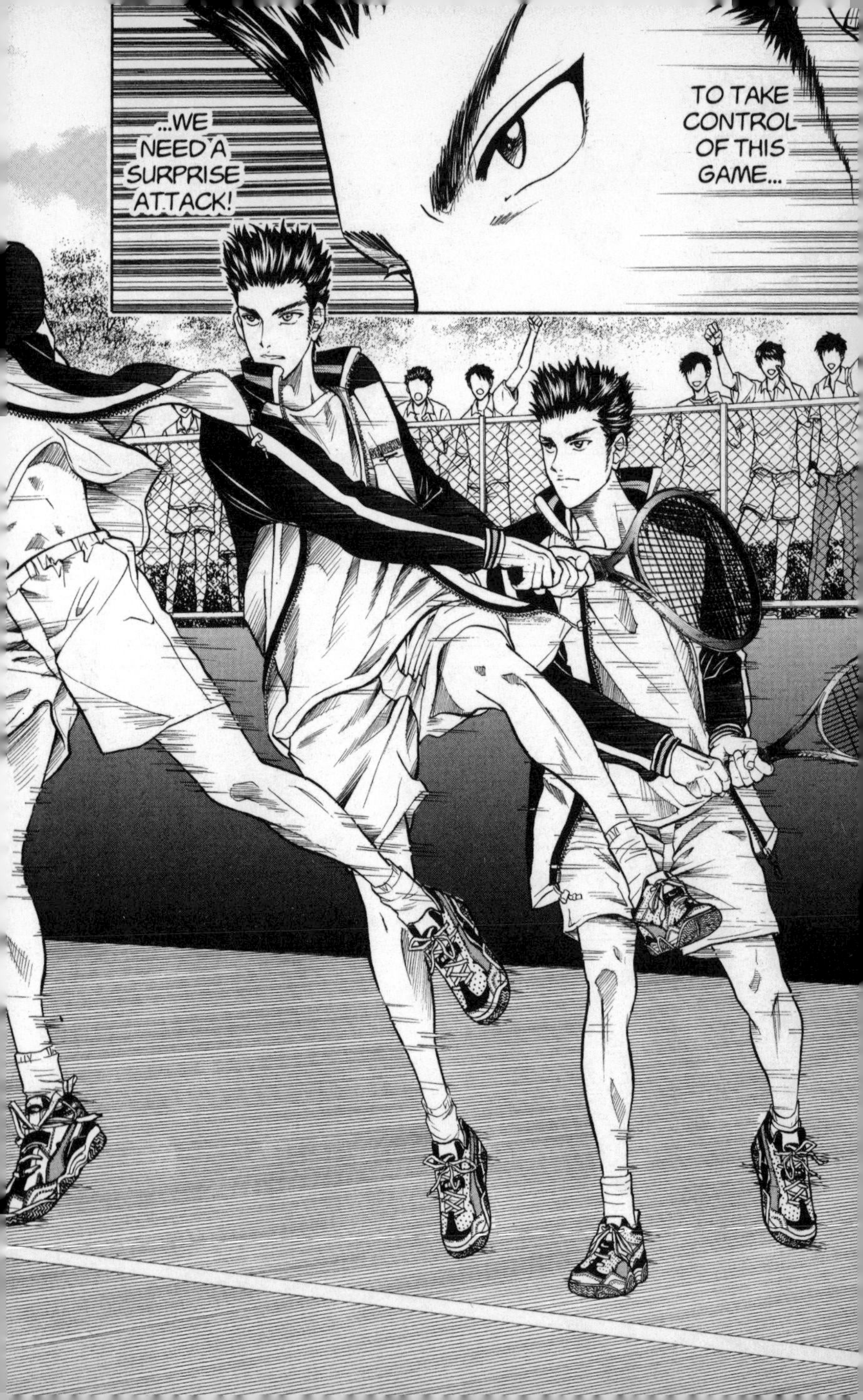
TO TAKE CONTROL OF THIS GAME...
...WE NEED A SURPRISE ATTACK!

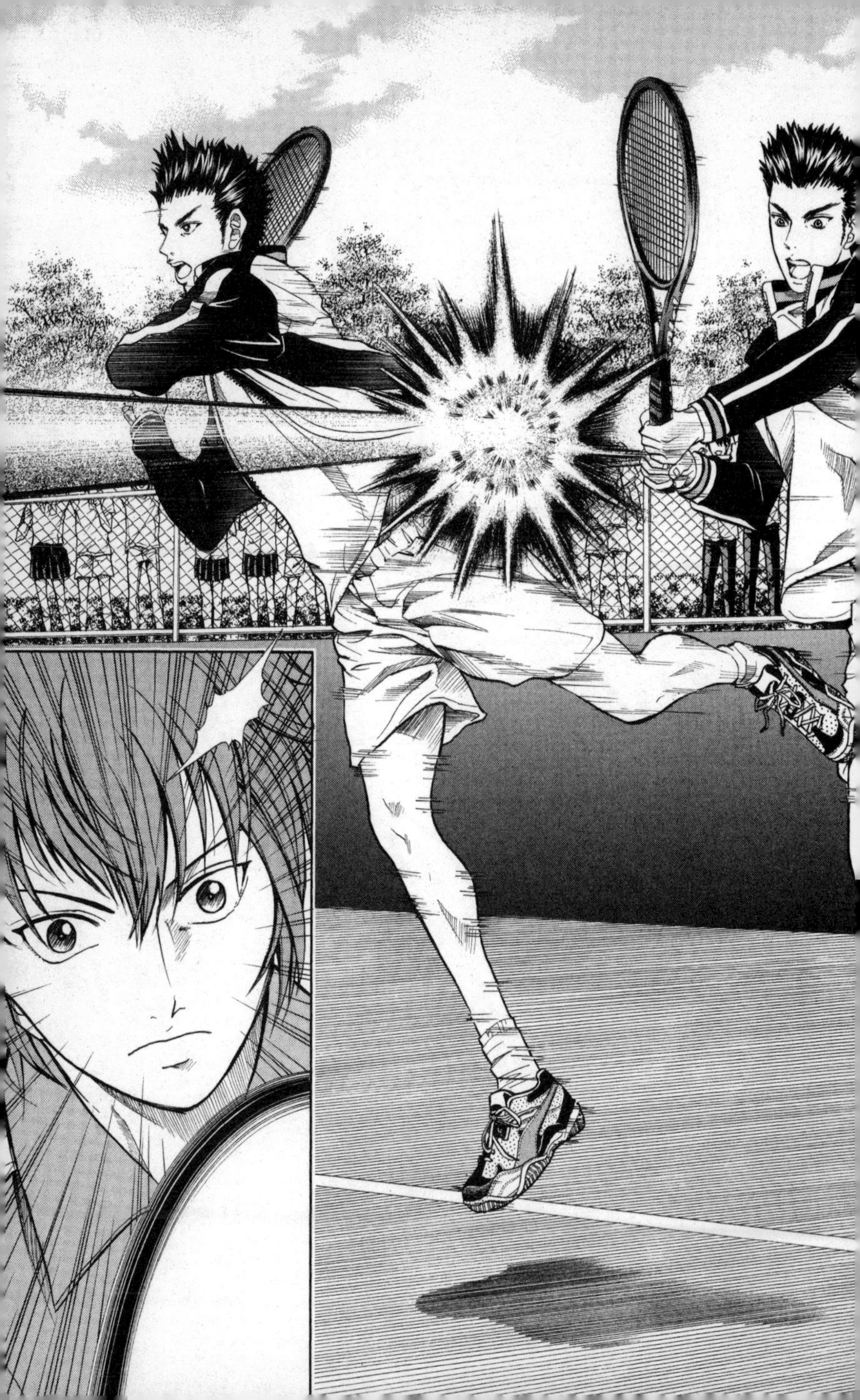

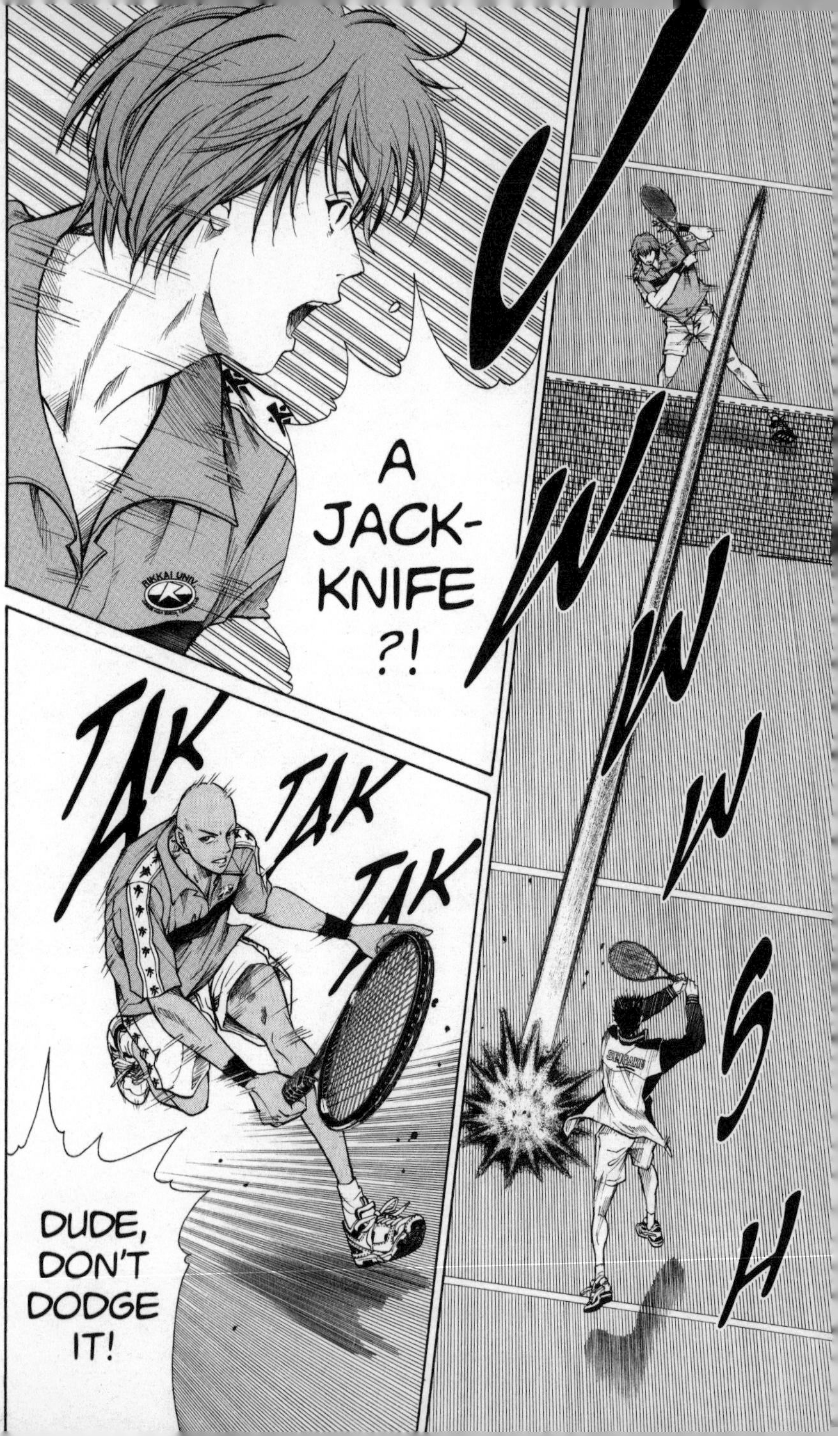
A JACK-KNIFE ?!
TAK
TAK
TAK
DUDE, DON'T DODGE IT!

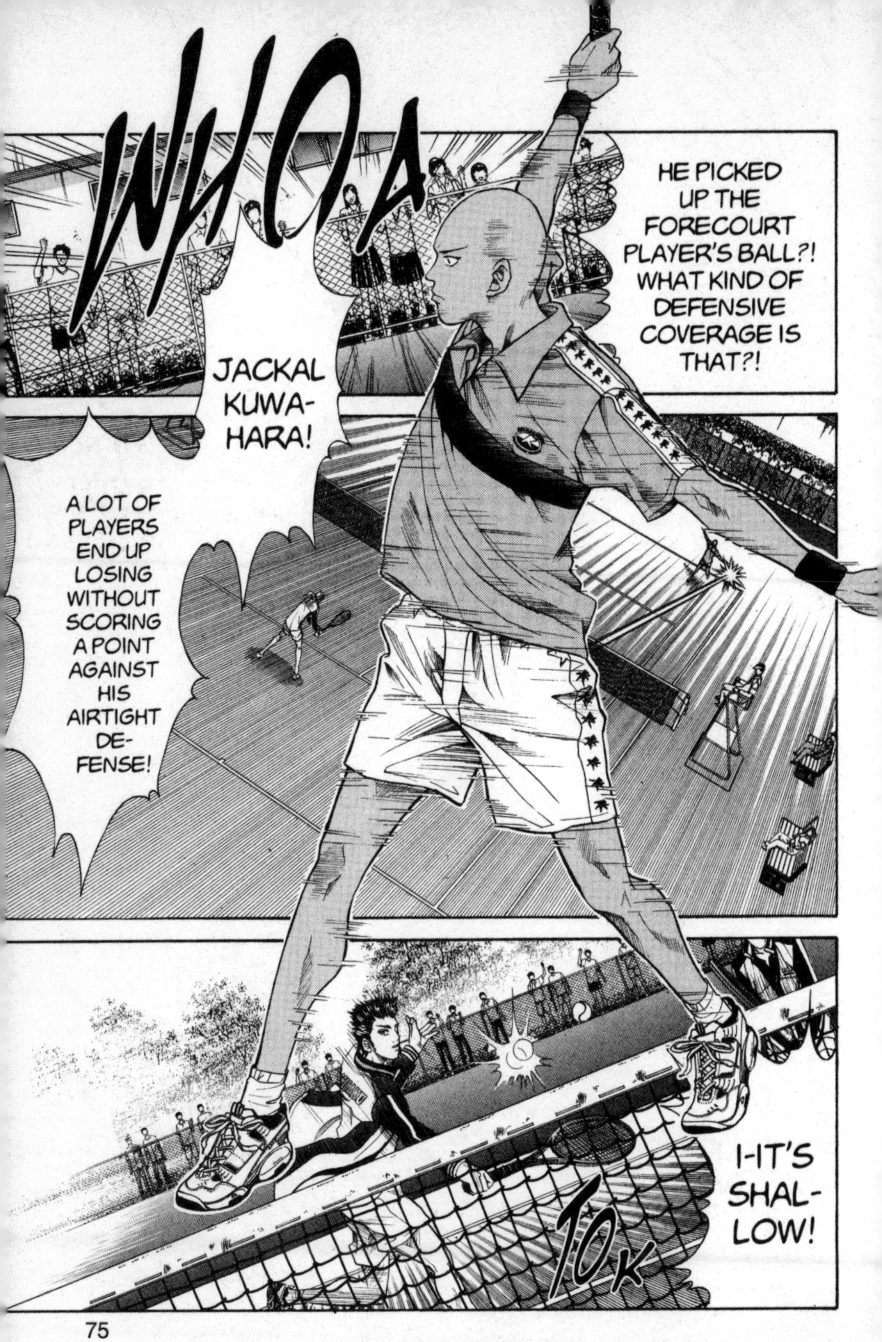
HE PICKED UP THE FORECOURT PLAYER'S BALL?! WHAT KIND OF DEFENSIVE COVERAGE IS THAT?!
WHOA
JACKAL KUWA-HARA!
A LOT OF PLAYERS END UP LOSING WITHOUT SCORING A POINT AGAINST HIS AIRTIGHT DE-FENSE!
I-IT'S SHAL-LOW!
TOK

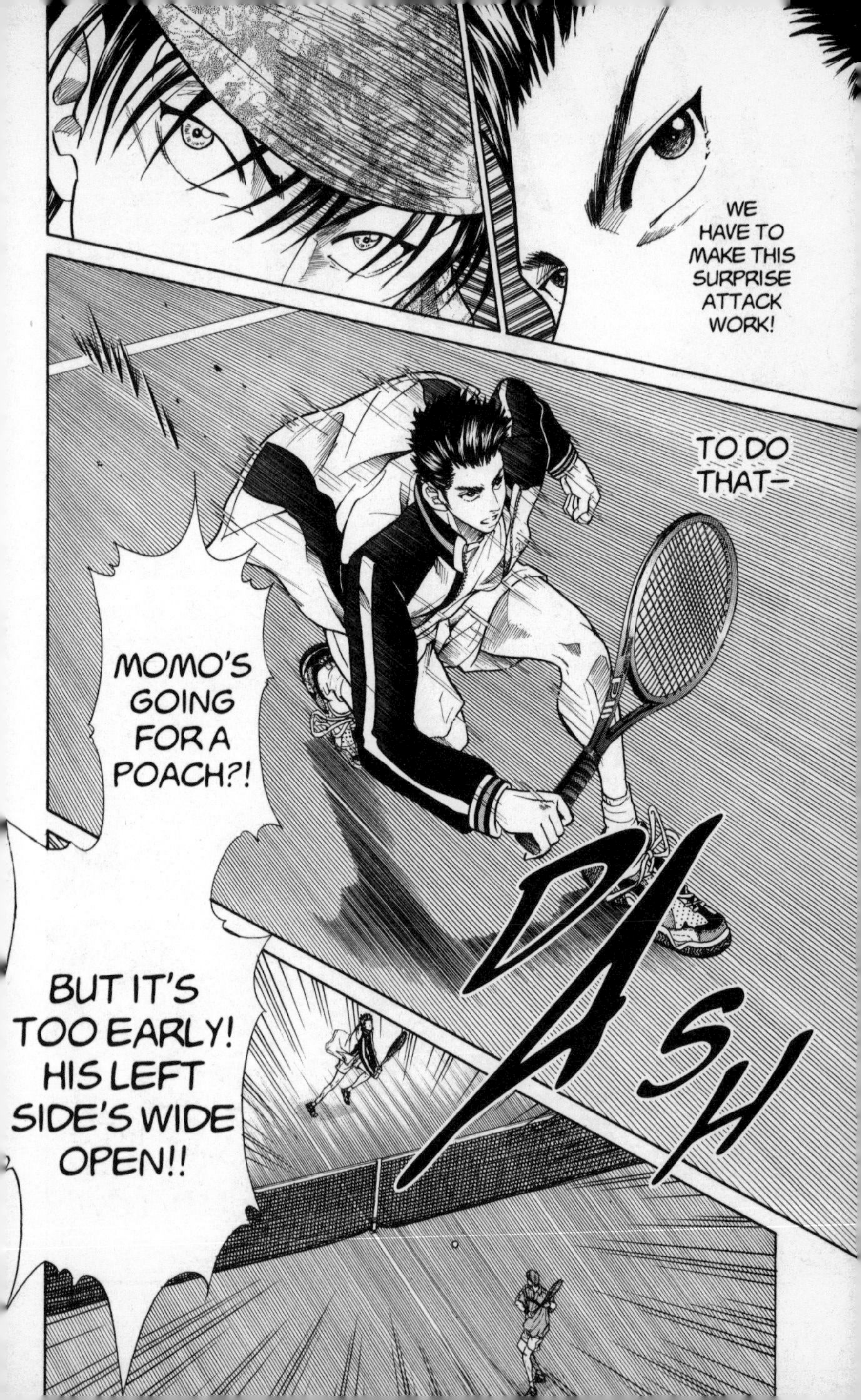
WE HAVE TO MAKE THIS SURPRISE ATTACK WORK!
TO DO THAT—
MOMO'S GOING FOR A POACH?!
DASH
BUT IT'S TOO EARLY! HIS LEFT SIDE'S WIDE OPEN!!

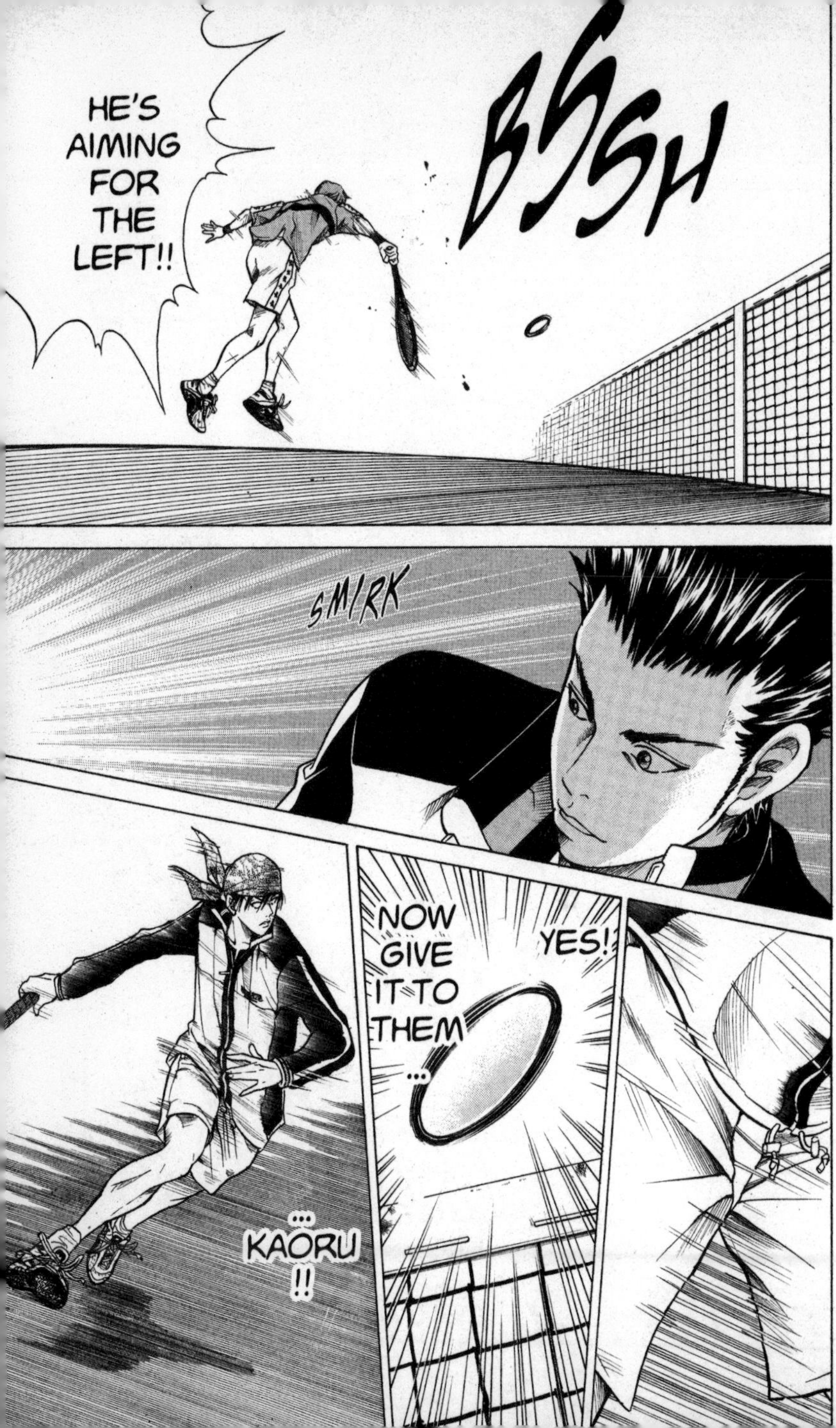
BSSH
HE'S AIMING FOR THE LEFT!!
SMIRK
NOW GIVE IT TO THEM ...
YES!
... KAORU !!

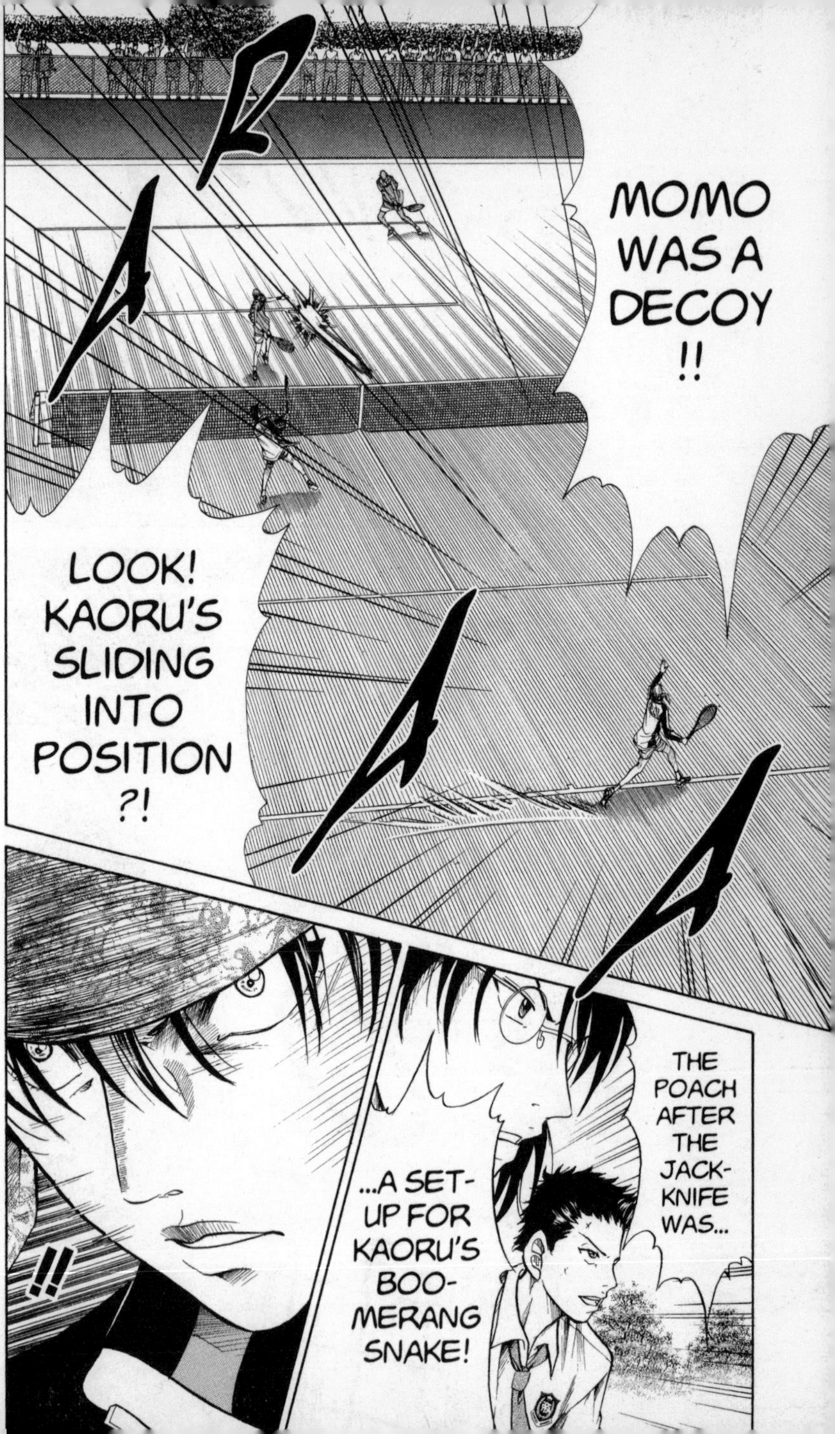
MOMO WAS A DECOY !!
LOOK! KAORU'S SLIDING INTO POSITION ?!
THE POACH AFTER THE JACK-KNIFE WAS...
...A SET-UP FOR KAORU'S BOOMERANG SNAKE!
!!

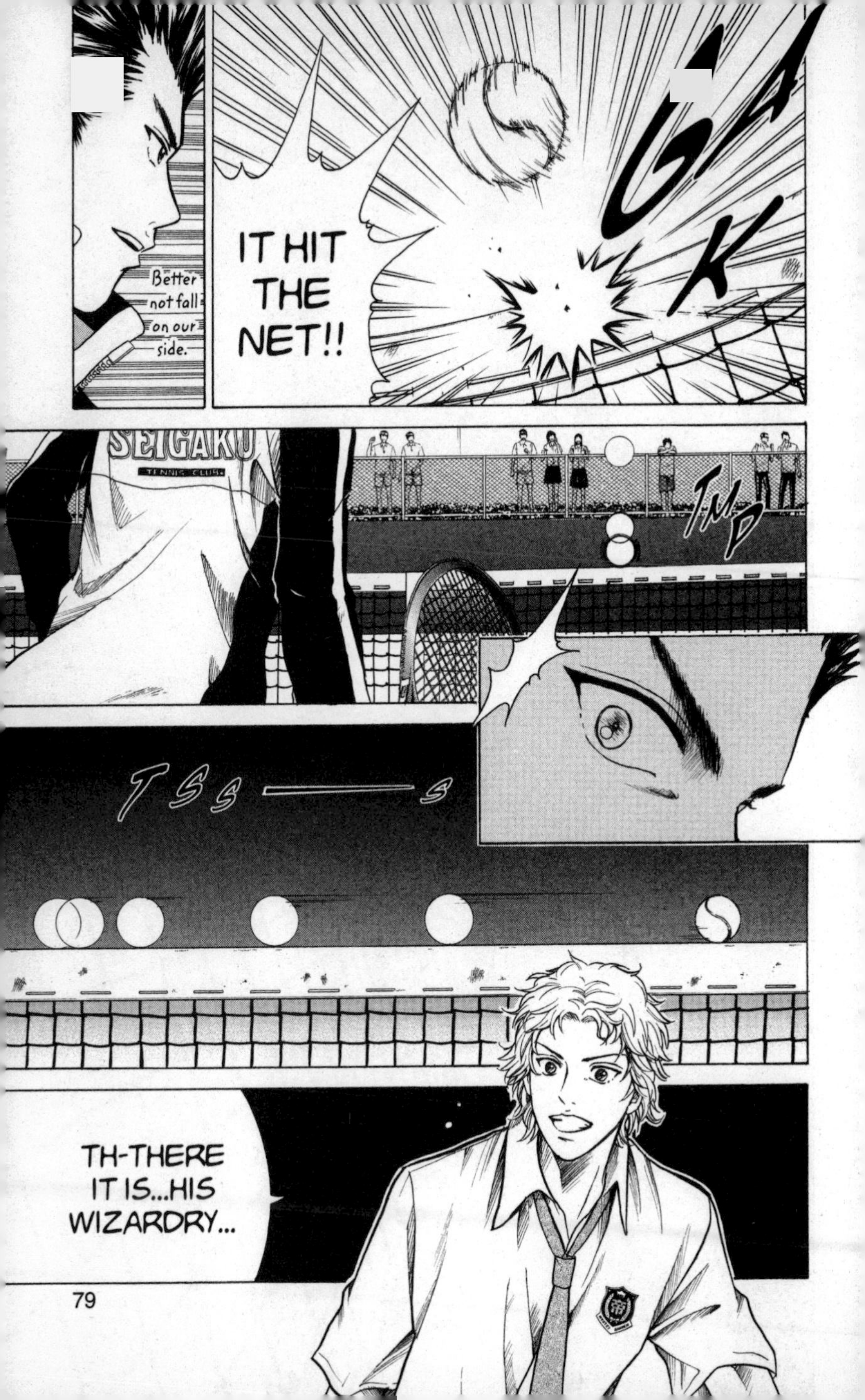
GAK
IT HIT THE NET!!
Better not fall on our side.
SEIGAKU TENNIS CLUB
TMP
TSS—S
TH-THERE IT IS...HIS WIZARDRY...

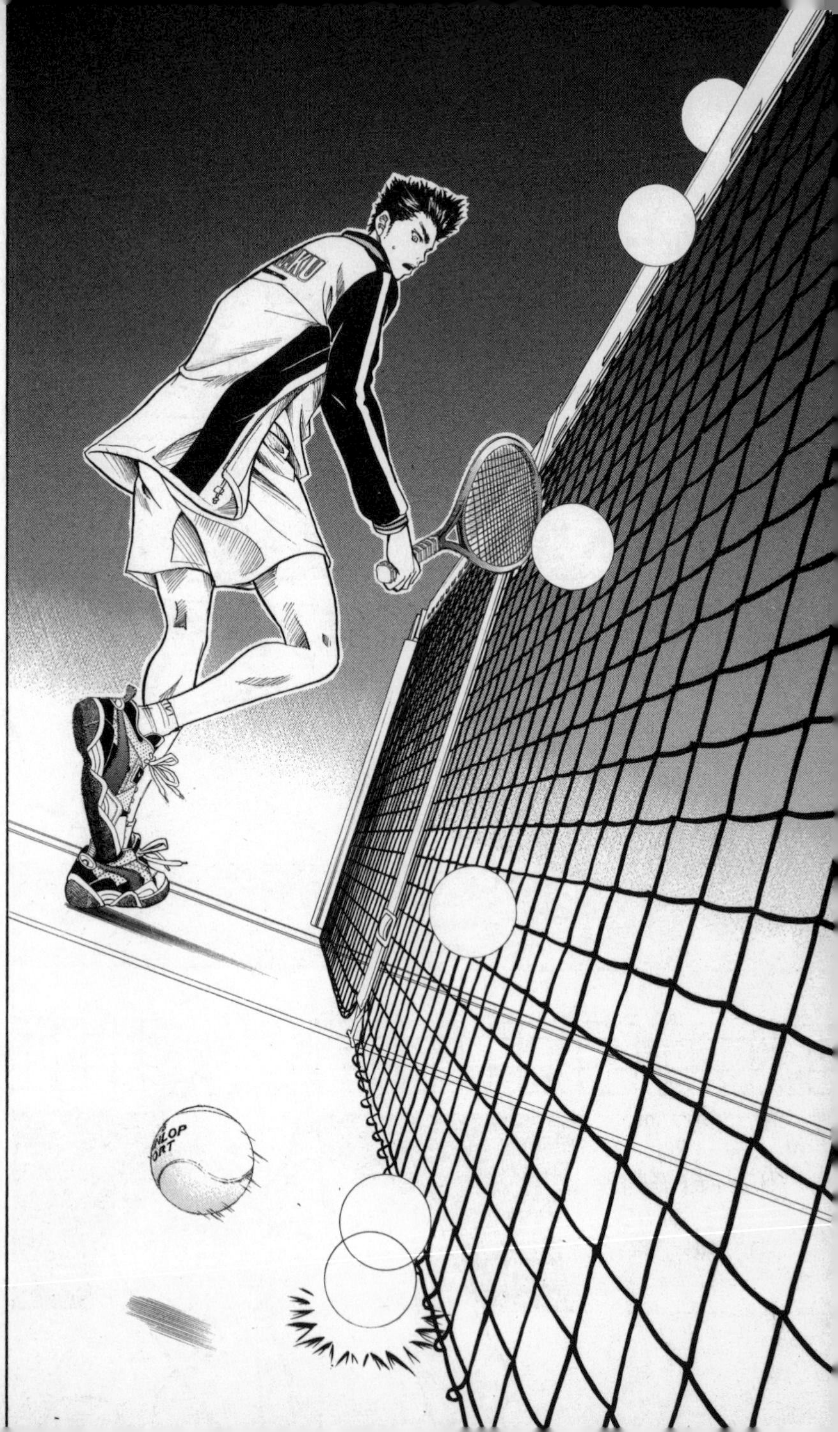

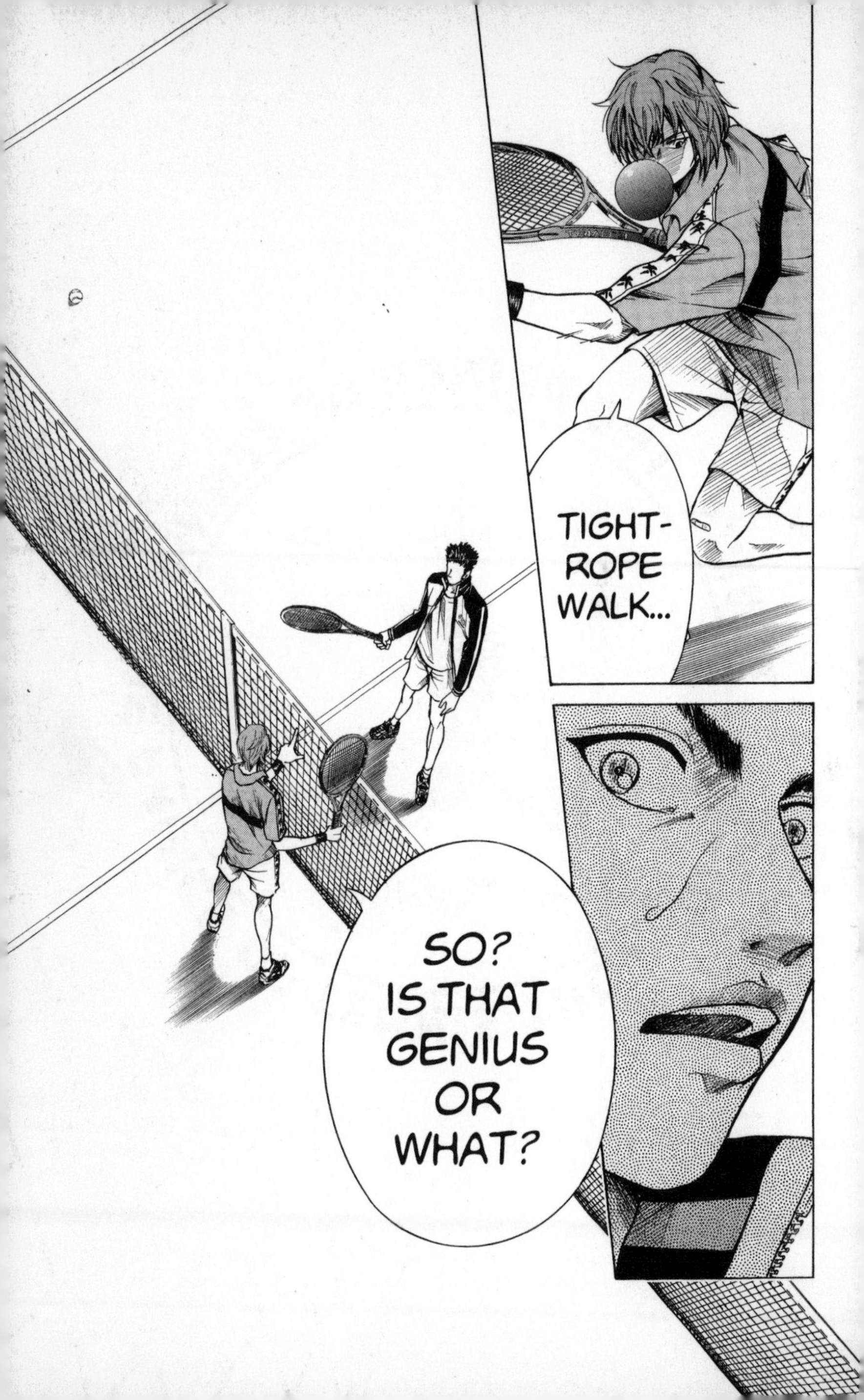
TIGHT-ROPE WALK...
SO? IS THAT GENIUS OR WHAT?

THE PRINCE OF TENNIS THE PRINCE OF TENNIS THE PRINCE OF TENNIS THE PRINCE OF TENNIS

Bunta's Must-Have Item

Green Apple Flavor

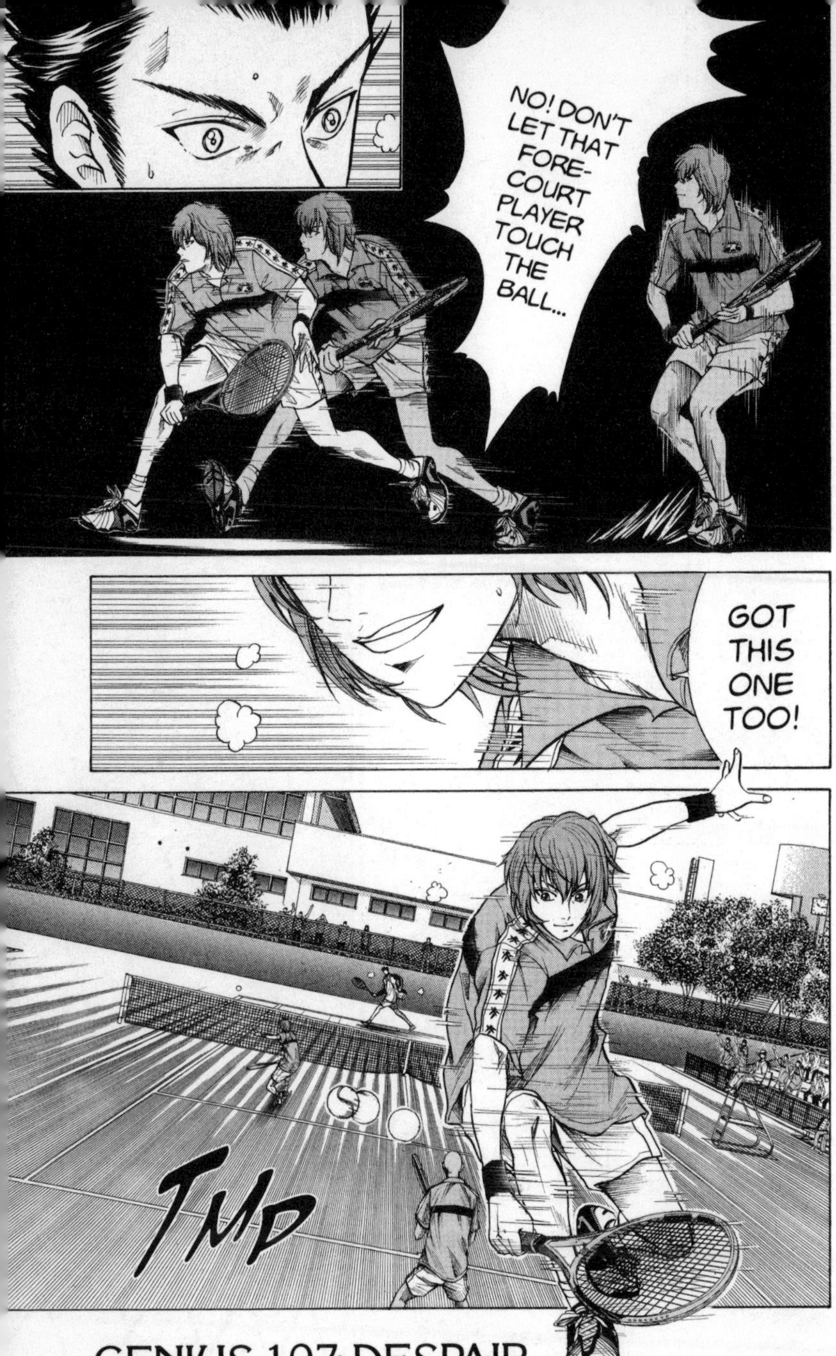
NO! DON'T LET THAT FORE-COURT PLAYER TOUCH THE BALL...
GOT THIS ONE TOO!
TMP

GENIUS 197: DESPAIR

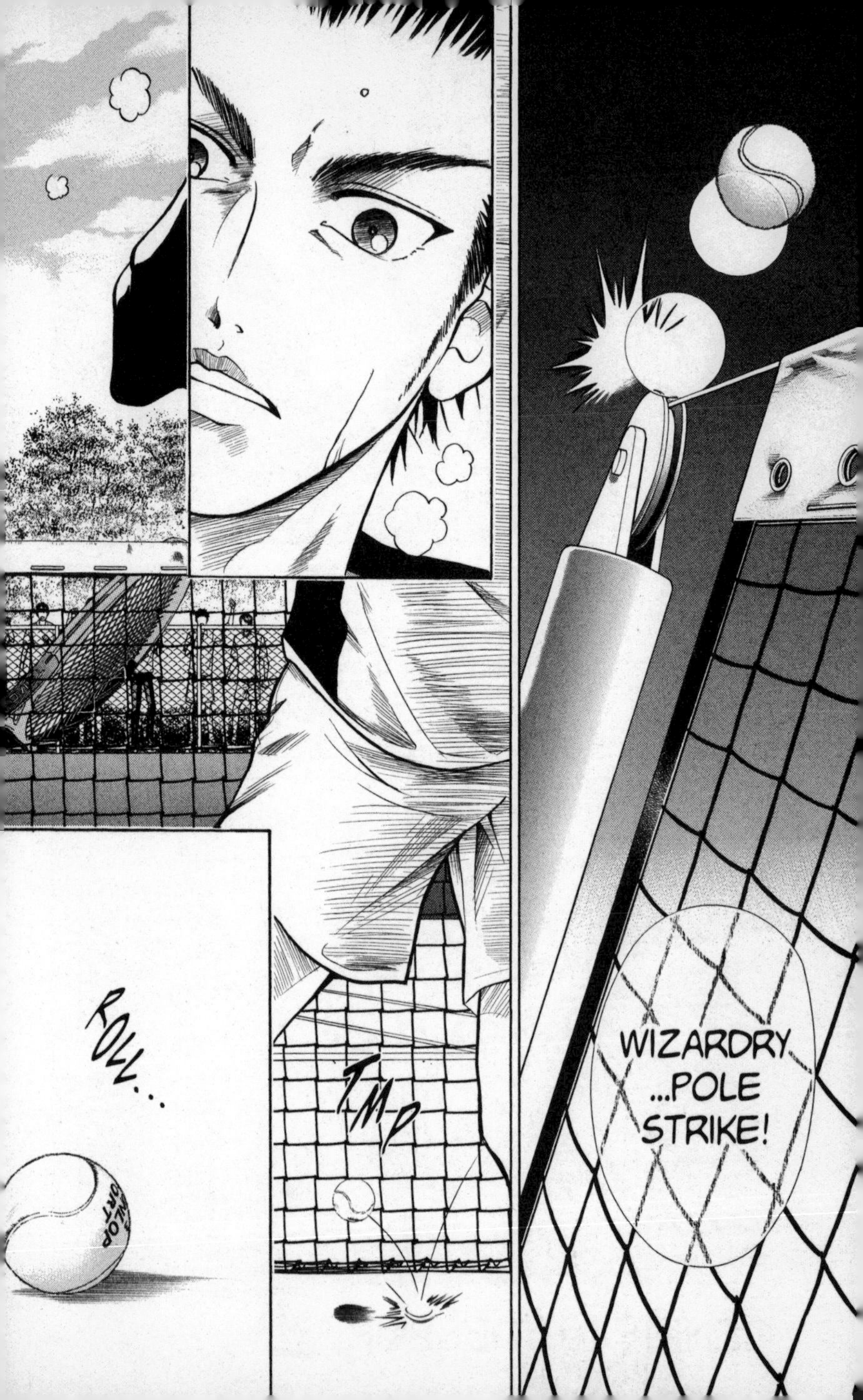
WIZARDRY ...POLE STRIKE!
TMP
ROLL...

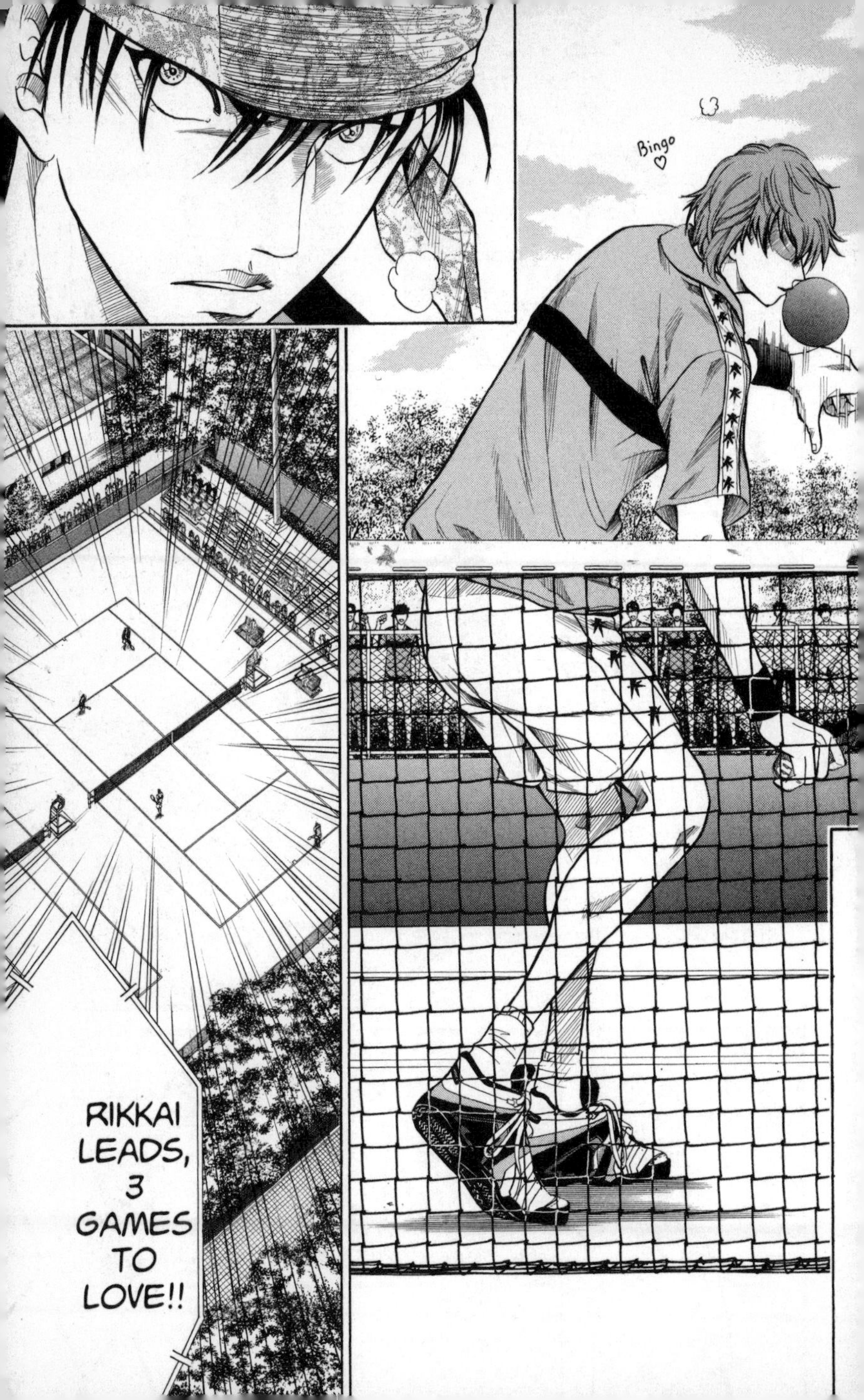
Bingo ♡
RIKKAI LEADS, 3 GAMES TO LOVE!!

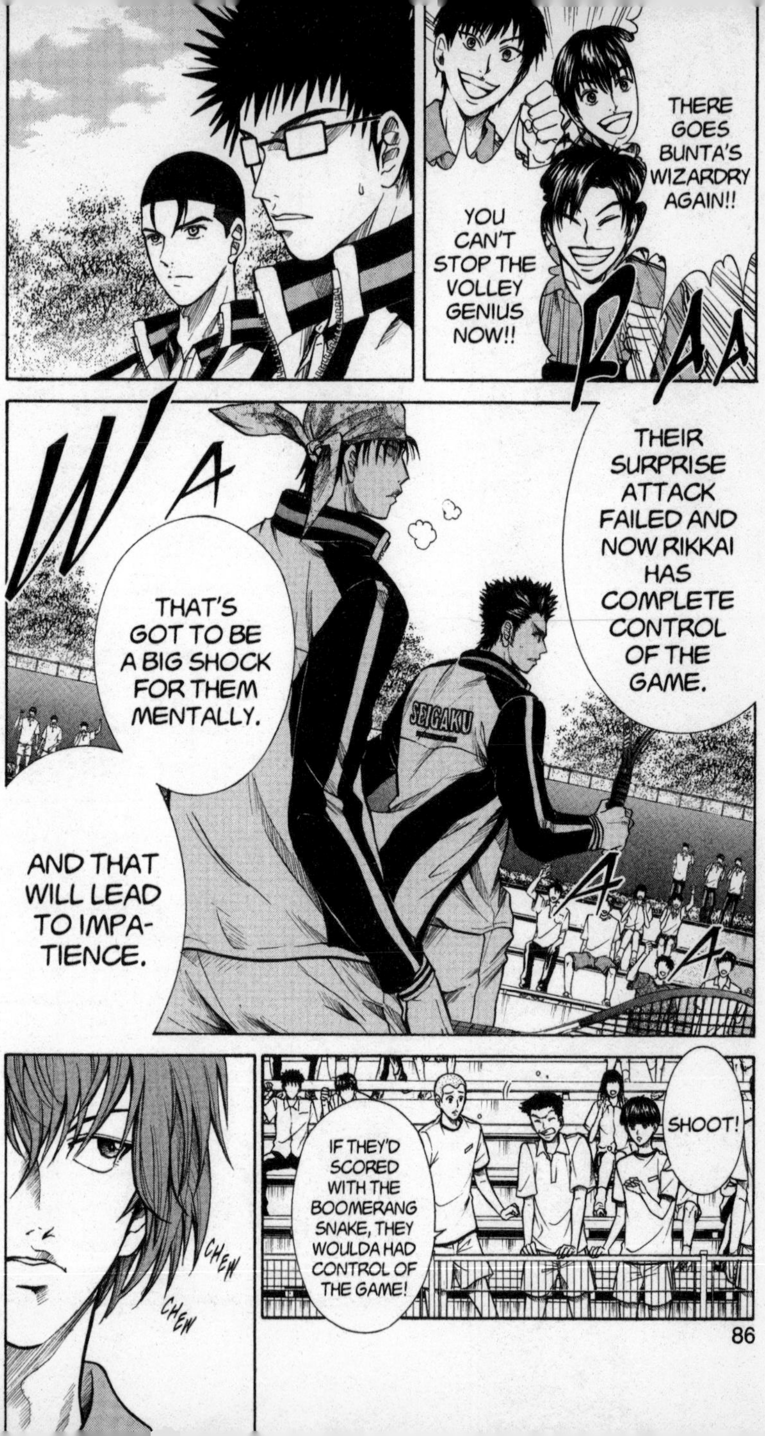

THERE GOES BUNTA'S WIZARDRY AGAIN!!
YOU CAN'T STOP THE VOLLEY GENIUS NOW!!
RAA
THEIR SURPRISE ATTACK FAILED AND NOW RIKKAI HAS COMPLETE CONTROL OF THE GAME.
WA
THAT'S GOT TO BE A BIG SHOCK FOR THEM MENTALLY.
AND THAT WILL LEAD TO IMPA-TIENCE.
A
A
SEIGAKU
SHOOT!
IF THEY'D SCORED WITH THE BOOMERANG SNAKE, THEY WOULDA HAD CONTROL OF THE GAME!
CHEW
CHEW

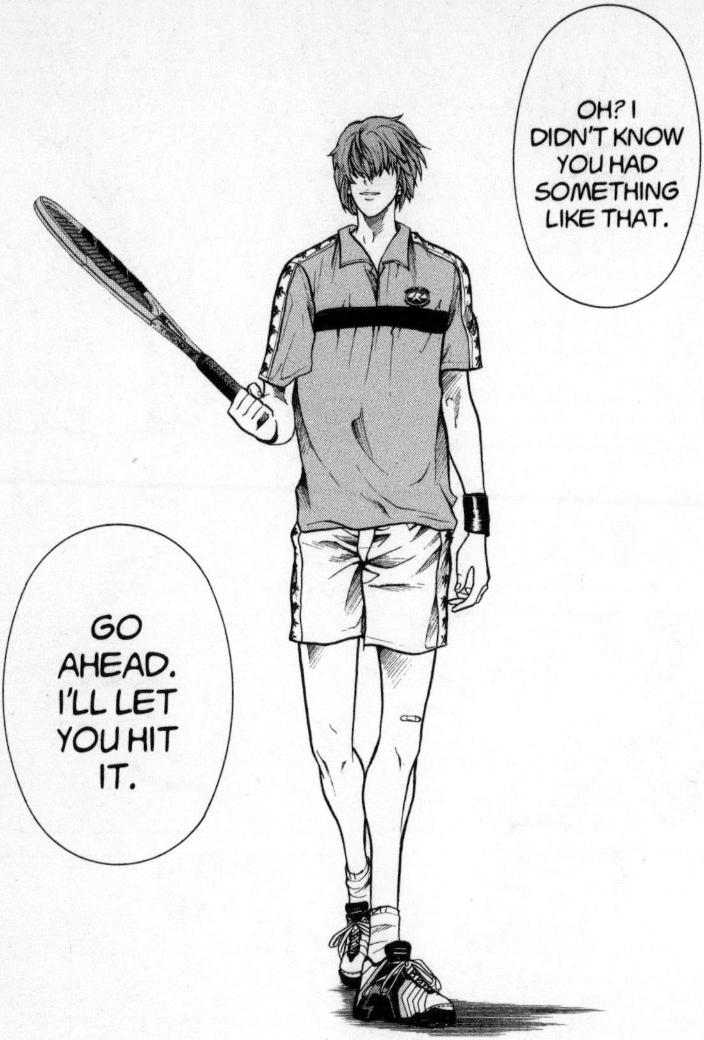
OH? I DIDN'T KNOW YOU HAD SOMETHING LIKE THAT.
GO AHEAD. I'LL LET YOU HIT IT.

GENIUS 197: DESPAIR

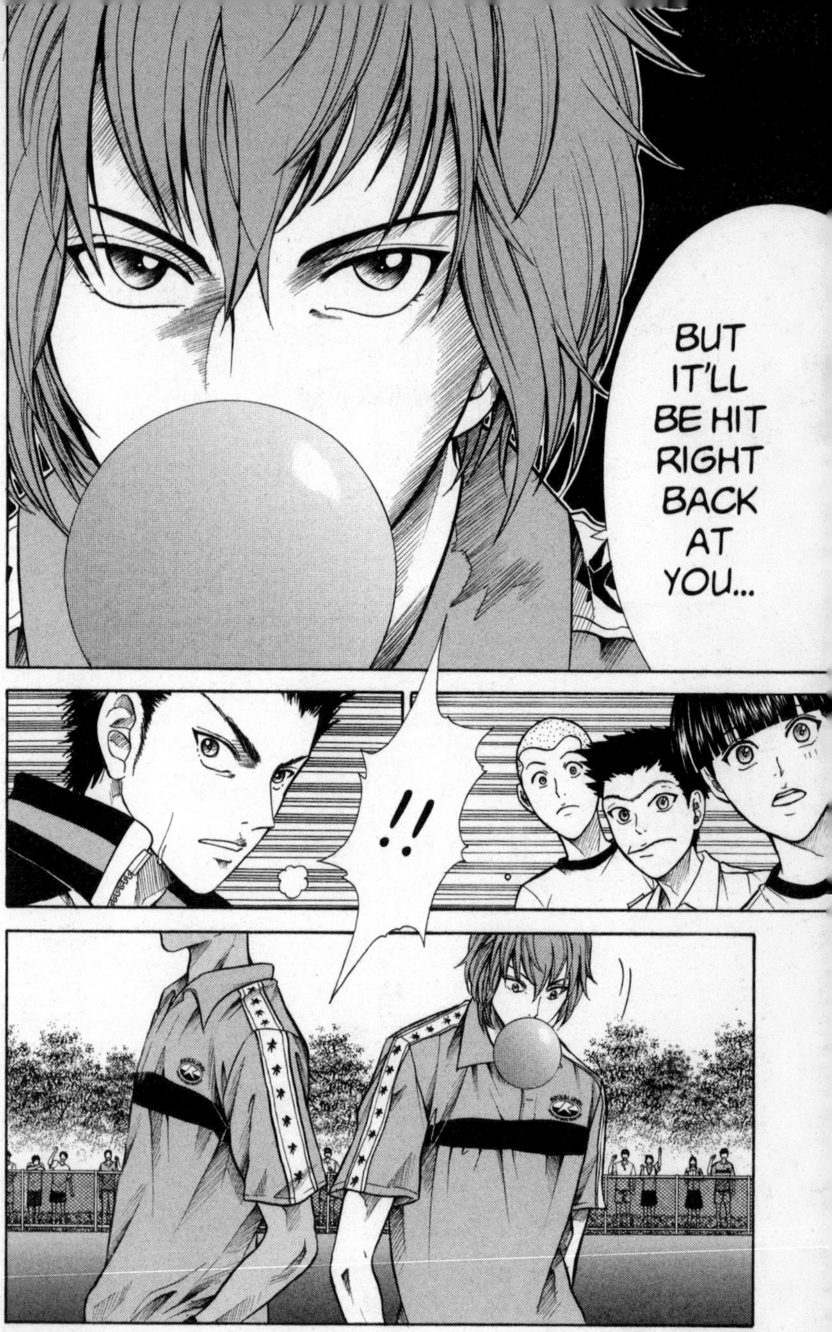
BUT IT'LL BE HIT RIGHT BACK AT YOU...
!!

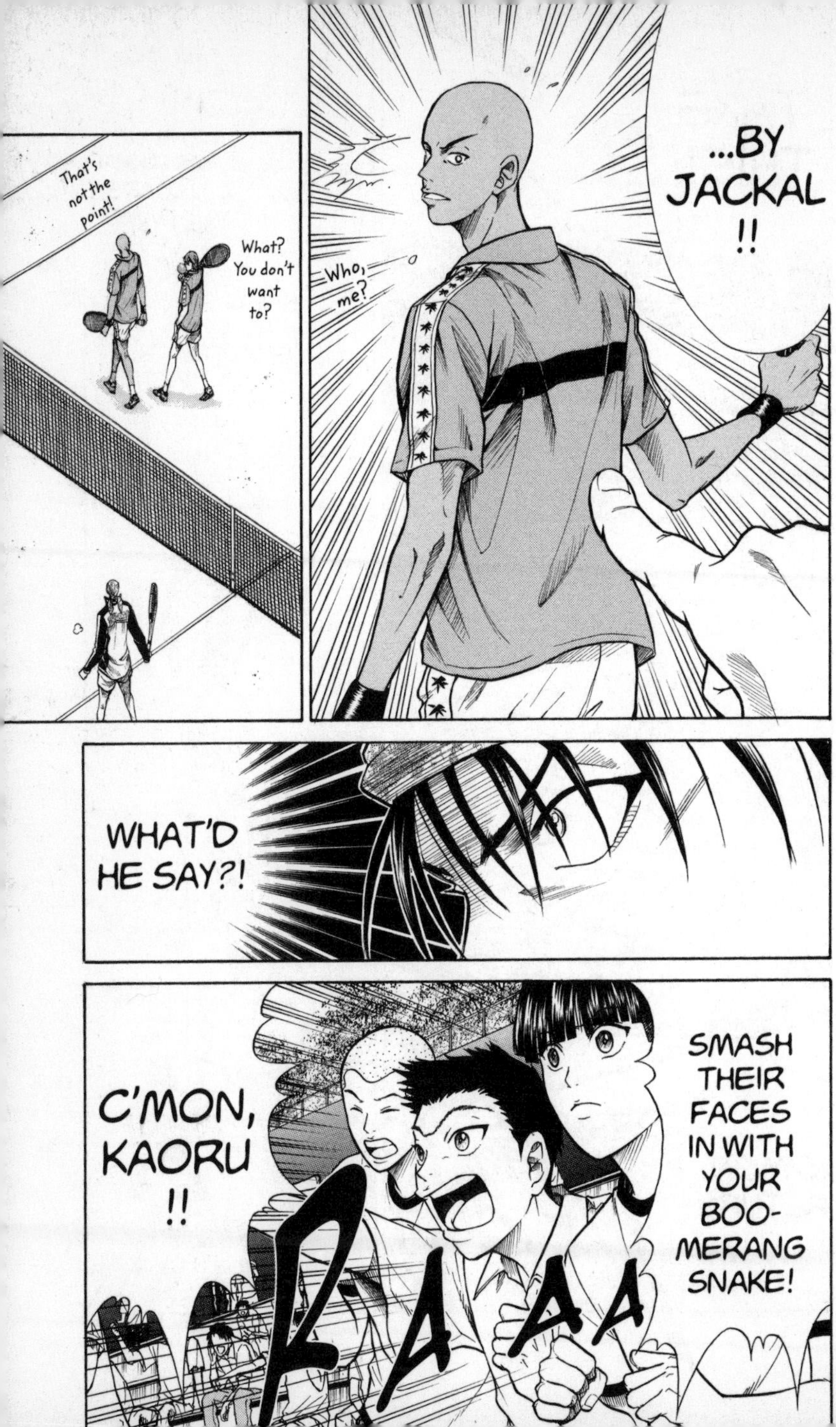
...BY JACKAL !!
Who, me?
What? You don't want to?
That's not the point!
WHAT'D HE SAY?!
SMASH THEIR FACES IN WITH YOUR BOO-MERANG SNAKE!
C'MON, KAORU !!
RAAA

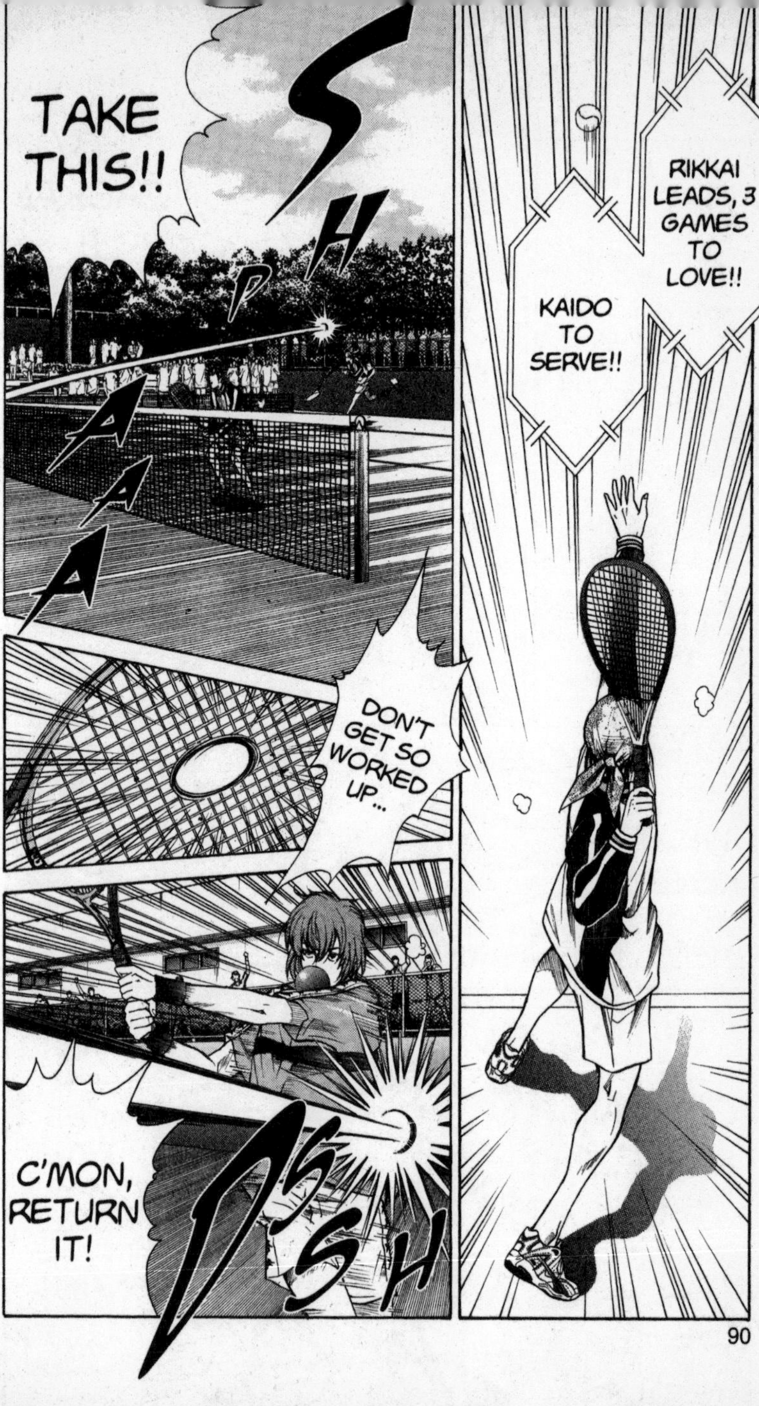
RIKKAI LEADS, 3 GAMES TO LOVE!!
KAIDO TO SERVE!!
TAKE THIS!!
SHPAAA
DON'T GET SO WORKED UP...
C'MON, RETURN IT!

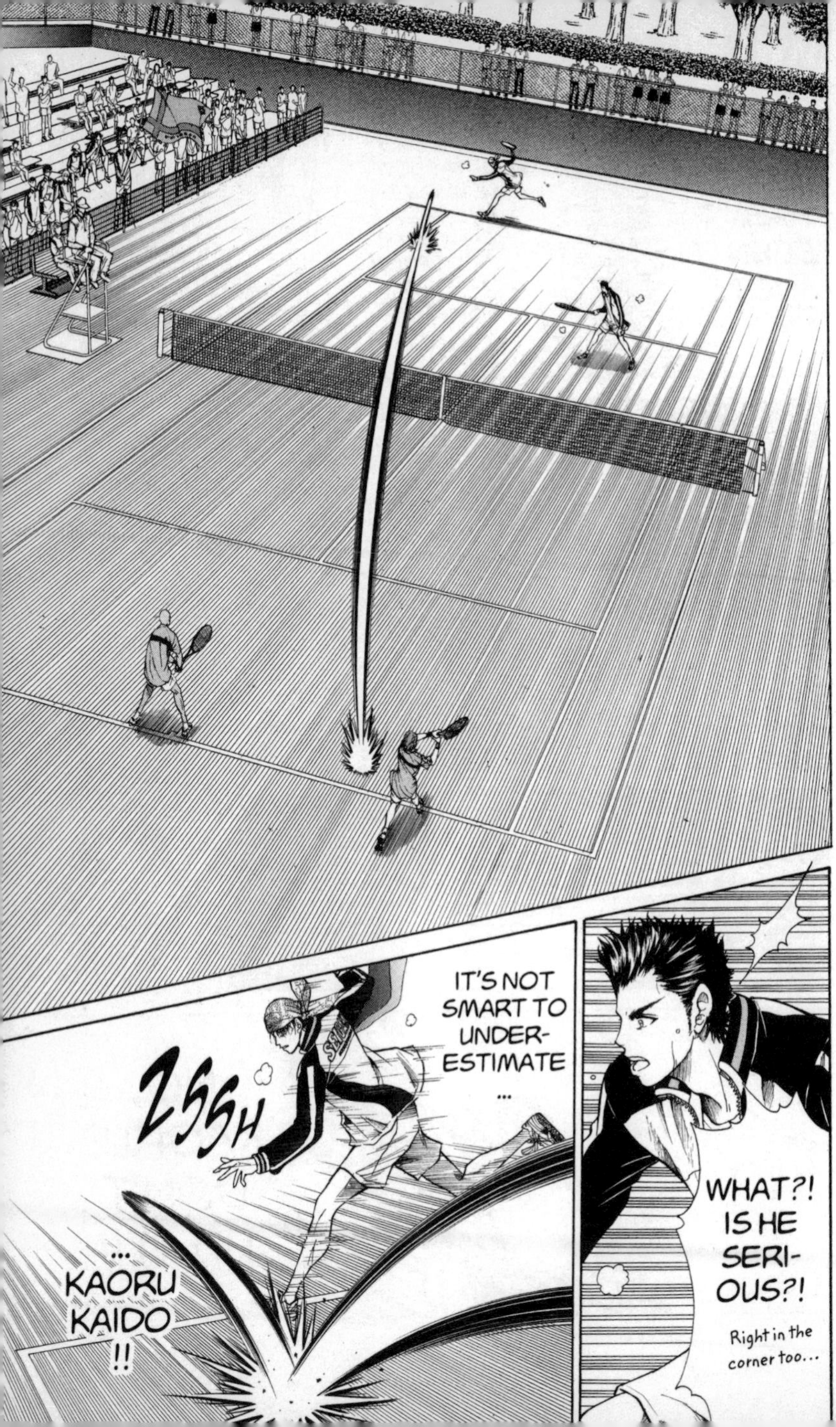
WHAT?! IS HE SERI-OUS?!
Right in the corner too...
IT'S NOT SMART TO UNDER-ESTIMATE ...
ZSSH
... KAORU KAIDO !!

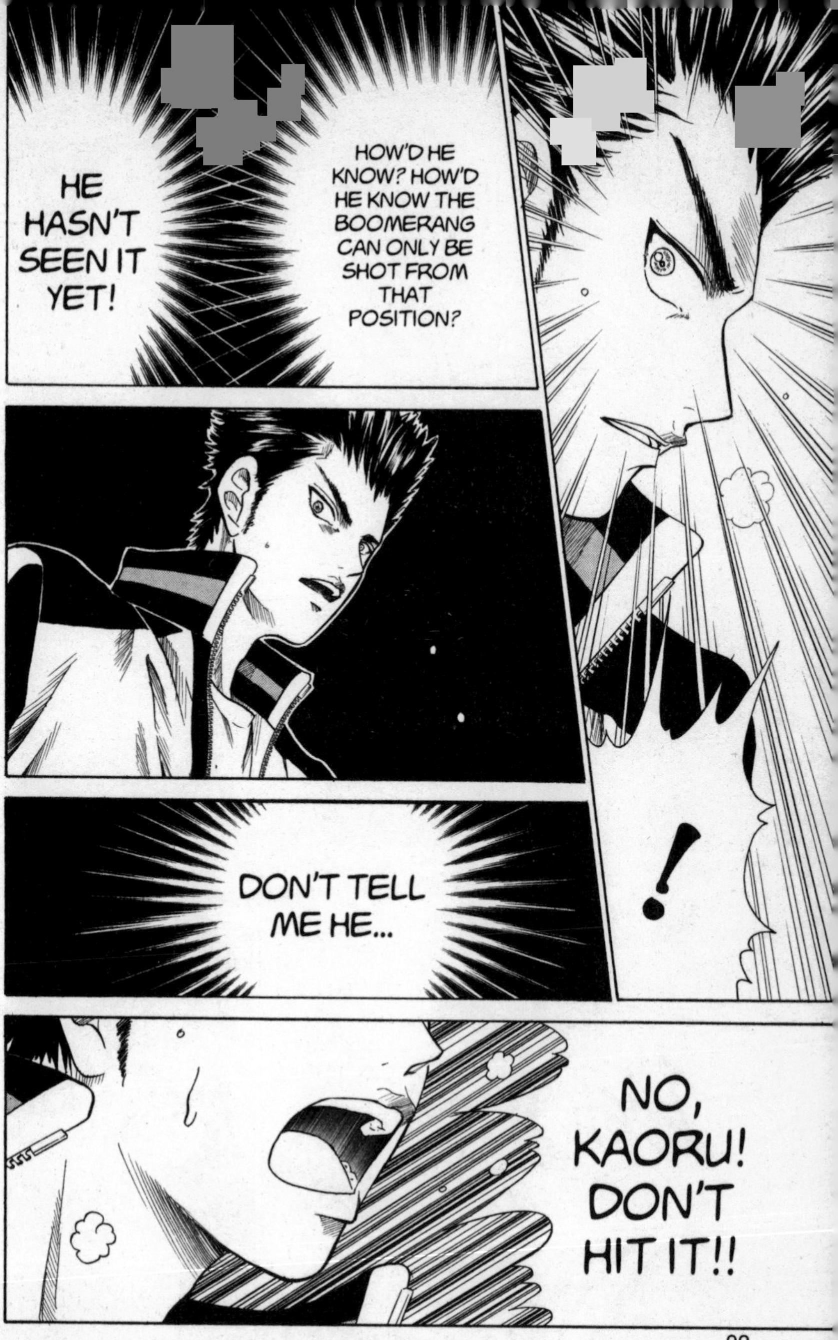
!
HOW'D HE KNOW? HOW'D HE KNOW THE BOOMERANG CAN ONLY BE SHOT FROM THAT POSITION?
HE HASN'T SEEN IT YET!
DON'T TELL ME HE...
NO, KAORU! DON'T HIT IT!!

READ THIS WAY

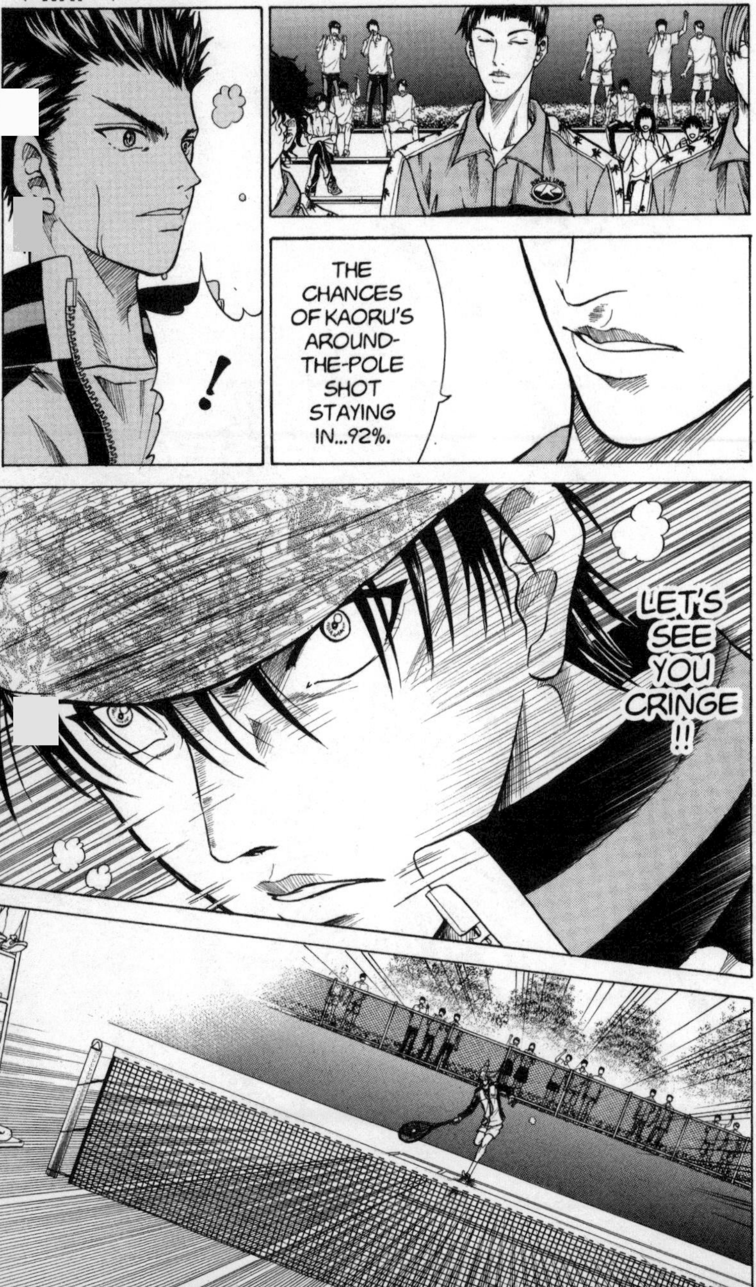
THE CHANCES OF KAORU'S AROUND-THE-POLE SHOT STAYING IN...92%.
!
LET'S SEE YOU CRINGE !!

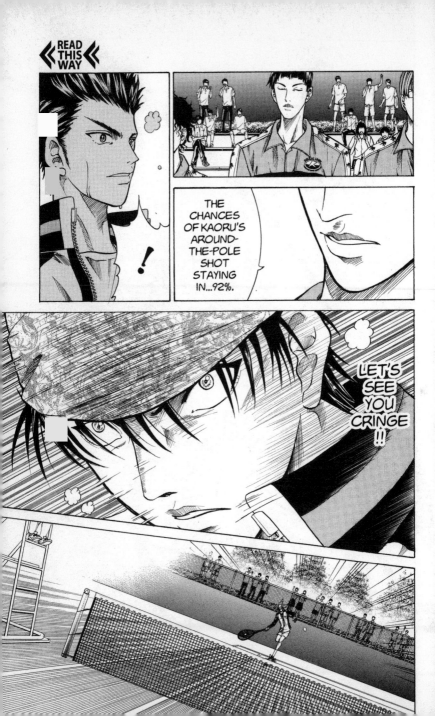

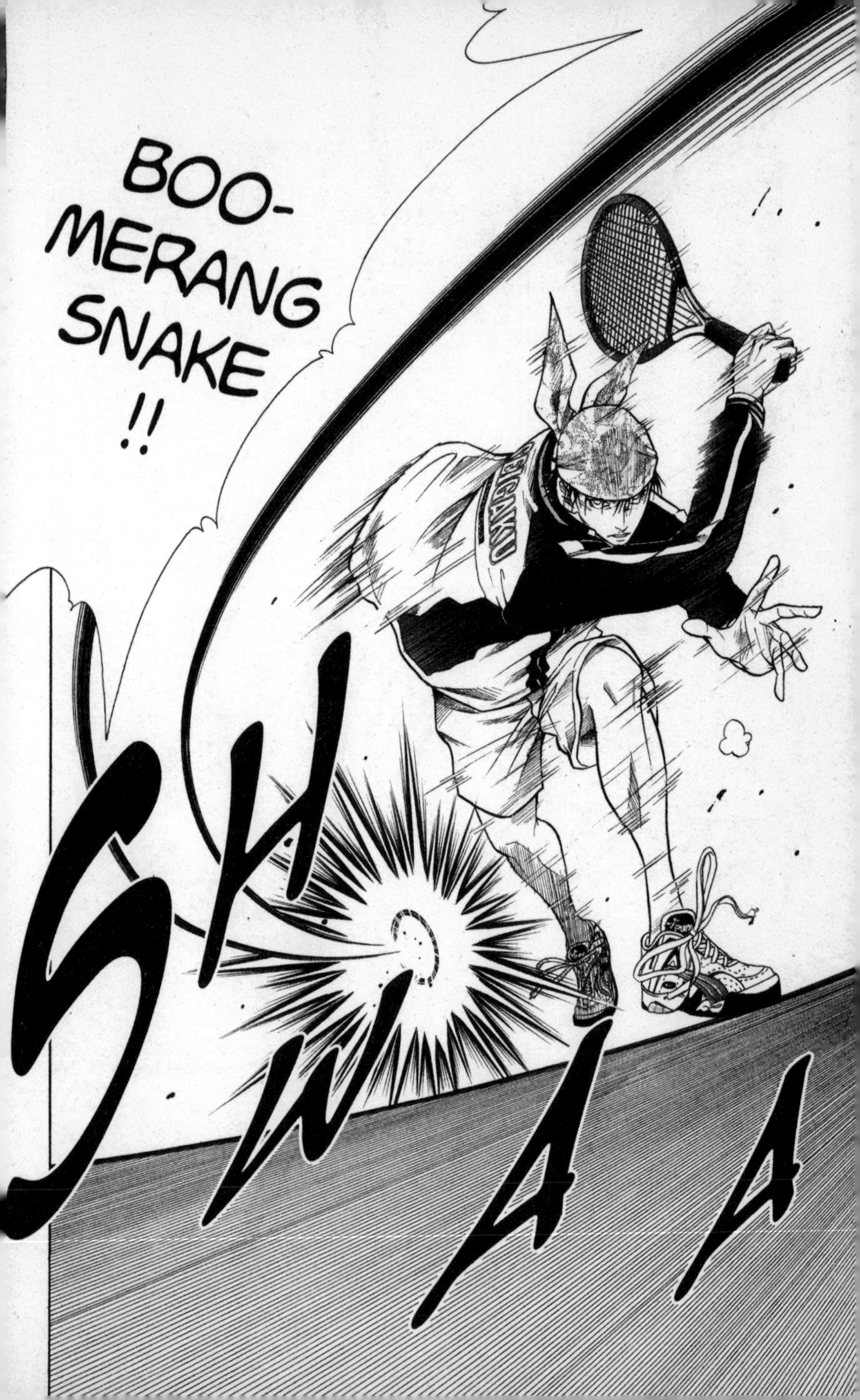
BOO-
MERANG
SNAKE
!!
SEIGAKU
SHWAA

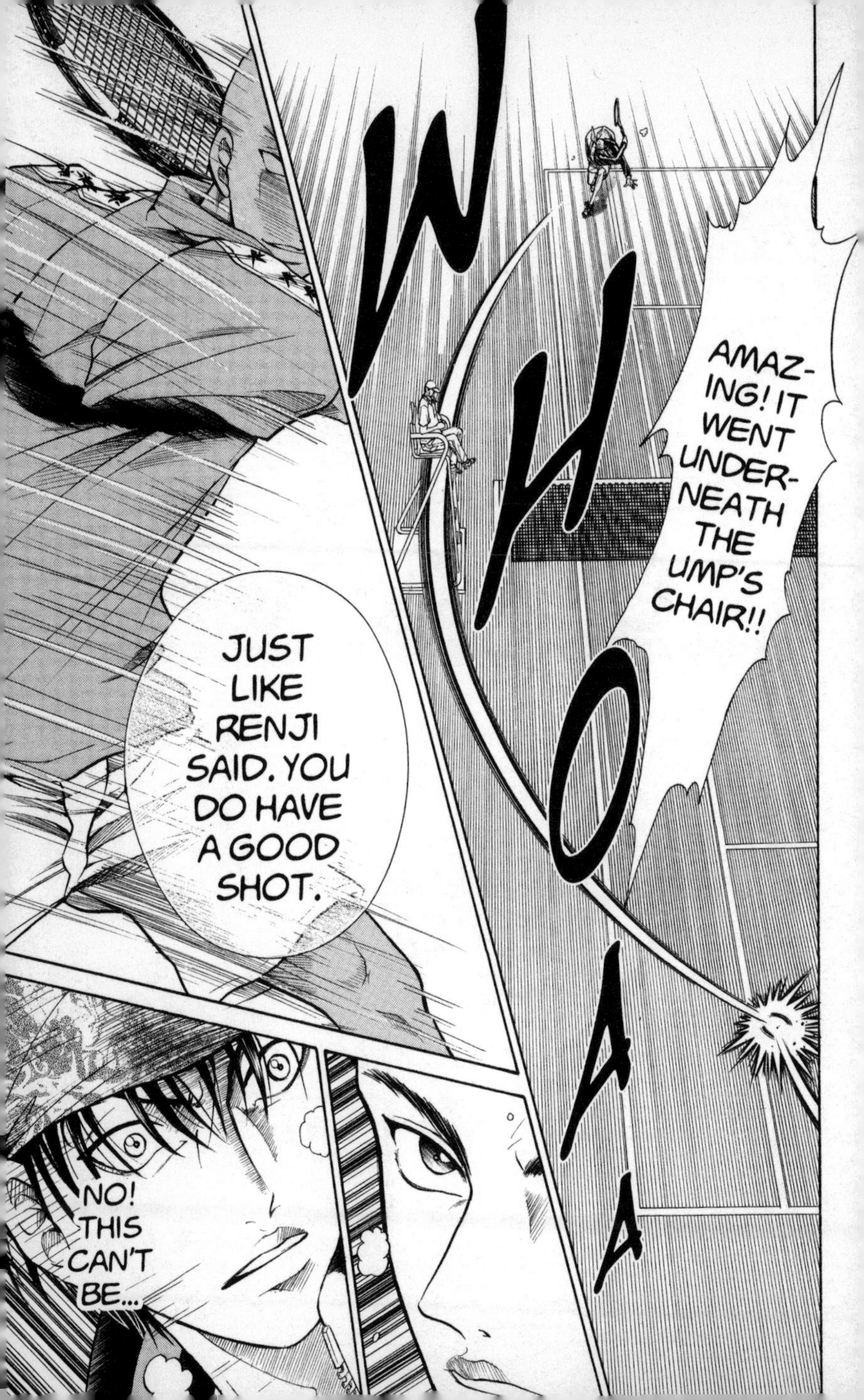
WHOAA
AMAZ-ING! IT WENT UNDER-NEATH THE UMP'S CHAIR!!
JUST LIKE RENJI SAID. YOU DO HAVE A GOOD SHOT.
NO! THIS CAN'T BE...

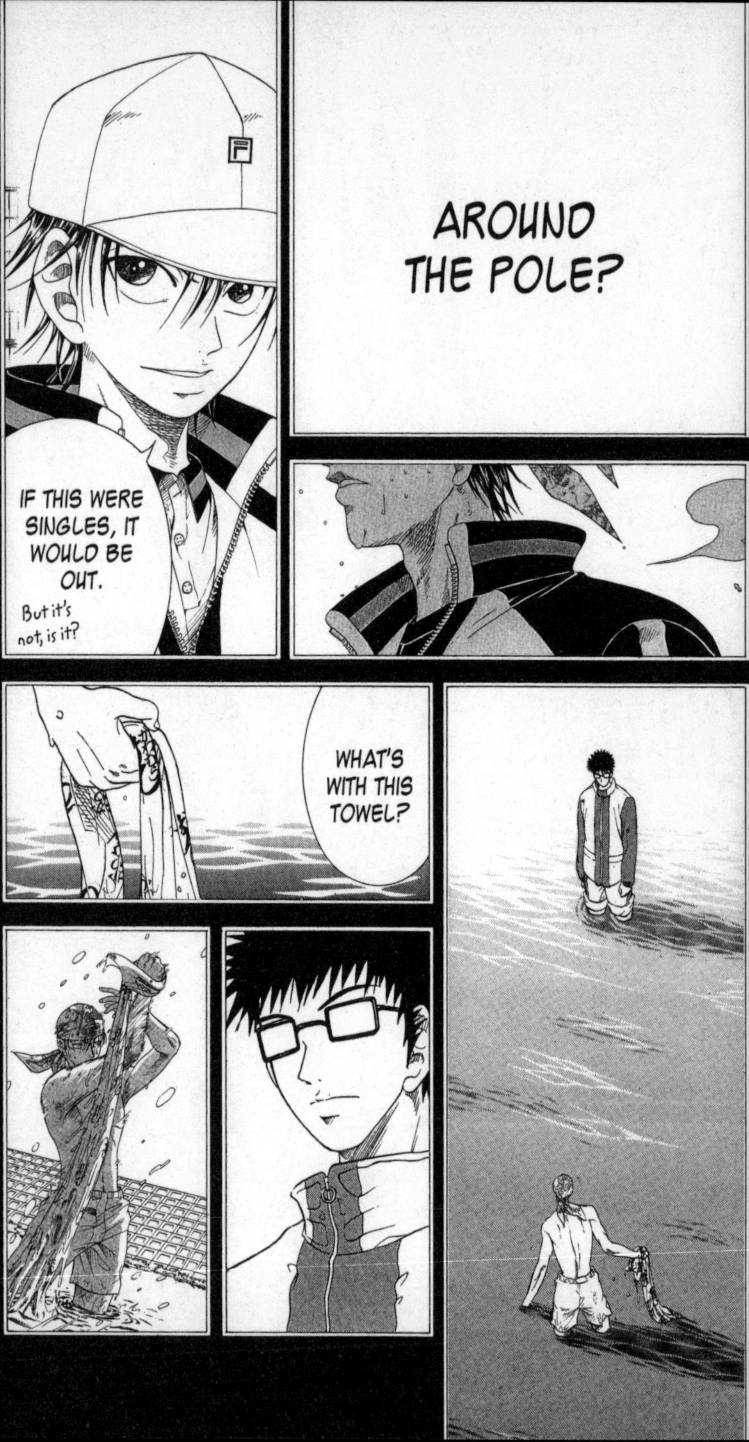
AROUND THE POLE?
IF THIS WERE SINGLES, IT WOULD BE OUT.
But it's not, is it?
WHAT'S WITH THIS TOWEL?

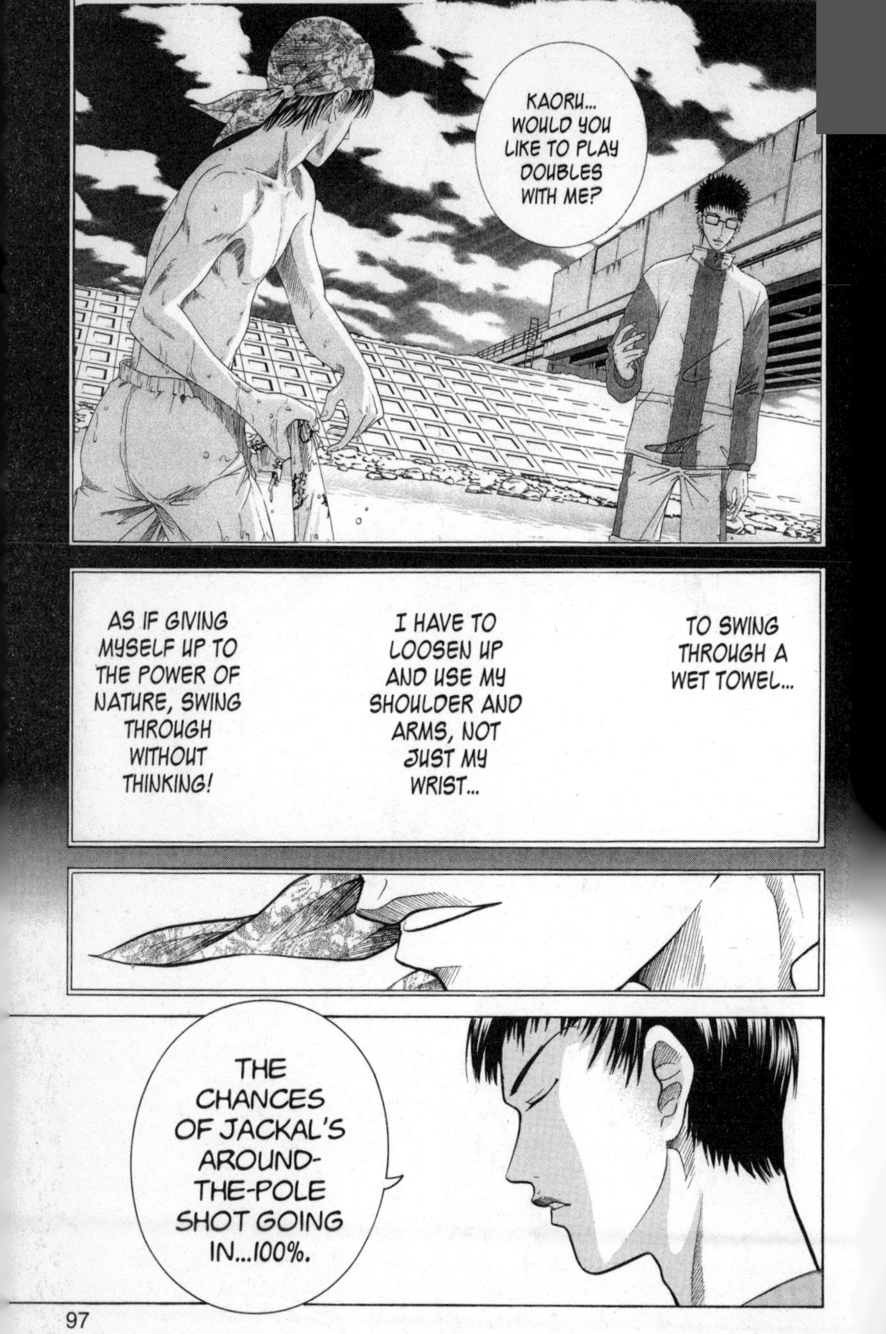
KAORU... WOULD YOU LIKE TO PLAY DOUBLES WITH ME?
TO SWING THROUGH A WET TOWEL...
I HAVE TO LOOSEN UP AND USE MY SHOULDER AND ARMS, NOT JUST MY WRIST...
AS IF GIVING MYSELF UP TO THE POWER OF NATURE, SWING THROUGH WITHOUT THINKING!
THE CHANCES OF JACKAL'S AROUND-THE-POLE SHOT GOING IN...100%.

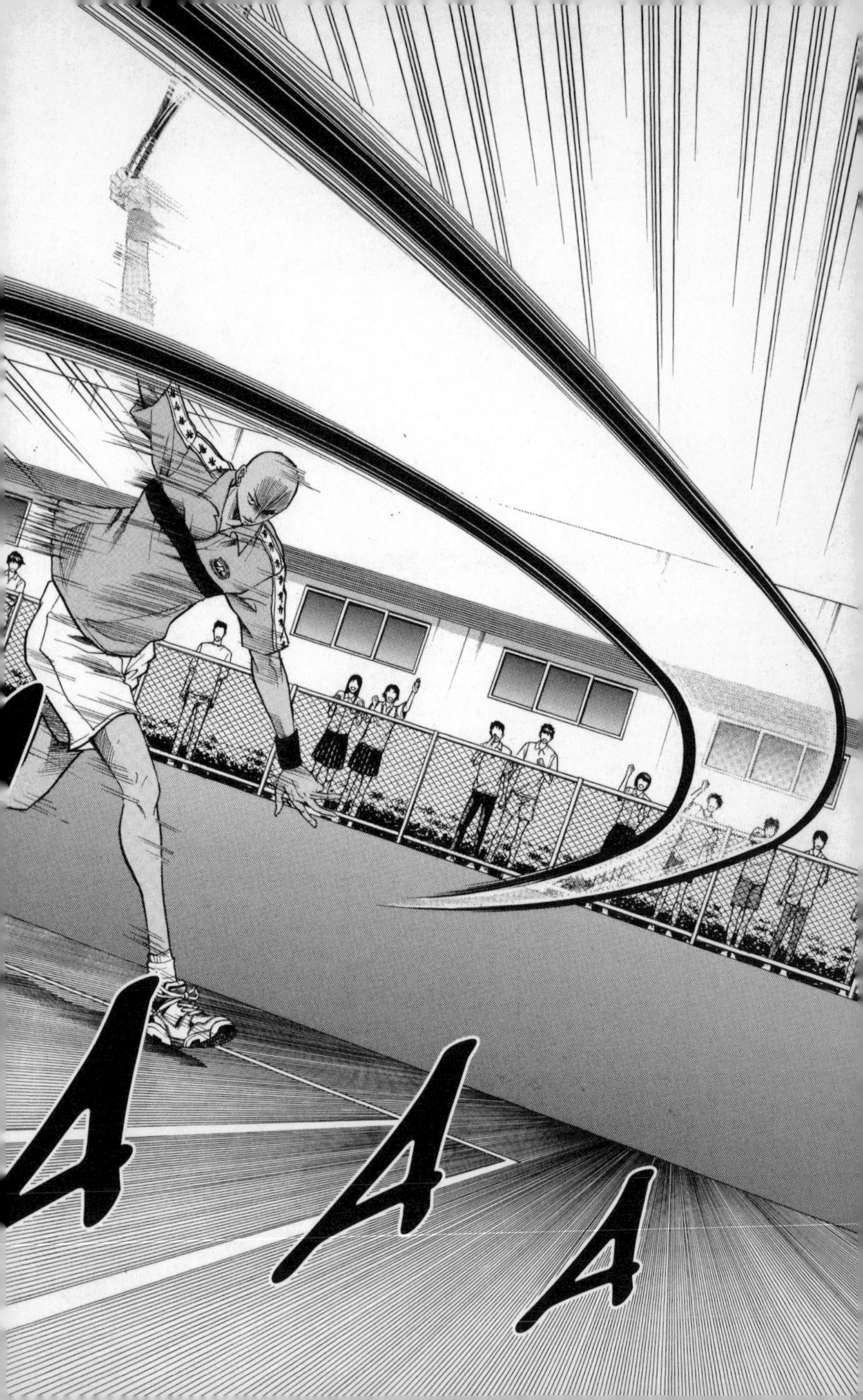

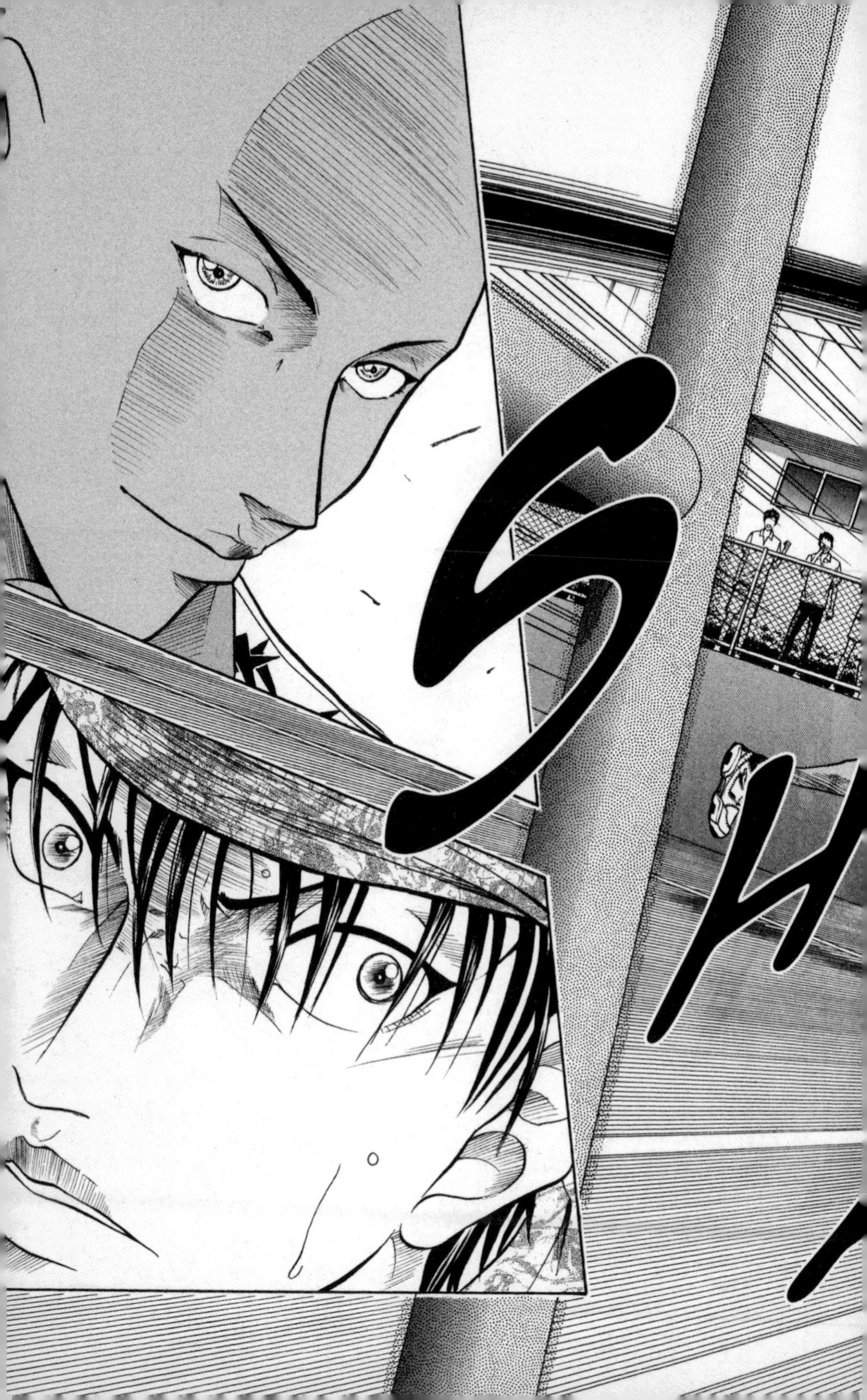

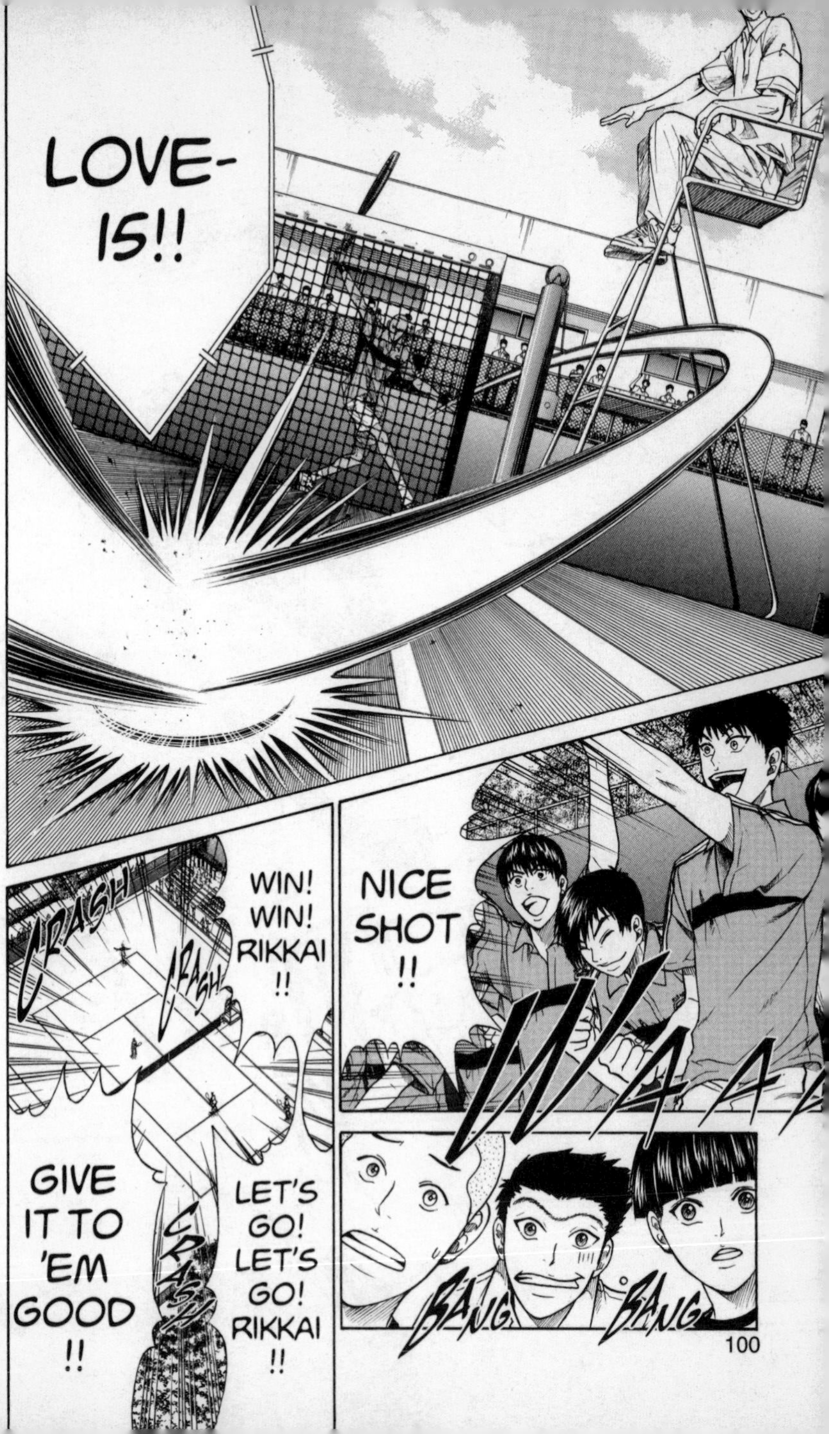

LOVE-15!!
NICE SHOT!!
WAA
BANG
BANG
WIN! WIN! RIKKAI!!
CRASH
CRASH
LET'S GO! LET'S GO! RIKKAI!!
GIVE IT TO 'EM GOOD!!
CRASH

READ THIS WAY

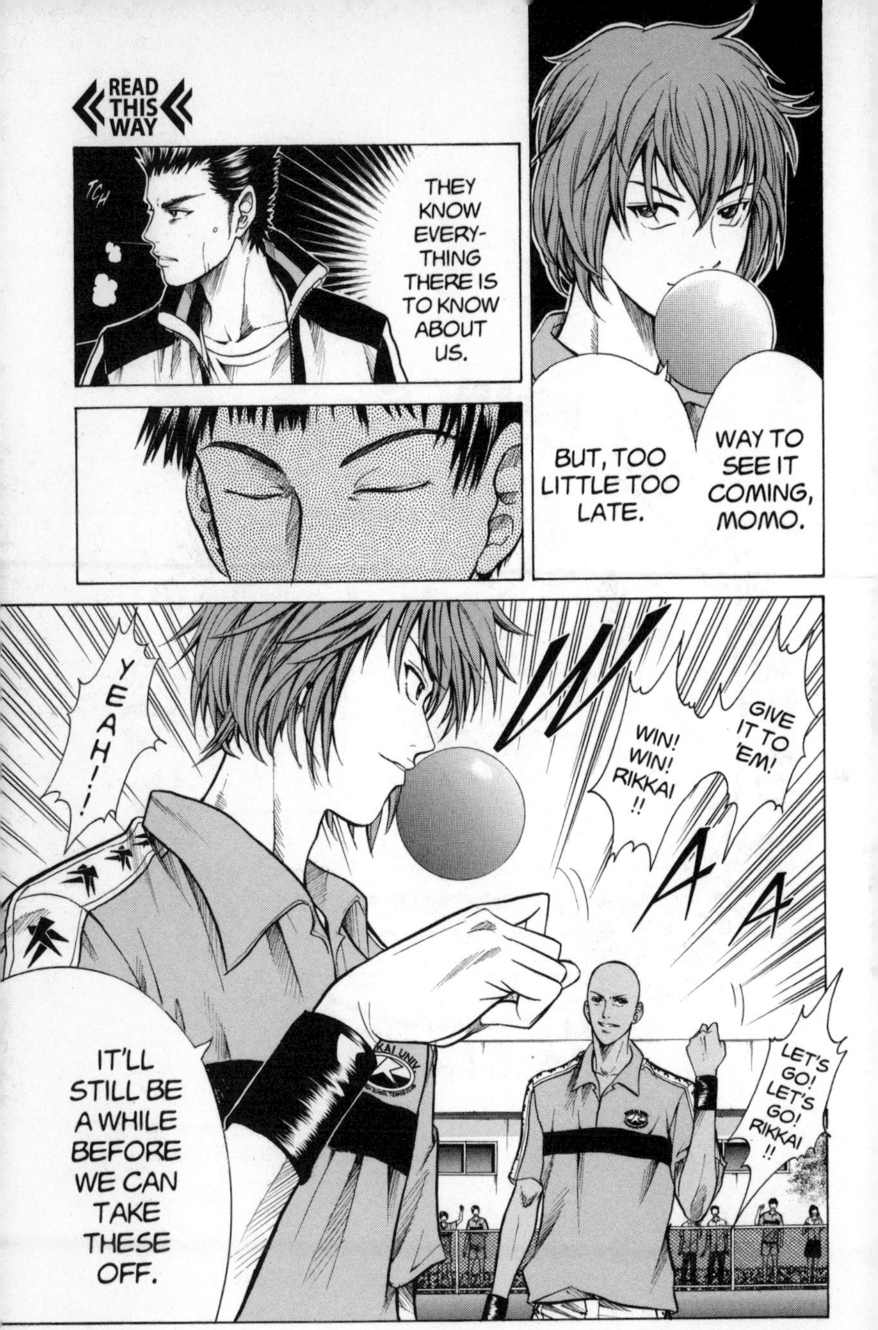
WAY TO SEE IT COMING, MOMO.
BUT, TOO LITTLE TOO LATE.
TCH
THEY KNOW EVERY-THING THERE IS TO KNOW ABOUT US.
GIVE IT TO 'EM!
WIN! WIN! RIKKAI!!
WAA
YEAH!!
LET'S GO! LET'S GO! RIKKAI!!
IT'LL STILL BE A WHILE BEFORE WE CAN TAKE THESE OFF.

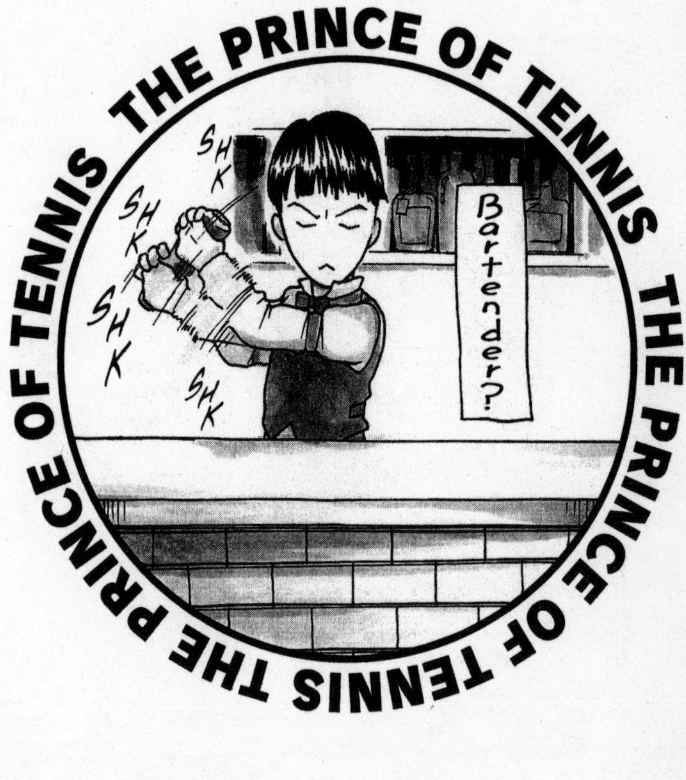
THE PRINCE OF TENNIS THE PRINCE OF TENNIS THE PRINCE OF TENNIS
Bartender?
SHK
SHK
SHK
SHK

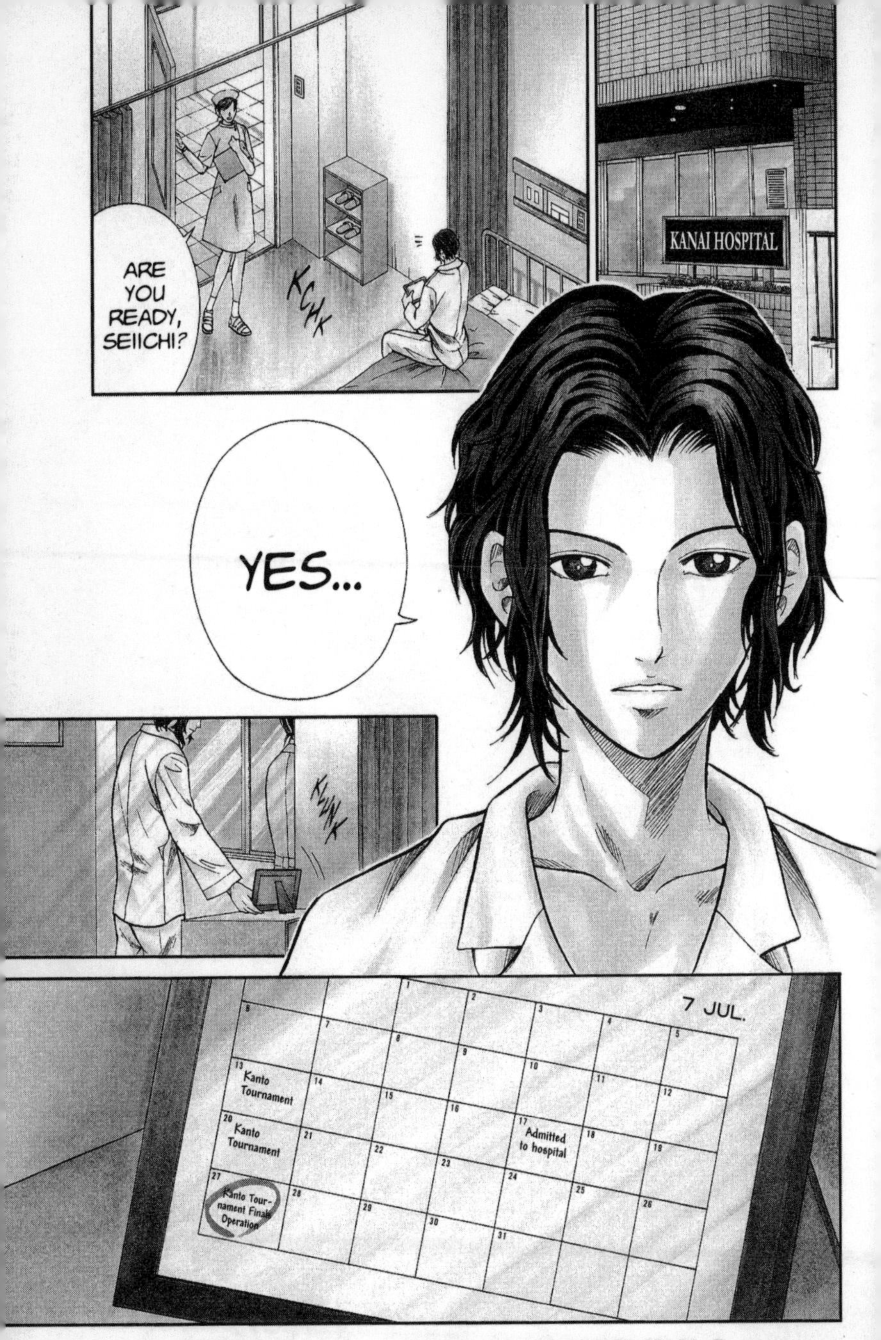
KANAI HOSPITAL
ARE YOU READY, SEIICHI?
KCHK
YES...
KLUNK
7 JUL.
Kanto Tournament
Kanto Tournament
Admitted to hospital
Kanto Tournament Finals Operation

GENIUS 198: AS A RIVAL

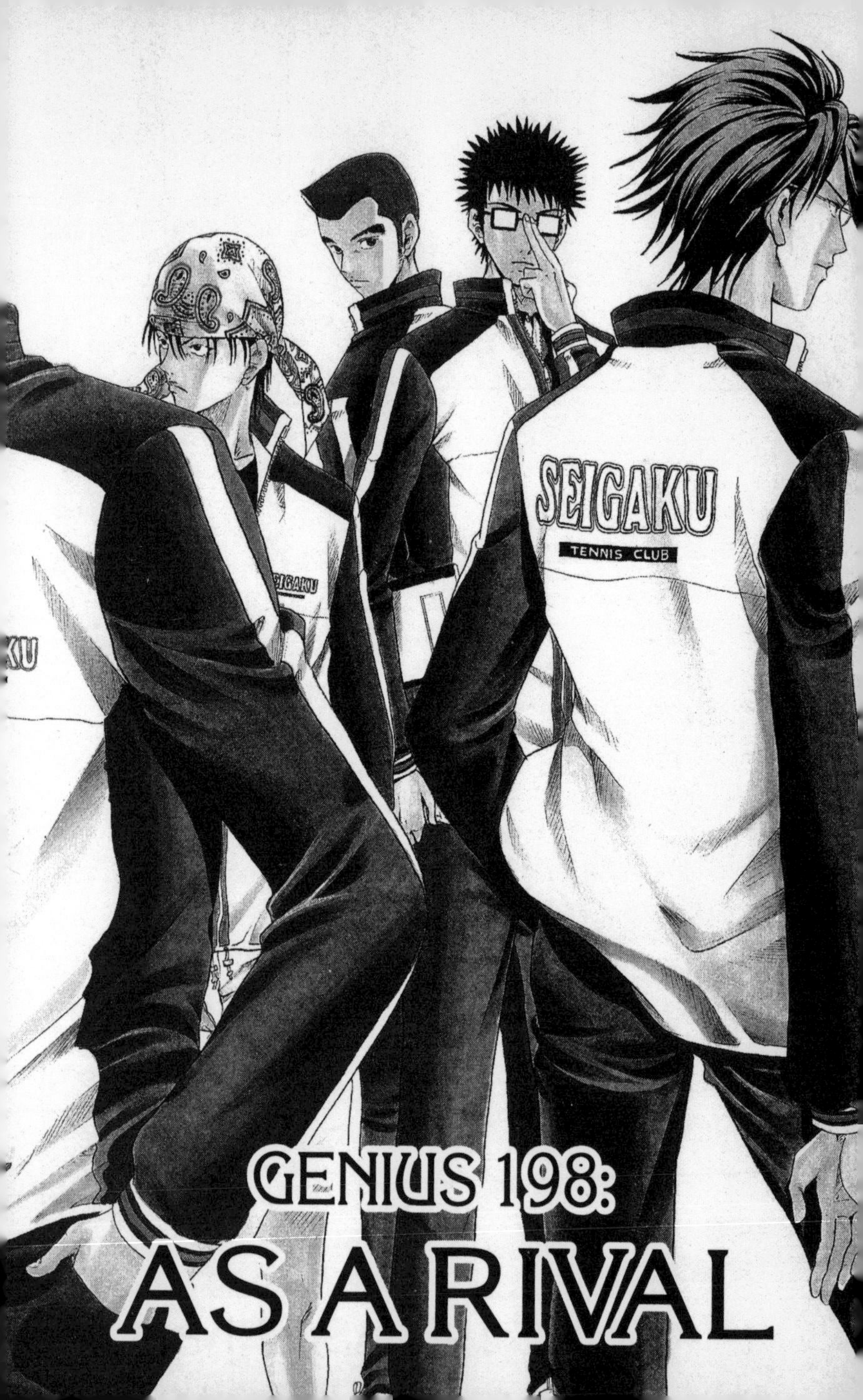
SEIGAKU
TENNIS CLUB
GENIUS 198:
AS A RIVAL

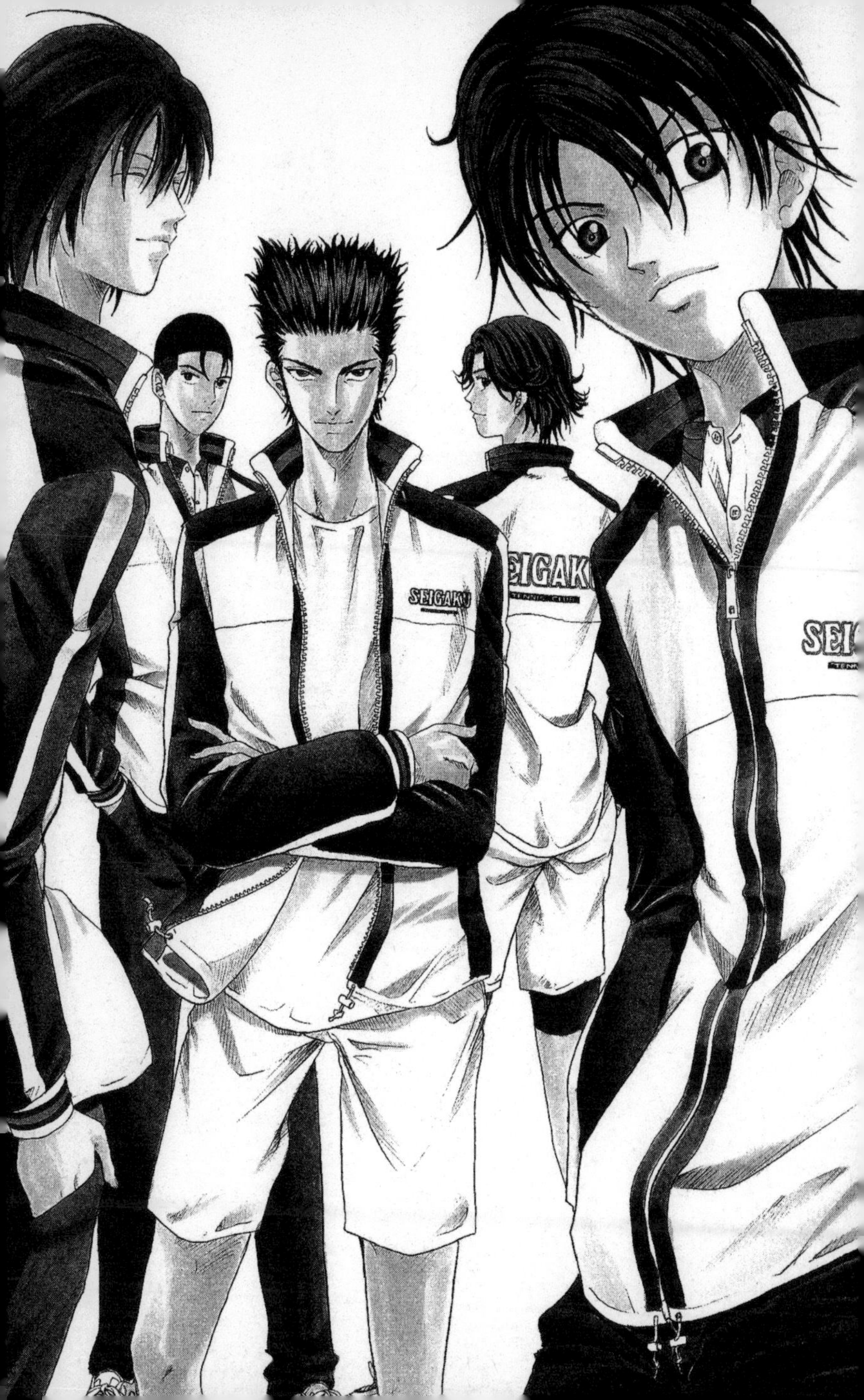
SEIGAKU

テニスの王子様

THE PRINCE OF TENNIS

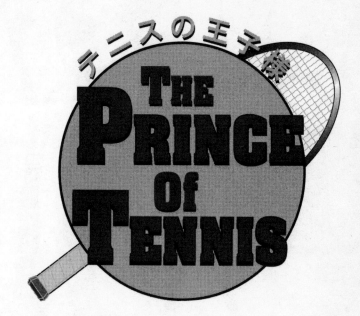

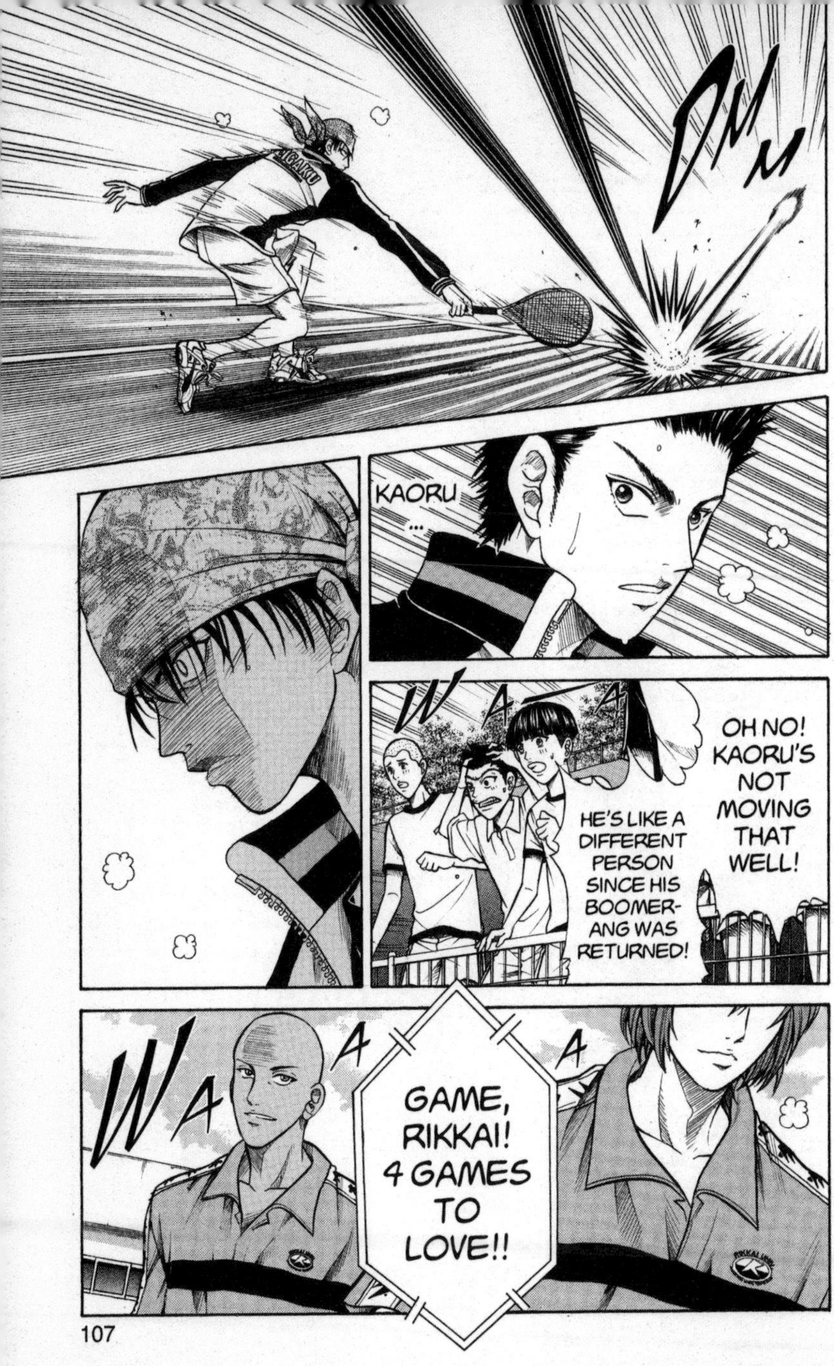
DMM
KAORU ...
WAA
OH NO! KAORU'S NOT MOVING THAT WELL!
HE'S LIKE A DIFFERENT PERSON SINCE HIS BOOMER-ANG WAS RETURNED!
WAA
A
GAME, RIKKAI! 4 GAMES TO LOVE!!

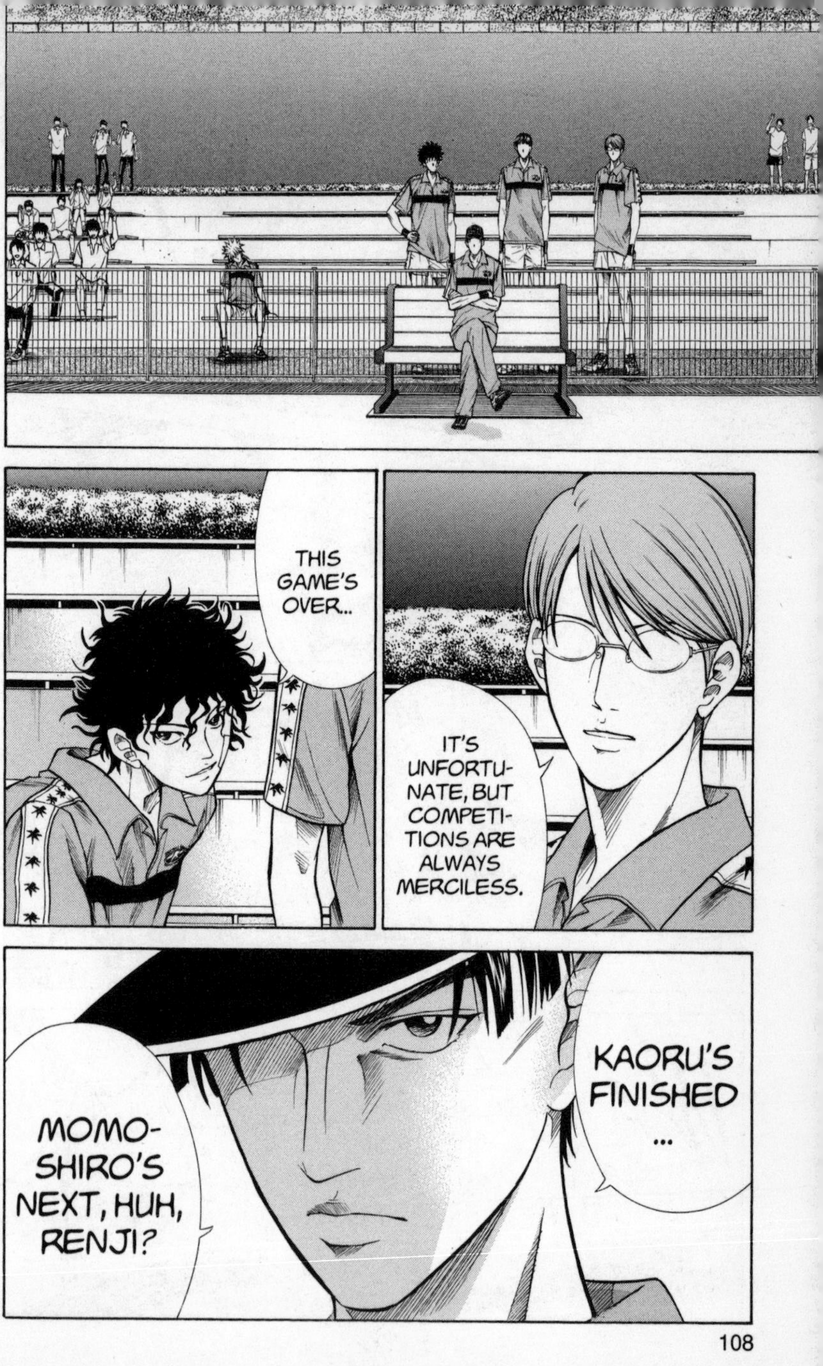
IT'S UNFORTUNATE, BUT COMPETITIONS ARE ALWAYS MERCILESS.
THIS GAME'S OVER...
KAORU'S FINISHED ...
MOMOSHIRO'S NEXT, HUH, RENJI?

READ THIS WAY

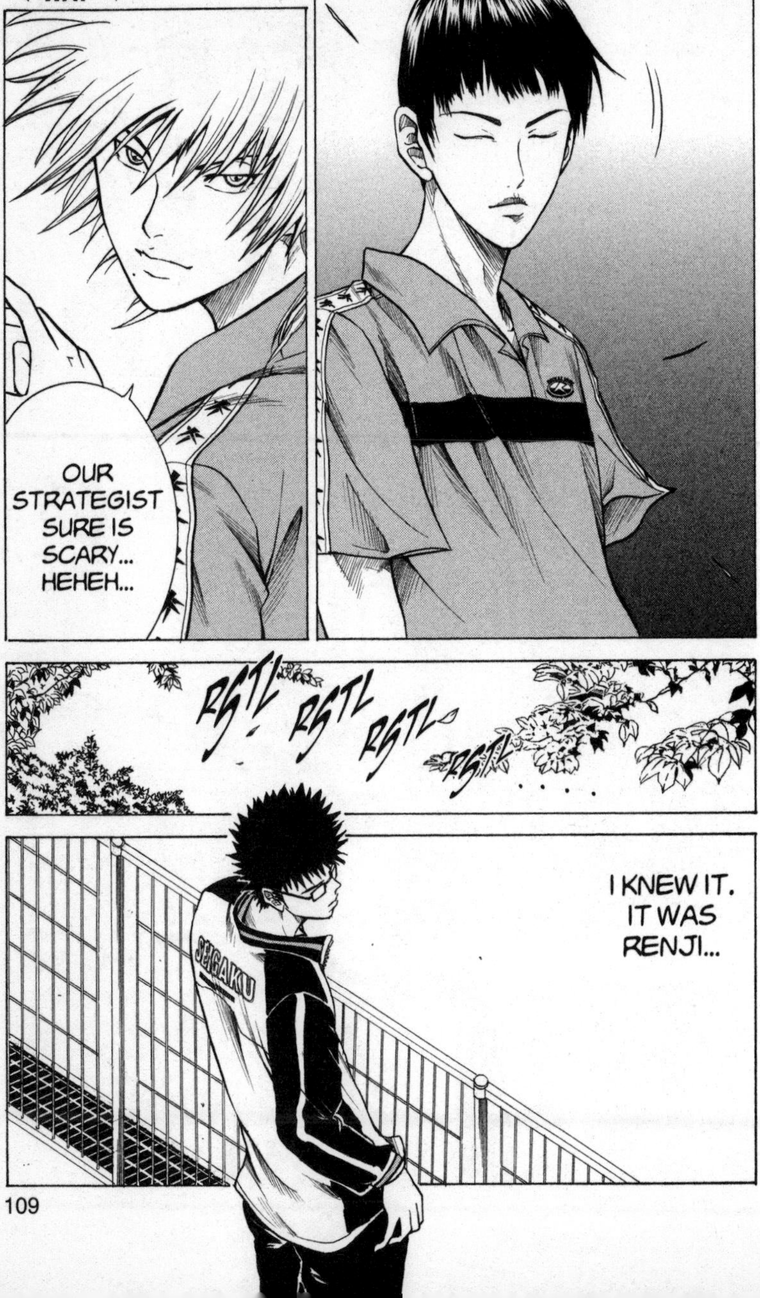
OUR STRATEGIST SURE IS SCARY... HEHEH...
RSTL RSTL RSTL RSTL
I KNEW IT. IT WAS RENJI...

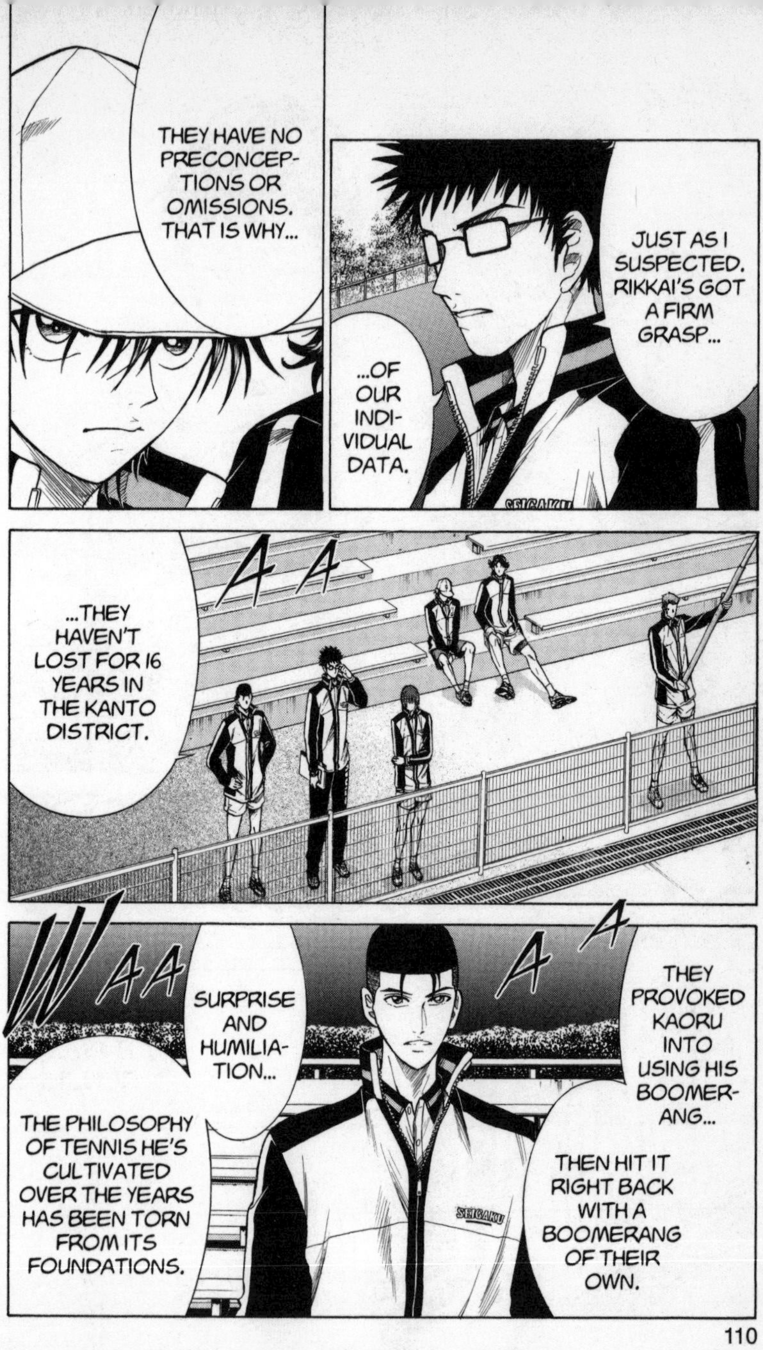
JUST AS I SUSPECTED. RIKKAI'S GOT A FIRM GRASP...
...OF OUR INDIVIDUAL DATA.
THEY HAVE NO PRECONCEPTIONS OR OMISSIONS. THAT IS WHY...
AA
...THEY HAVEN'T LOST FOR 16 YEARS IN THE KANTO DISTRICT.
WAAAA
THEY PROVOKED KAORU INTO USING HIS BOOMERANG...
THEN HIT IT RIGHT BACK WITH A BOOMERANG OF THEIR OWN.
SURPRISE AND HUMILIATION...
THE PHILOSOPHY OF TENNIS HE'S CULTIVATED OVER THE YEARS HAS BEEN TORN FROM ITS FOUNDATIONS.

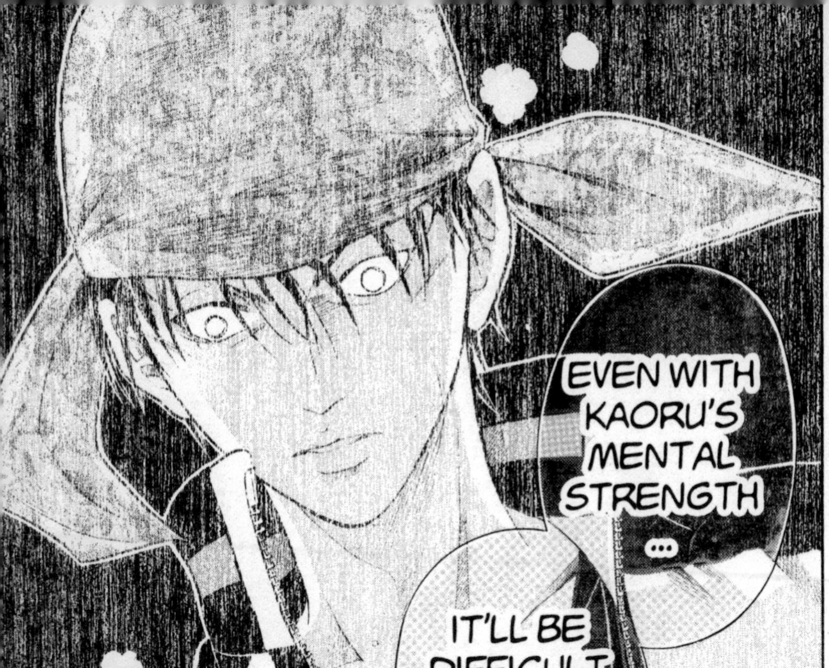
EVEN WITH KAORU'S MENTAL STRENGTH...
IT'LL BE DIFFICULT FOR HIM TO PLAY CALMLY.
SEIGA
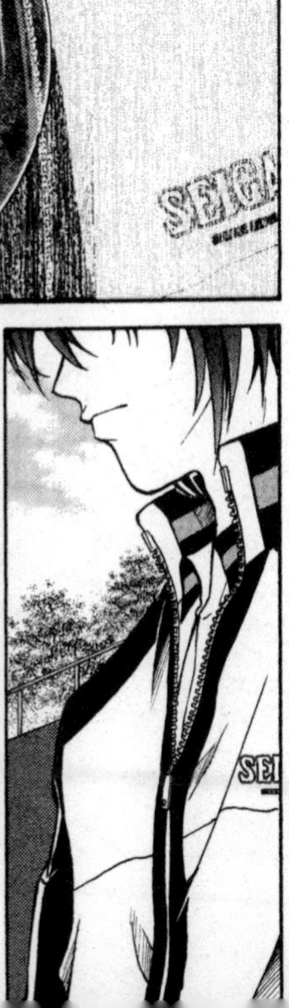
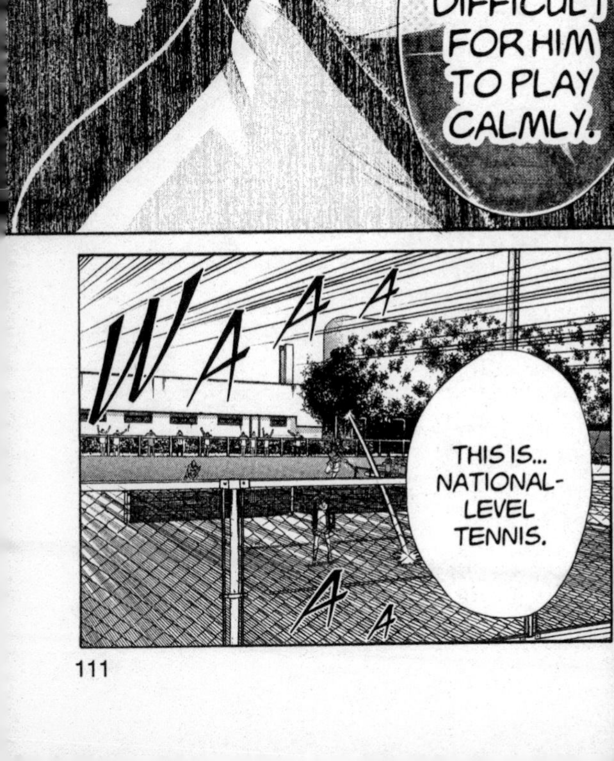
WAAAA
THIS IS... NATIONAL-LEVEL TENNIS.

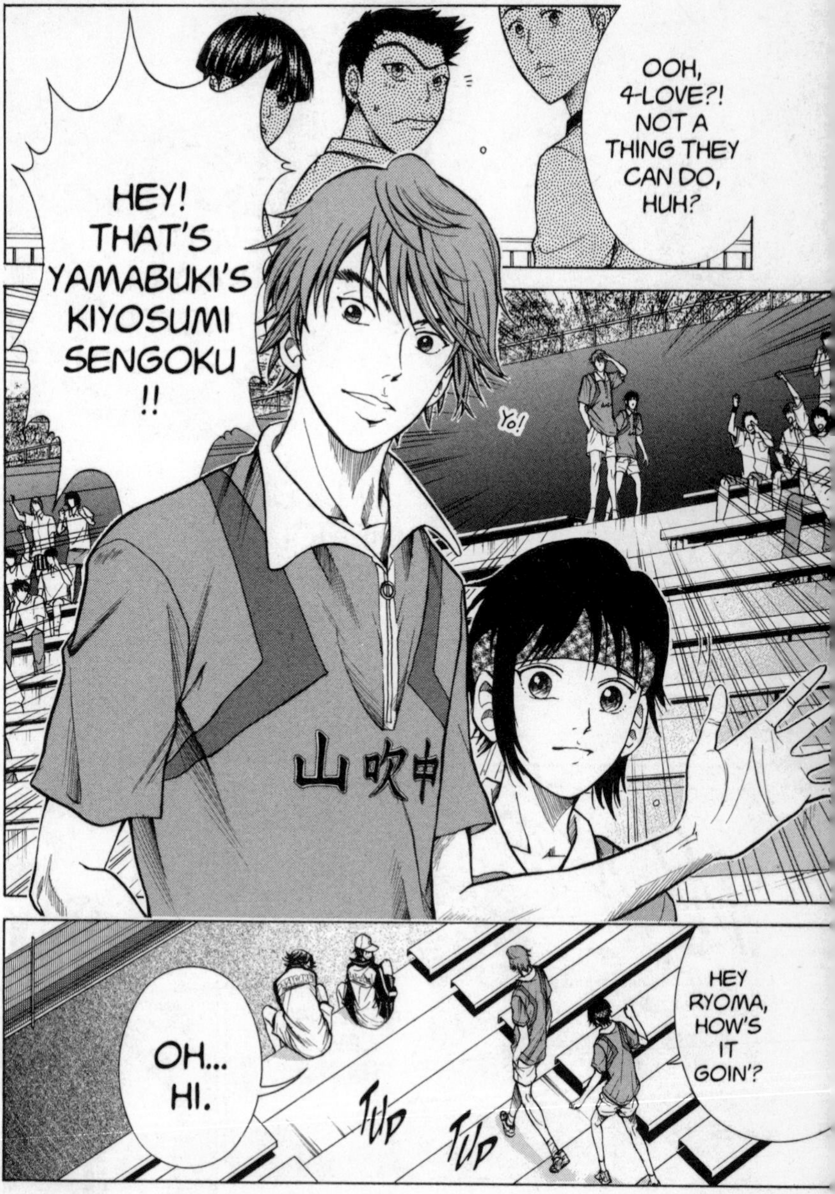
OOH, 4-LOVE?! NOT A THING THEY CAN DO, HUH?
HEY! THAT'S YAMABUKI'S KIYOSUMI SENGOKU !!
Yo!
HEY RYOMA, HOW'S IT GOIN'?
TUP
TUP
OH... HI.

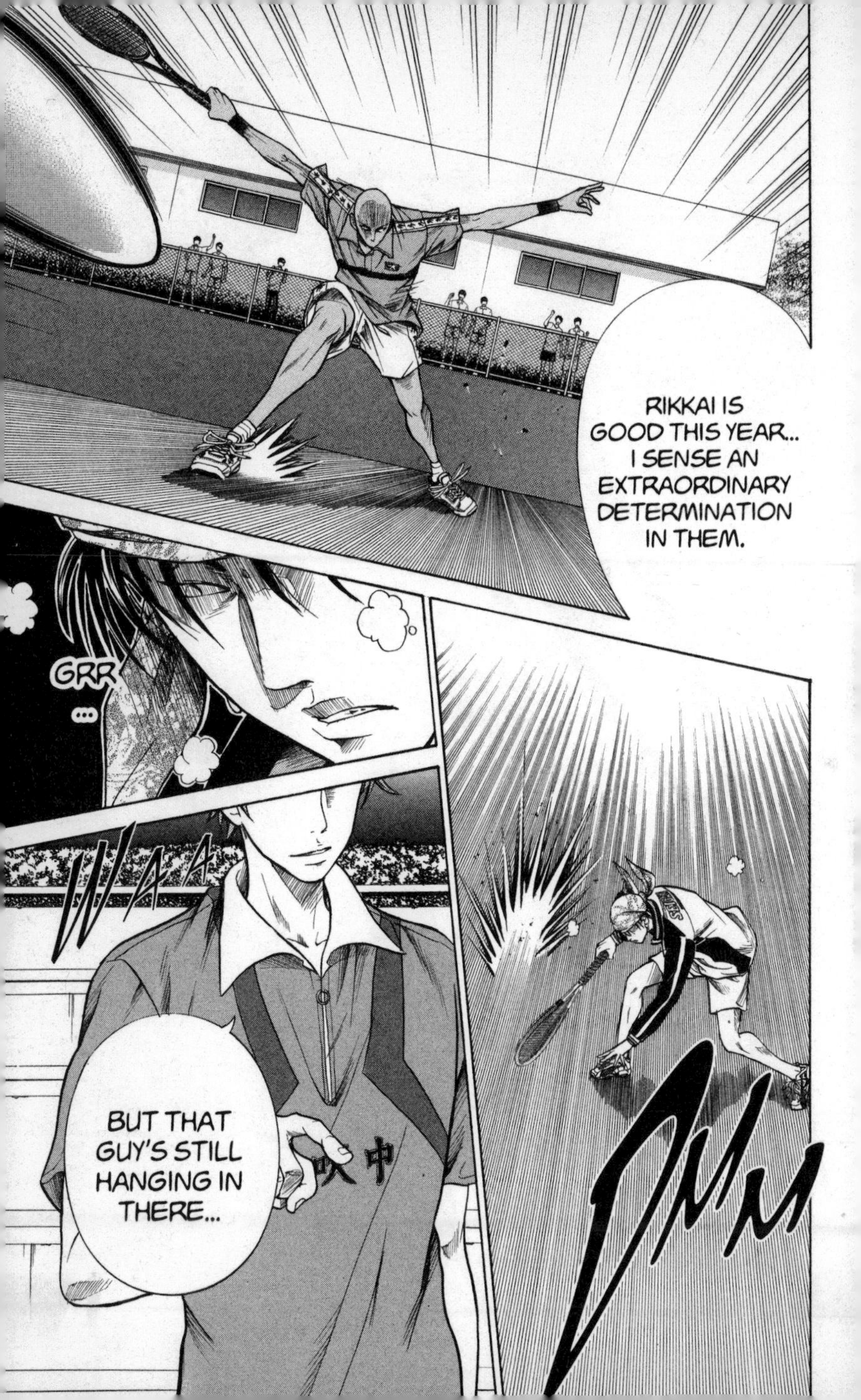
RIKKAI IS GOOD THIS YEAR... I SENSE AN EXTRAORDINARY DETERMINATION IN THEM.
DMM
GRR ...
WAA
BUT THAT GUY'S STILL HANGING IN THERE...

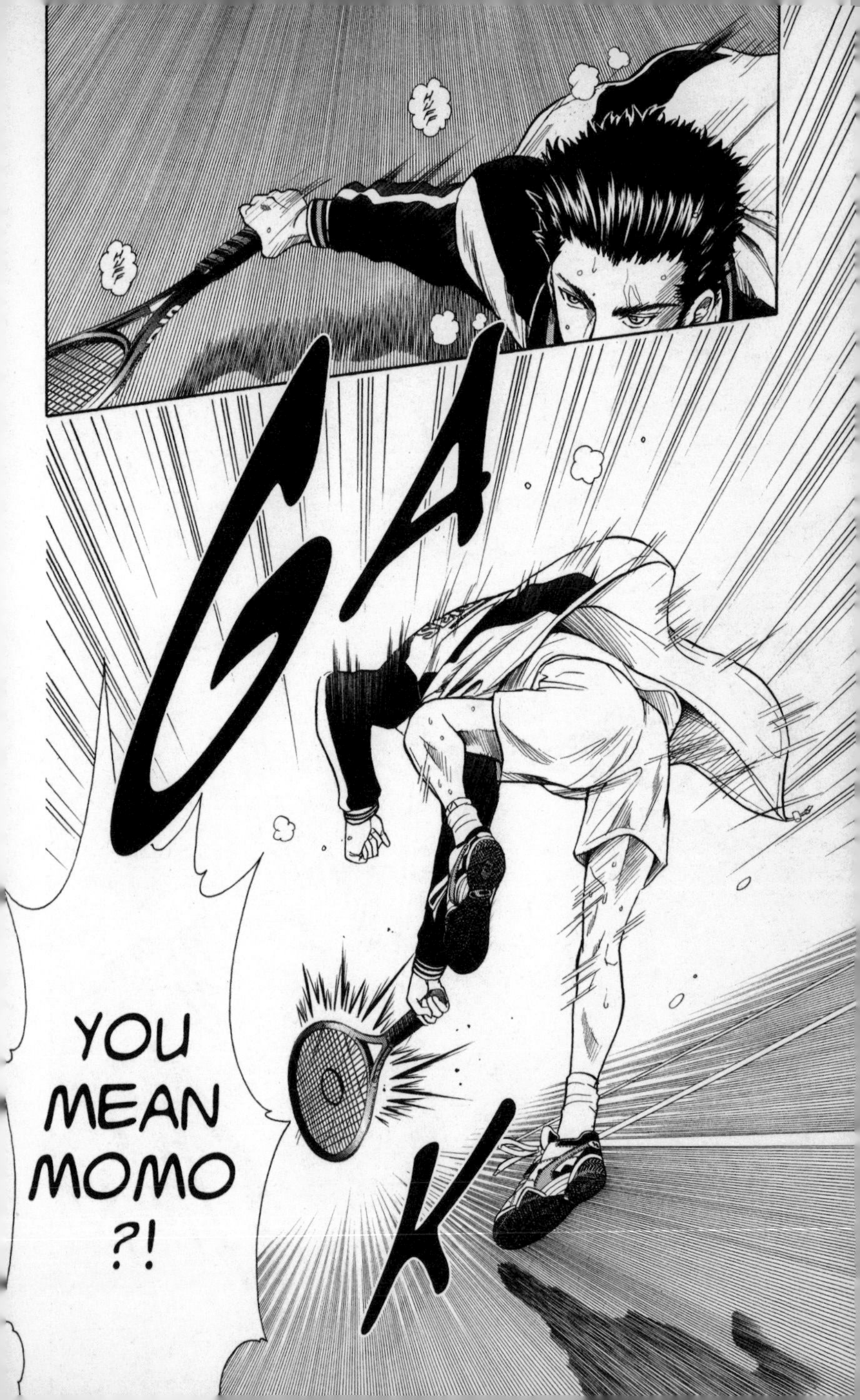
GA
K
YOU MEAN MOMO?!

READ THIS WAY

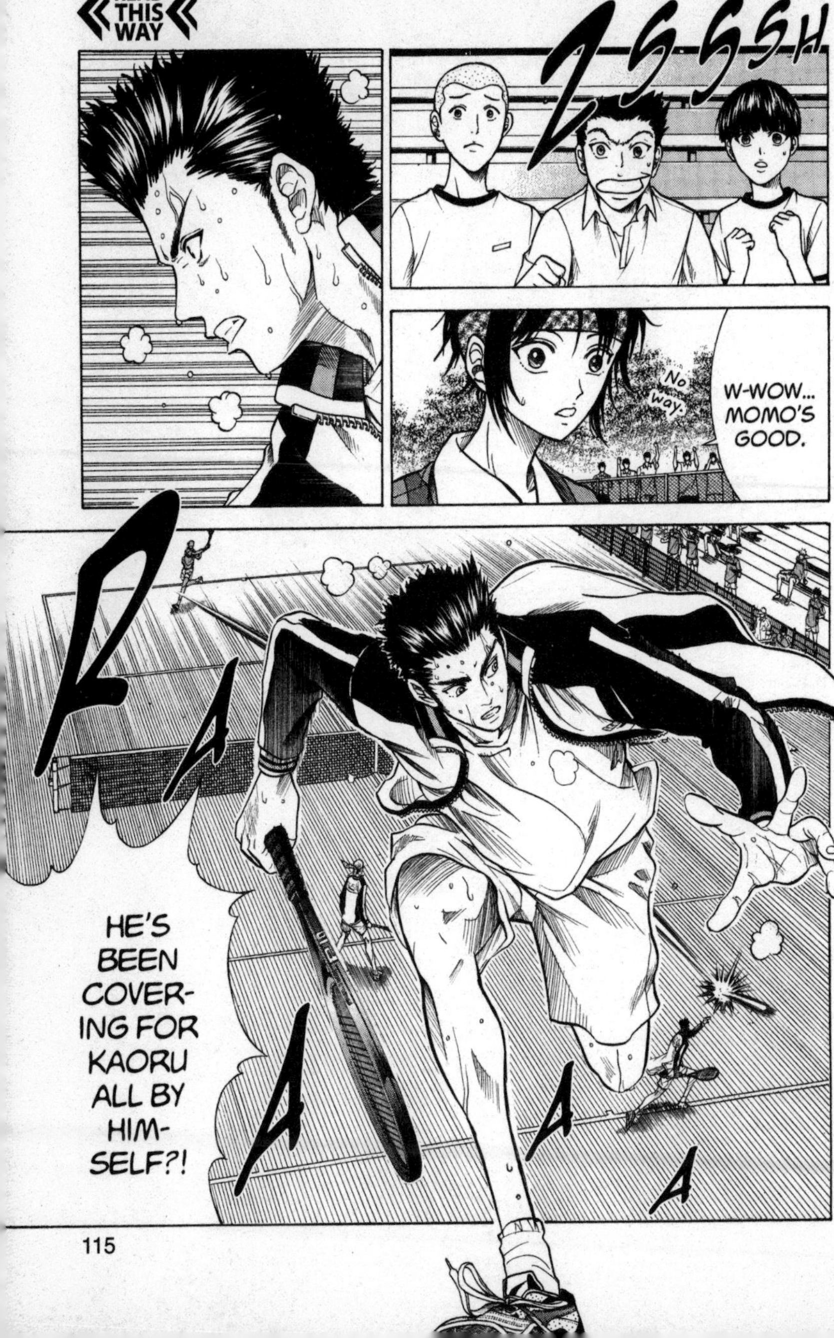

ZSSSH
W-WOW... MOMO'S GOOD.
No way.
RAAAA
HE'S BEEN COVERING FOR KAORU ALL BY HIMSELF?!

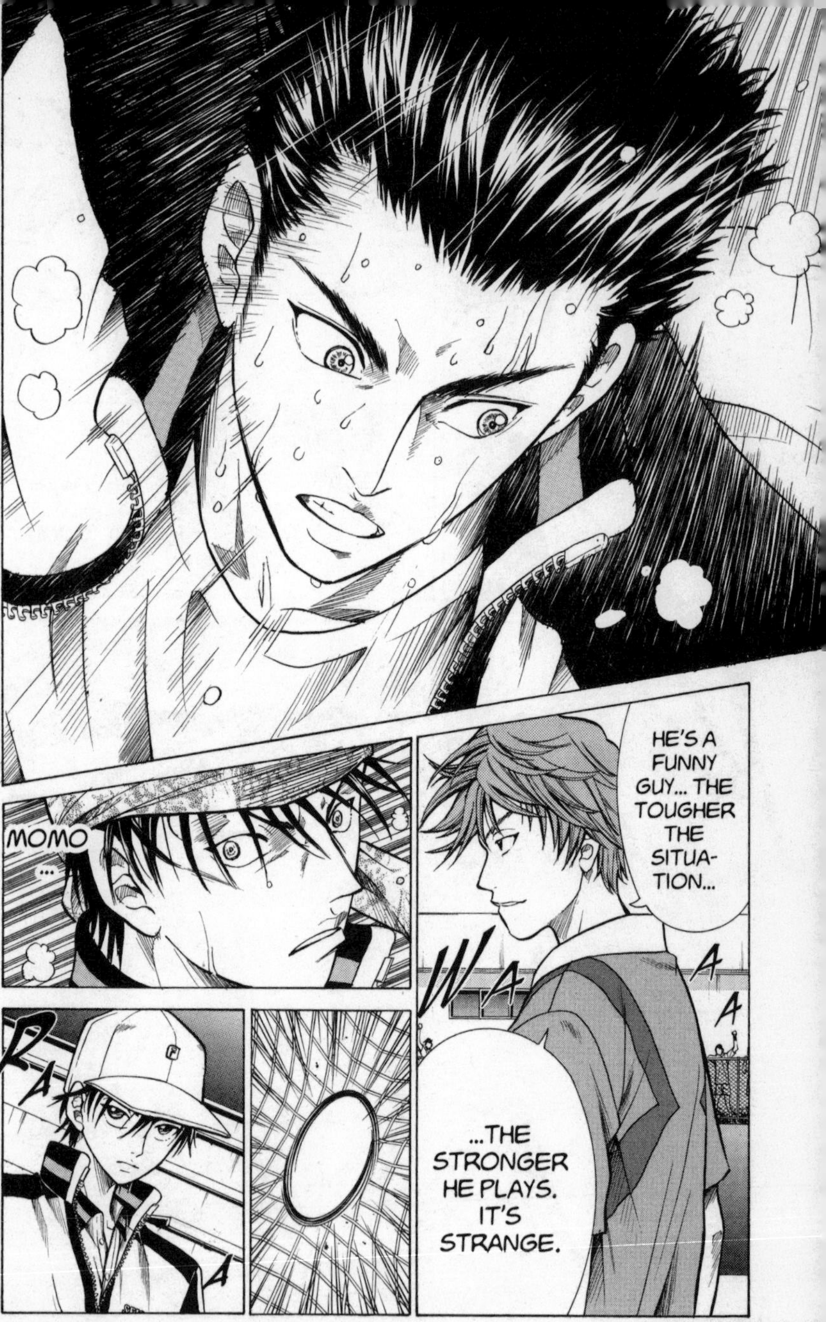
HE'S A FUNNY GUY... THE TOUGHER THE SITUATION...
MOMO ...
WA A A
...THE STRONGER HE PLAYS. IT'S STRANGE.
RA A

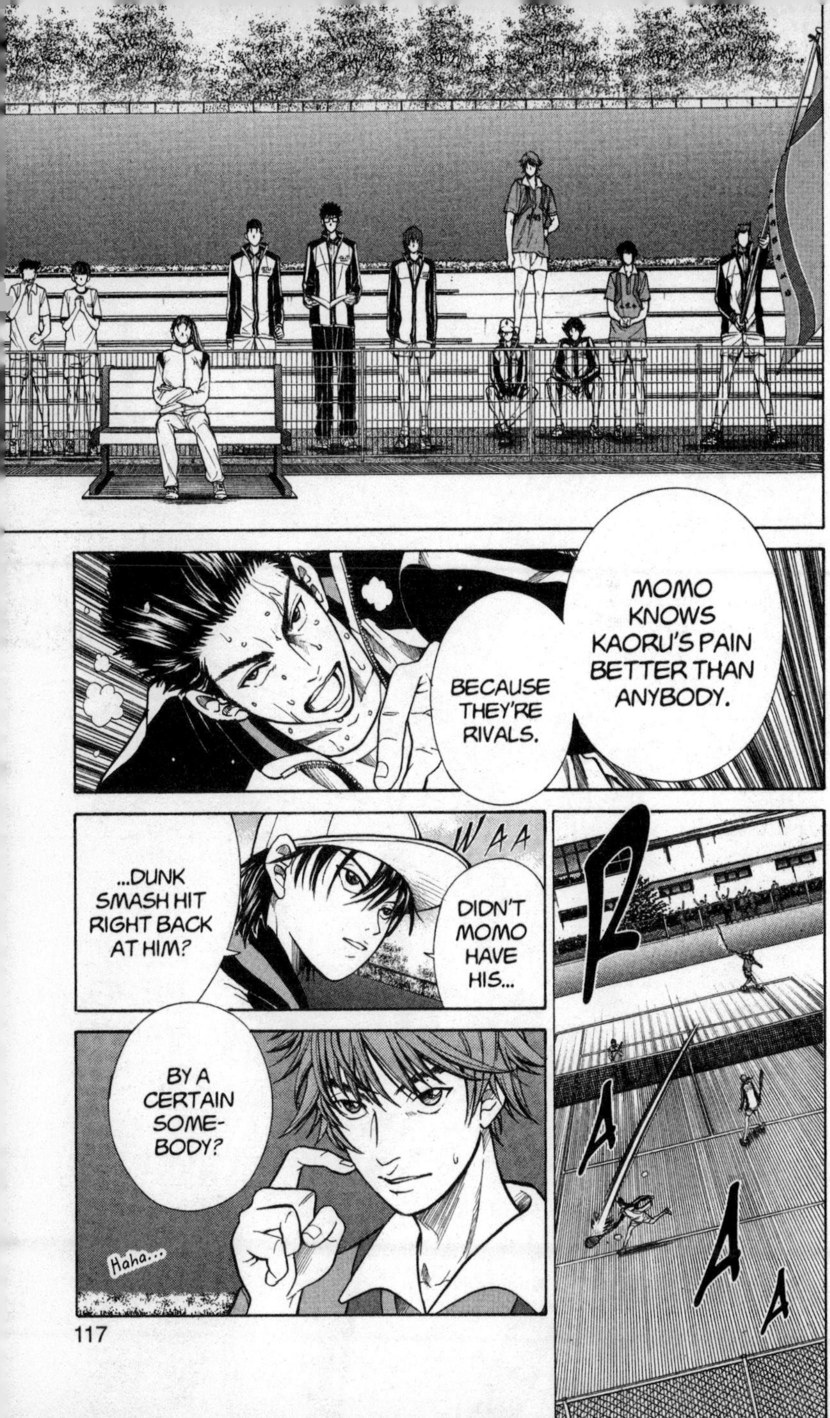
MOMO KNOWS KAORU'S PAIN BETTER THAN ANYBODY.
BECAUSE THEY'RE RIVALS.
WAA
DIDN'T MOMO HAVE HIS...
...DUNK SMASH HIT RIGHT BACK AT HIM?
BY A CERTAIN SOMEBODY?
Haha...

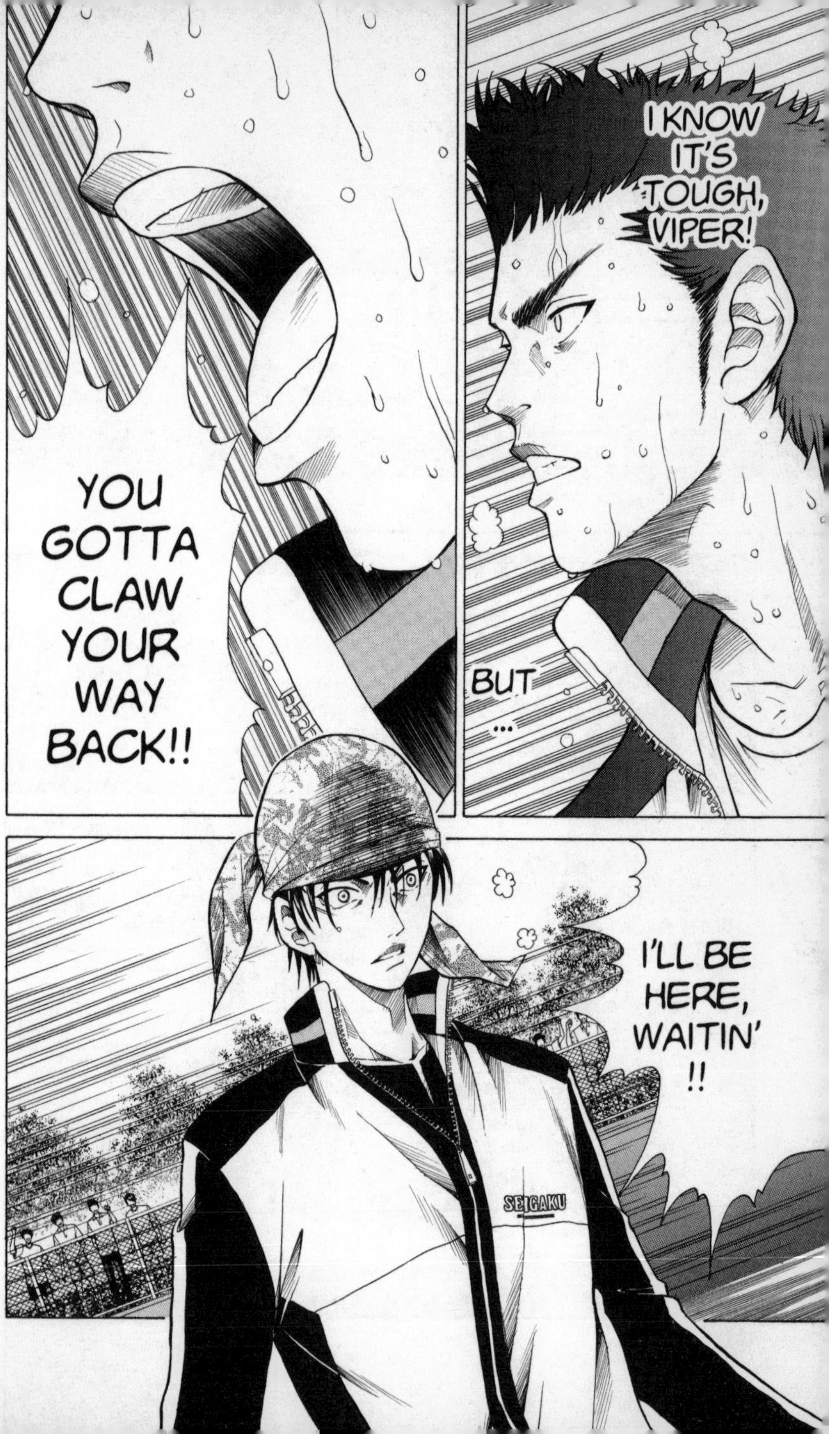
I KNOW IT'S TOUGH, VIPER!
BUT ...
YOU GOTTA CLAW YOUR WAY BACK!!
I'LL BE HERE, WAITIN' !!

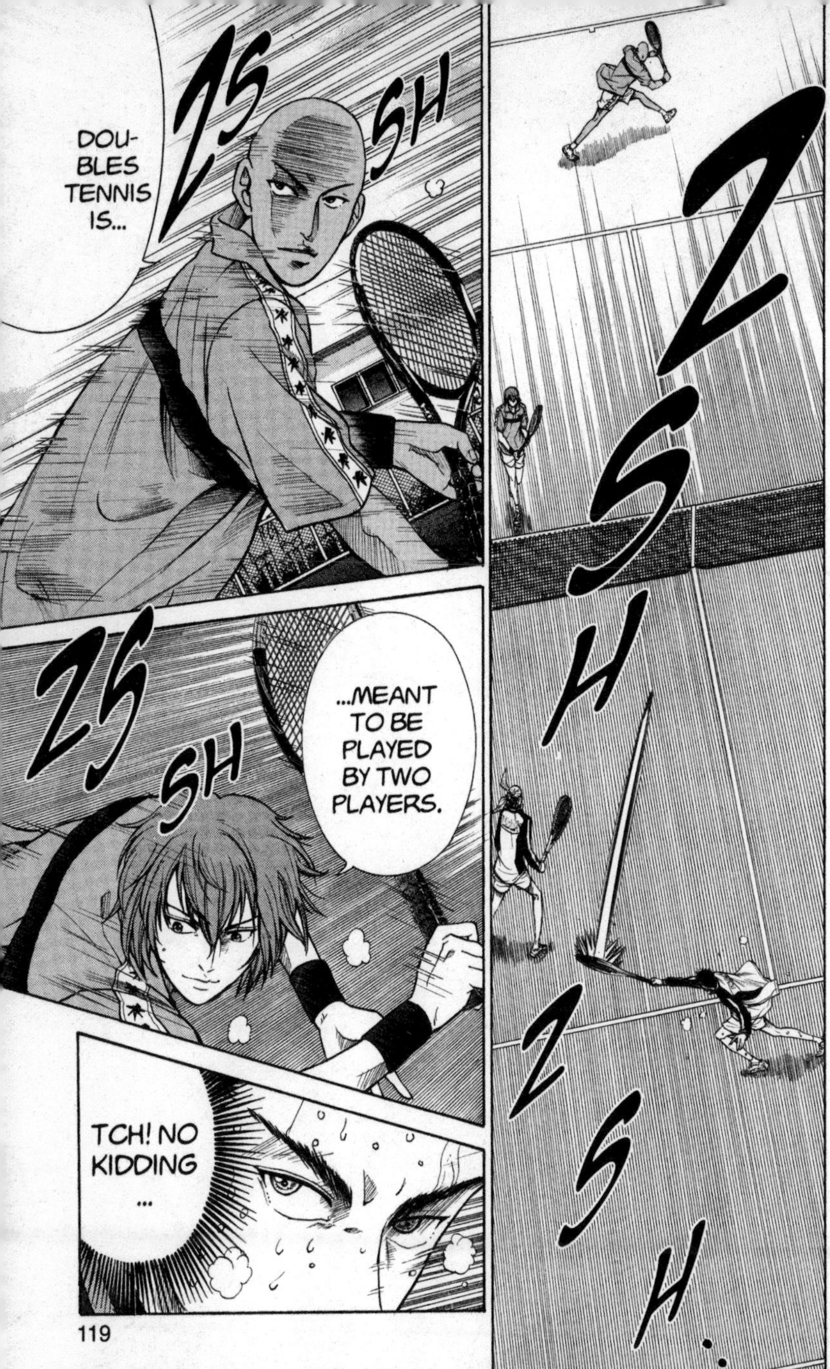
ZSSH
ZSSH..
ZSSH
DOU-BLES TENNIS IS...
ZSSH
...MEANT TO BE PLAYED BY TWO PLAYERS.
TCH! NO KIDDING ...

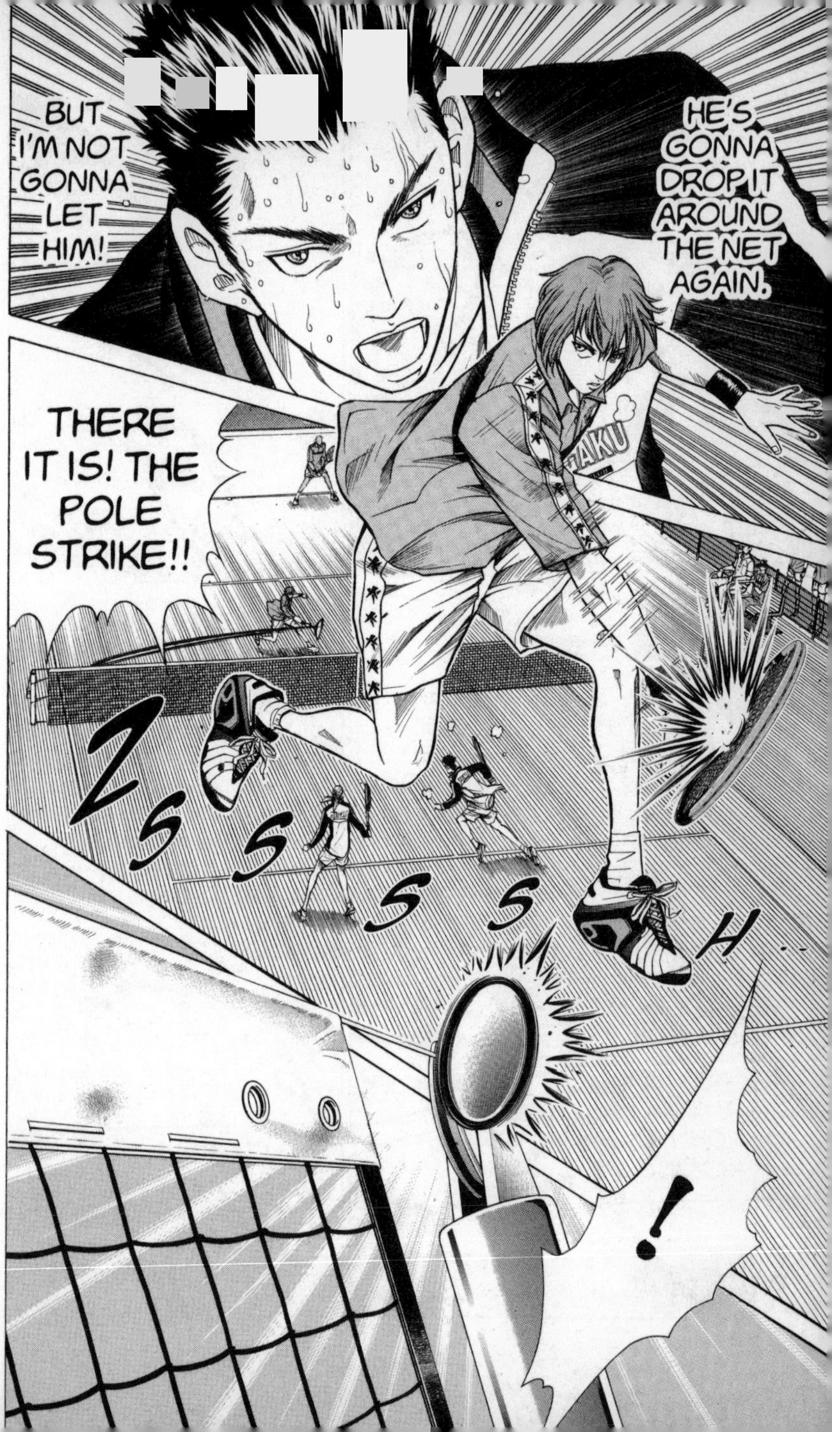
HE'S GONNA DROP IT AROUND THE NET AGAIN.
BUT I'M NOT GONNA LET HIM!
THERE IT IS! THE POLE STRIKE!!
ZSSSSSH...
!

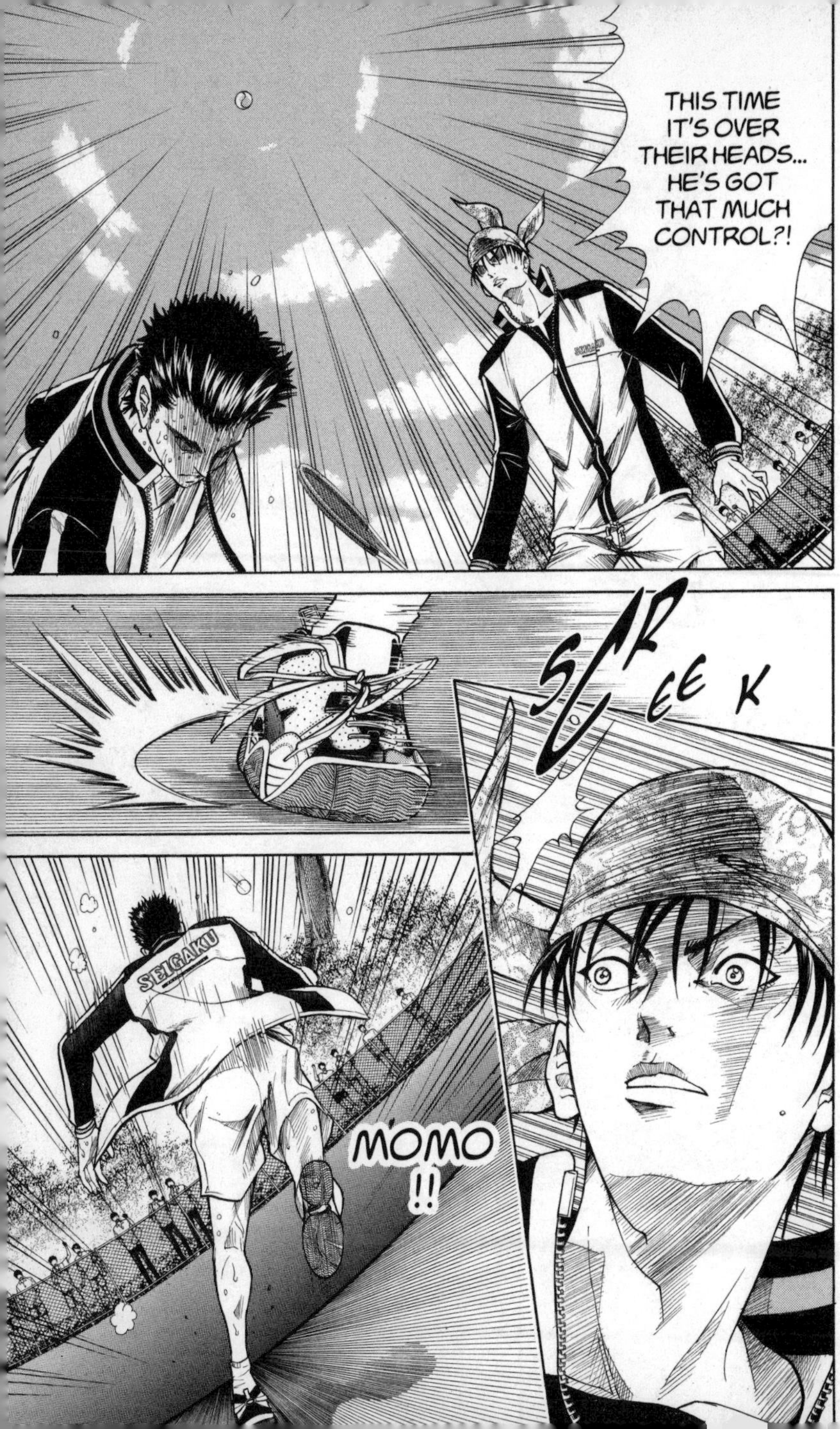
THIS TIME IT'S OVER THEIR HEADS... HE'S GOT THAT MUCH CONTROL?!
SCREEK
SEIGAKU
MOMO !!

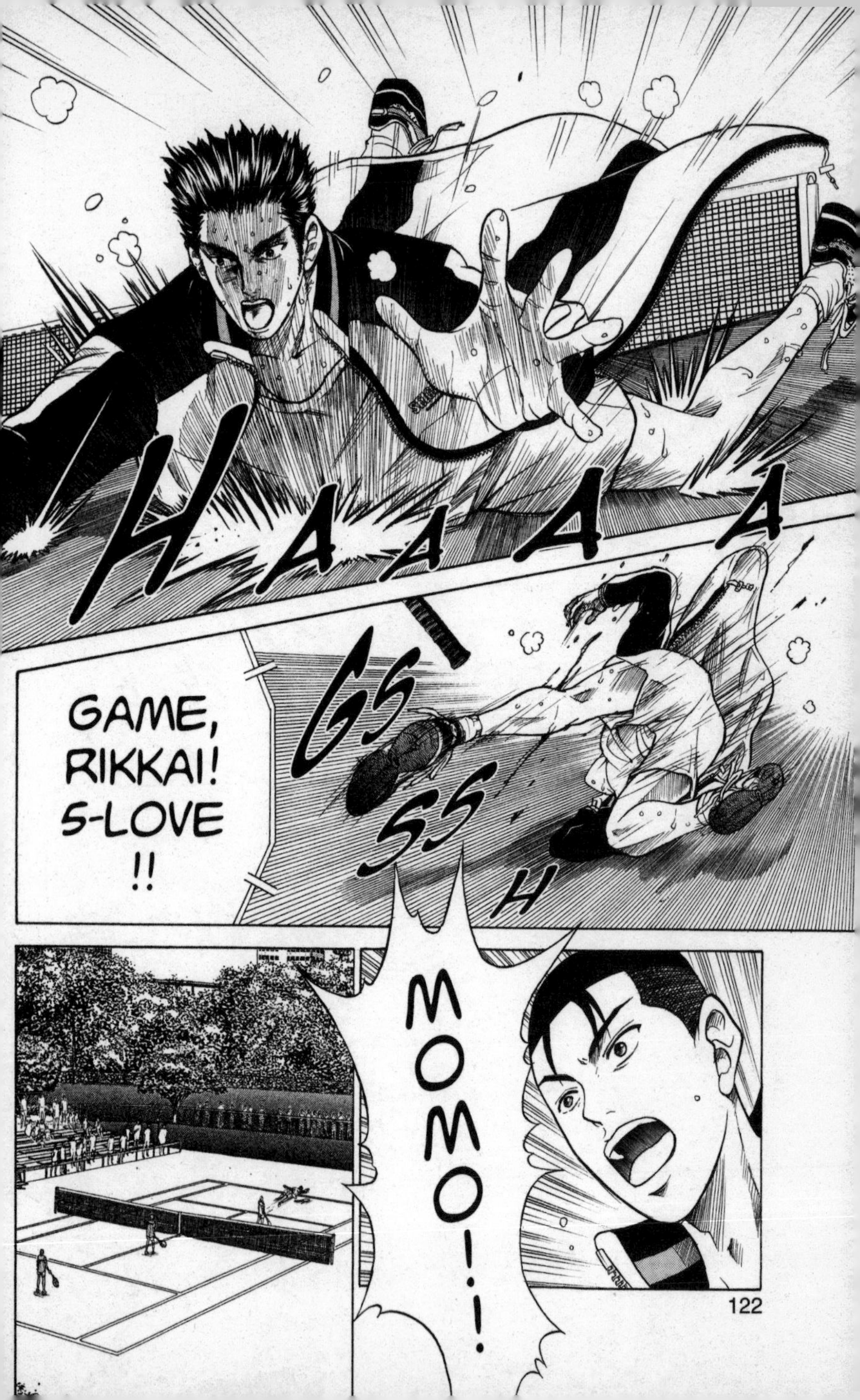
HAAAA
GSSSH
GAME, RIKKAI! 5-LOVE !!
MOMO!!

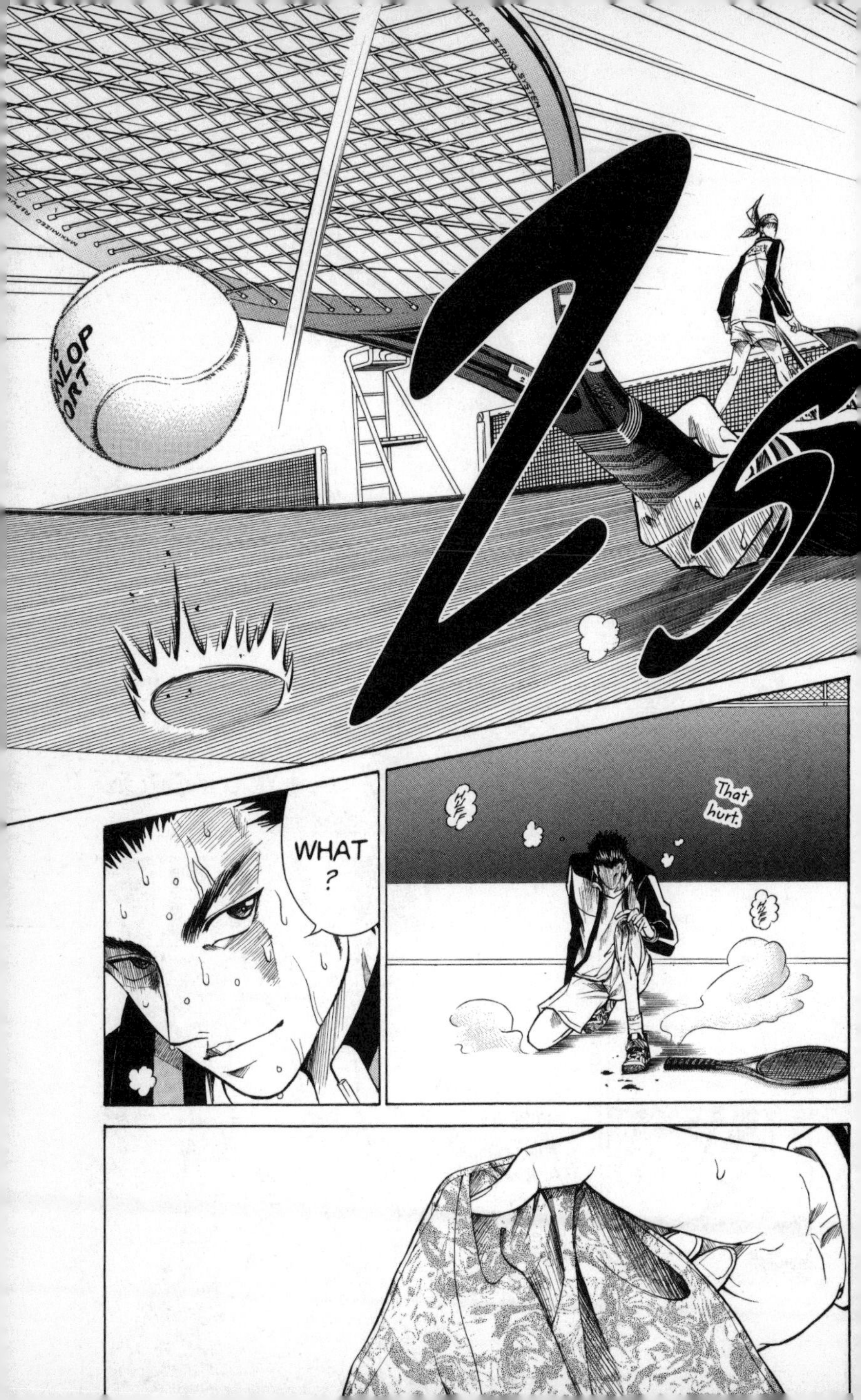
That hurt.
WHAT ?

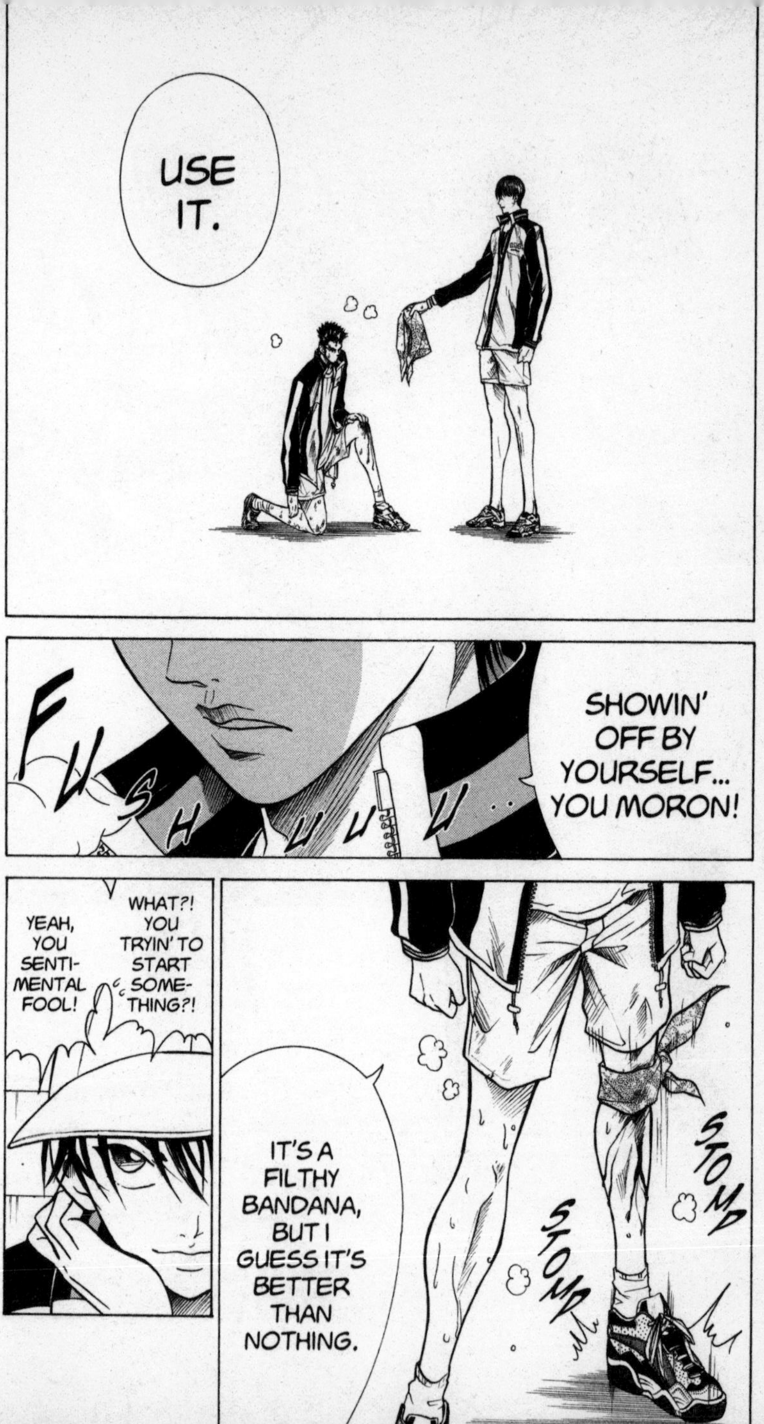
USE IT.
FUSHUUU...
SHOWIN' OFF BY YOURSELF... YOU MORON!
IT'S A FILTHY BANDANA, BUT I GUESS IT'S BETTER THAN NOTHING.
STOMP
STOMP
WHAT?! YOU TRYIN' TO START SOMETHING?!
YEAH, YOU SENTIMENTAL FOOL!

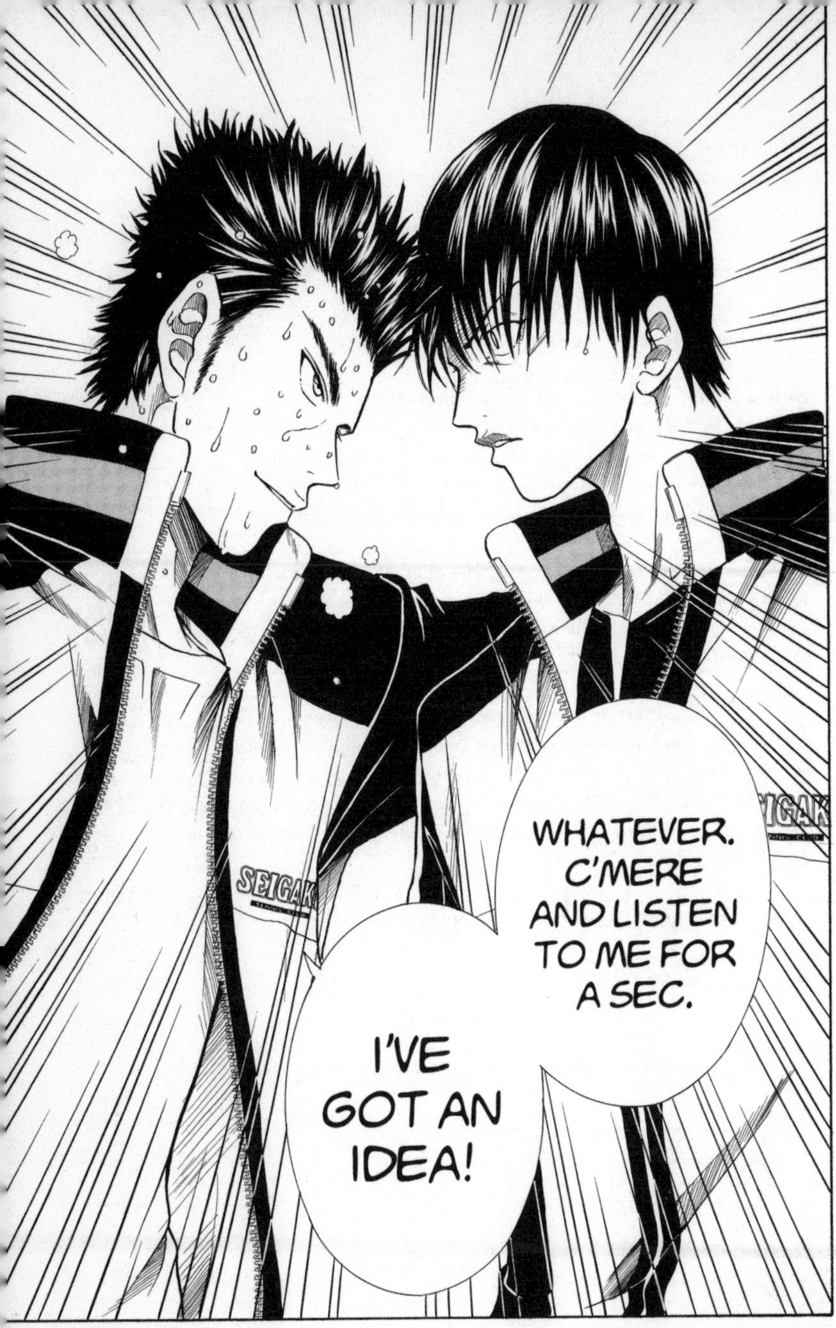
WHATEVER. C'MERE AND LISTEN TO ME FOR A SEC.
I'VE GOT AN IDEA!

THE PRINCE OF TENNIS

Thank you for reading *The Prince of Tennis*, volume 23.

Before I knew it, a lot of loveable new characters appeared in this story. I'm gonna keep working hard 'til there's a hundred of them!! And until each and every one of them is sent boxes of chocolates with heartfelt messages written to them... They really are lucky. I thank you on their behalf...[laughs].

Last year we were too busy to count the number of chocolates received and announce the total, but this year we worked our butts off to do the count!! We'll announce the chocolate rankings at the end of the volume, so please look forward to it.

Thanks to the support of a lot of people, the Kanto Tournament has reached the finals at last. I'll give the Rikkai matches everything I have, so please keep up the support!! By the way, to those of you who're thinking that *The Prince of Tennis* will end after the Rikkai matches: think again! The Nationals will be even more exciting. So please continue watching the characters grow.

So, how should I surprise you guys this year [smiles]?

See you in the next volume!!

Takeshi Konomi
2004.3.8

Send fan letters to: Takeshi Konomi, *The Prince of Tennis*, c/o VIZ Media LLC, P.O. Box 77010, San Francisco, CA 94107

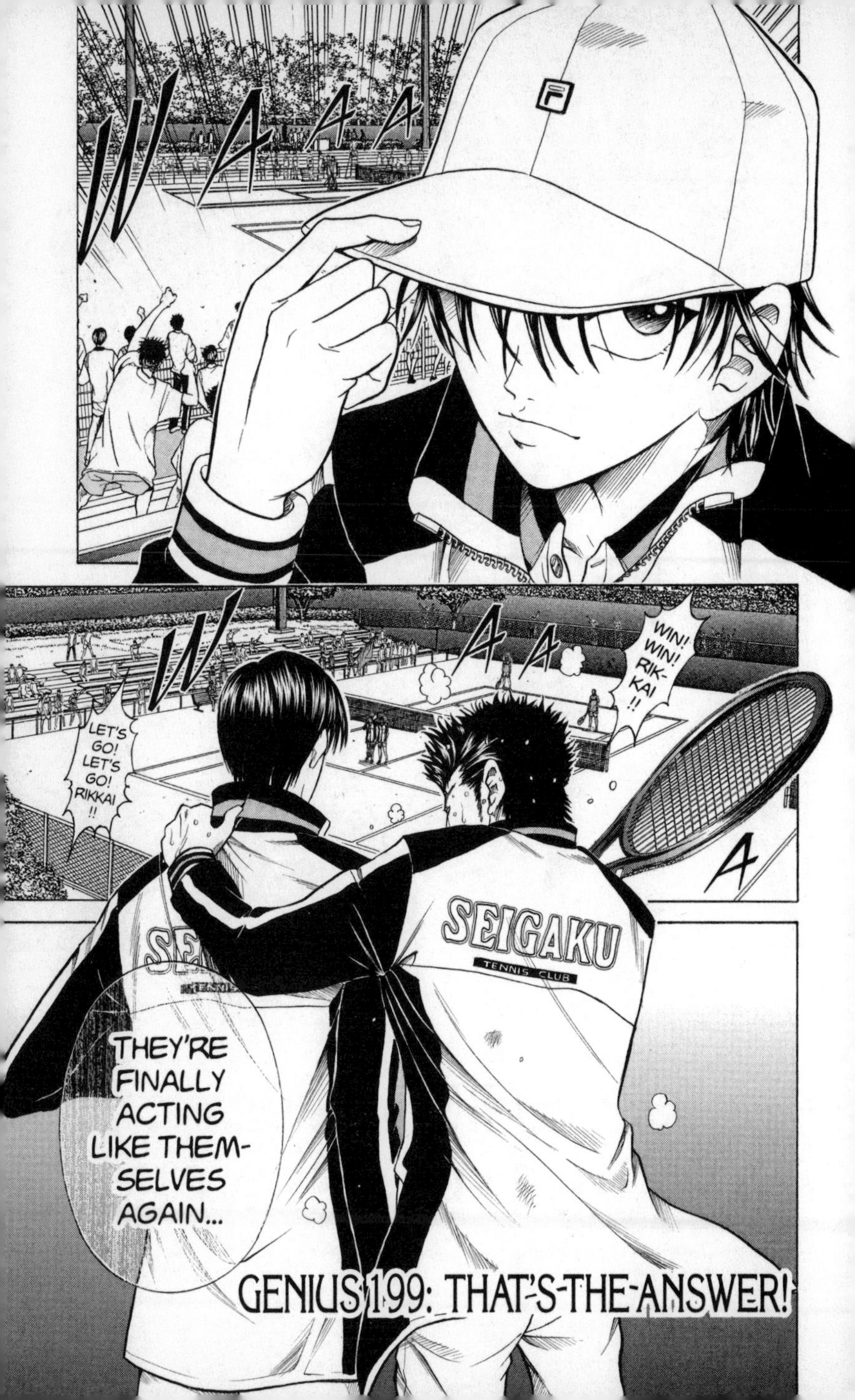
WAAAA
WIN! WIN! RIK-KAI!!
WAAA
LET'S GO! LET'S GO! RIKKAI!!
A
SEIGAKU TENNIS CLUB
THEY'RE FINALLY ACTING LIKE THEM-SELVES AGAIN...
GENIUS 199: THAT'S-THE-ANSWER!

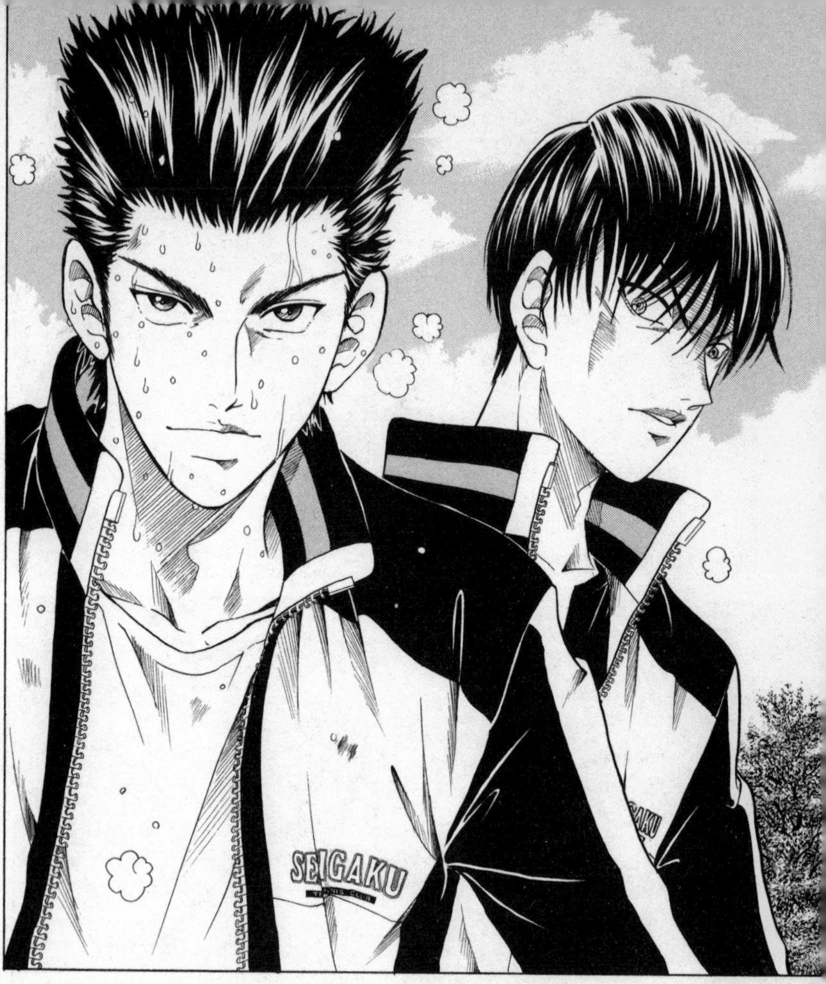
SEIGAKU

GENIUS 199:
THAT'S THE ANSWER!

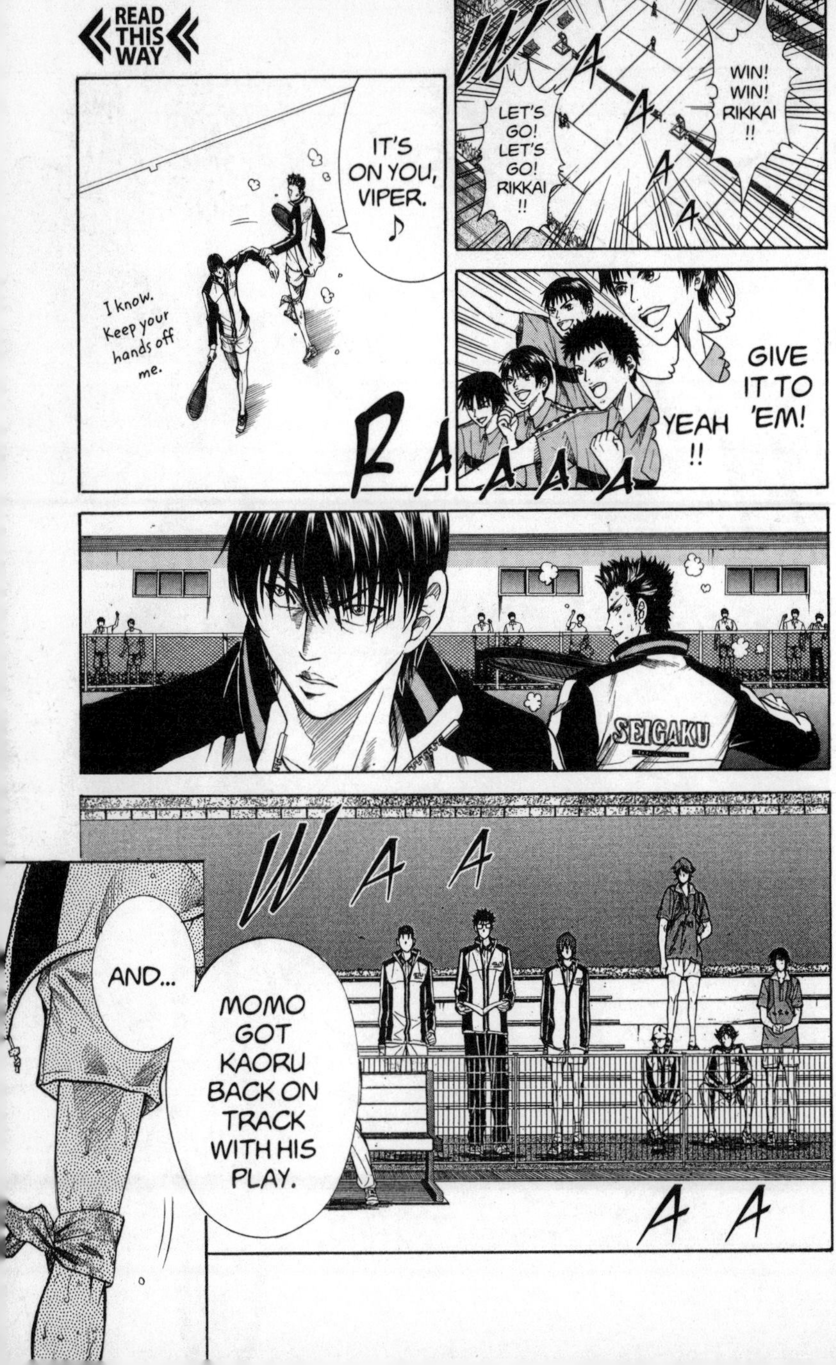
READ THIS WAY
WIN! WIN! RIKKAI!!
LET'S GO! LET'S GO! RIKKAI!!
WAAAAA
GIVE IT TO 'EM!
YEAH!!
RAAAA
IT'S ON YOU, VIPER. ♪
I know. Keep your hands off me.
WAA
AA
AND...
MOMO GOT KAORU BACK ON TRACK WITH HIS PLAY.

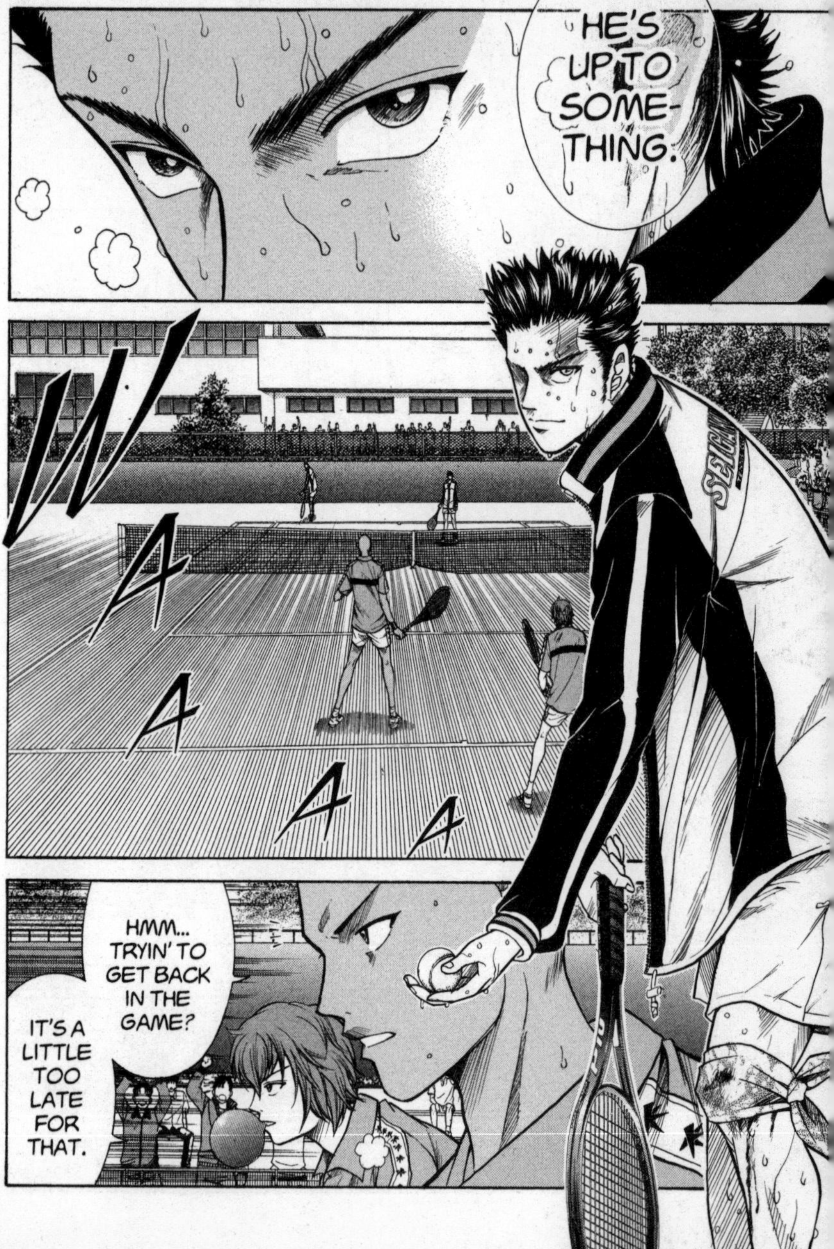
HE'S UP TO SOME-THING.
WAAAAA
HMM... TRYIN' TO GET BACK IN THE GAME?
IT'S A LITTLE TOO LATE FOR THAT.

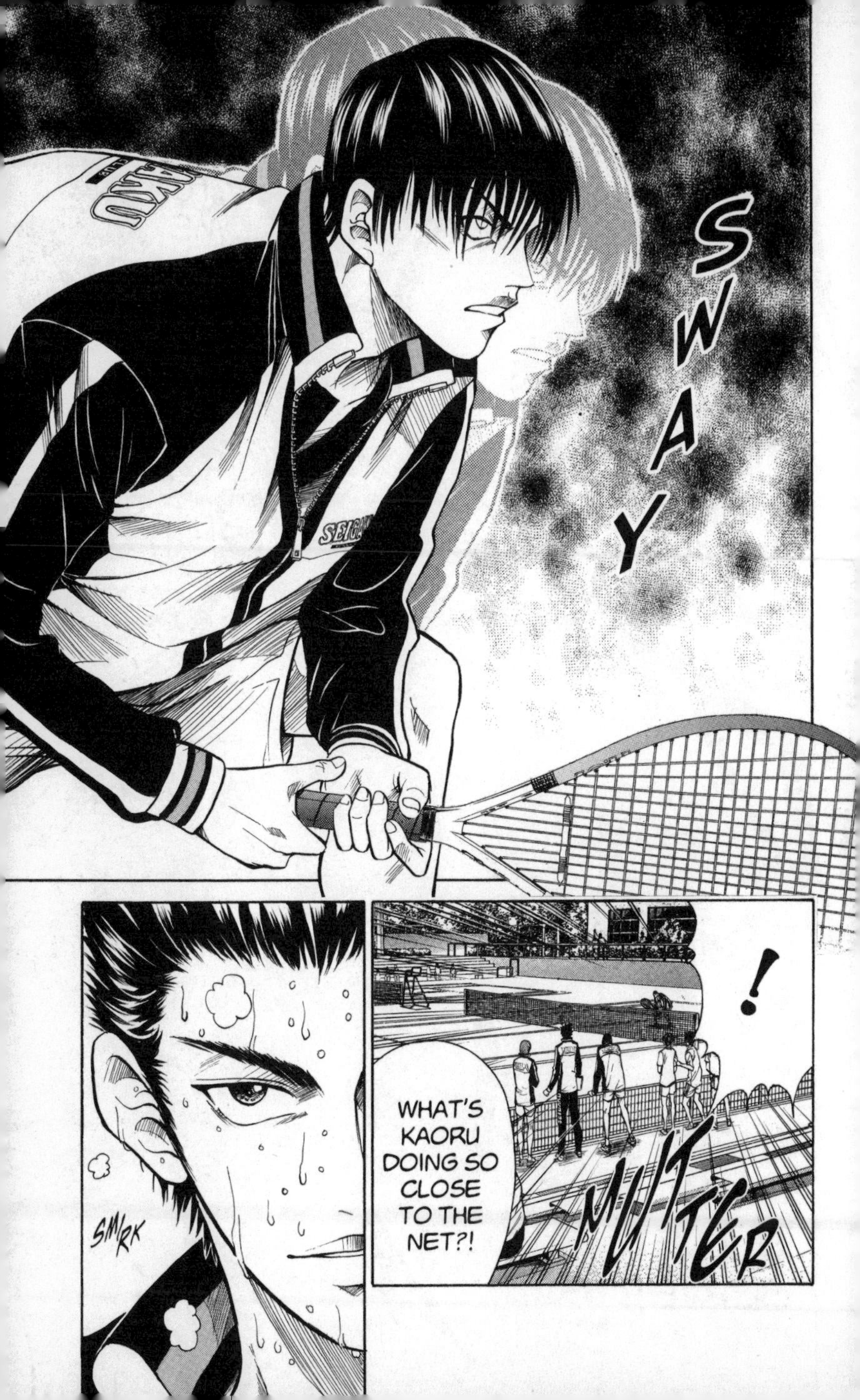
SWAY
!
WHAT'S KAORU DOING SO CLOSE TO THE NET?!
MUTTER
SMIRK

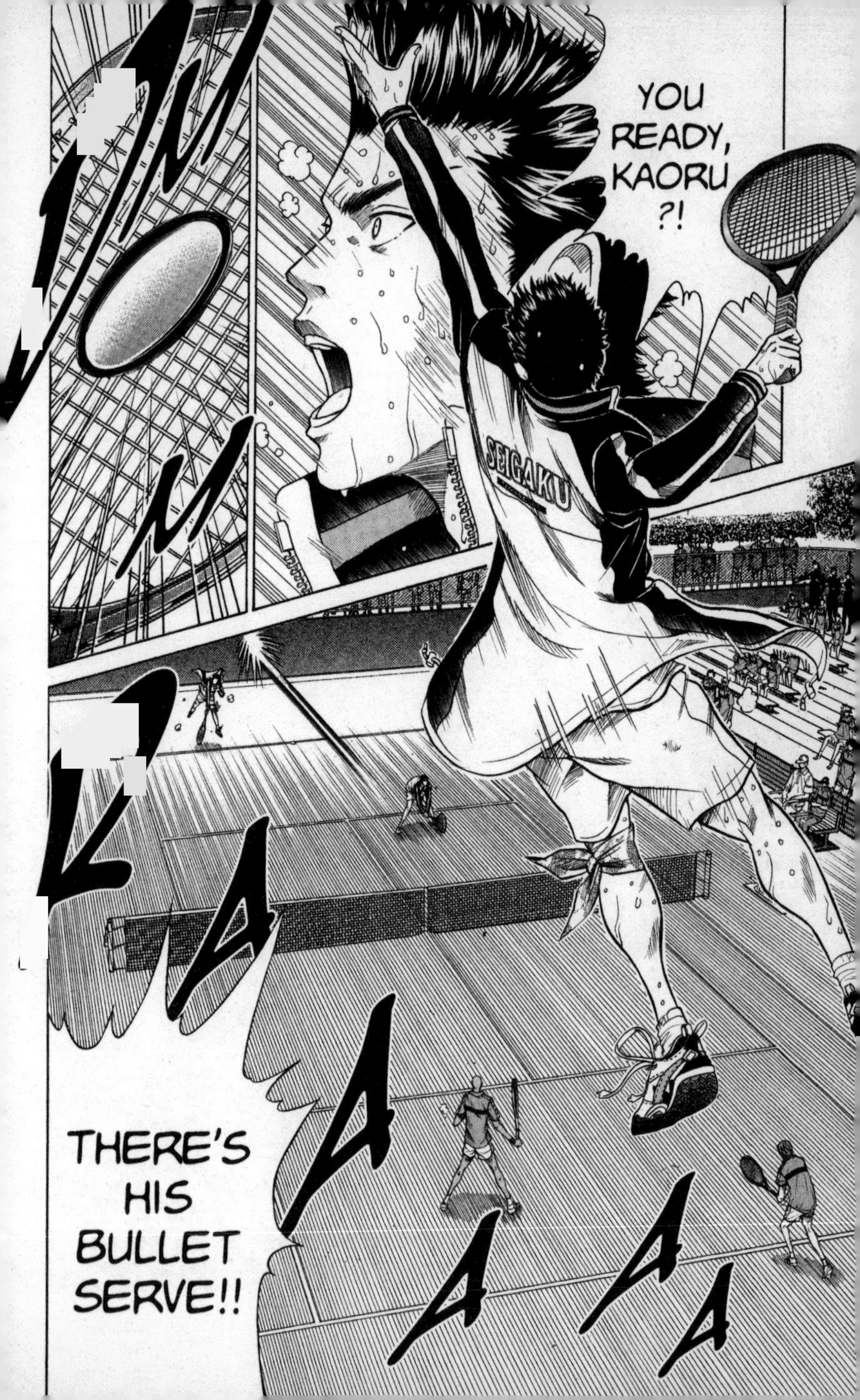
YOU READY, KAORU?!
THERE'S HIS BULLET SERVE!!

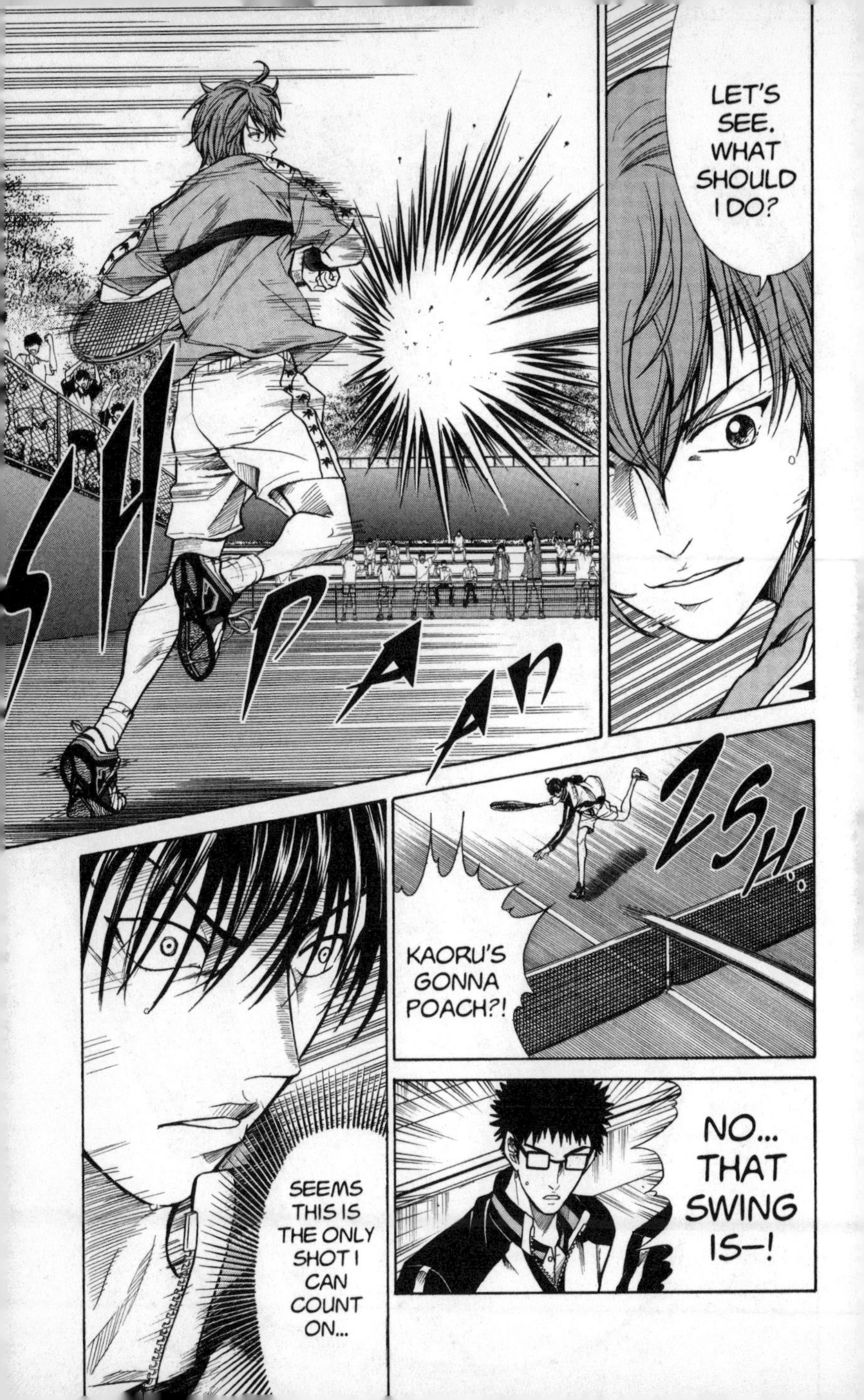
LET'S SEE. WHAT SHOULD I DO?
SHPAAN
ZSH
KAORU'S GONNA POACH?!
NO... THAT SWING IS—!
SEEMS THIS IS THE ONLY SHOT I CAN COUNT ON...

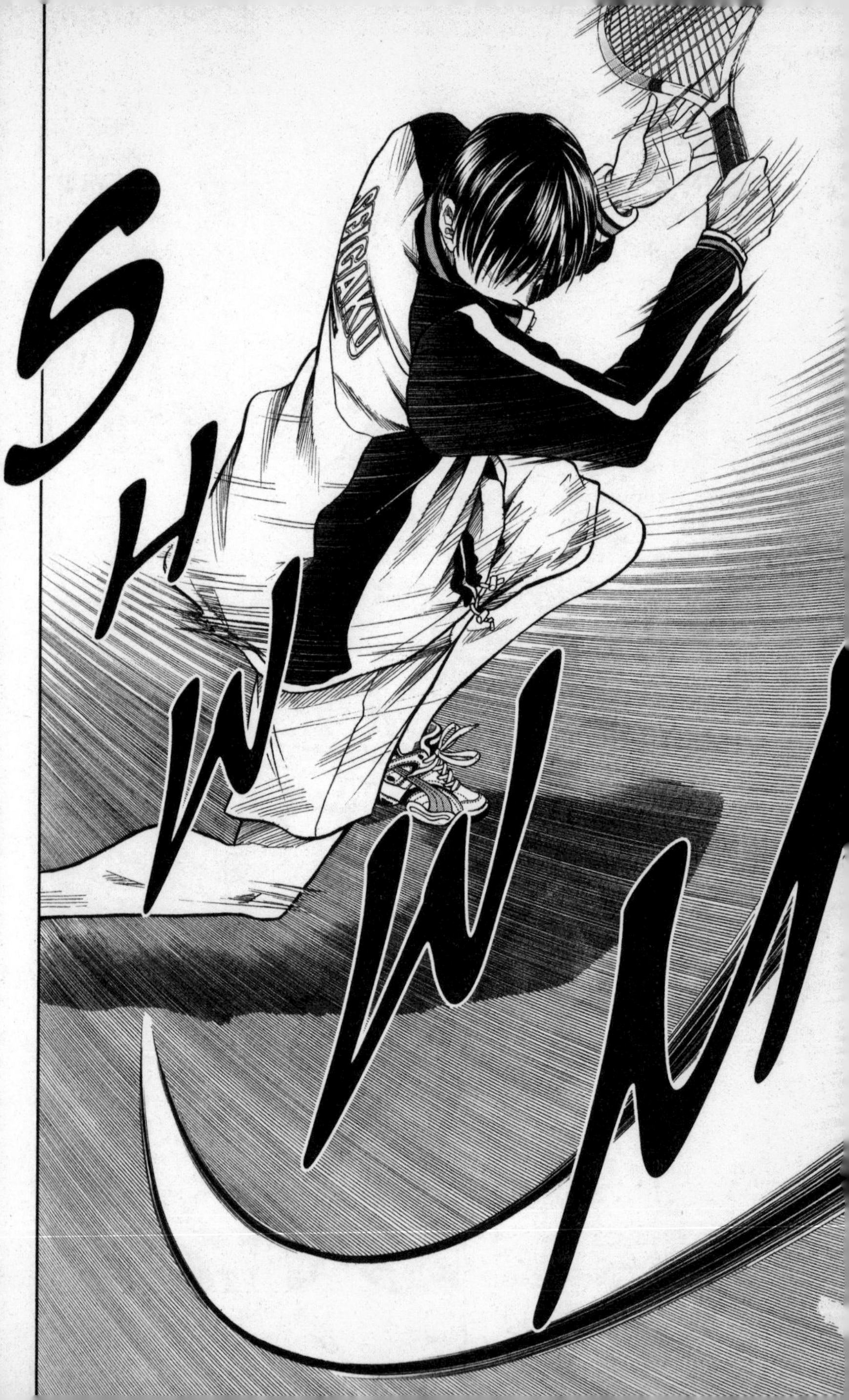
SEIGAKU

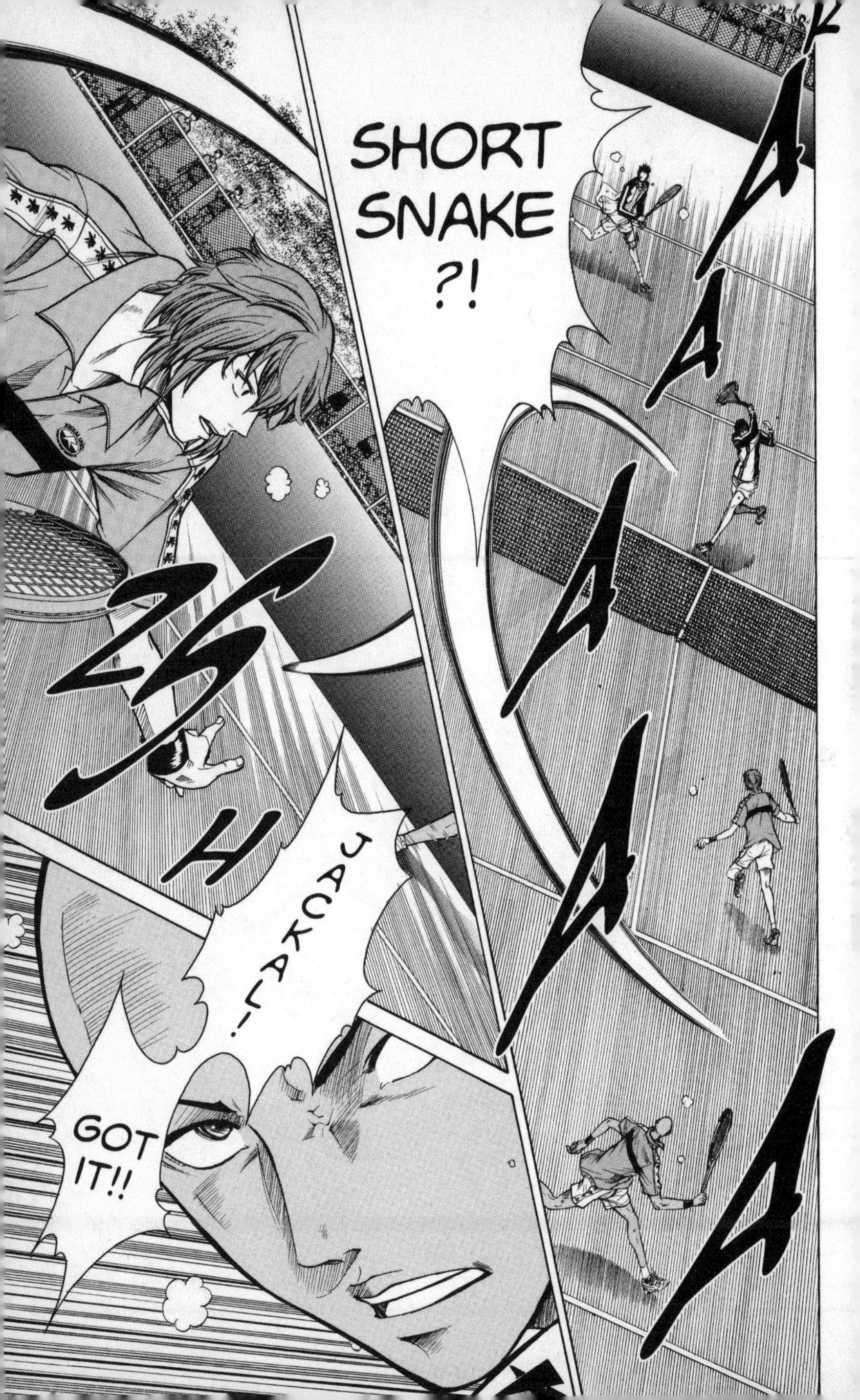
SHORT SNAKE ?!
JACKAL!
GOT IT!!

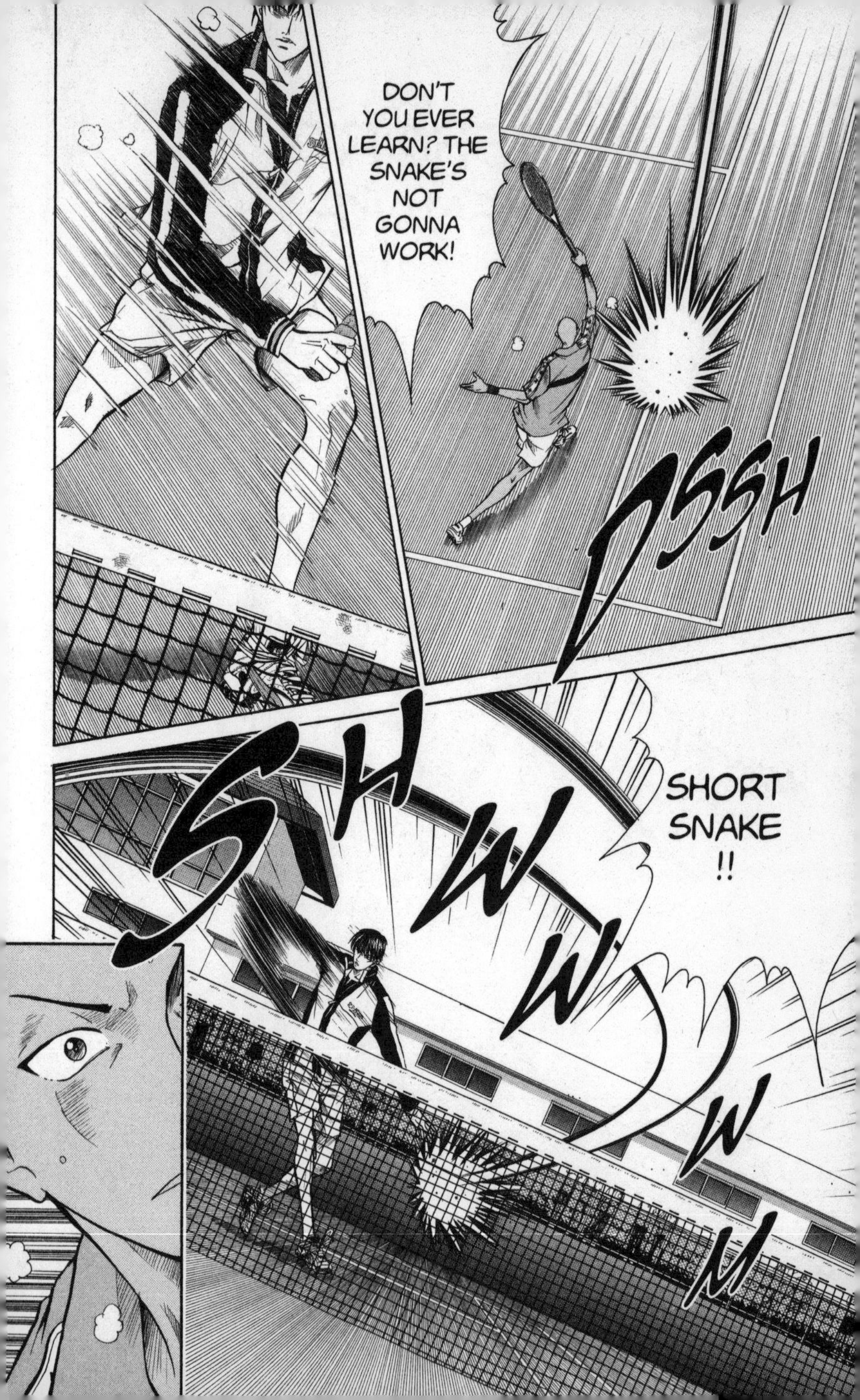
DON'T YOU EVER LEARN? THE SNAKE'S NOT GONNA WORK!
DSSH
SHORT SNAKE !!
SHWWWWM

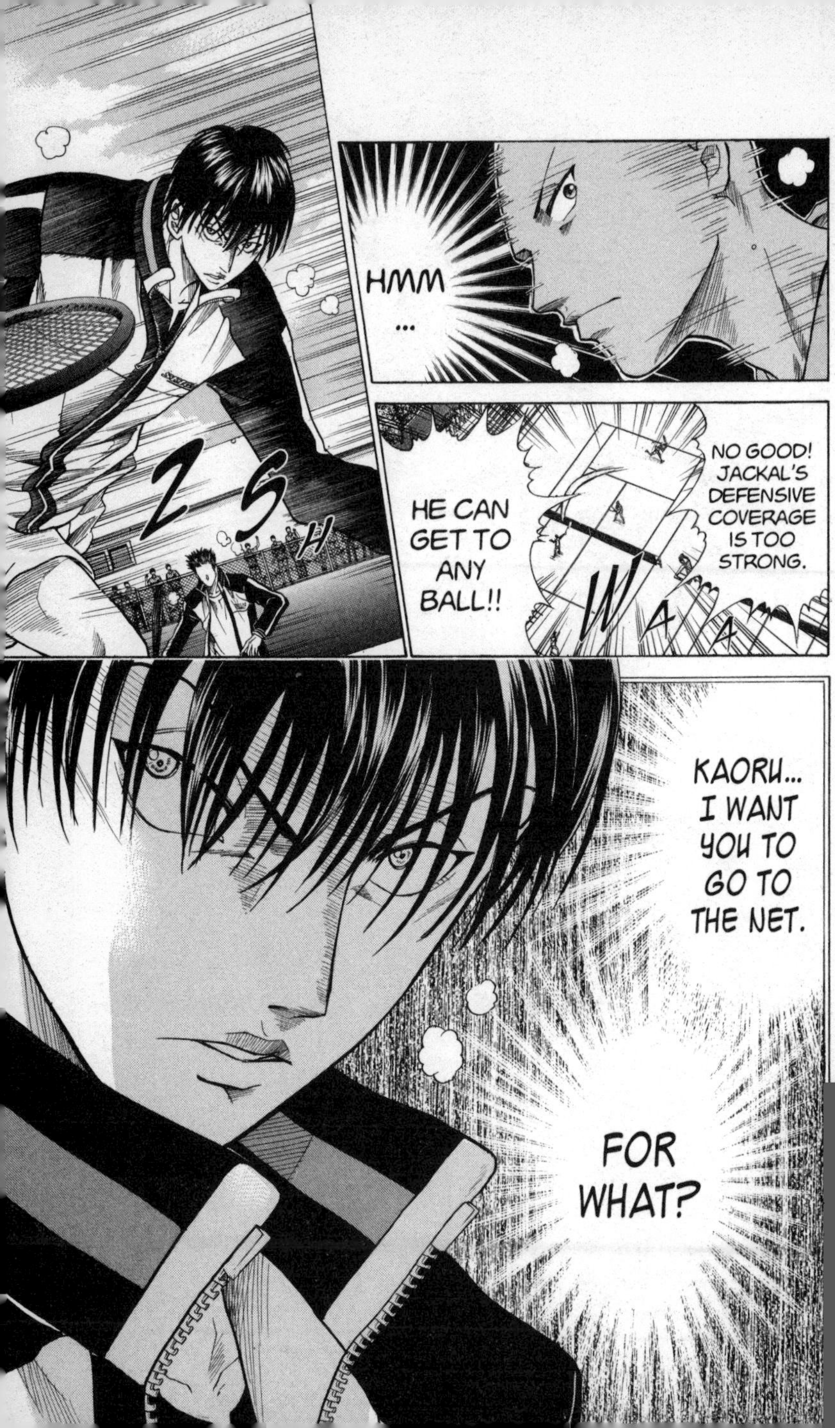
HMM ...
NO GOOD! JACKAL'S DEFENSIVE COVERAGE IS TOO STRONG.
HE CAN GET TO ANY BALL!!
WAA
ZSH
KAORU... I WANT YOU TO GO TO THE NET.
FOR WHAT?

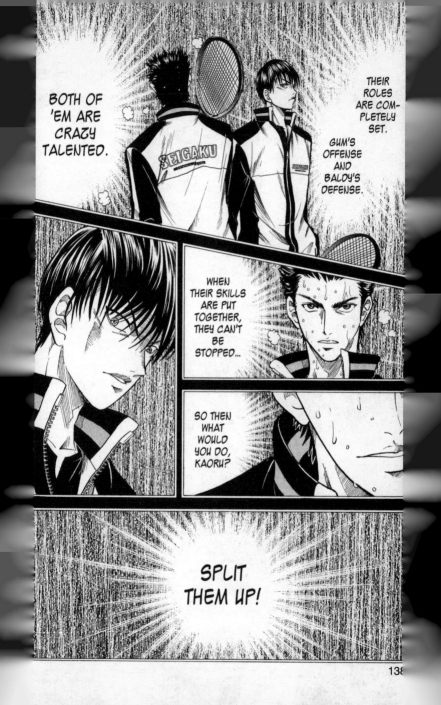

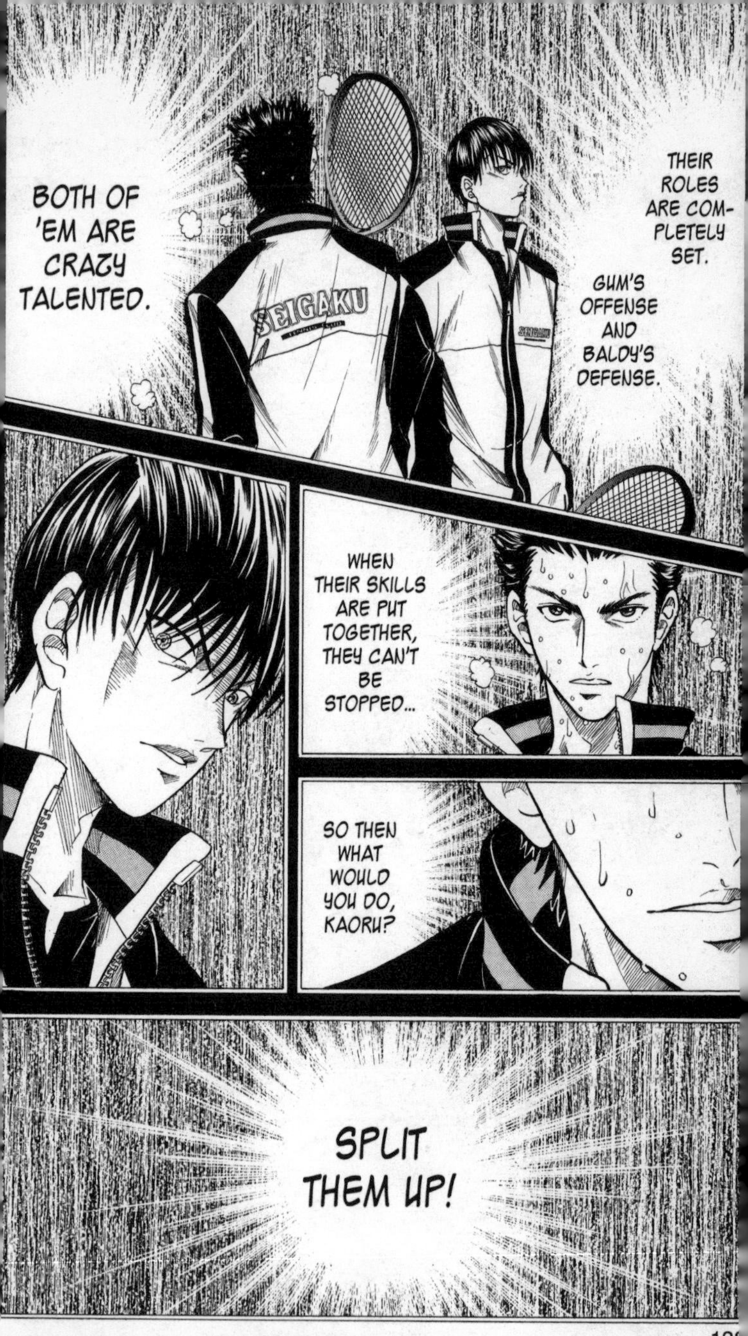
THEIR ROLES ARE COM-PLETELY SET.
GUM'S OFFENSE AND BALDY'S DEFENSE.
BOTH OF 'EM ARE CRAZY TALENTED.
WHEN THEIR SKILLS ARE PUT TOGETHER, THEY CAN'T BE STOPPED...
SO THEN WHAT WOULD YOU DO, KAORU?
SPLIT THEM UP!

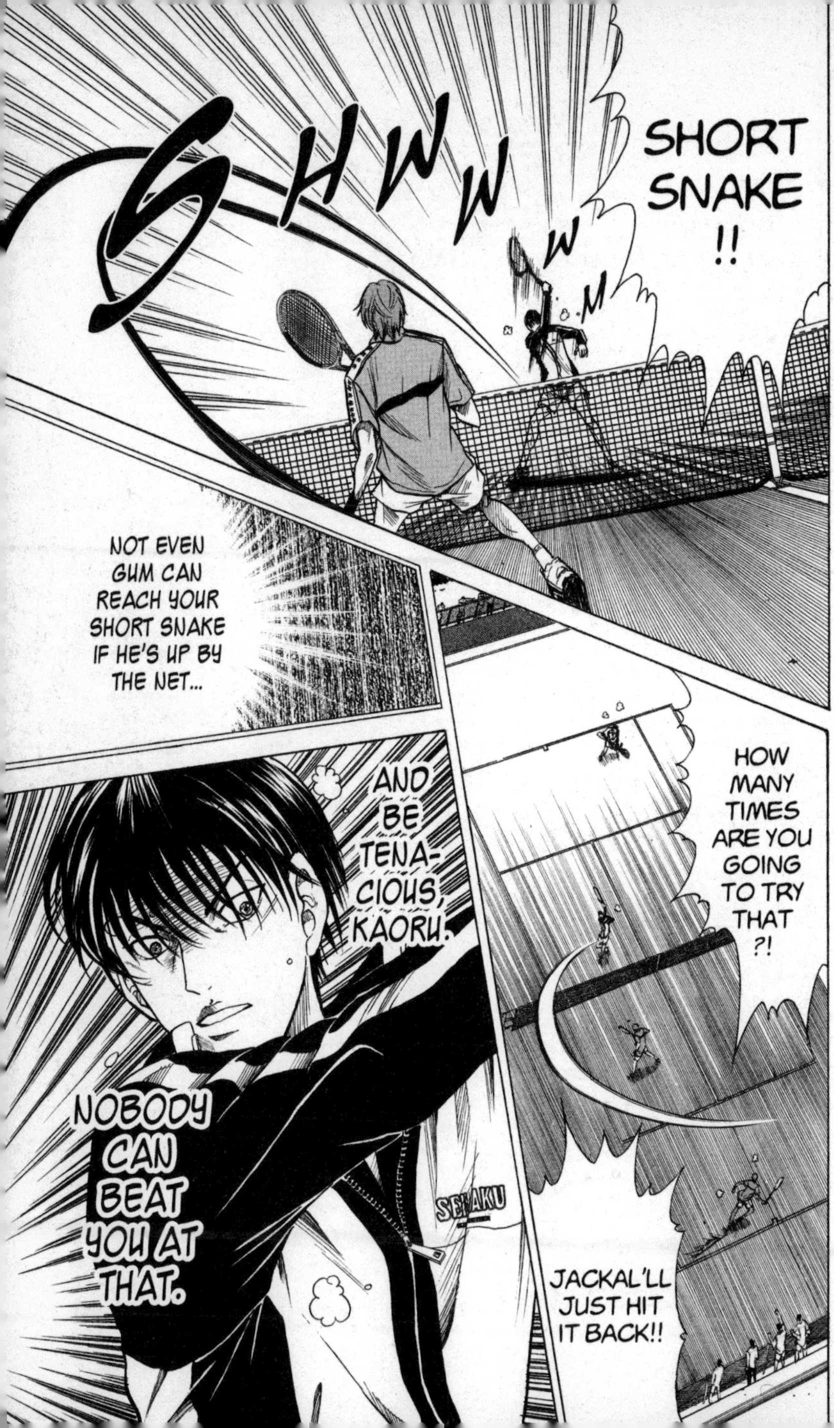
SHWWWM
SHORT SNAKE !!
HOW MANY TIMES ARE YOU GOING TO TRY THAT ?!
JACKAL'LL JUST HIT IT BACK!!
NOT EVEN GUM CAN REACH YOUR SHORT SNAKE IF HE'S UP BY THE NET...
AND BE TENA-CIOUS, KAORU.
NOBODY CAN BEAT YOU AT THAT.

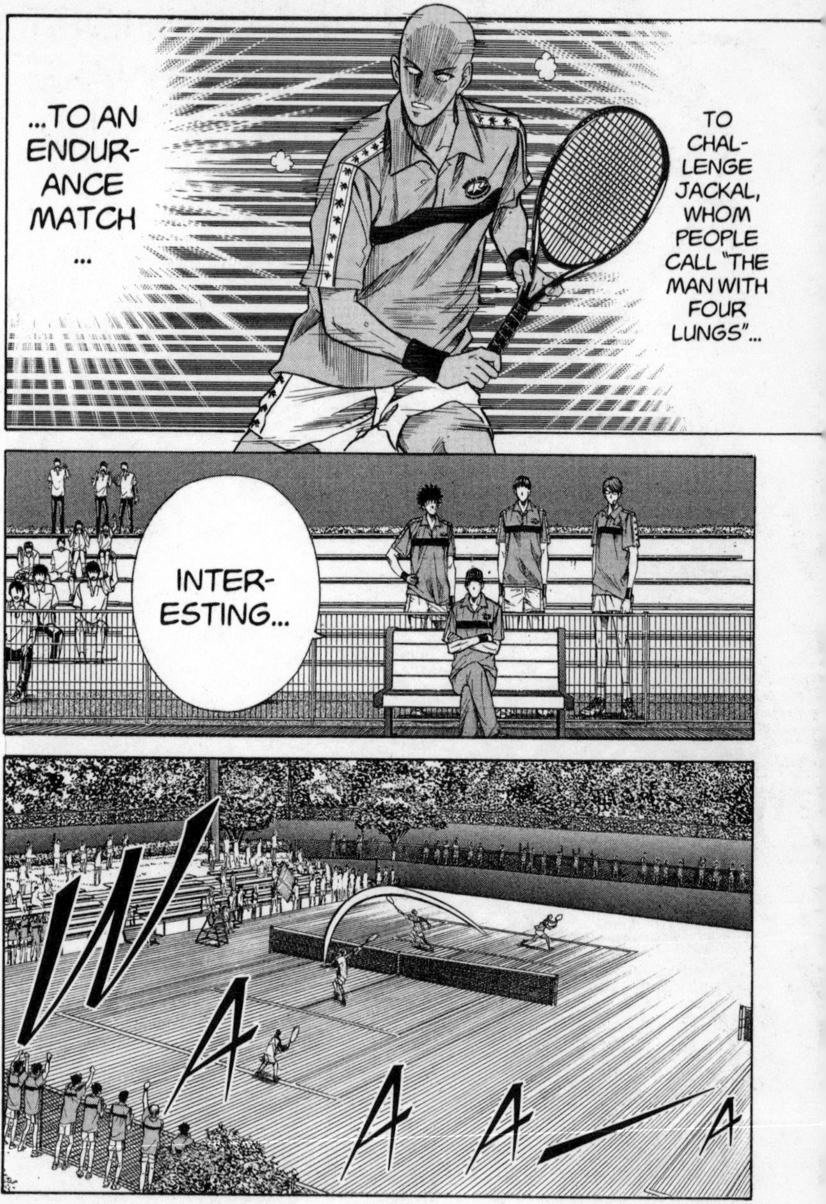
TO CHALLENGE JACKAL, WHOM PEOPLE CALL "THE MAN WITH FOUR LUNGS"...
...TO AN ENDURANCE MATCH...
INTERESTING...
WAAA—A

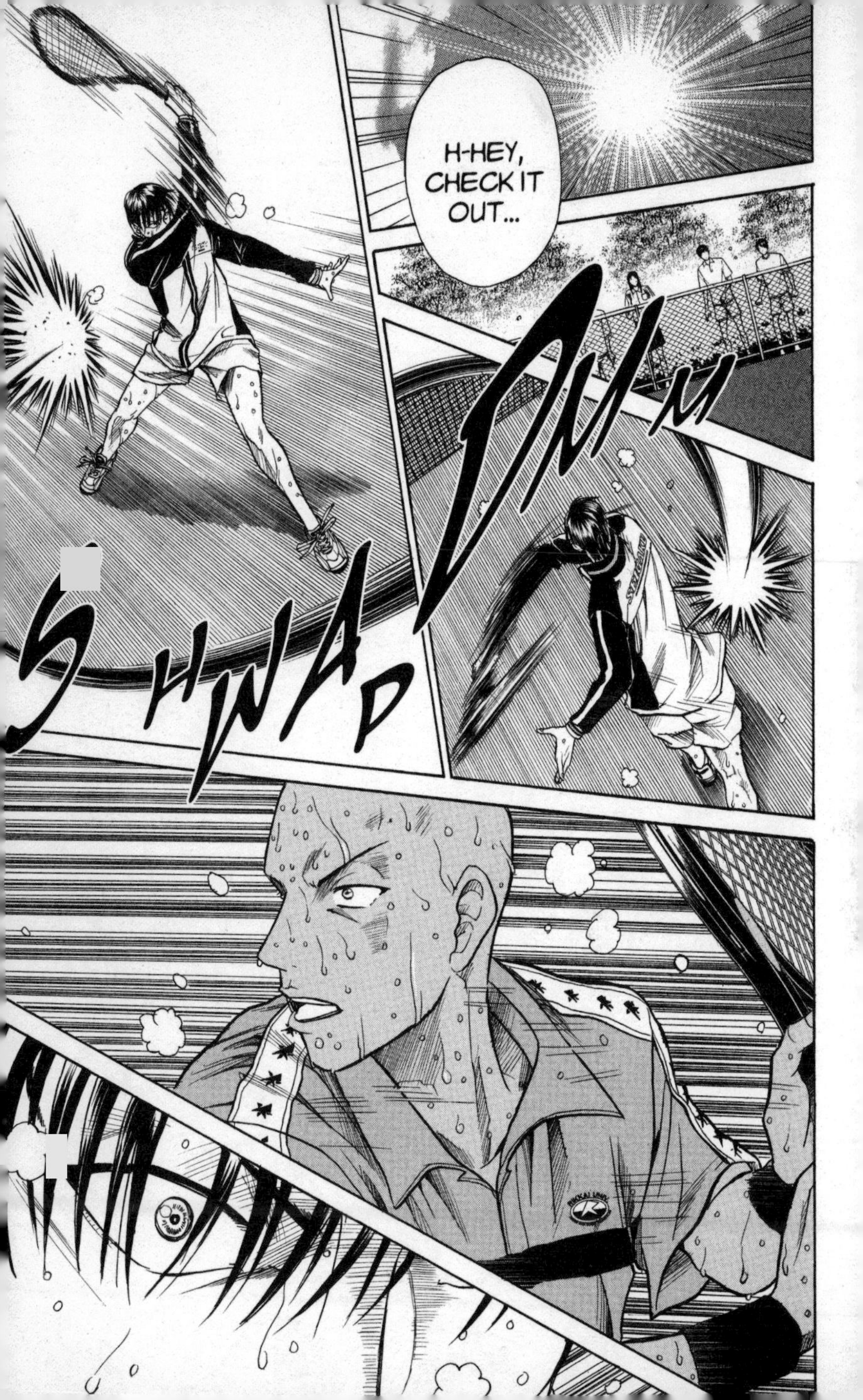
H-HEY, CHECK IT OUT...

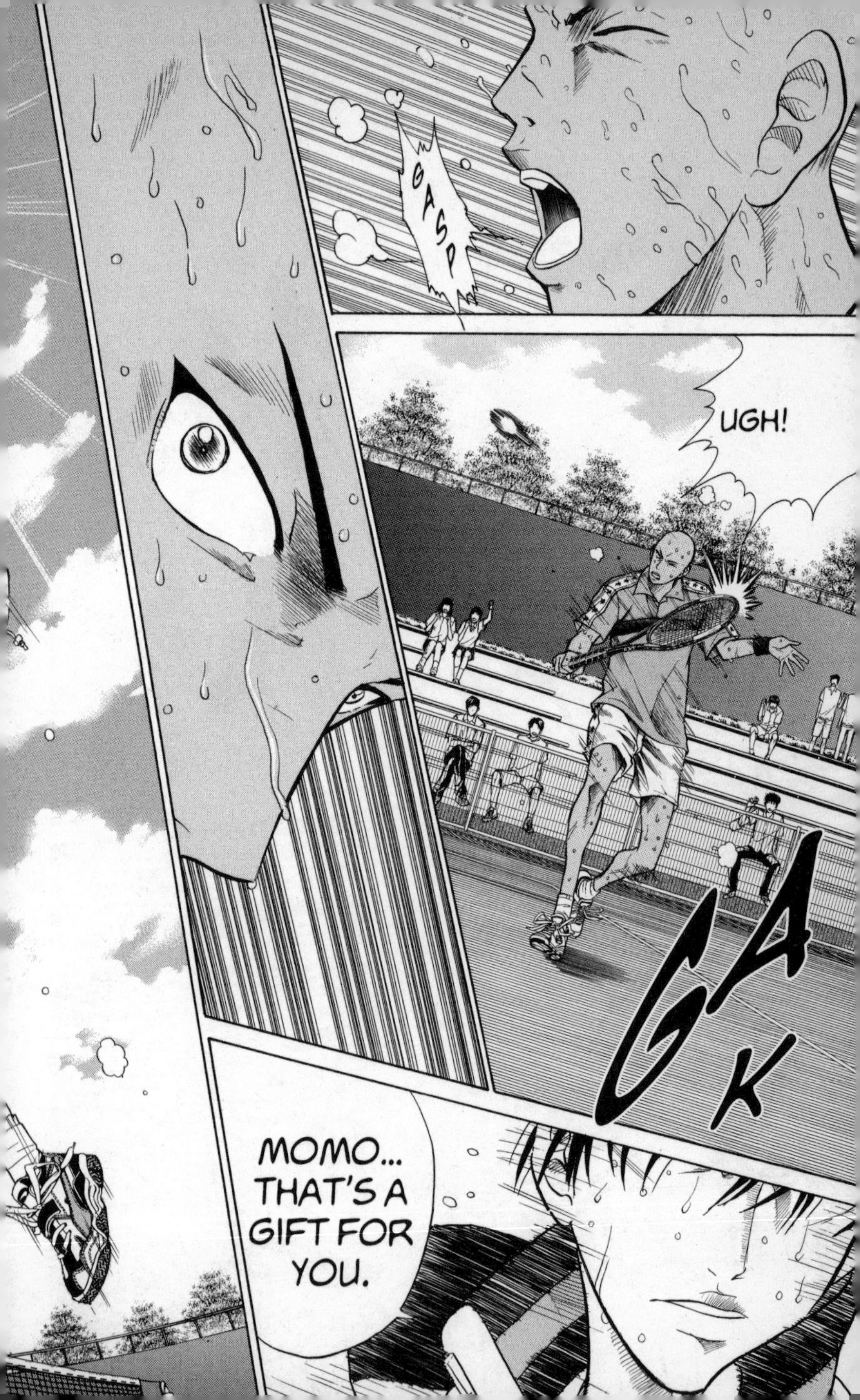
GASP
UGH!
GAK
MOMO... THAT'S A GIFT FOR YOU.

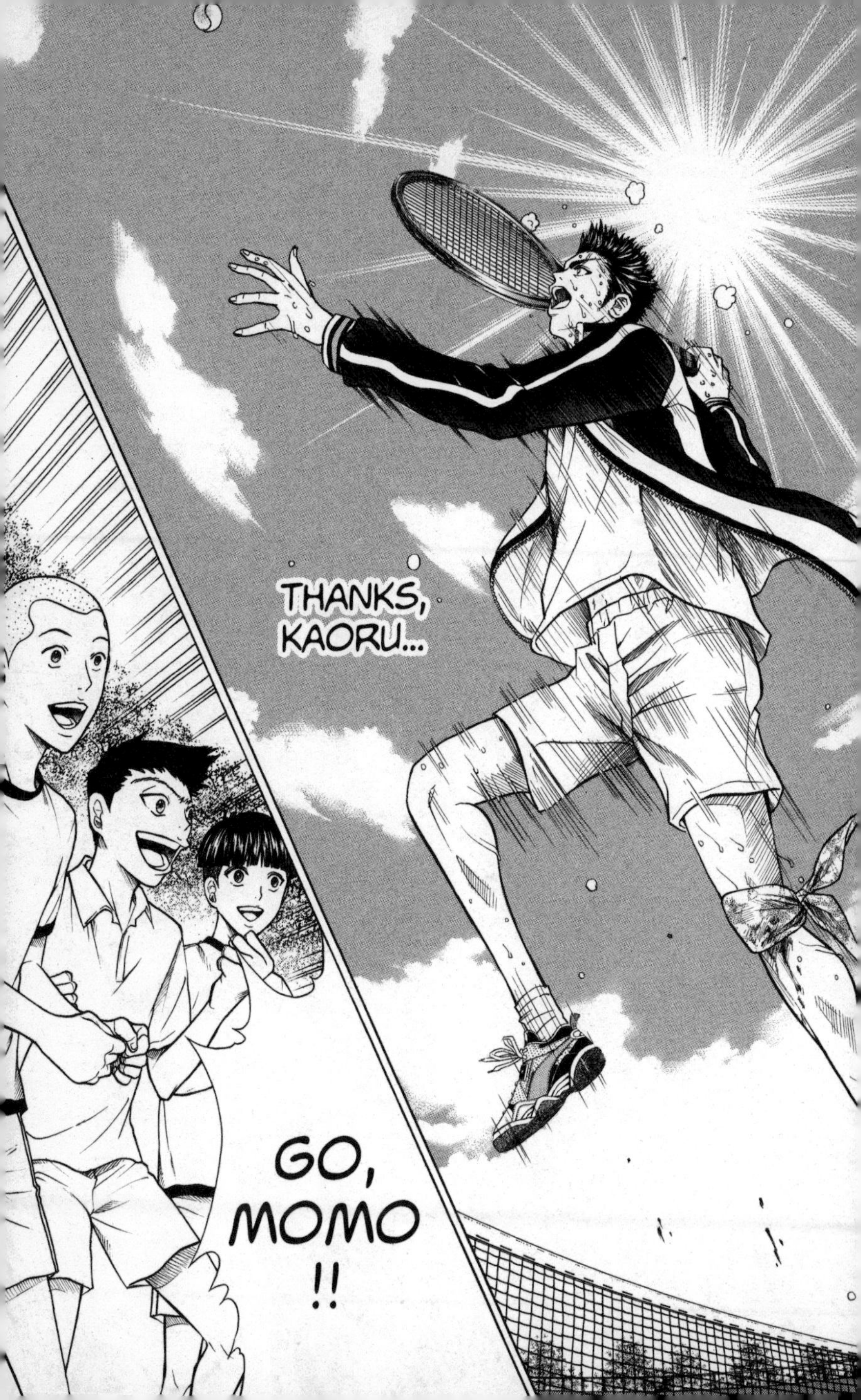
THANKS, KAORU...
GO, MOMO!!

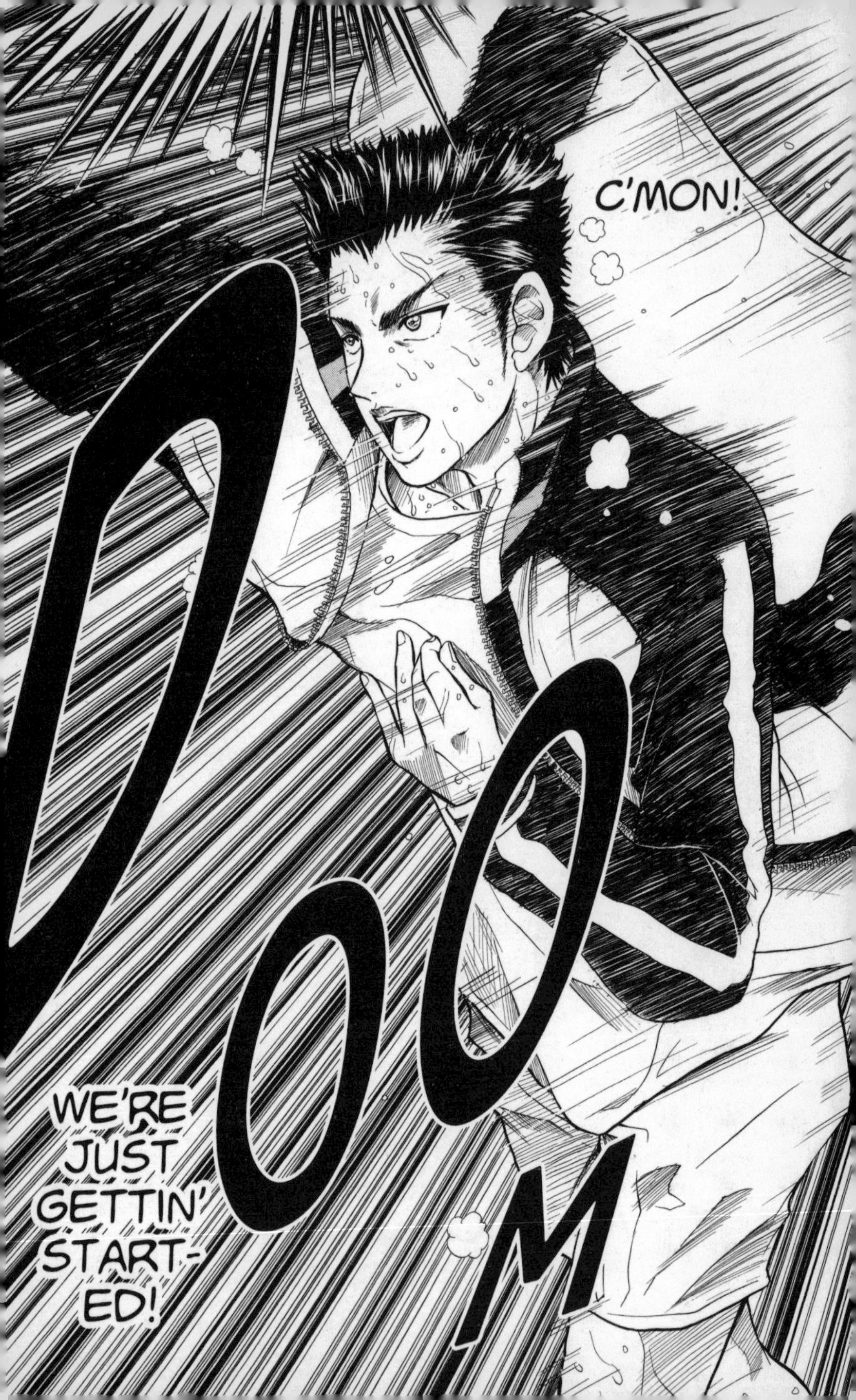
C'MON!
DOOM
WE'RE JUST GETTIN' START-ED!

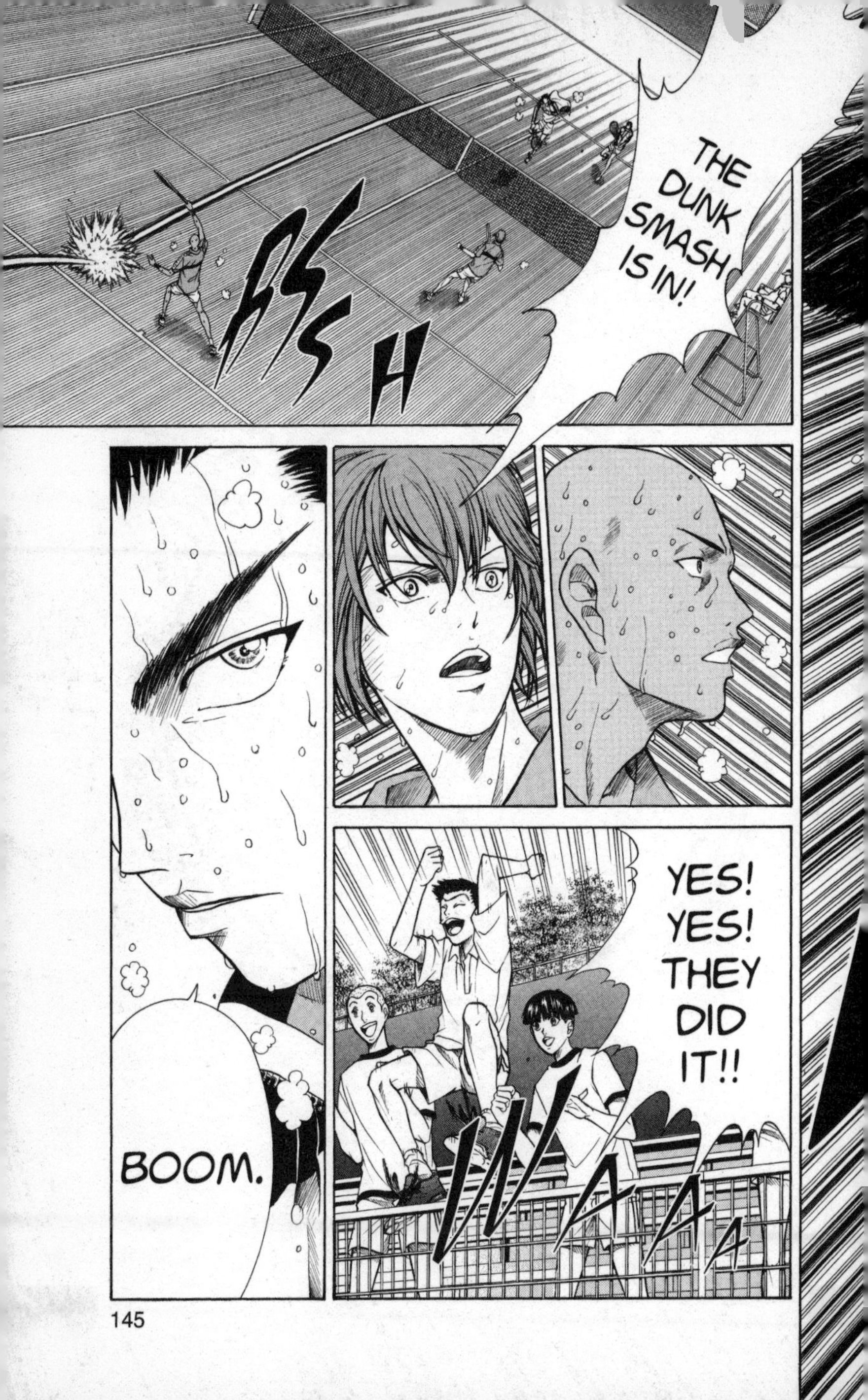
RSSH
THE DUNK SMASH IS IN!
YES! YES! THEY DID IT!!
WAAA
BOOM.

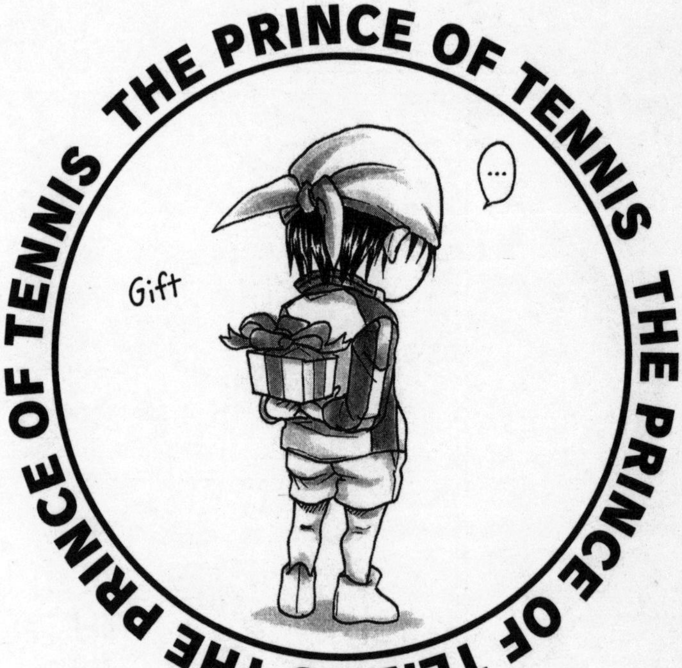
THE PRINCE OF TENNIS THE PRINCE OF TENNIS THE PRINCE OF TENNIS
...
Gift

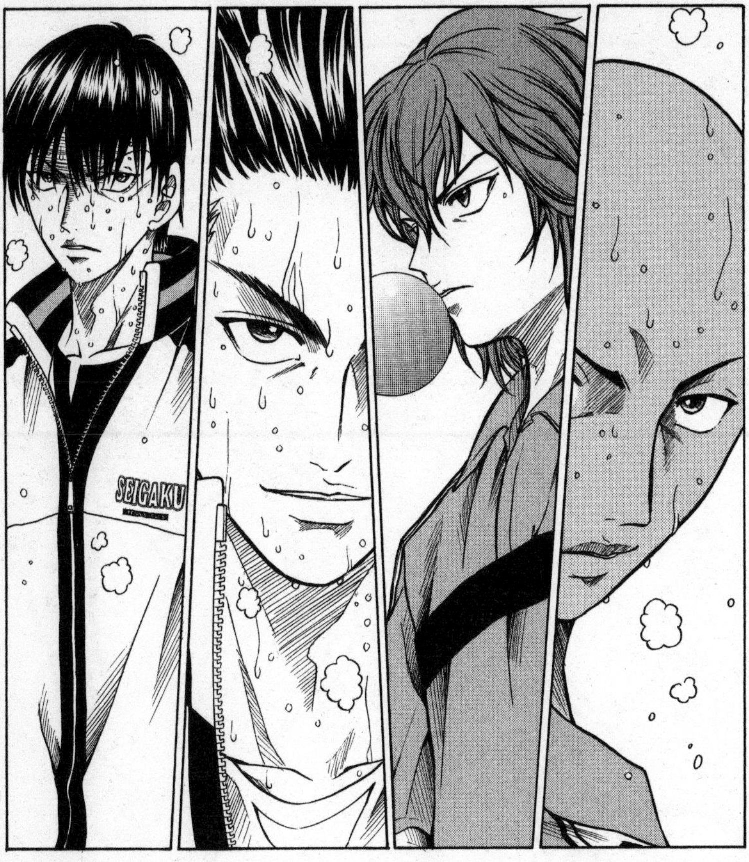
SEIGAKU

GENIUS 200:
PRIDE

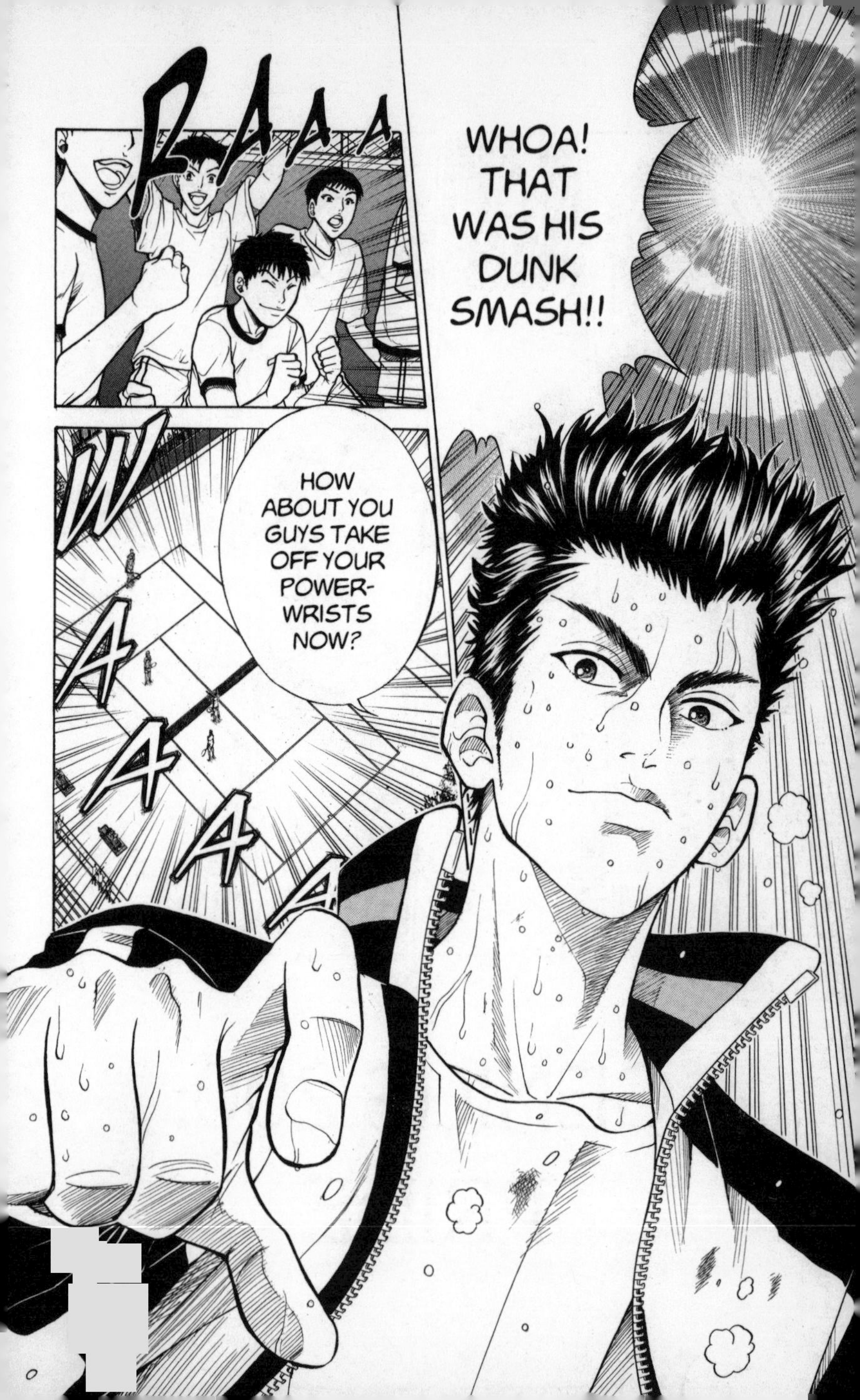
WHOA! THAT WAS HIS DUNK SMASH!!
HOW ABOUT YOU GUYS TAKE OFF YOUR POWER-WRISTS NOW?
RAAAA
WAAAAA

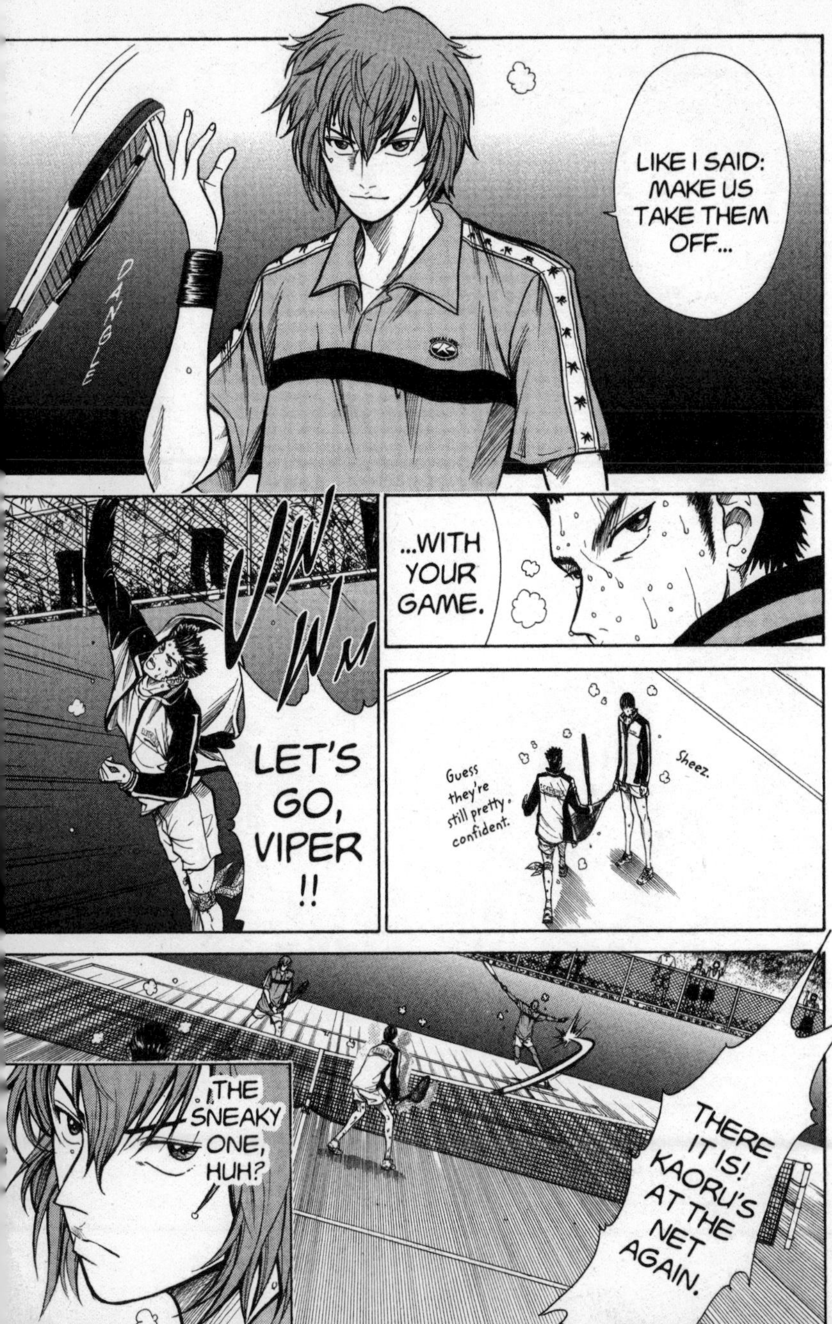
LIKE I SAID: MAKE US TAKE THEM OFF...
DANGLE
...WITH YOUR GAME.
Sheez.
Guess they're still pretty confident.
LET'S GO, VIPER!!
THERE IT IS! KAORU'S AT THE NET AGAIN.
THE SNEAKY ONE, HUH?

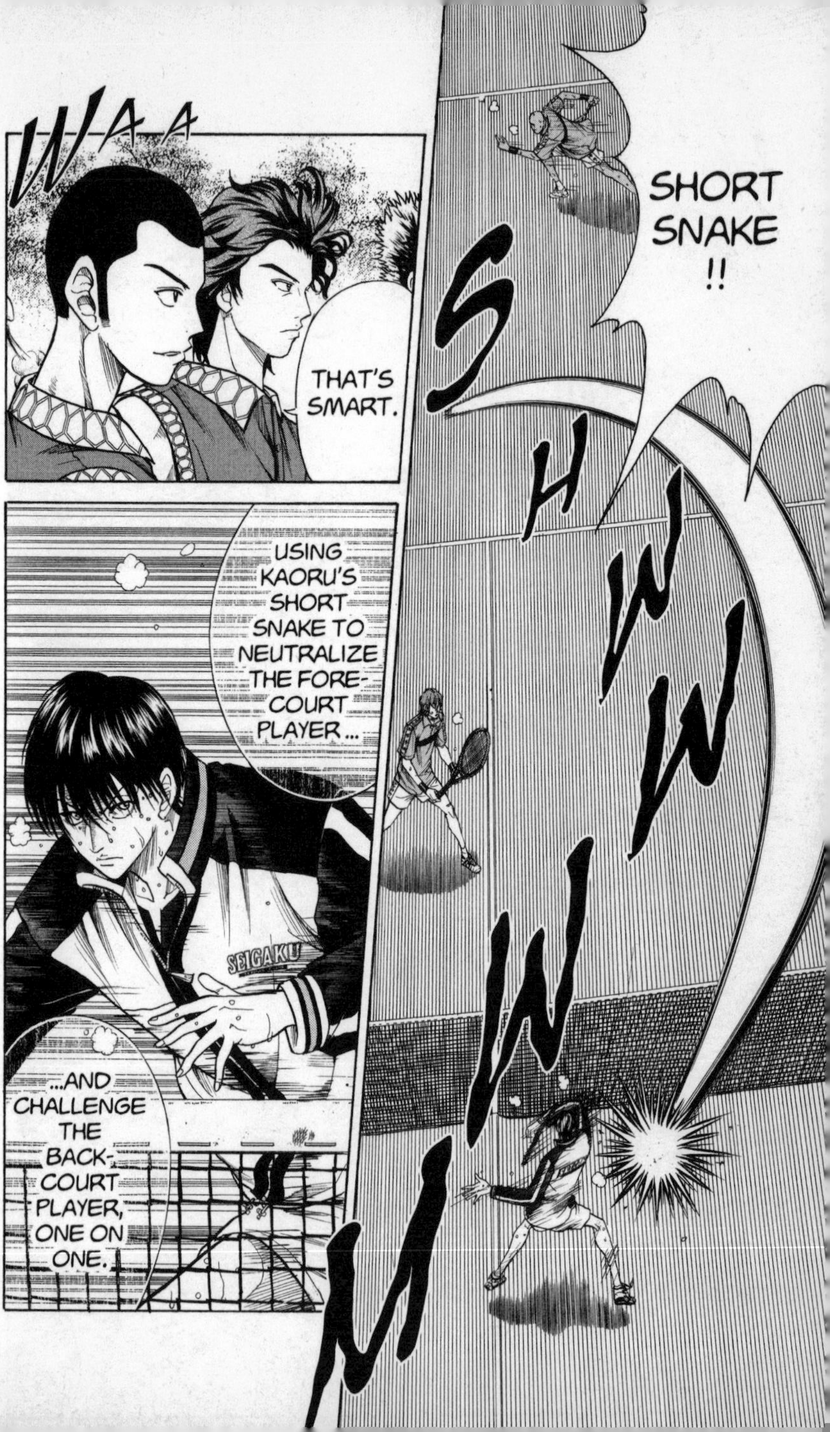
SHWWWM
SHORT SNAKE !!
WAAA
THAT'S SMART.
USING KAORU'S SHORT SNAKE TO NEUTRALIZE THE FORE-COURT PLAYER...
...AND CHALLENGE THE BACK-COURT PLAYER, ONE ON ONE.
SEIGAKU

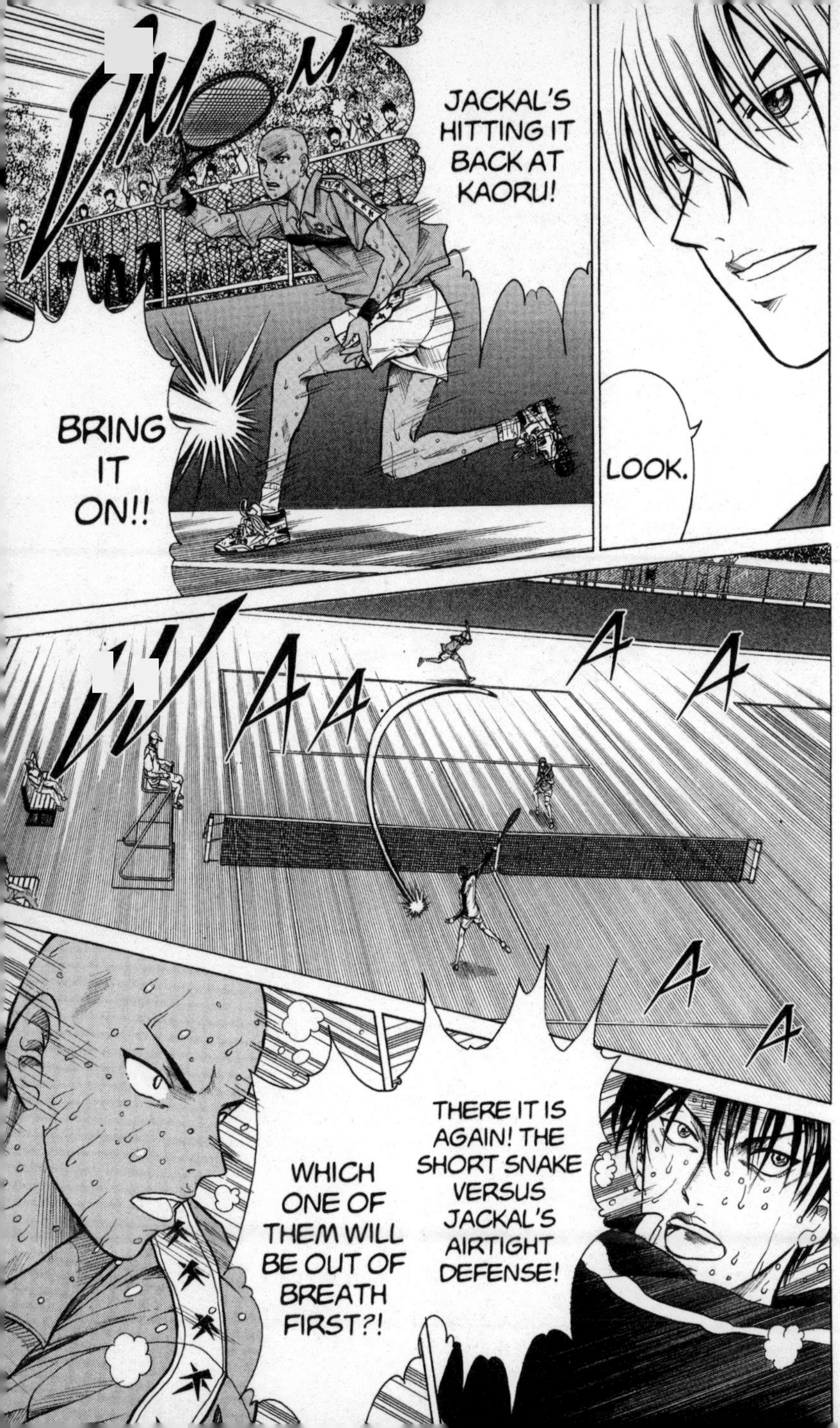
LOOK.
JACKAL'S HITTING IT BACK AT KAORU!
BRING IT ON!!
THERE IT IS AGAIN! THE SHORT SNAKE VERSUS JACKAL'S AIRTIGHT DEFENSE!
WHICH ONE OF THEM WILL BE OUT OF BREATH FIRST?!

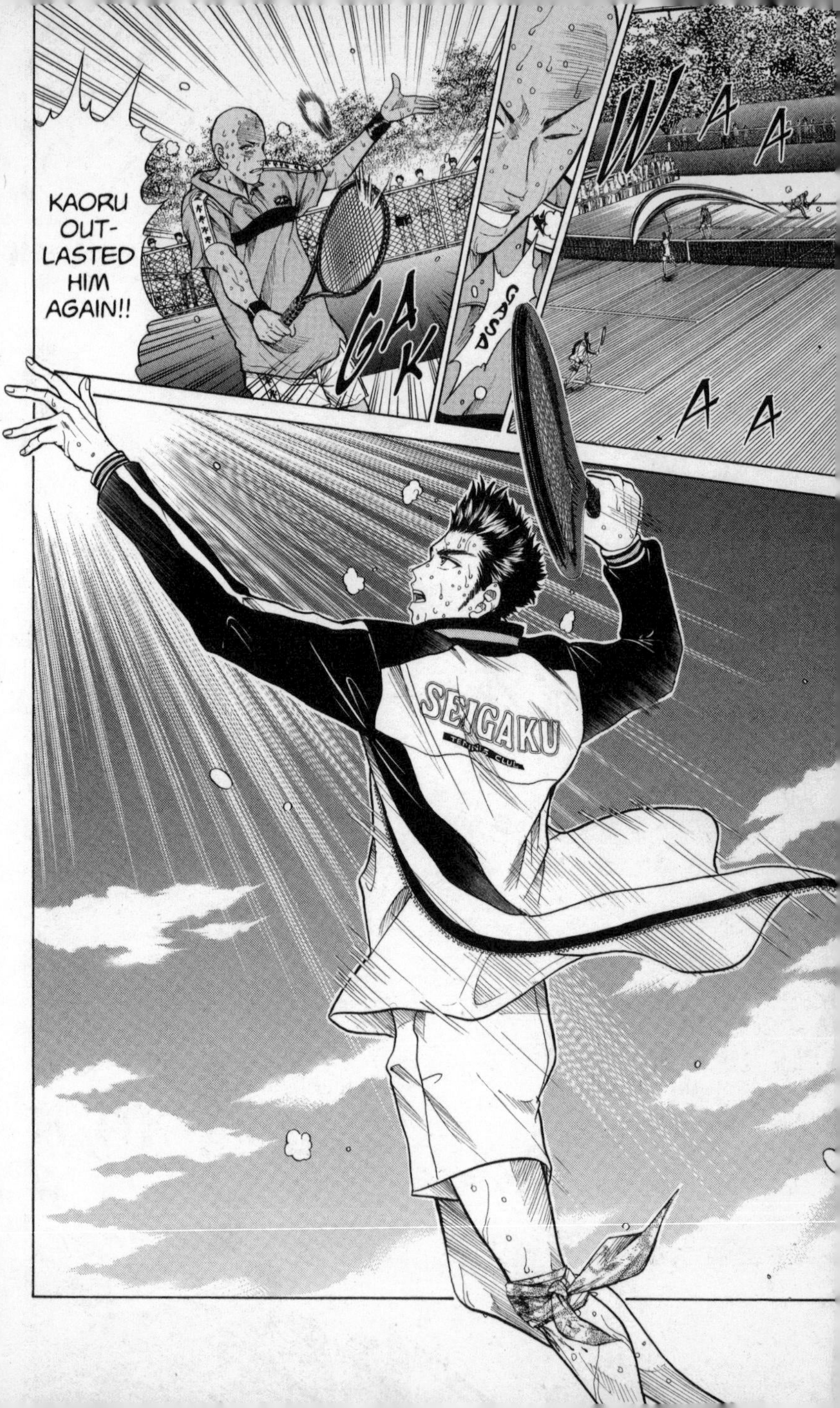
WAAA
AA
GASA
GAK
KAORU OUT-LASTED HIM AGAIN!!
SEIGAKU
TENNIS CLUB

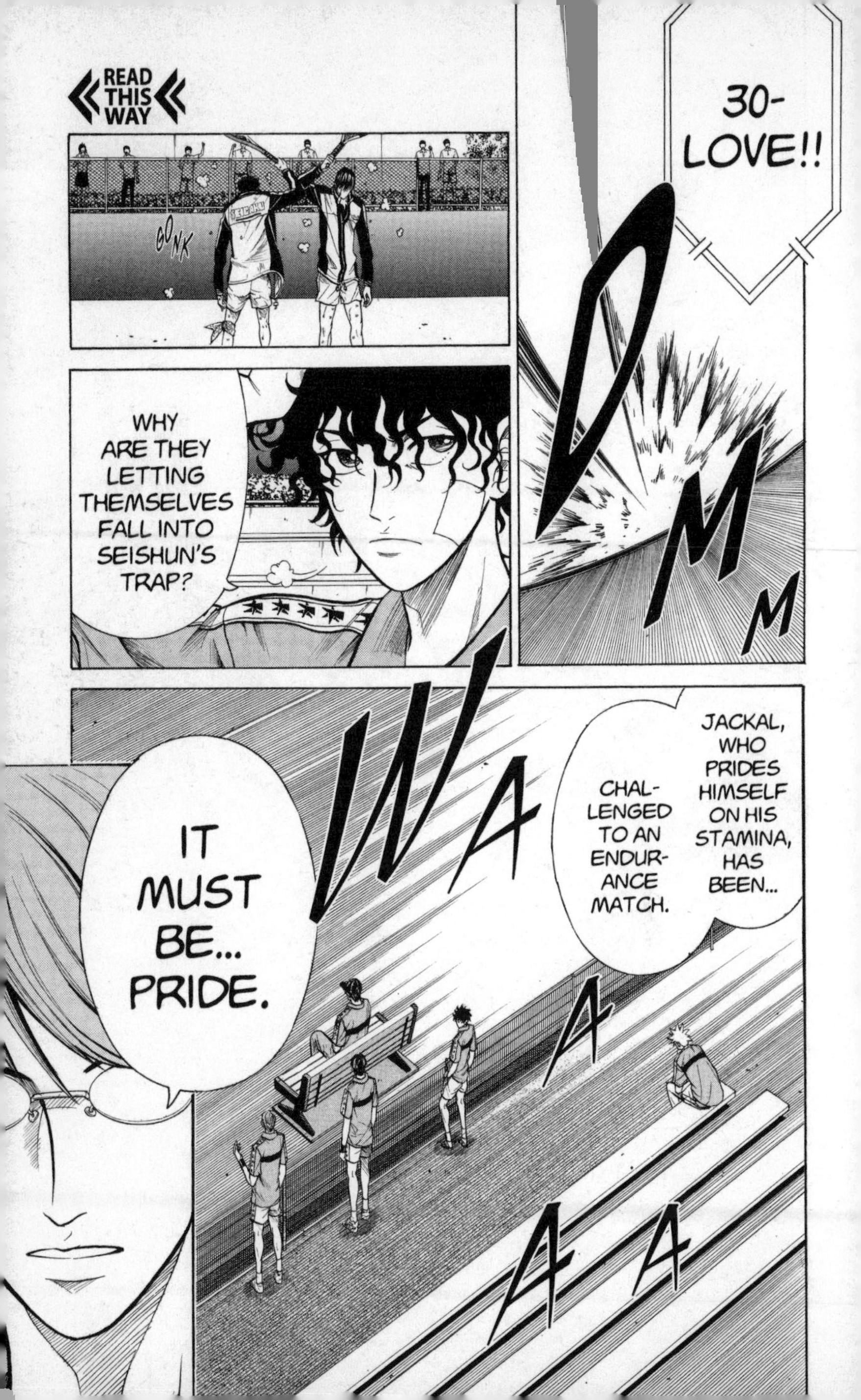
READ THIS WAY
30-LOVE!!
DOMMM
GONK
WHY ARE THEY LETTING THEMSELVES FALL INTO SEISHUN'S TRAP?
WAAAA
JACKAL, WHO PRIDES HIMSELF ON HIS STAMINA, HAS BEEN...
CHAL-LENGED TO AN ENDUR-ANCE MATCH.
IT MUST BE... PRIDE.

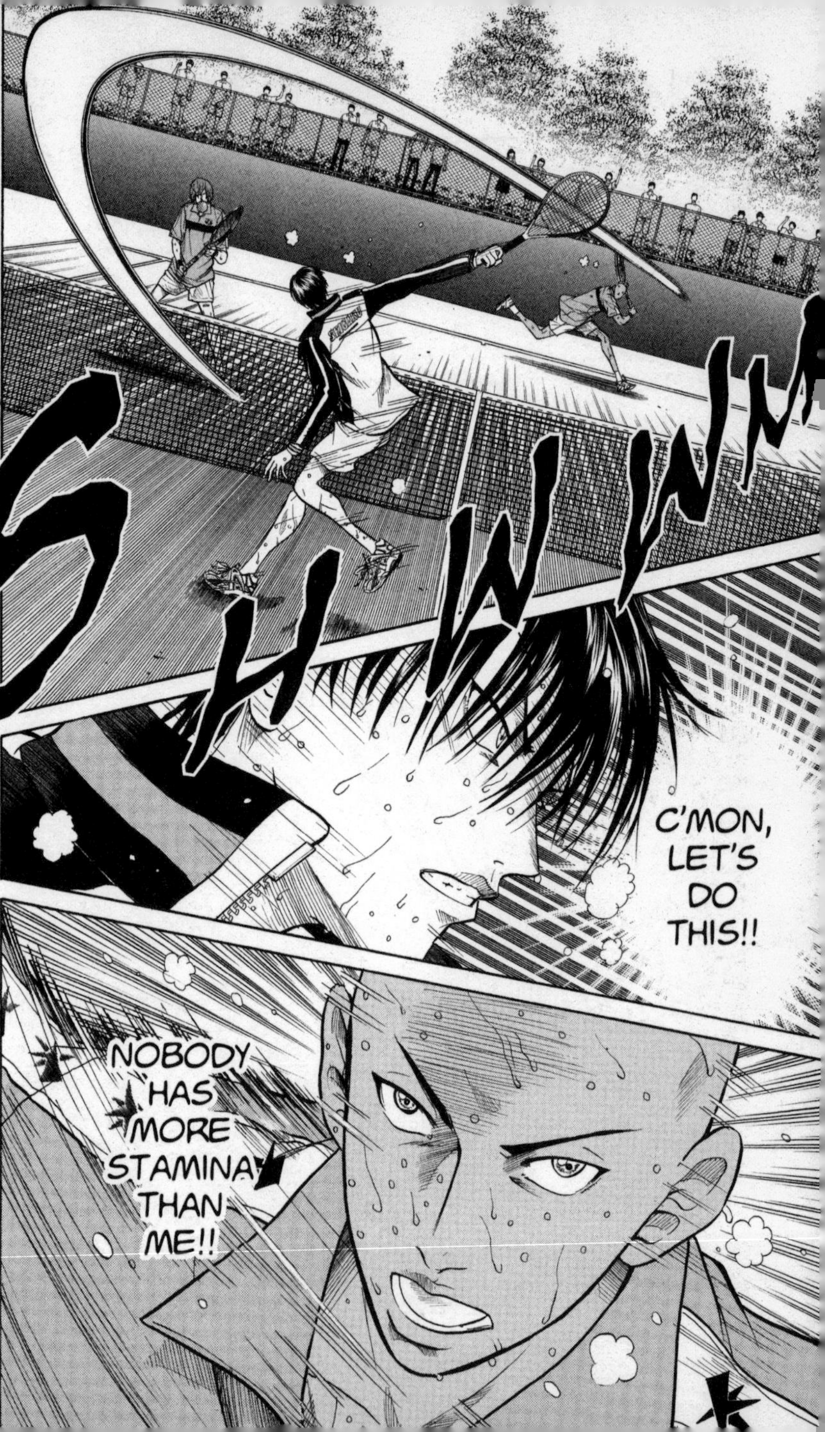
SHWINN
C'MON, LET'S DO THIS!!
NOBODY HAS MORE STAMINA THAN ME!!

READ THIS WAY

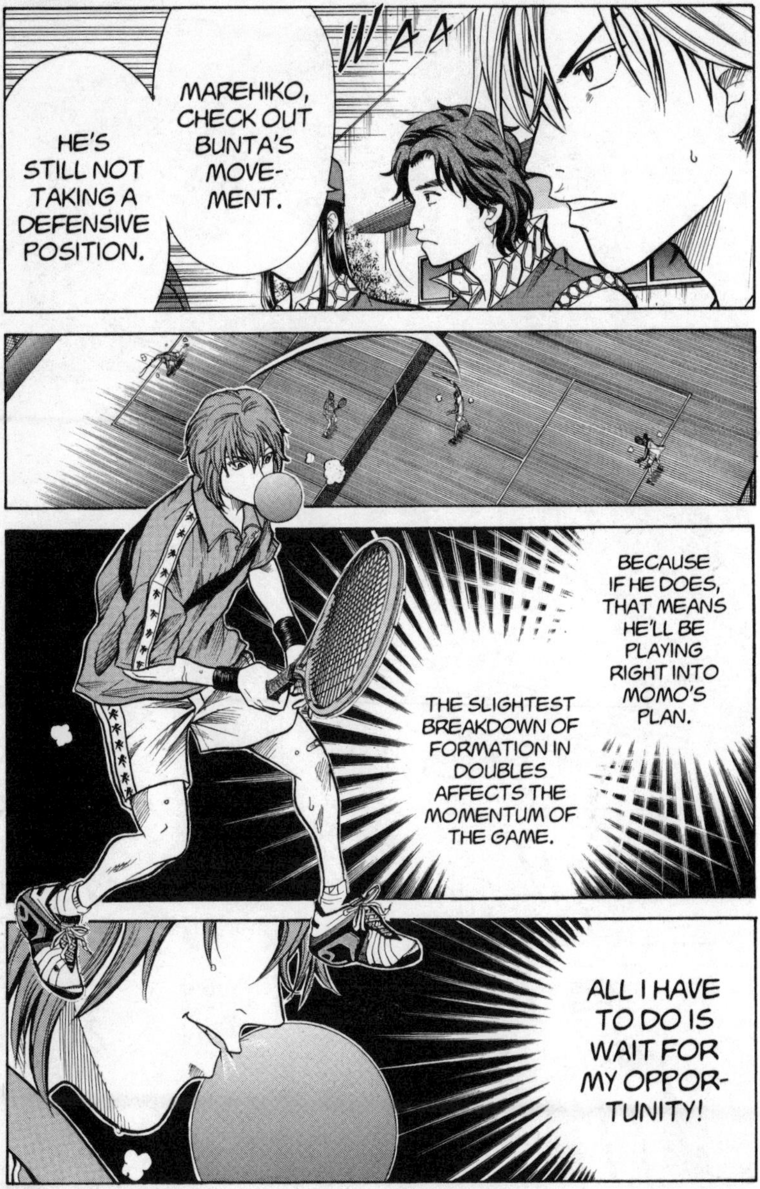
WAA
MAREHIKO, CHECK OUT BUNTA'S MOVE-MENT.
HE'S STILL NOT TAKING A DEFENSIVE POSITION.
BECAUSE IF HE DOES, THAT MEANS HE'LL BE PLAYING RIGHT INTO MOMO'S PLAN.
THE SLIGHTEST BREAKDOWN OF FORMATION IN DOUBLES AFFECTS THE MOMENTUM OF THE GAME.
ALL I HAVE TO DO IS WAIT FOR MY OPPOR-TUNITY!

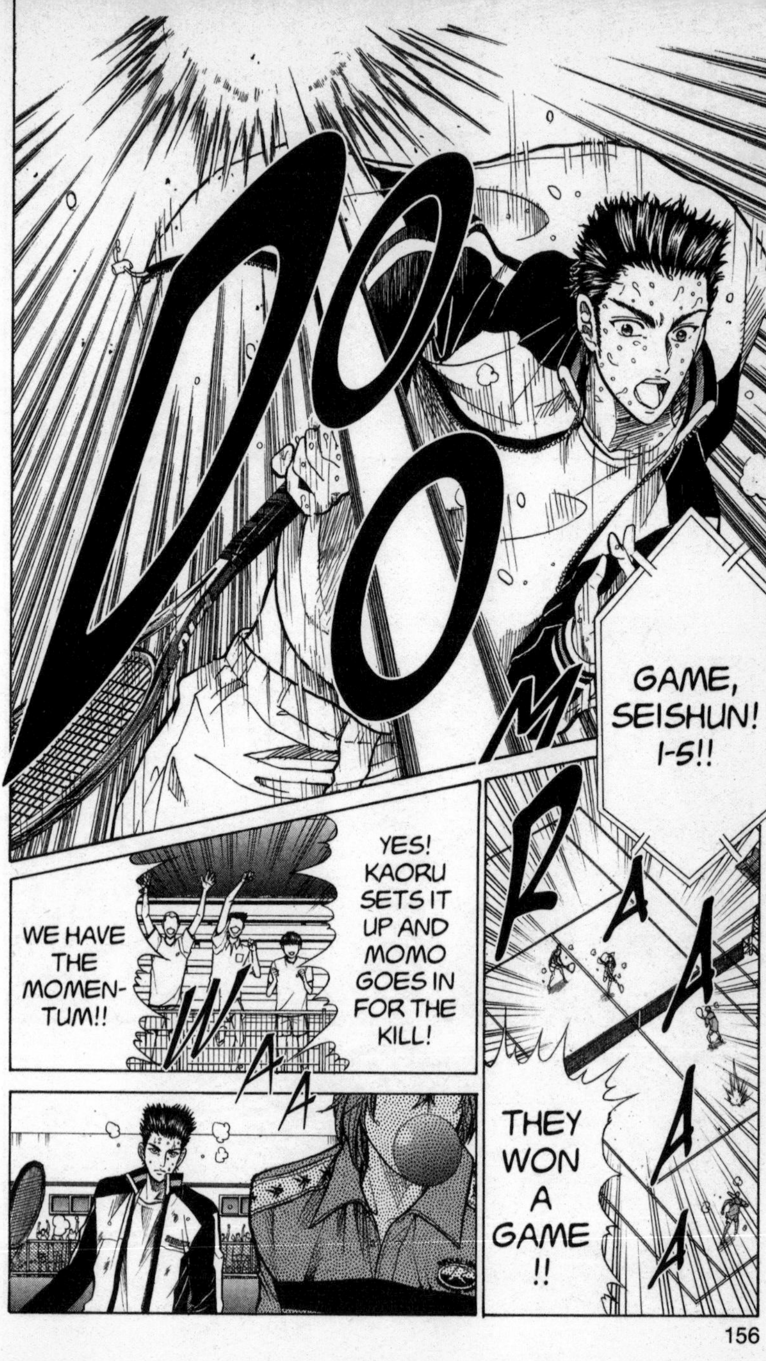
DOOM
GAME, SEISHUN! 1-5!!
RAAAA
THEY WON A GAME!!
YES! KAORU SETS IT UP AND MOMO GOES IN FOR THE KILL!
WE HAVE THE MOMEN-TUM!!
WAA

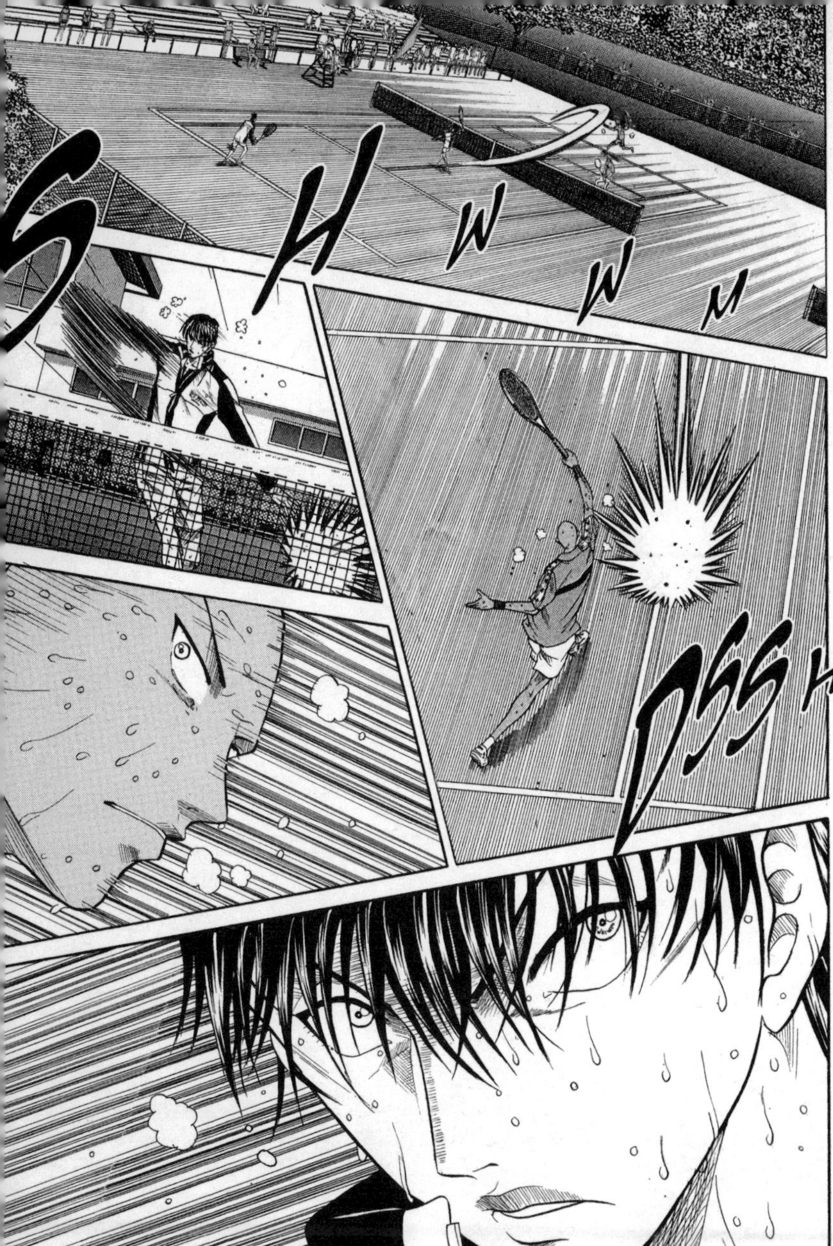
SHWWWM
DSSH

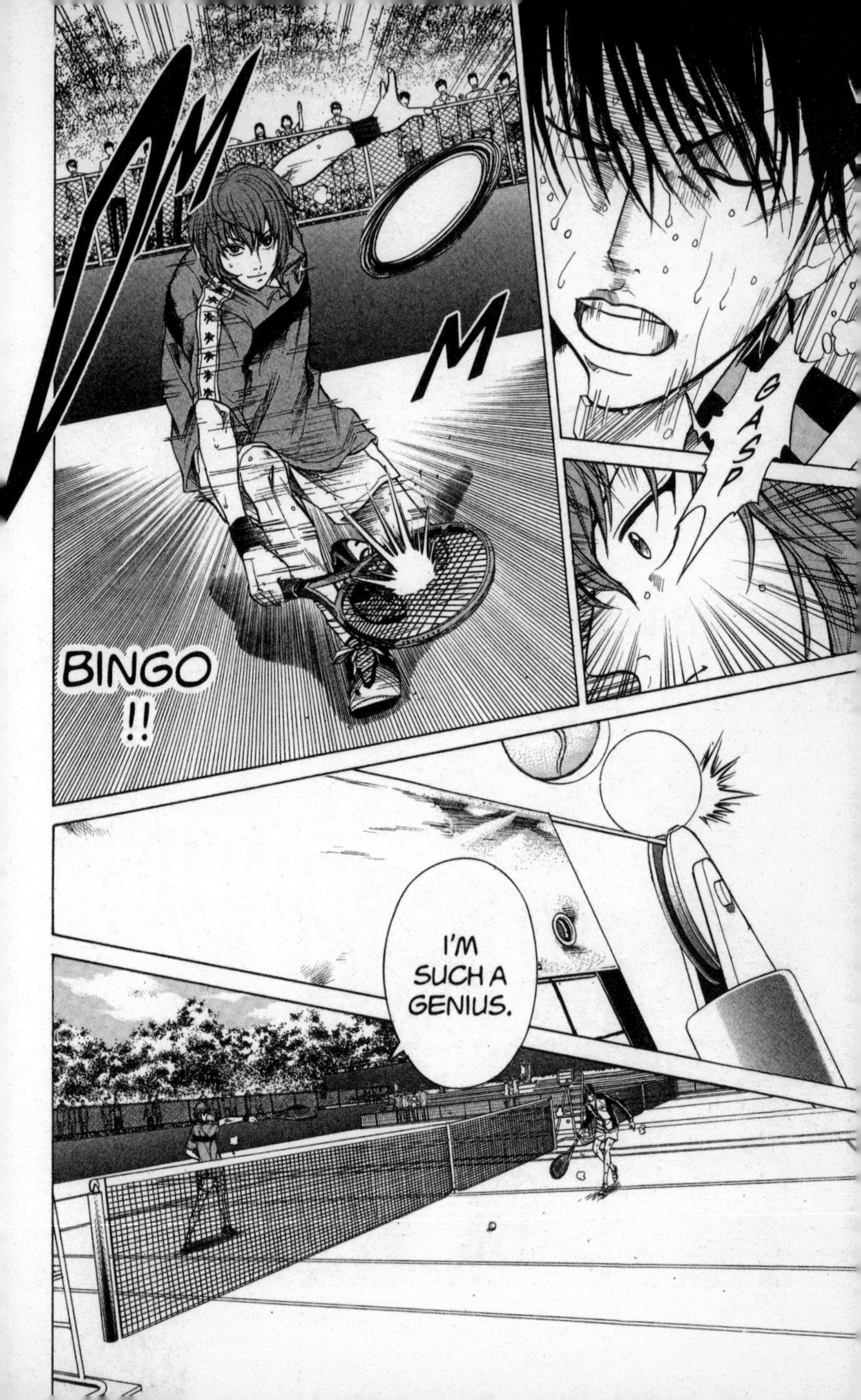
GASP
M
M
BINGO !!
I'M SUCH A GENIUS.

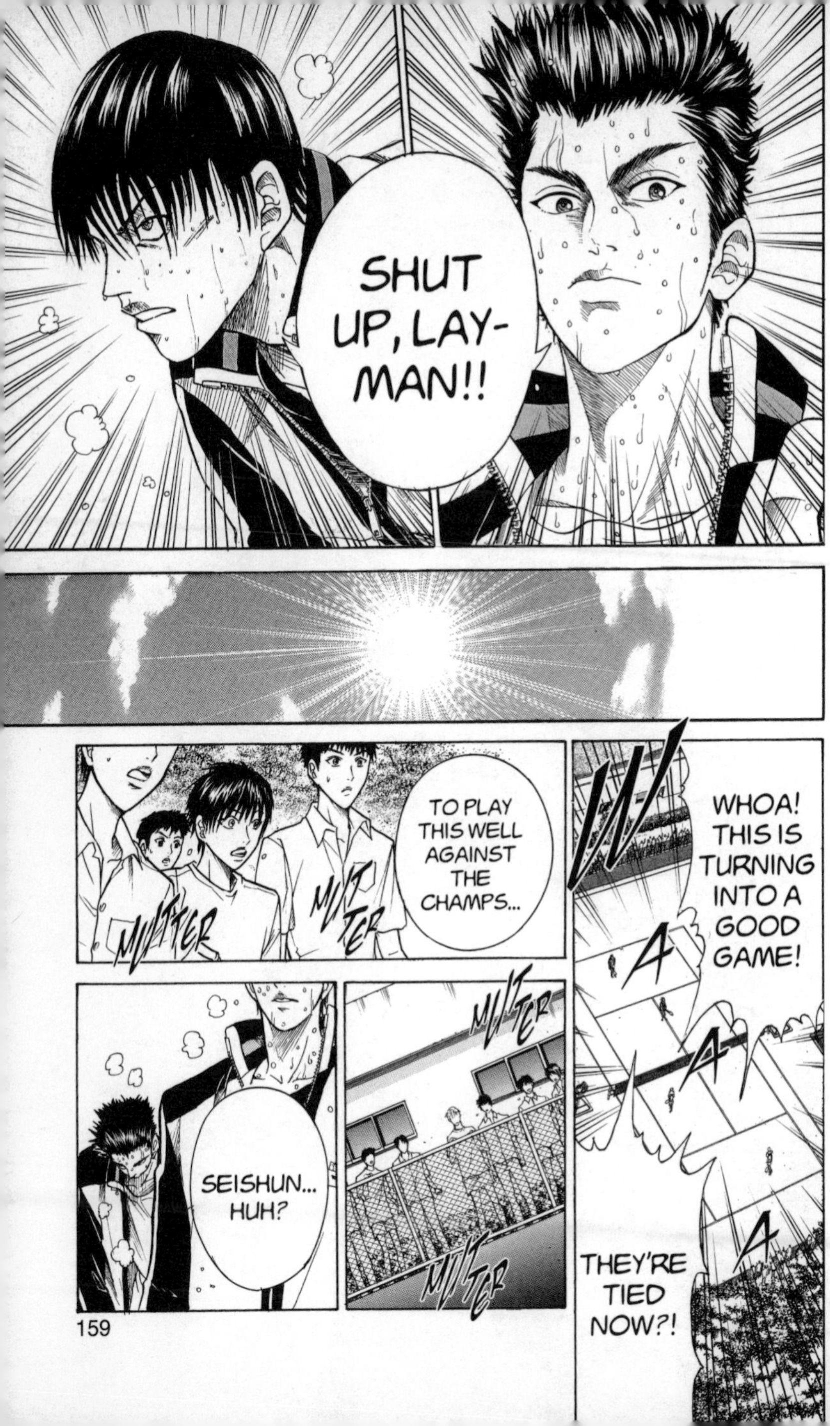
SHUT UP, LAYMAN!!
WAAA
WHOA! THIS IS TURNING INTO A GOOD GAME!
THEY'RE TIED NOW?!
TO PLAY THIS WELL AGAINST THE CHAMPS...
MUTTER MUTTER
MUTTER MUTTER
MUTTER MUTTER
SEISHUN... HUH?

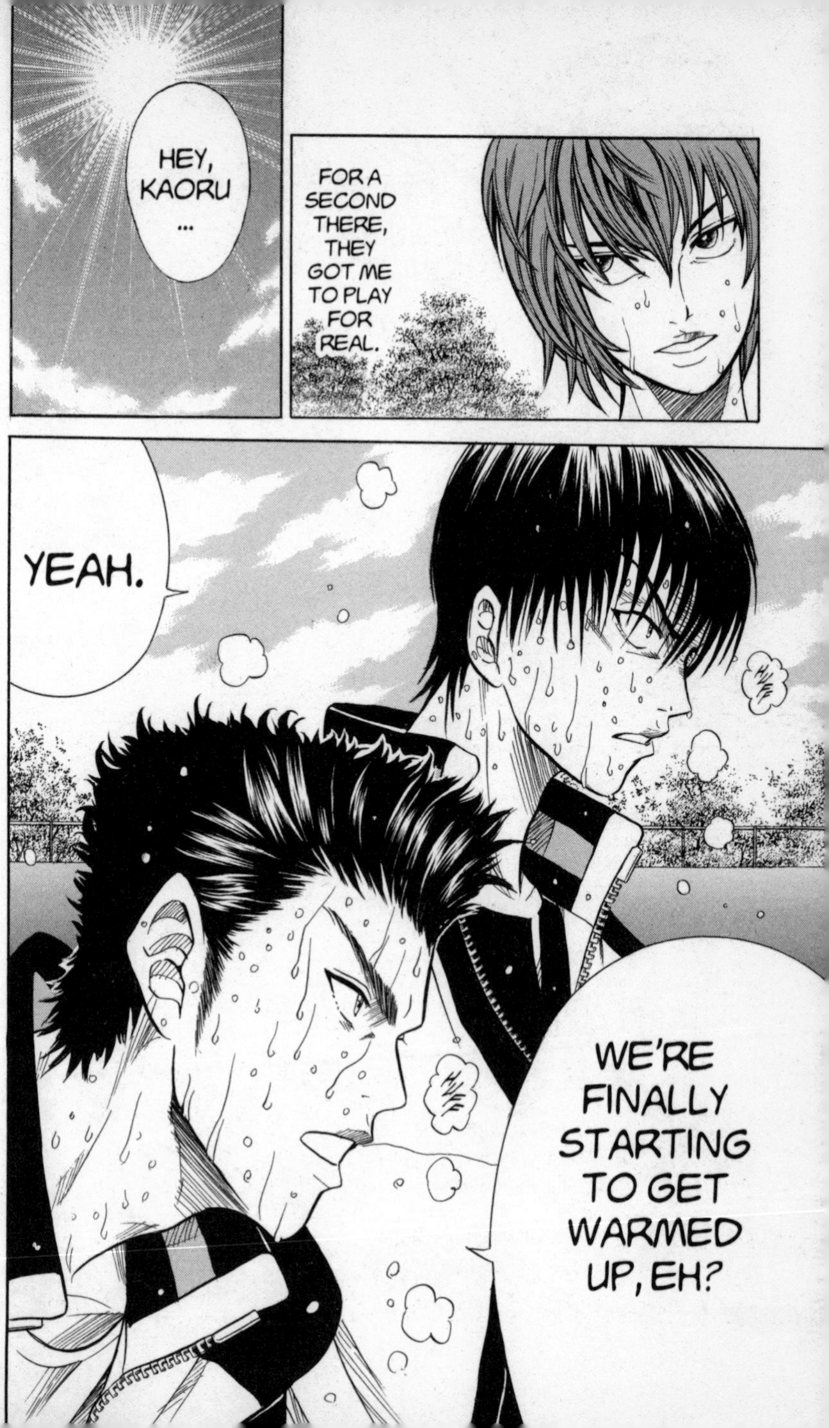
FOR A SECOND THERE, THEY GOT ME TO PLAY FOR REAL.
HEY, KAORU ...
WE'RE FINALLY STARTING TO GET WARMED UP, EH?
YEAH.

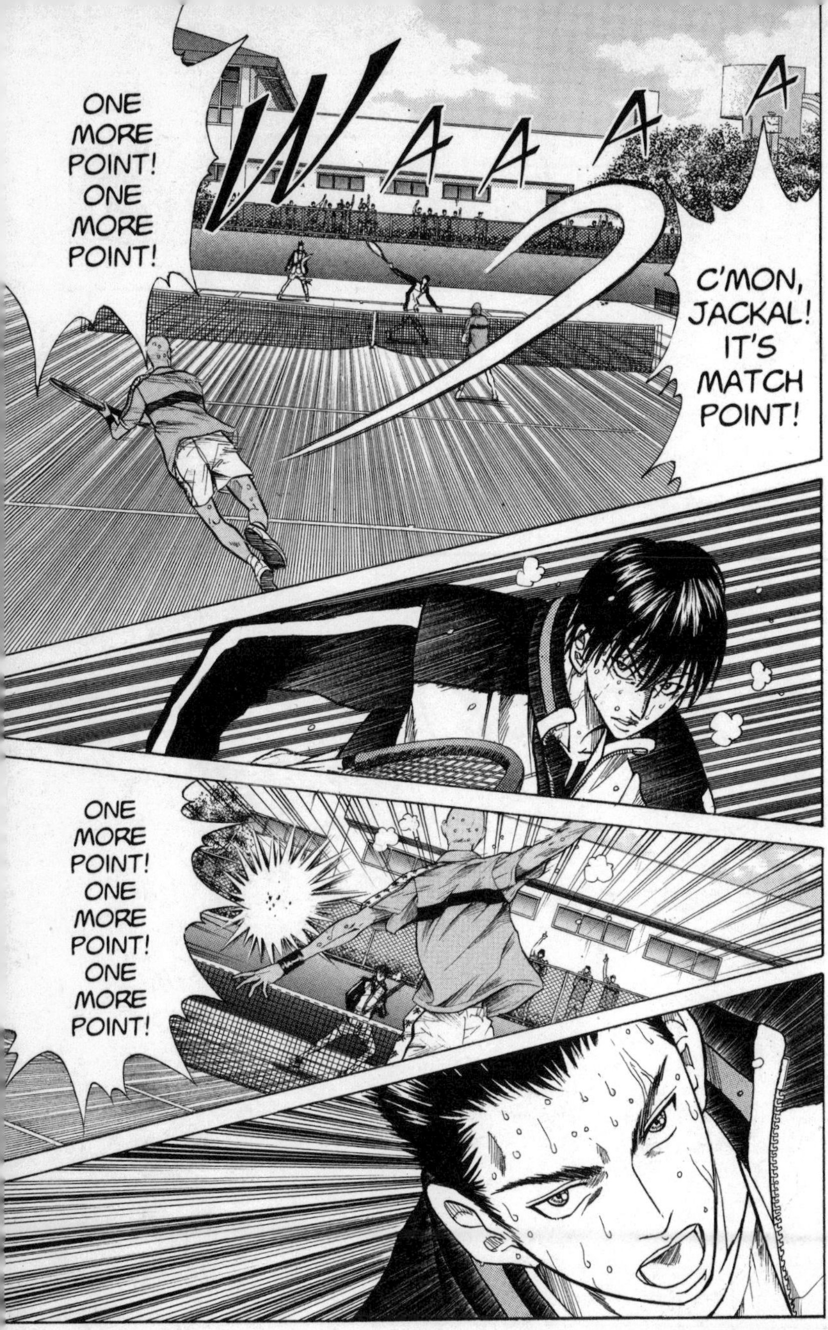
C'MON, JACKAL! IT'S MATCH POINT!
WAAAA
ONE MORE POINT! ONE MORE POINT!
ONE MORE POINT! ONE MORE POINT! ONE MORE POINT!

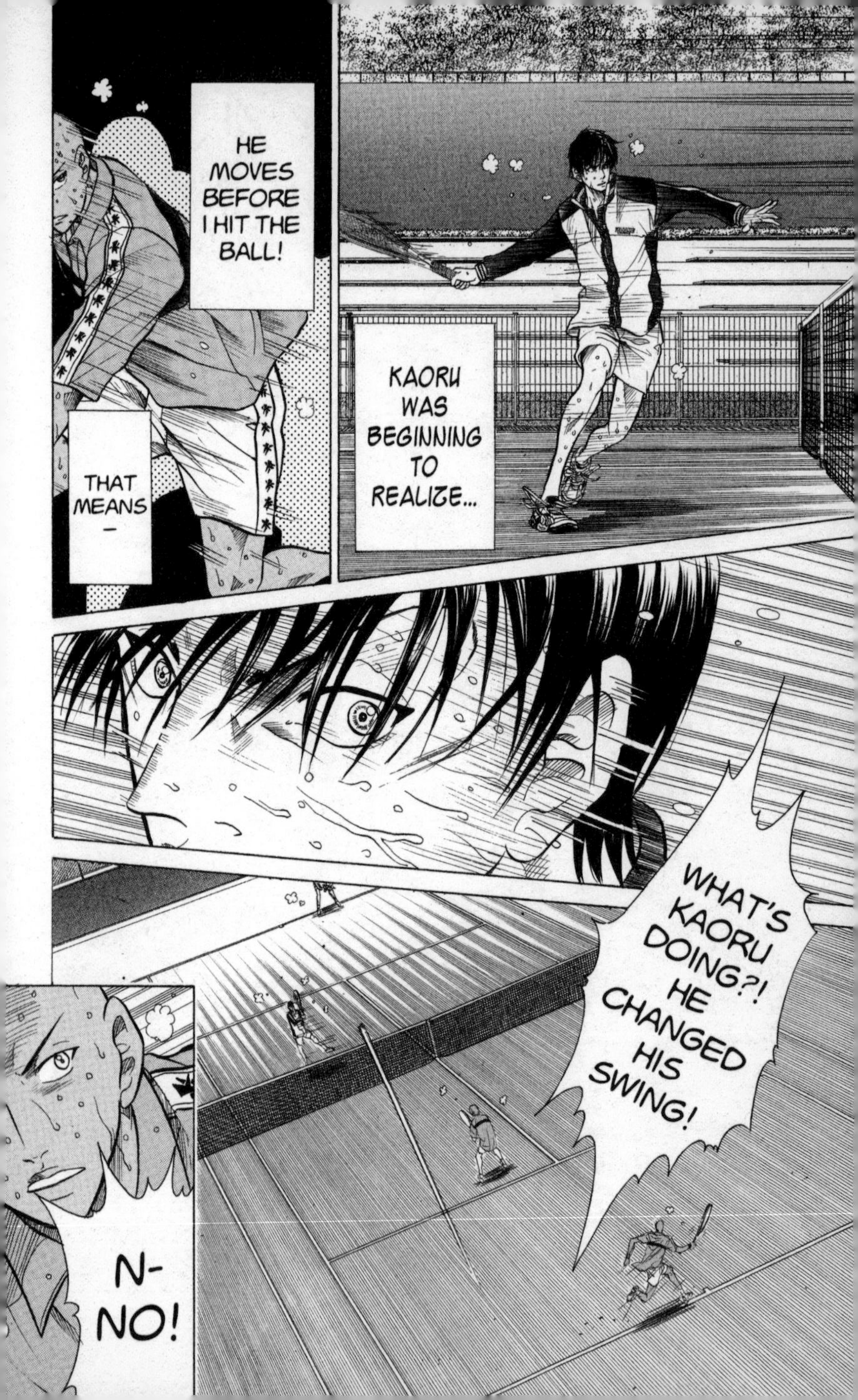
KAORU WAS BEGINNING TO REALIZE...
HE MOVES BEFORE I HIT THE BALL!
THAT MEANS —
WHAT'S KAORU DOING?! HE CHANGED HIS SWING!
N-NO!

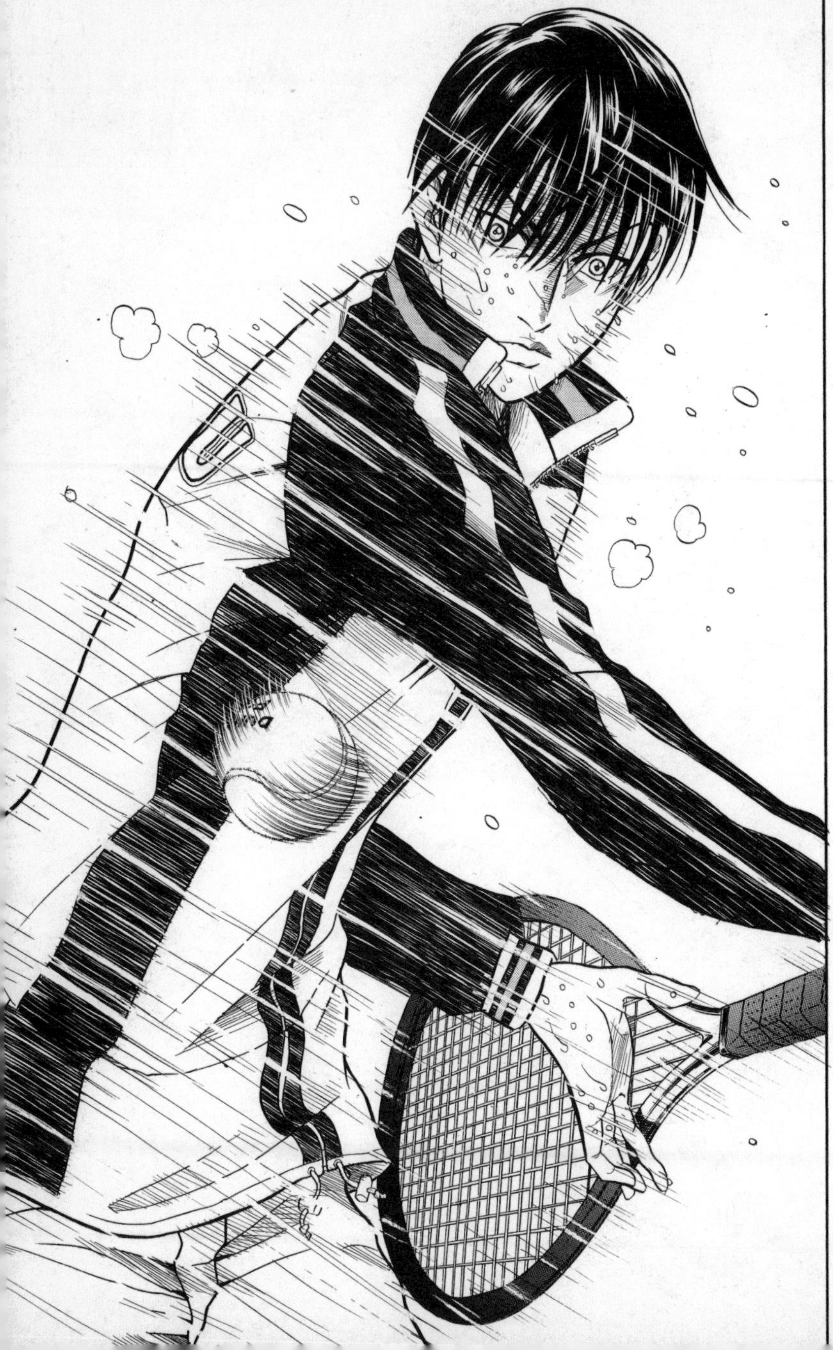

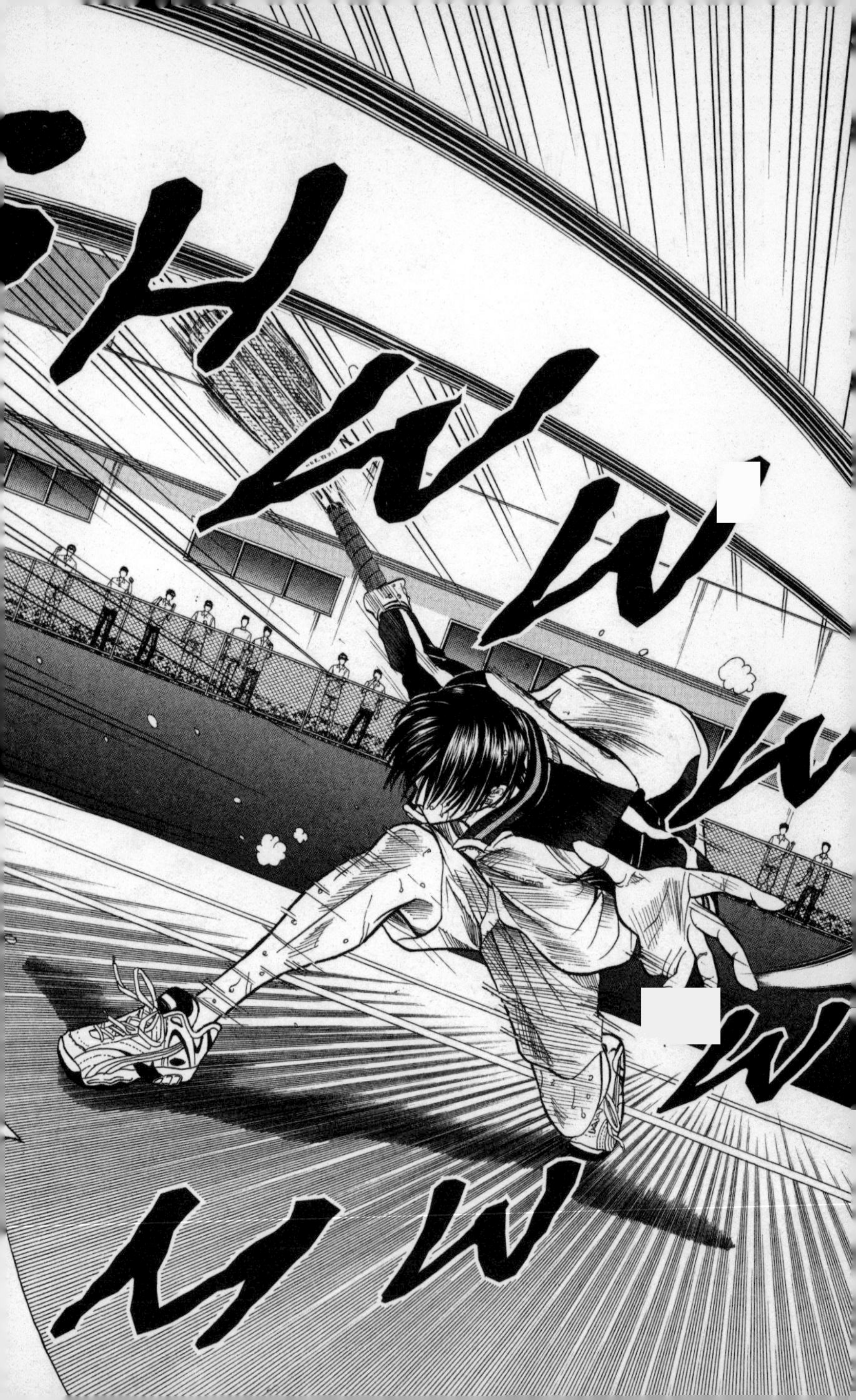

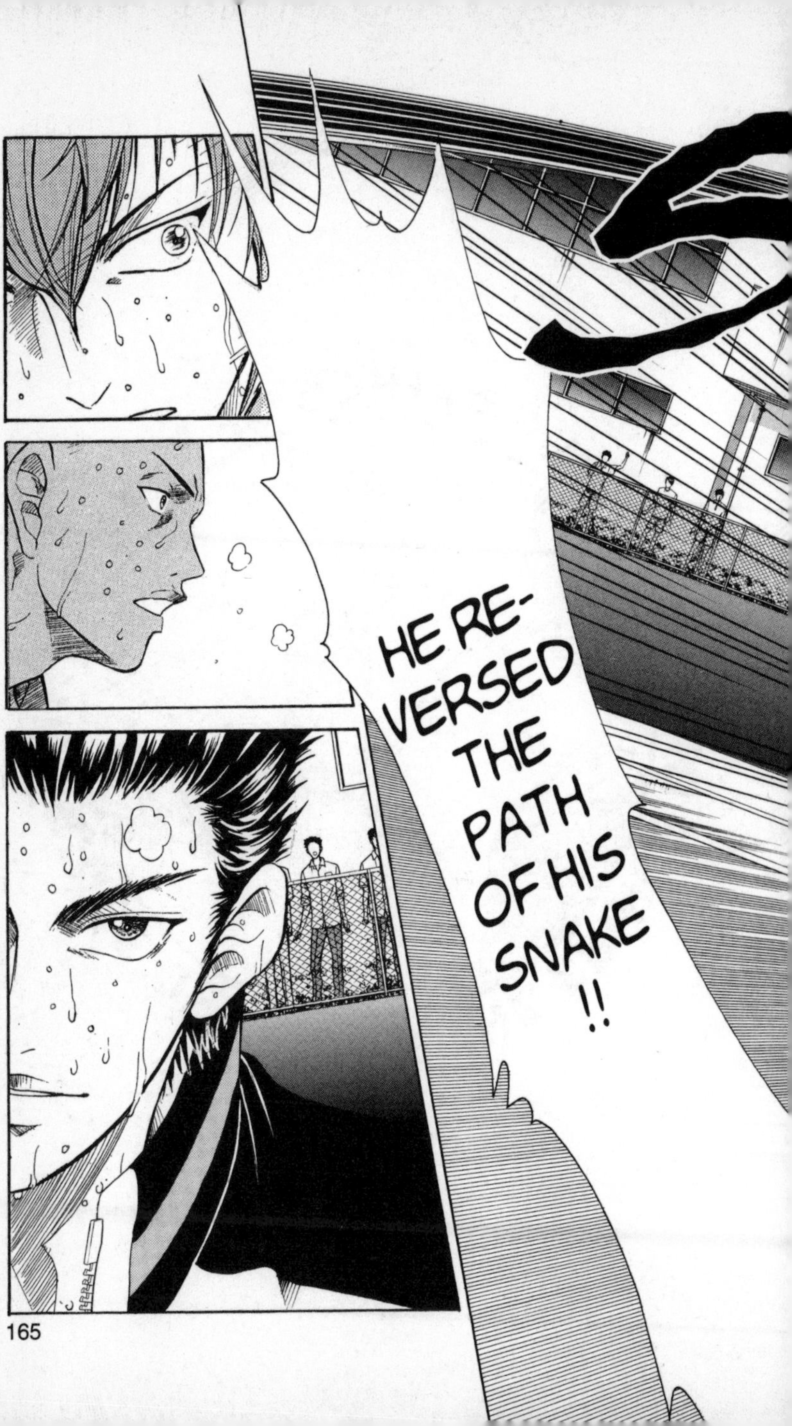
HE RE-
VERSED
THE
PATH
OF HIS
SNAKE
!!

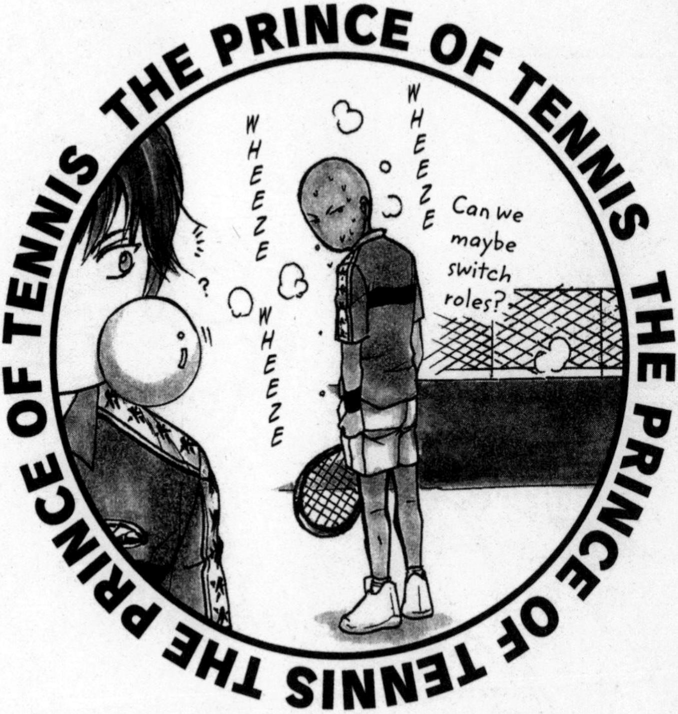
THE PRINCE OF TENNIS THE PRINCE OF TENNIS THE PRINCE OF TENNIS
Can we maybe switch roles?
WHEEZE
WHEEZE
WHEEZE
?

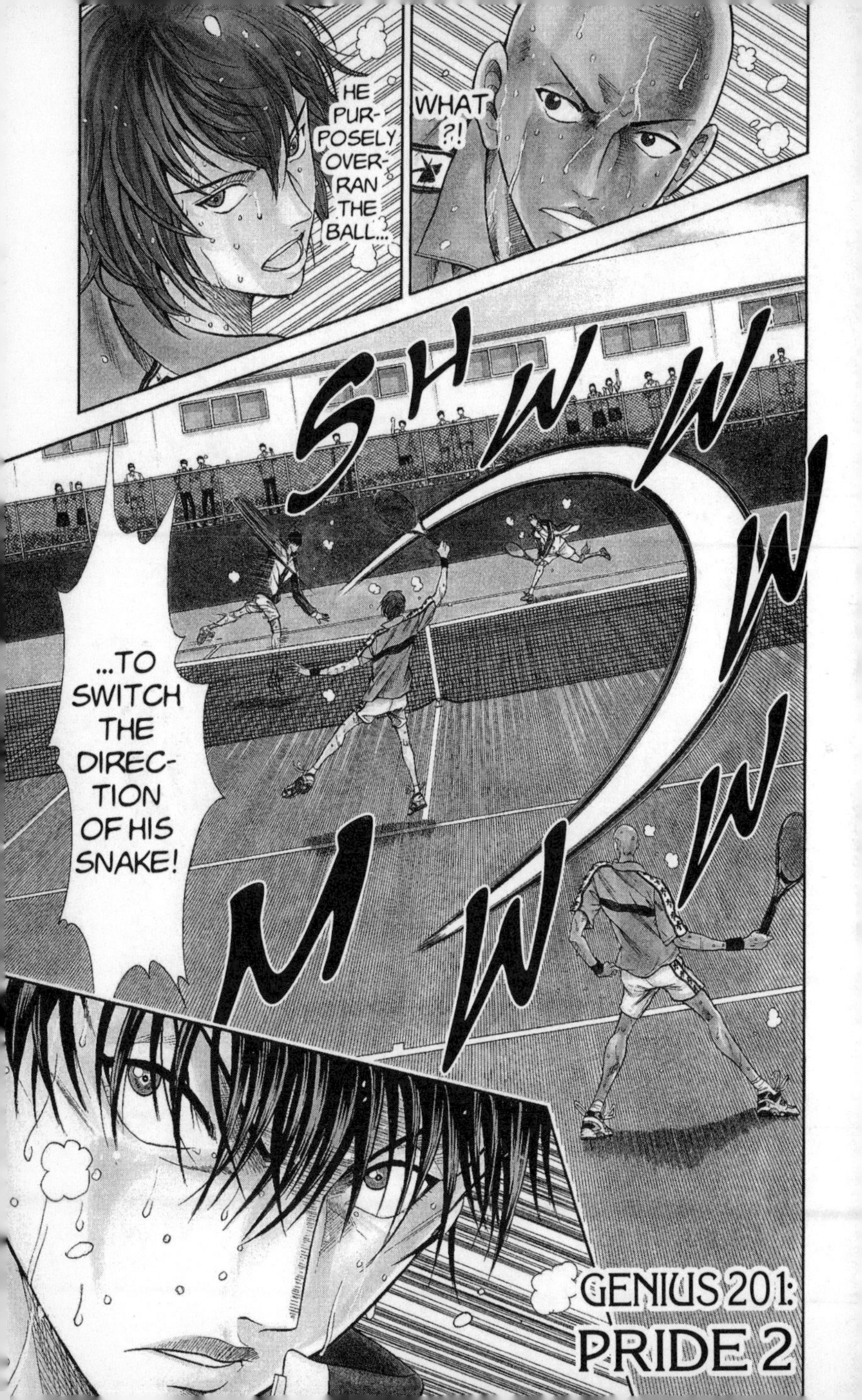
WHAT?!
HE PURPOSELY OVERRAN THE BALL...
SHWWWWWWWMM
...TO SWITCH THE DIRECTION OF HIS SNAKE!
GENIUS 201: PRIDE 2

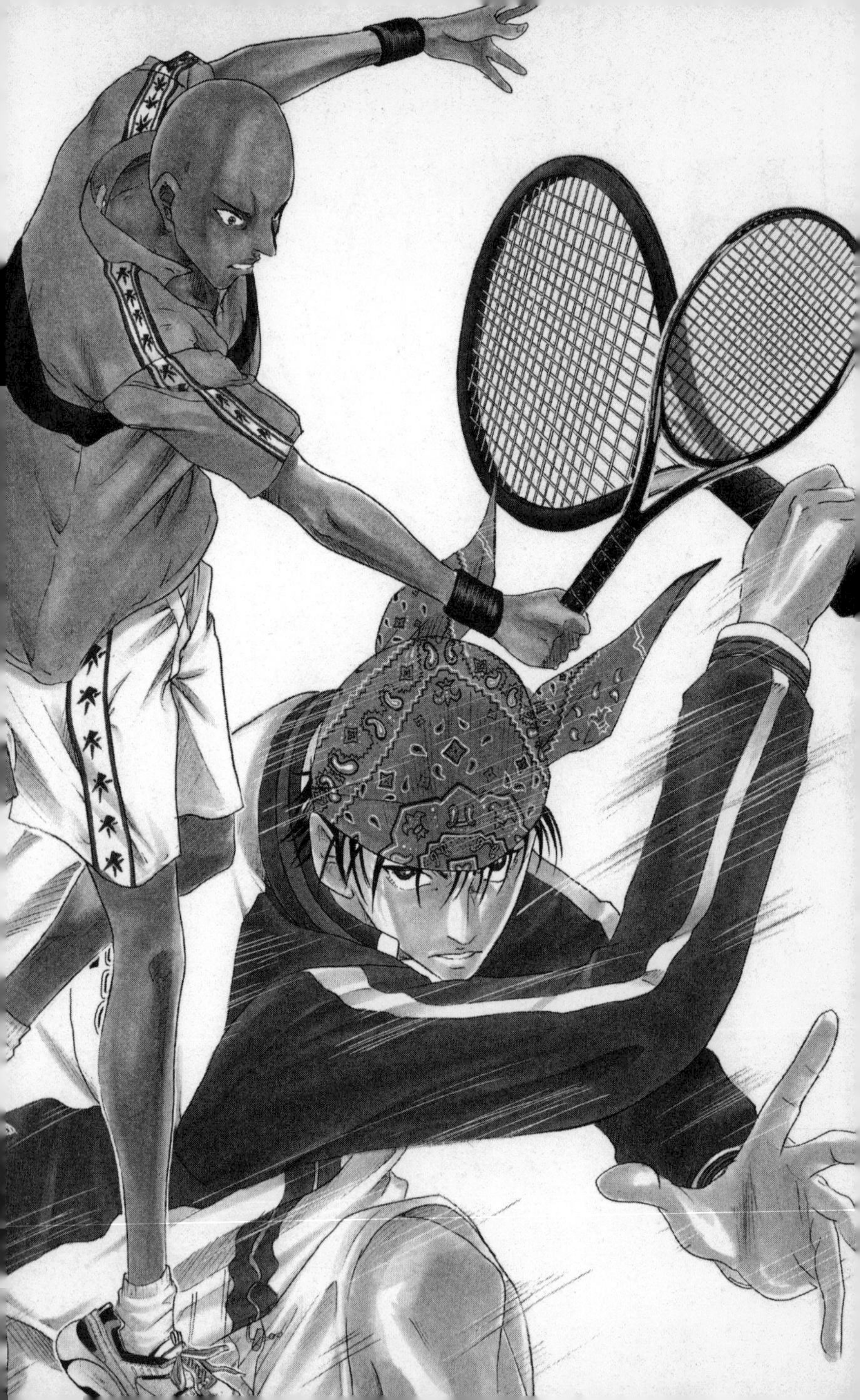

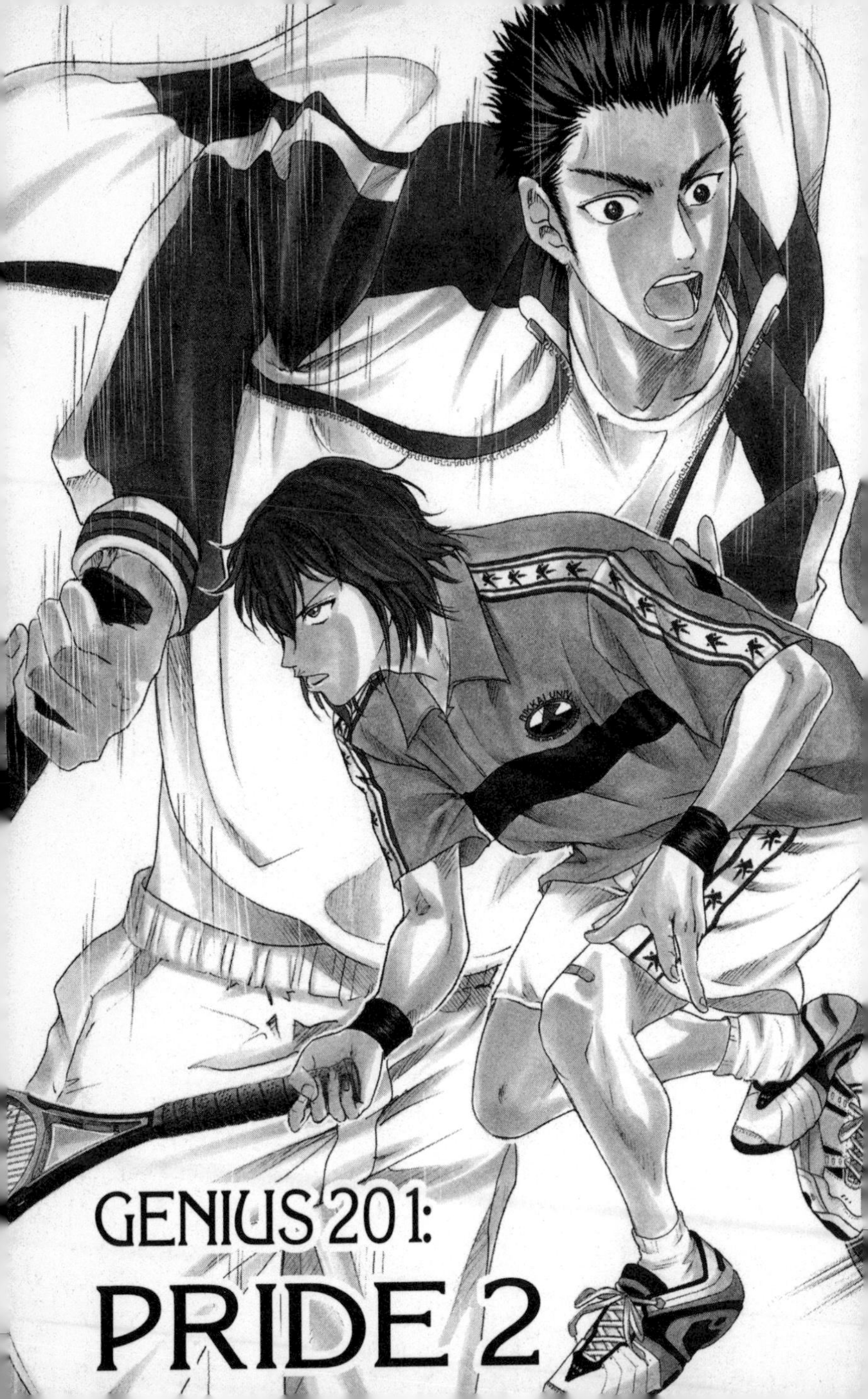

GENIUS 201:
PRIDE 2

テニスの王子様

THE PRINCE OF TENNIS

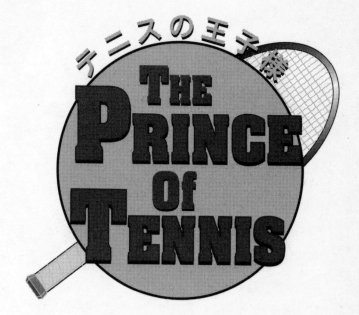

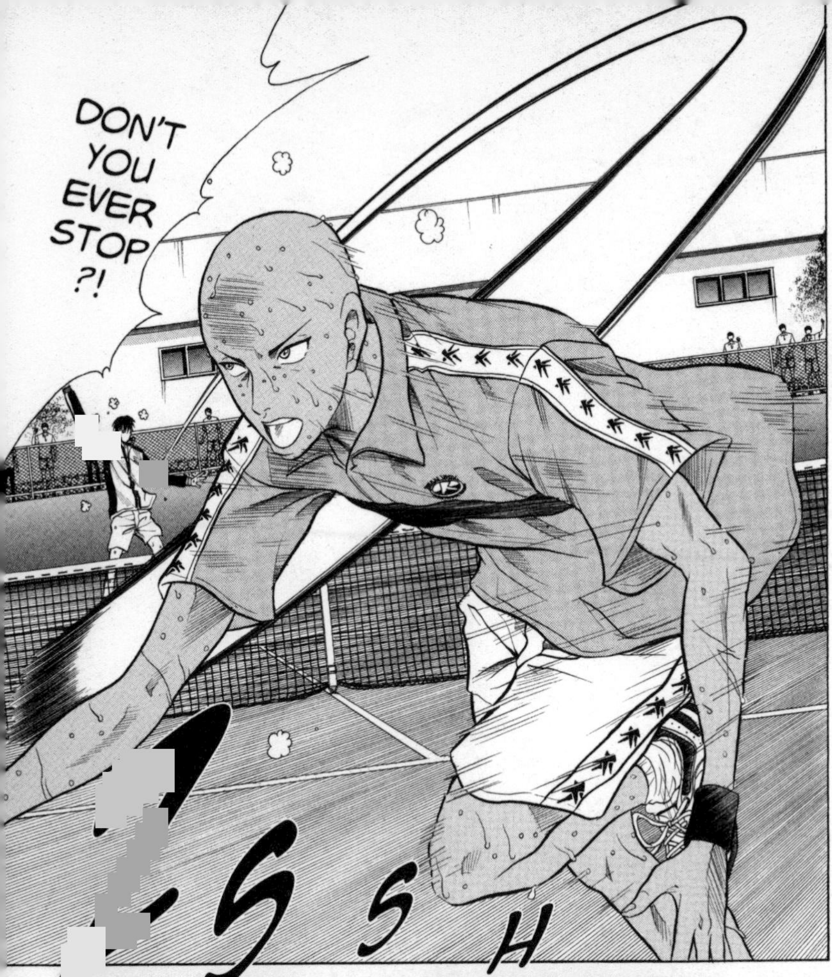
DON'T YOU EVER STOP ?!
SSH

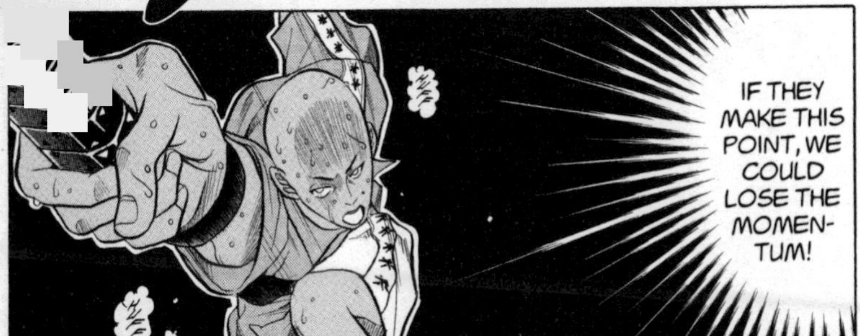
IF THEY MAKE THIS POINT, WE COULD LOSE THE MOMEN-TUM!

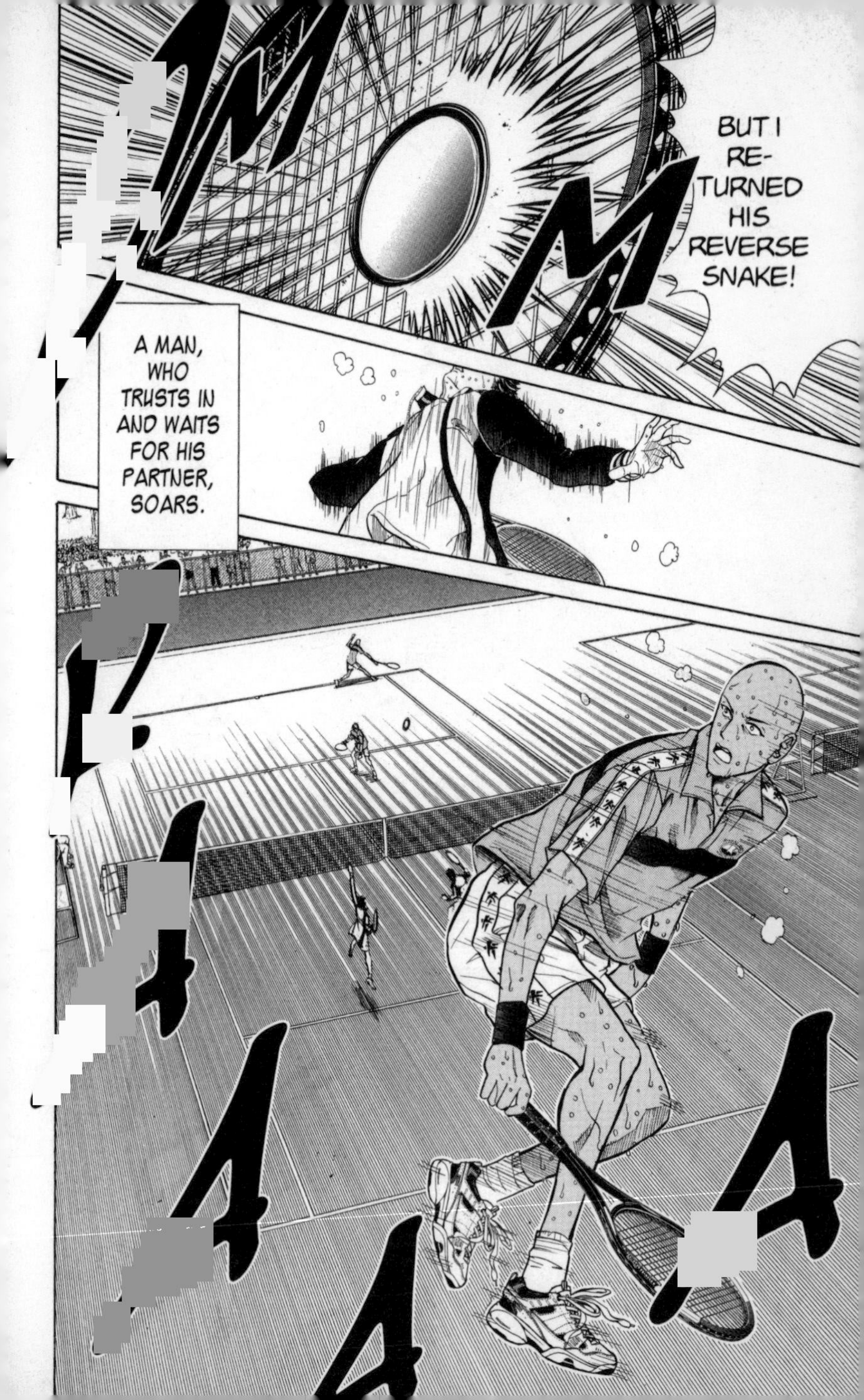
BUT I RE-TURNED HIS REVERSE SNAKE!
MOM
A MAN, WHO TRUSTS IN AND WAITS FOR HIS PARTNER, SOARS.

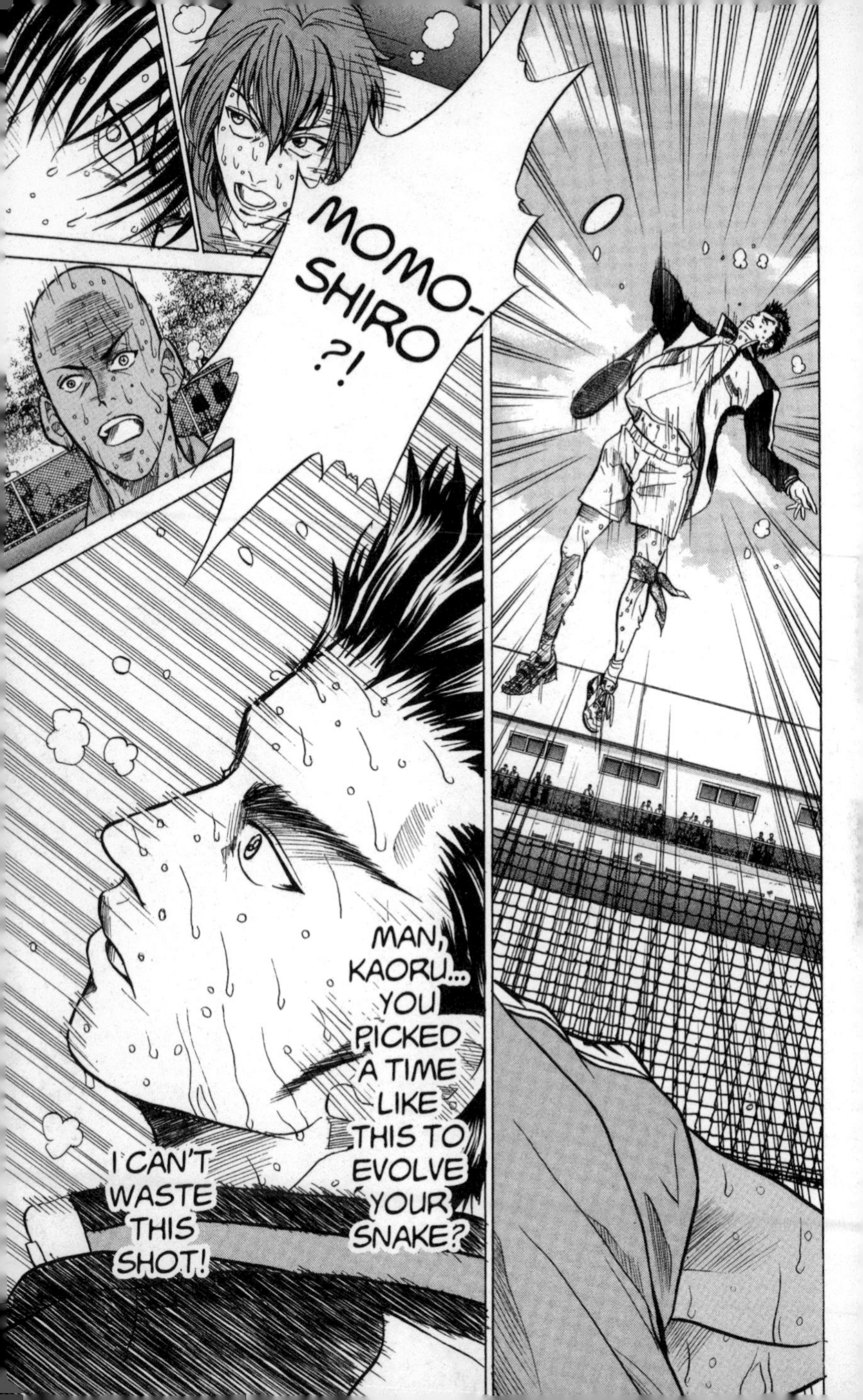
MOMO-SHIRO ?!
MAN, KAORU... YOU PICKED A TIME LIKE THIS TO EVOLVE YOUR SNAKE?
I CAN'T WASTE THIS SHOT!

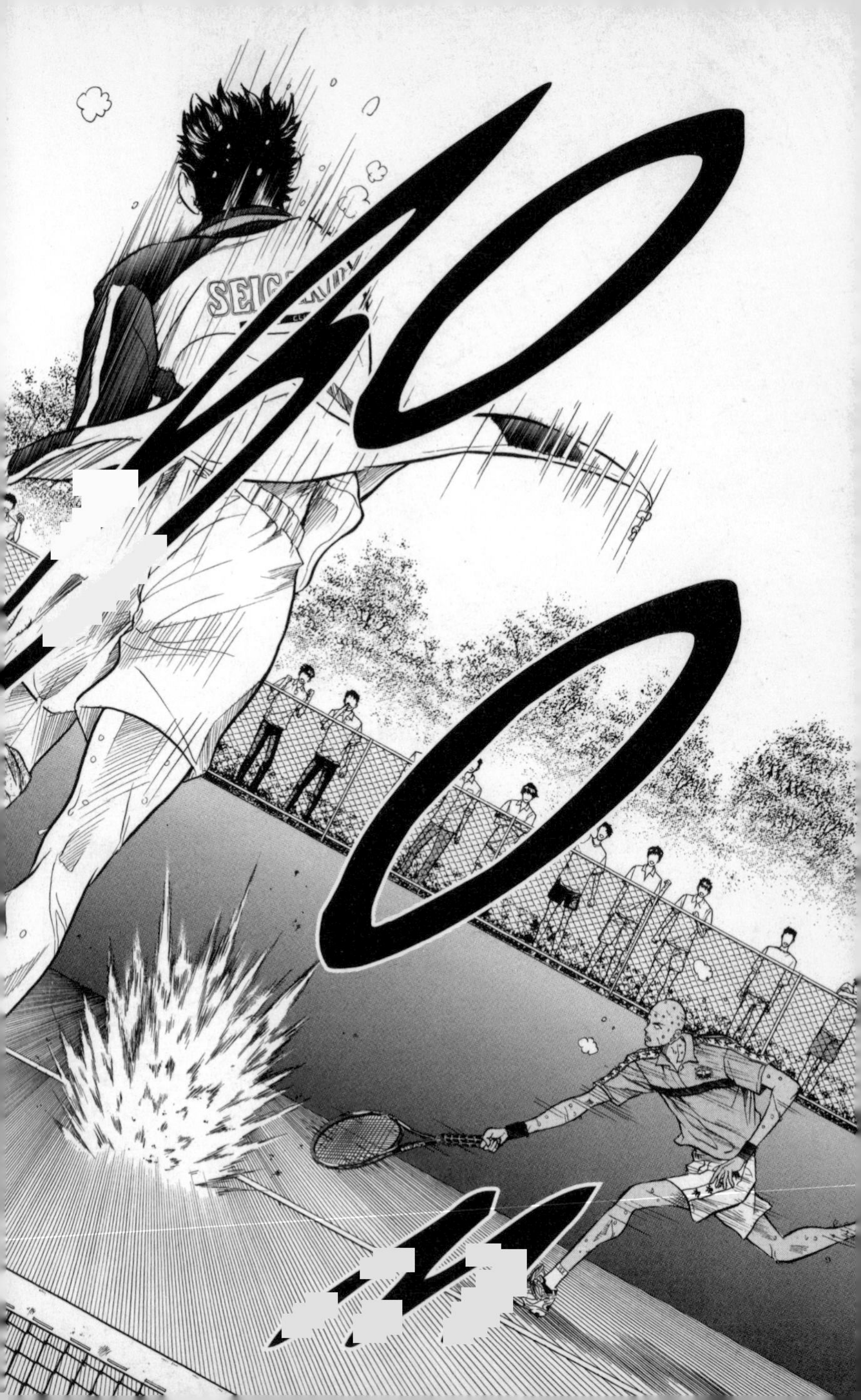

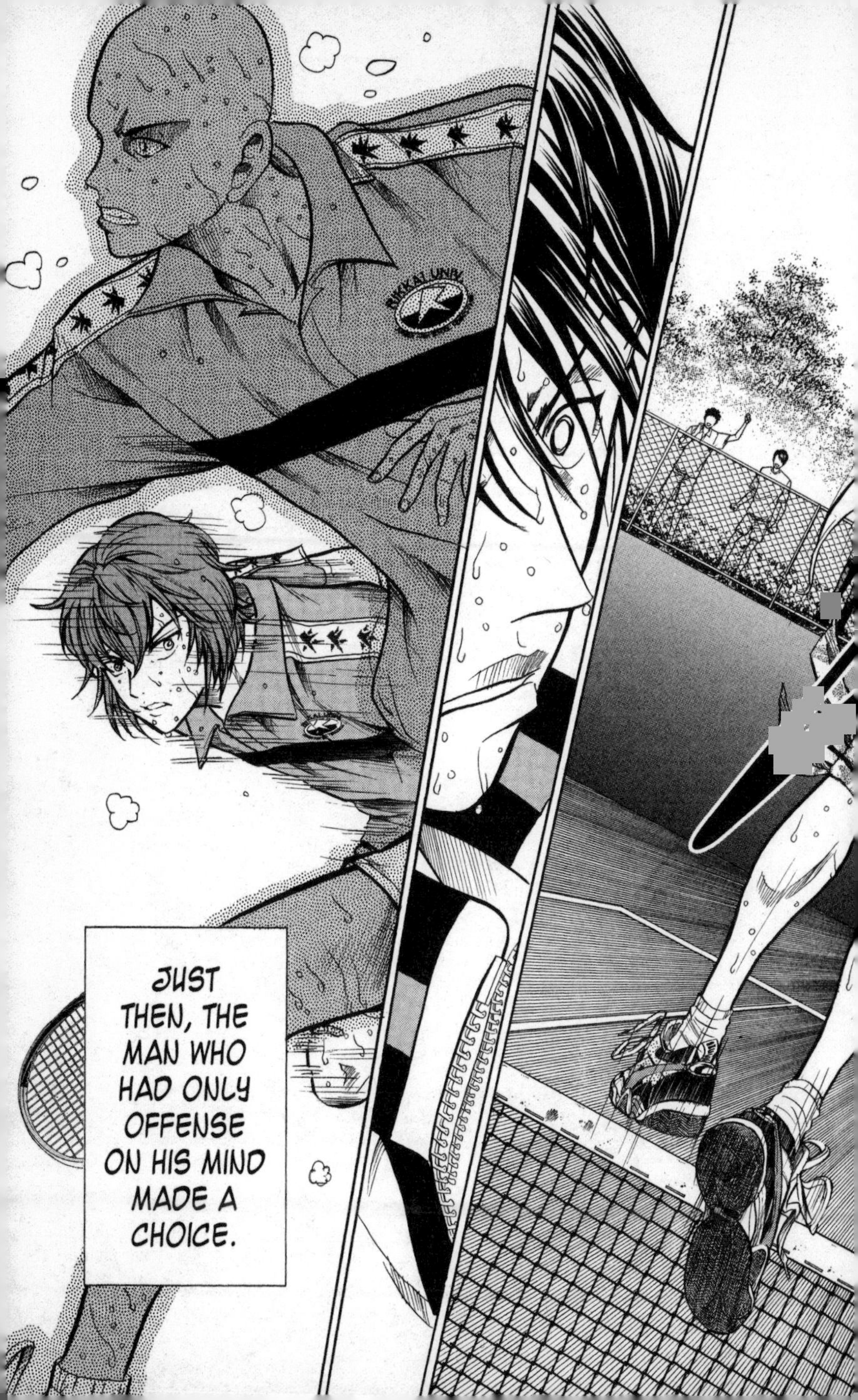
JUST THEN, THE MAN WHO HAD ONLY OFFENSE ON HIS MIND MADE A CHOICE.

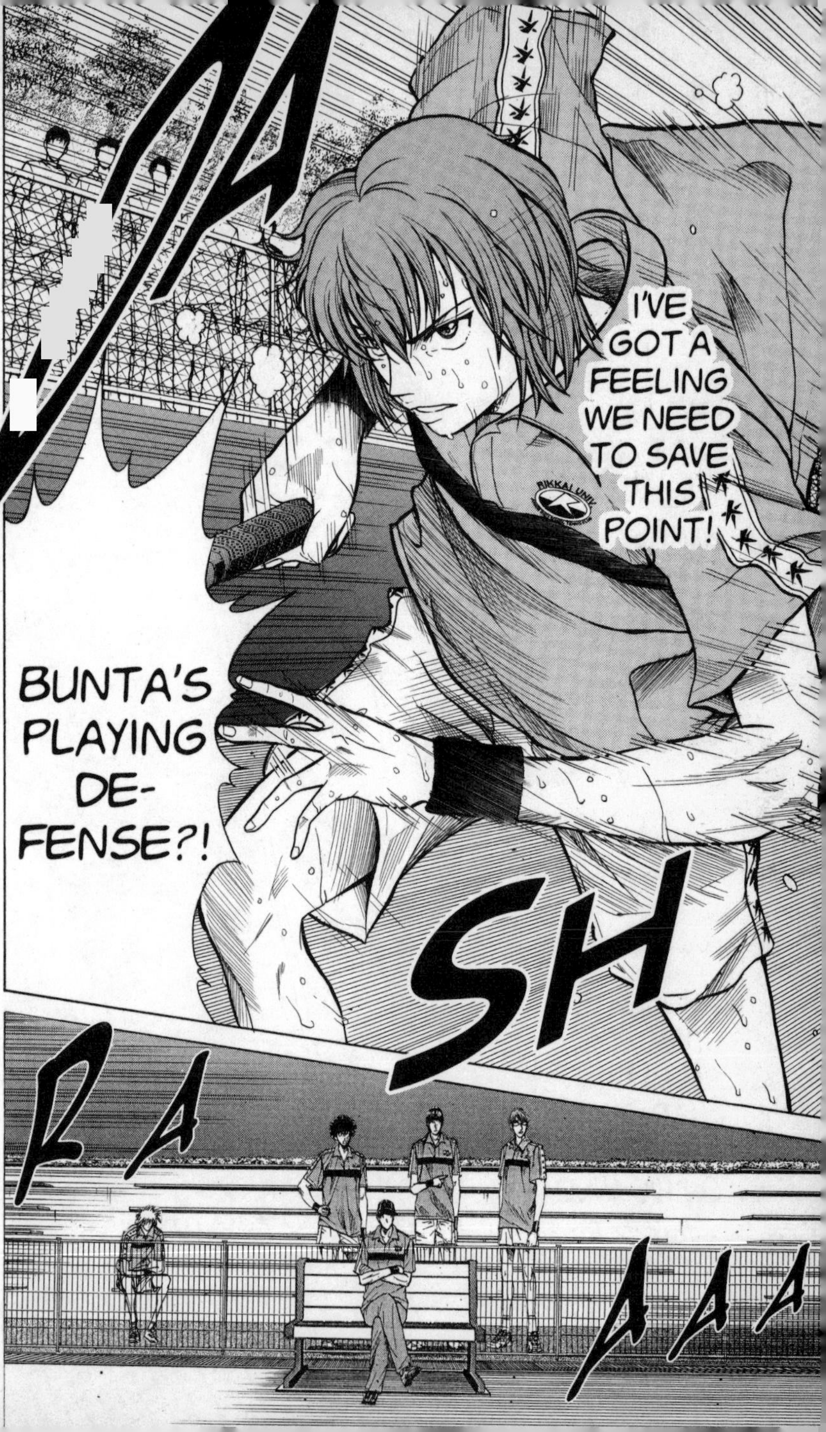
I'VE GOT A FEELING WE NEED TO SAVE THIS POINT!
BUNTA'S PLAYING DE-FENSE?!

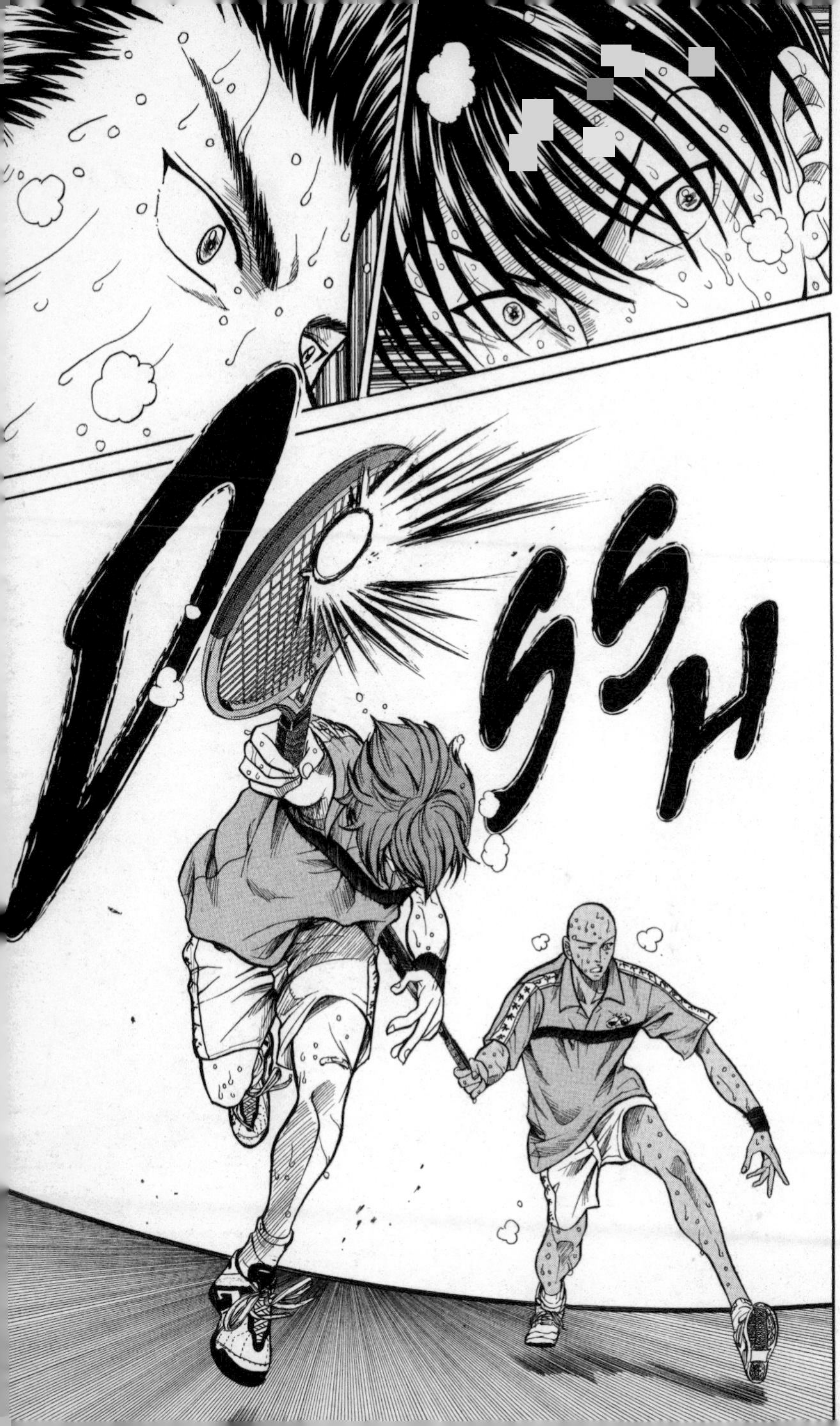
VSSH

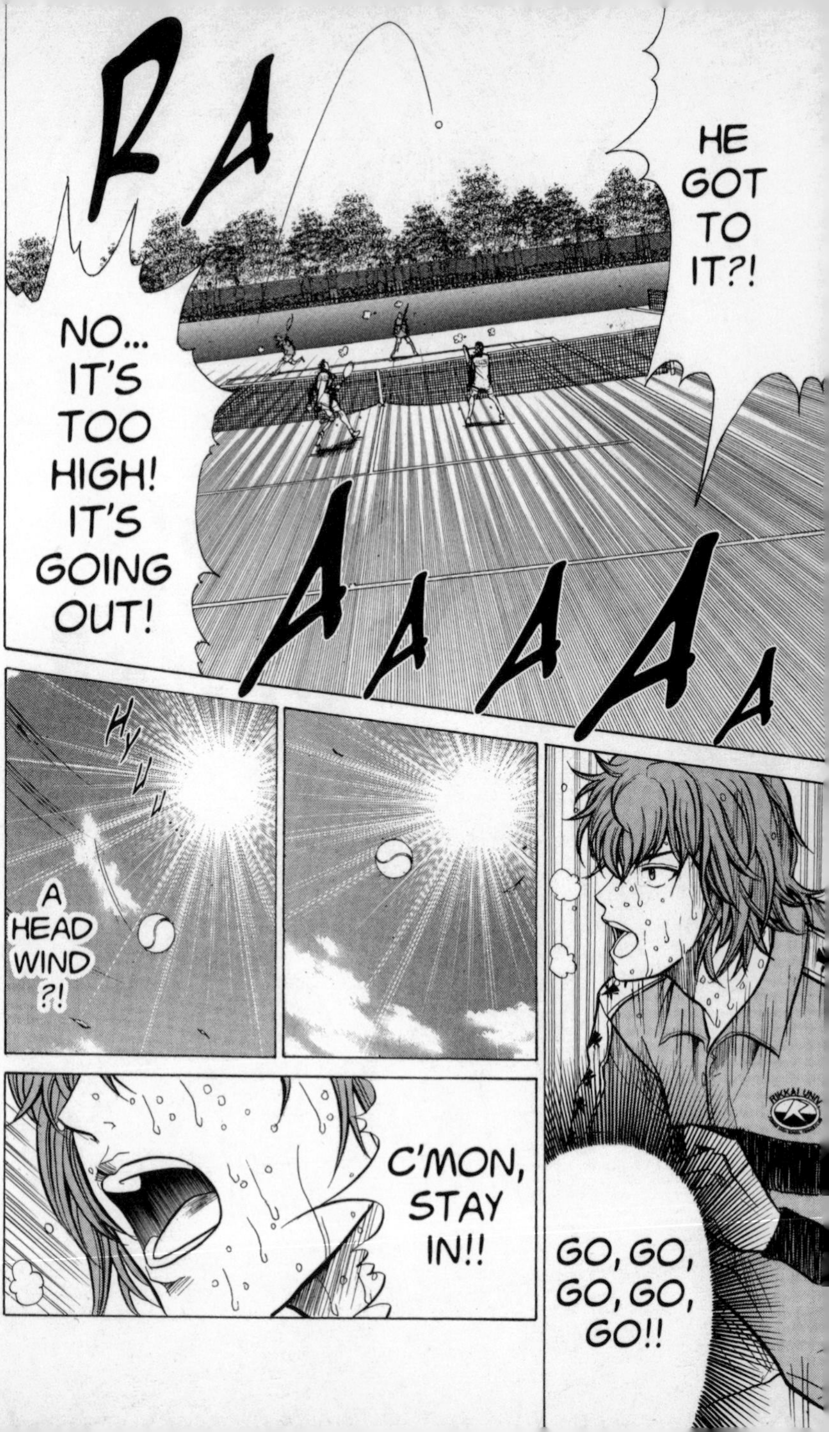
HE GOT TO IT?!
RAAAAAA
NO... IT'S TOO HIGH! IT'S GOING OUT!
RIKKAI UNIV.
GO, GO, GO, GO, GO!!
HYUUU
A HEAD WIND ?!
C'MON, STAY IN!!

READ THIS WAY

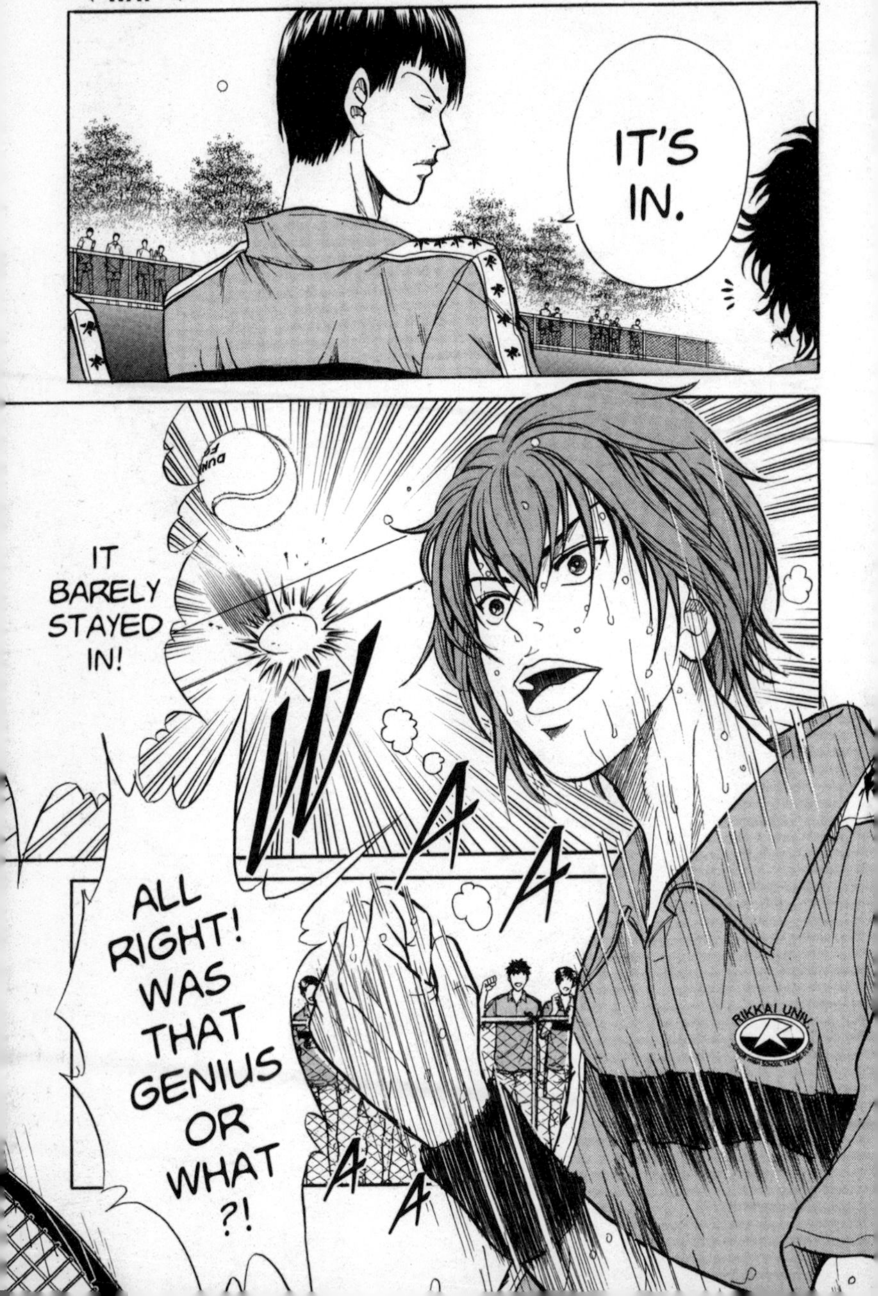
IT'S IN.
IT BARELY STAYED IN!
WAAAAA
RIKKAI UNIV.
ALL RIGHT! WAS THAT GENIUS OR WHAT?!

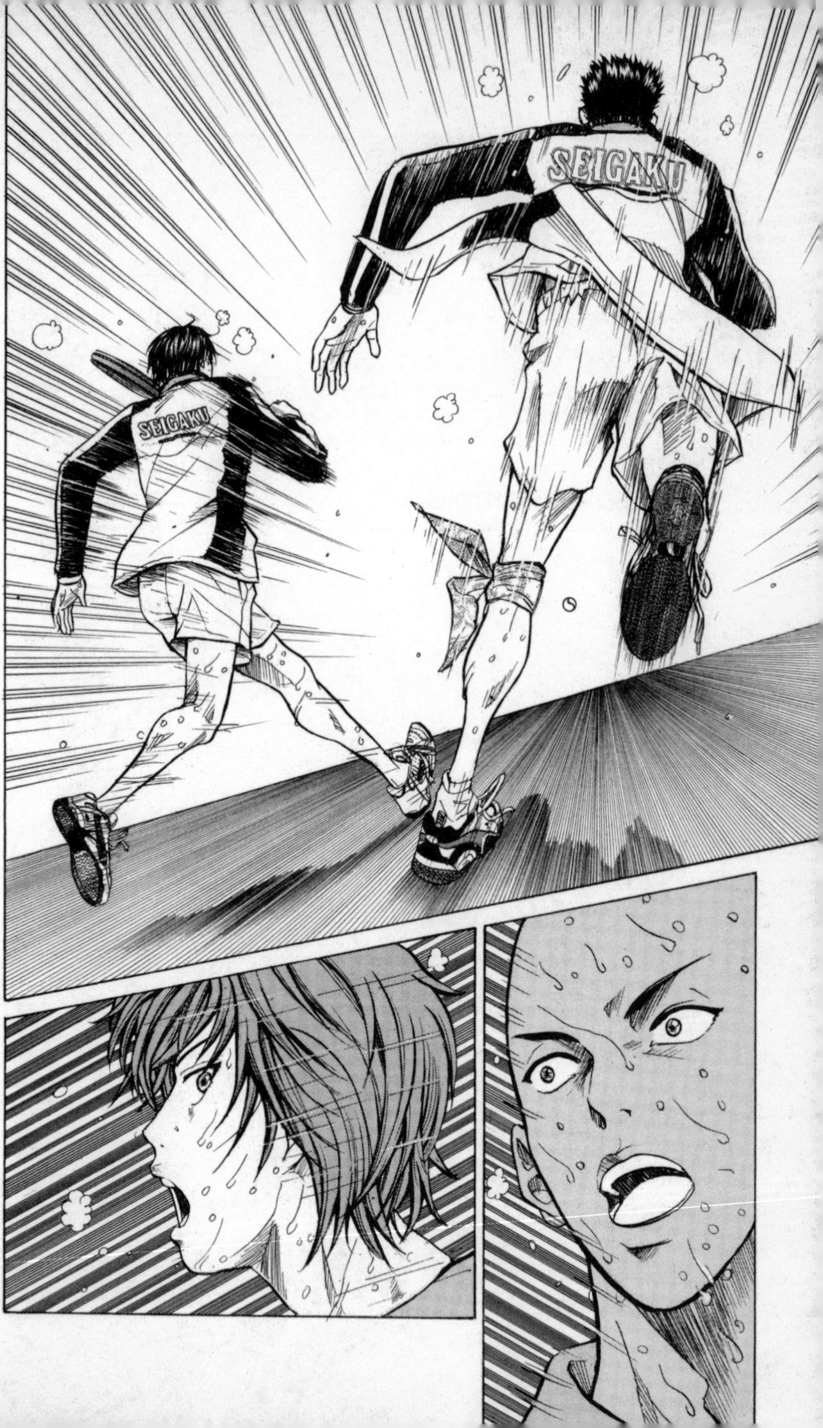
SEIGAKU
SEIGAKU

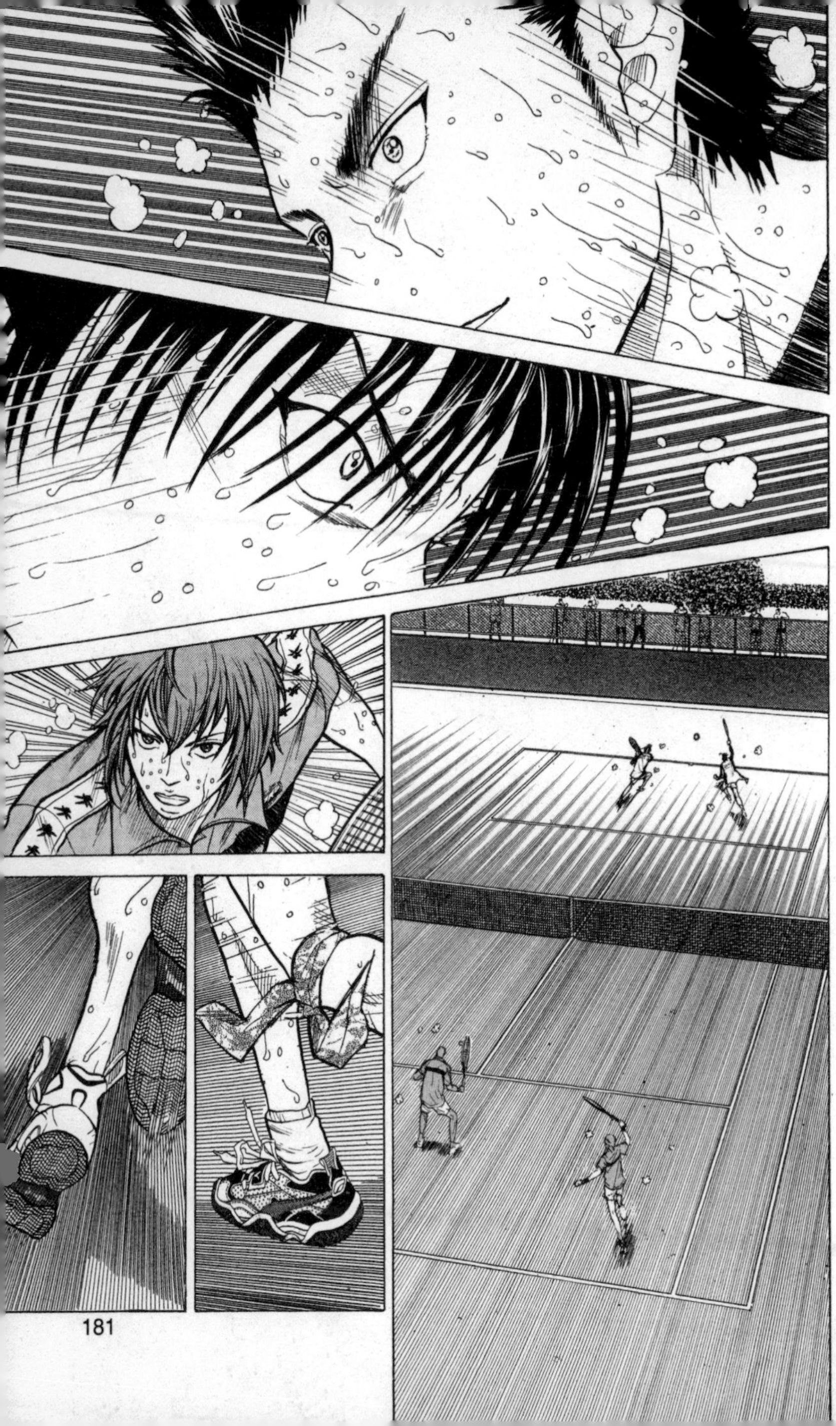

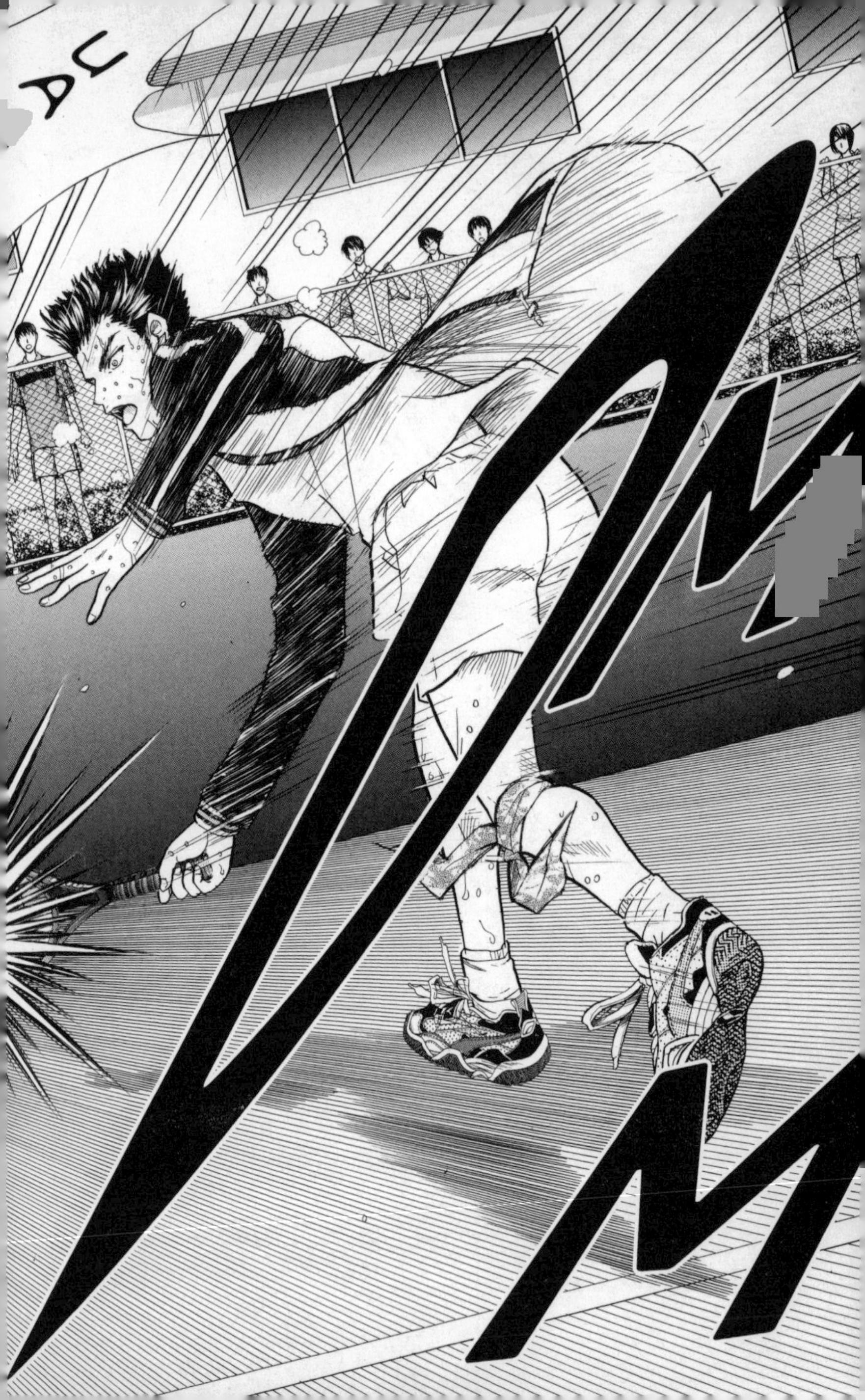

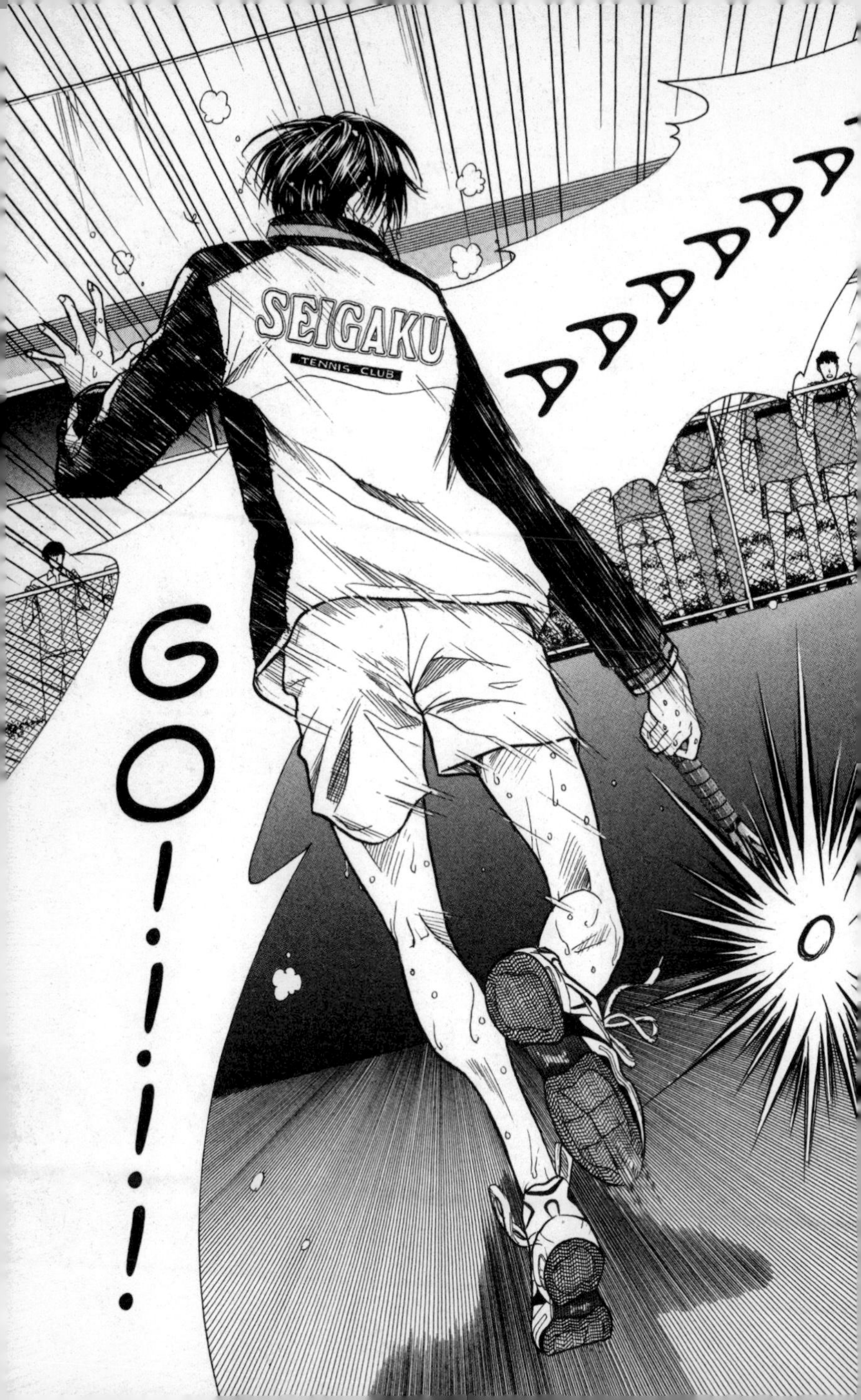
AAAAAAA
SEIGAKU
TENNIS CLUB
GO!!!!

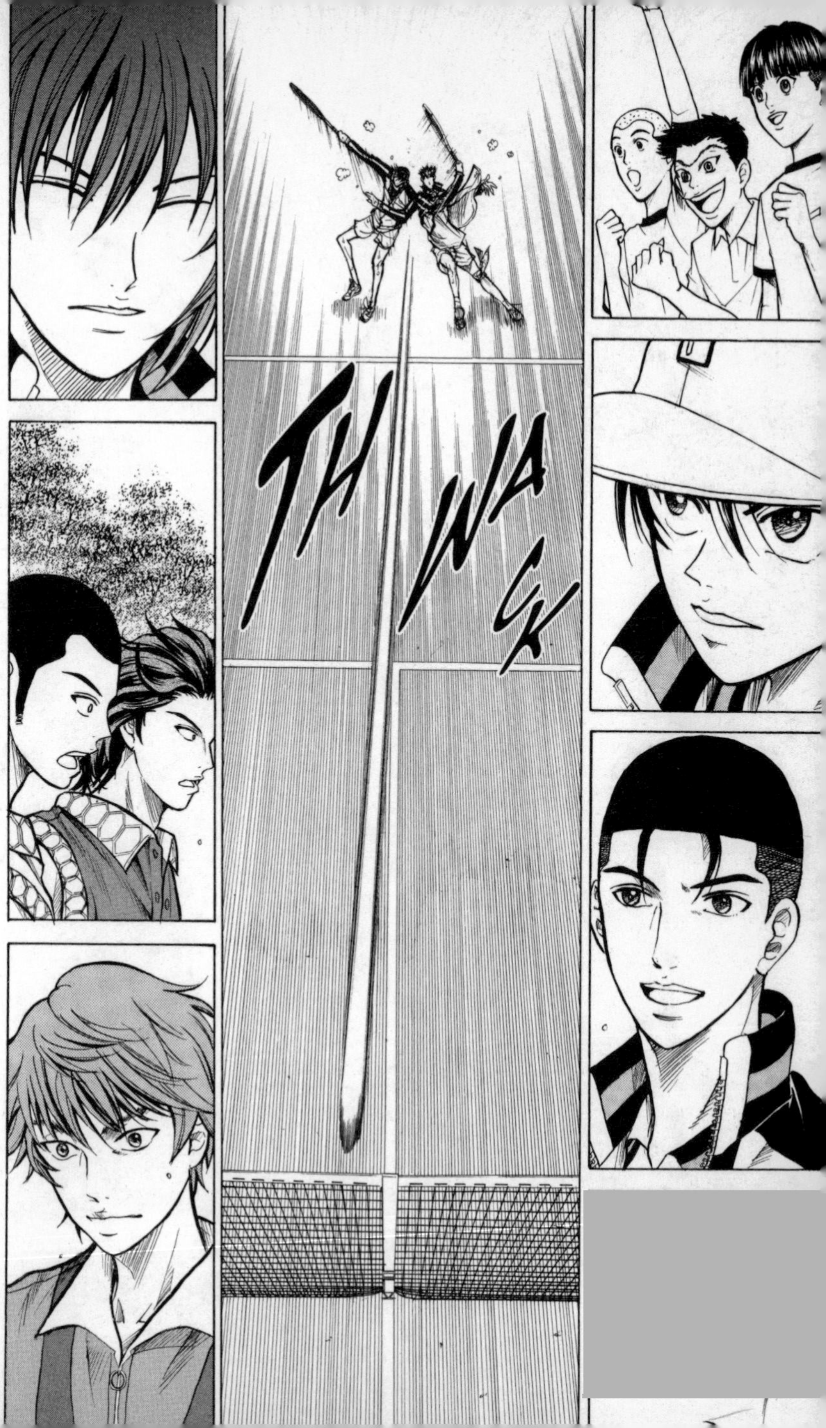
THWACK

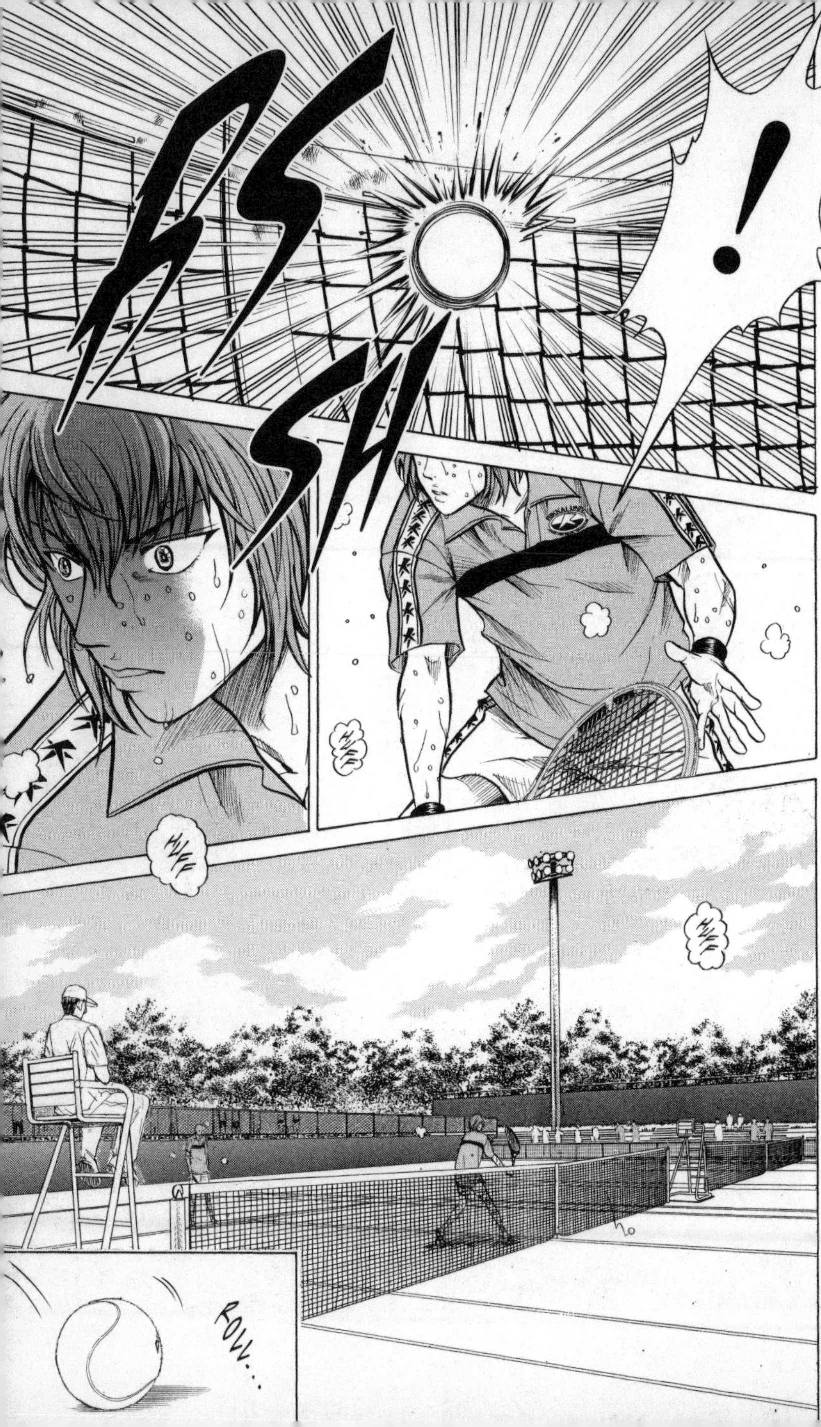
!
HUFF
HUFF
HUFF
ROLL...

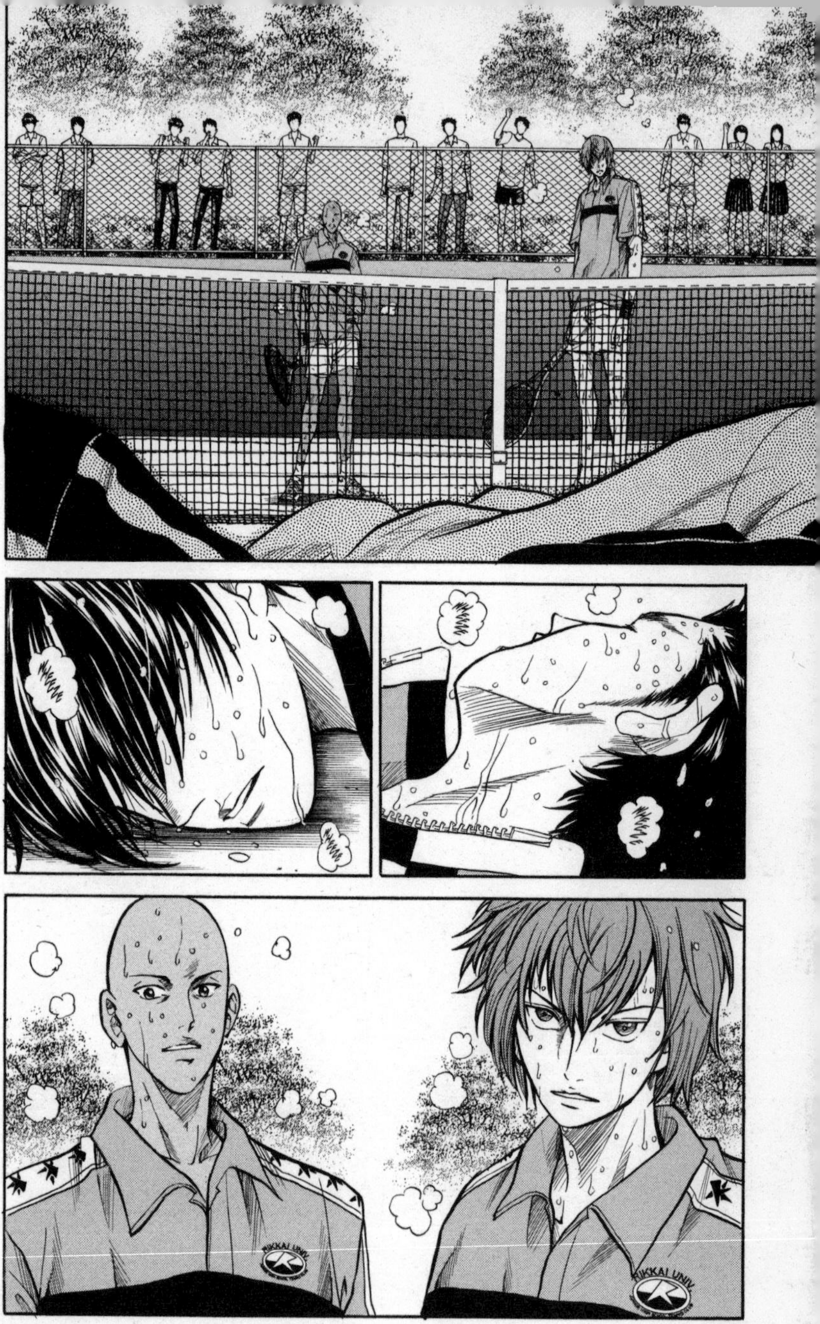

READ THIS WAY

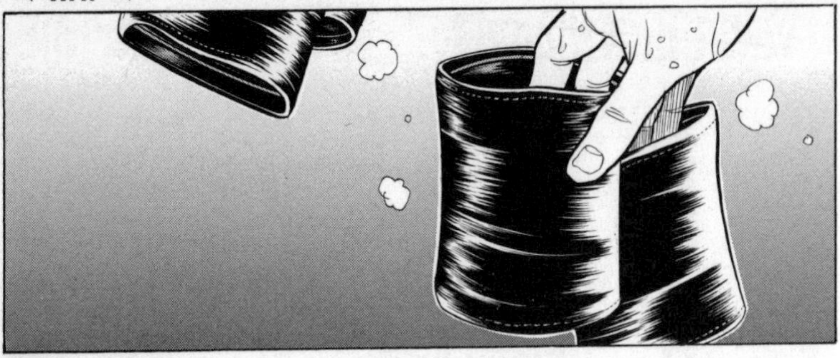

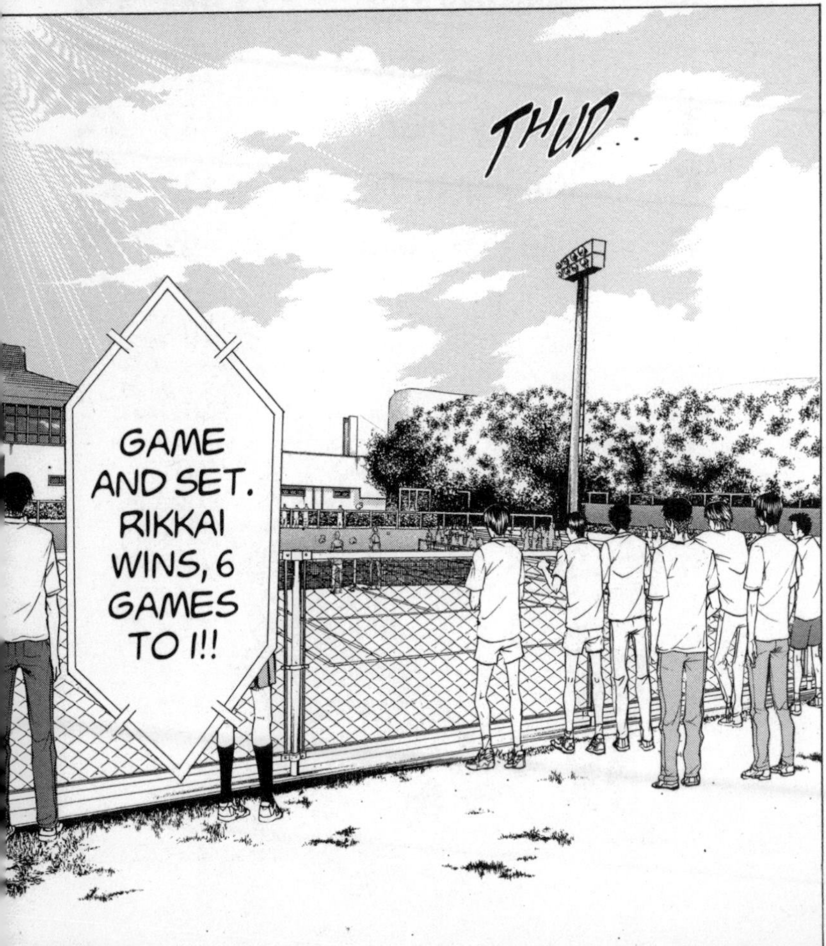
THUD...
GAME AND SET. RIKKAI WINS, 6 GAMES TO 1!!!

2004

Valentine's Day Chocolate Tally Results!!

(2,607 total)

1st	Takeshi Konomi	392
2nd	Keigo Atobe	255
3rd	Shusuke Fuji	243
4th	Ryoma Echizen	158
5th	Eiji Kikumaru	143
6th	Kunimitsu Tezuka	128
7th	Sadaharu Inui	97

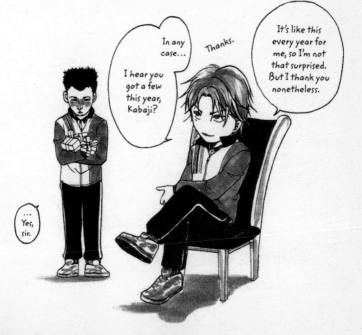

It's like this every year for me, so I'm not that surprised. But I thank you nonetheless.
Thanks.
In any case...
I hear you got a few this year, Kabaji?
...Yes, sir.

8th	Kaoru Kaido	92
9th	Yushi Oshitori	91
10th	Chotaro Otori	86
11th	Bunta Marui	70
12th	Ryo Shishido	67
13th	Takeshi Momoshiro	66
14th	Jiro Akutagawa	51
15th	Seiichi Yukimura	48
15th	Masaharu Nio	48
15th	Gakuto Mukahi	48
18th	Kiyosumi Sengoku	47
10th	Akaya Kirihara	46
20th	Shuichiro Oishi	44
21st	Wakashi Hiyoshi	33
22nd	Genichiro Sanada	29
23rd	Hiroshi Yagyu	27
24th	Kentaro Minami	24
25th	Hajime Mizuki	23
25th	Hikaru Amane	23
27th	Munehiro Kabaji	19
28th	Yuta Fuji	18
28th	Akira Kamio	18
30th	Atsushi Kisarazu	15
31st	Haginosuke Taki	10

And many others...

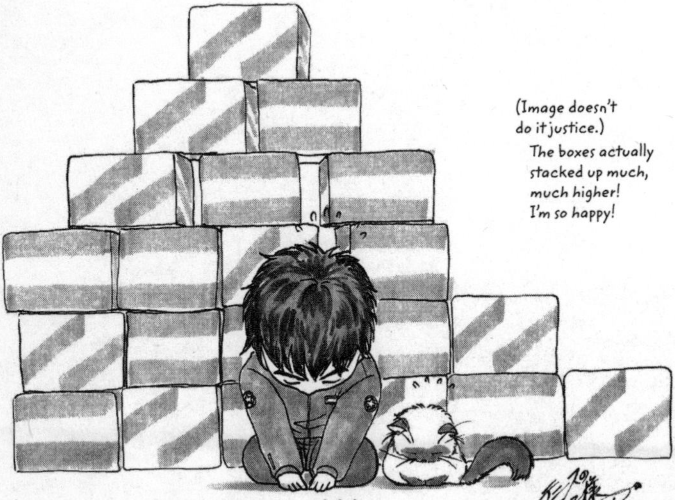

(Image doesn't do it justice.) The boxes actually stacked up much, much higher! I'm so happy!

Thank you!!!

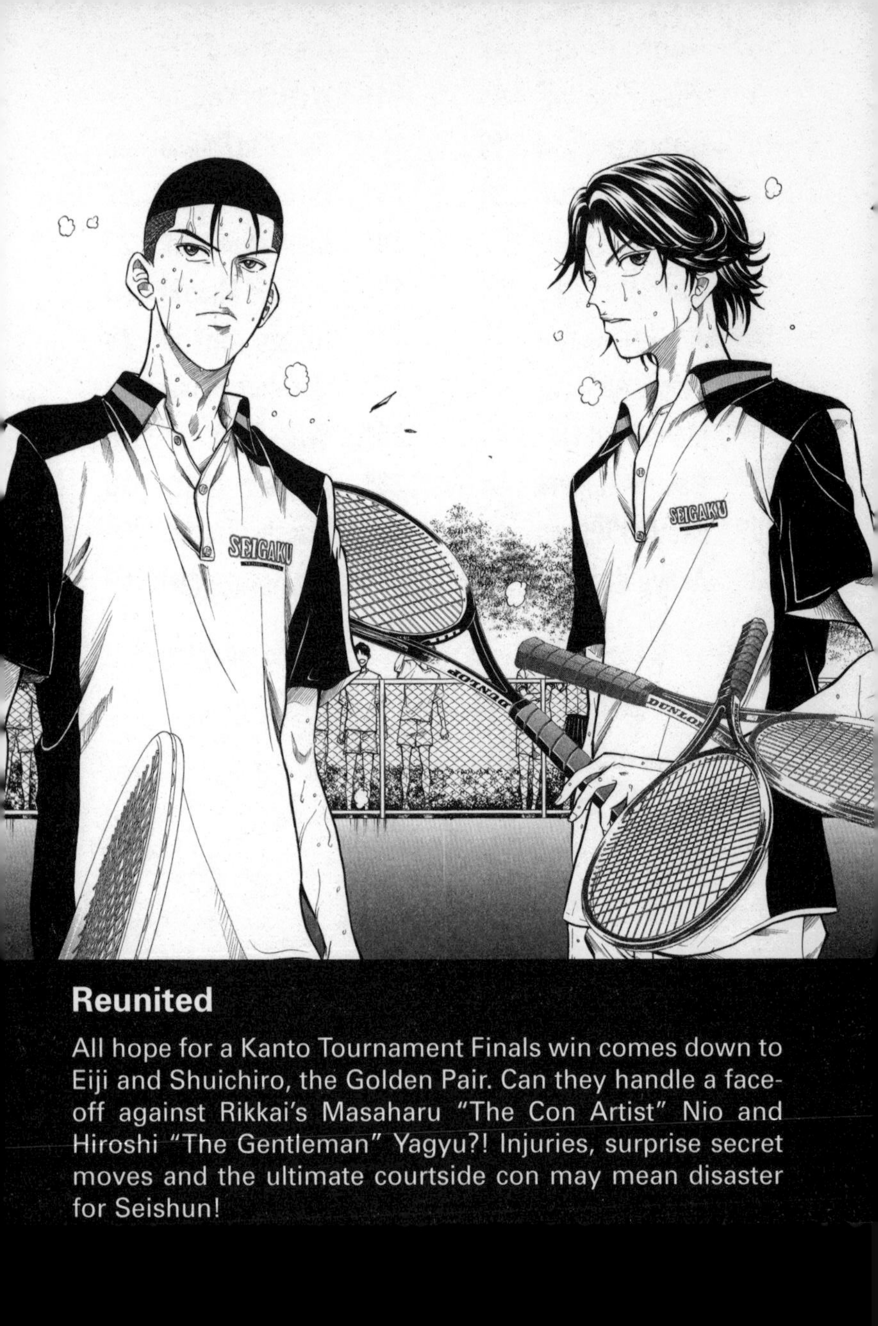
SEIGAKU
SEIGAKU

Reunited

All hope for a Kanto Tournament Finals win comes down to Eiji and Shuichiro, the Golden Pair. Can they handle a face-off against Rikkai's Masaharu "The Con Artist" Nio and Hiroshi "The Gentleman" Yagyu?! Injuries, surprise secret moves and the ultimate courtside con may mean disaster for Seishun!

テニスの王子様

THE PRINCE OF TENNIS

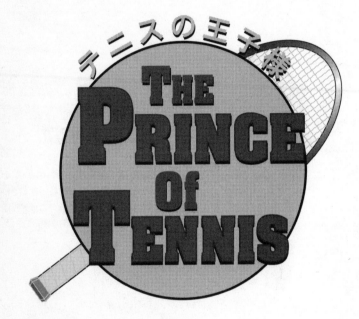

THE PERFECT MATCH!

SHONEN JUMP™

THE PRINCE OF TENNIS ™

WELCOME SHONEN JUMP HOME VIDEO'S NEWEST TEAM MEMBER

The Prince of Tennis anime is now being served in collectible DVD box sets. Get the complete *The Prince of Tennis* collection today!

13 episodes
3 discs

THE PRINCE OF TENNIS
DVD Box Set, Vol. 1
Buy yours today!

THE PRINCE OF TENNIS
BOX SET VOLUME 1

SHONEN JUMP
HOME VIDEO
www.shonenjump.com

Original works © 1999 TAKESHI KONOMI
Animation series and products derived thereof © 2001 NAS • TV TOKYO
All Rights Reserved.

viz media
www.viz.com

SJ

Hikaru no Go™

Manga on sale now!

$7.95

HIKARU NO GO 1
Yumi Hotta
Takeshi Obata

SHONEN JUMP GRAPHIC NOVEL

Hikaru no Go

Story by **Yumi Hotta** Art by **Takeshi Obata**
Supervised by **Yukari Umezawa (5 Dan)**

volume **1**

VIZ

An ancient ghost possesses Hikaru and unleashes his hidden genius!

SHONEN JUMP
MANGA

HIKARU-NO GO © 1998 by Yumi Hotta, Takeshi Obata/SHUEISHA Inc

On sale at:
www.shonenjump.com
Also available at your local
bookstore and comic store.

www.viz.com

WHISTLE!

Manga on sale now!

WHISTLE!

$7.⁹⁹

When the whistle blows, get ready for rip-roaring soccer action!

WHISTLE! © 1998 by Daisuke Higuchi/SHUEISHA Inc.

On sale at:
www.shonenjump.com
Also available at your local
bookstore and comic store.

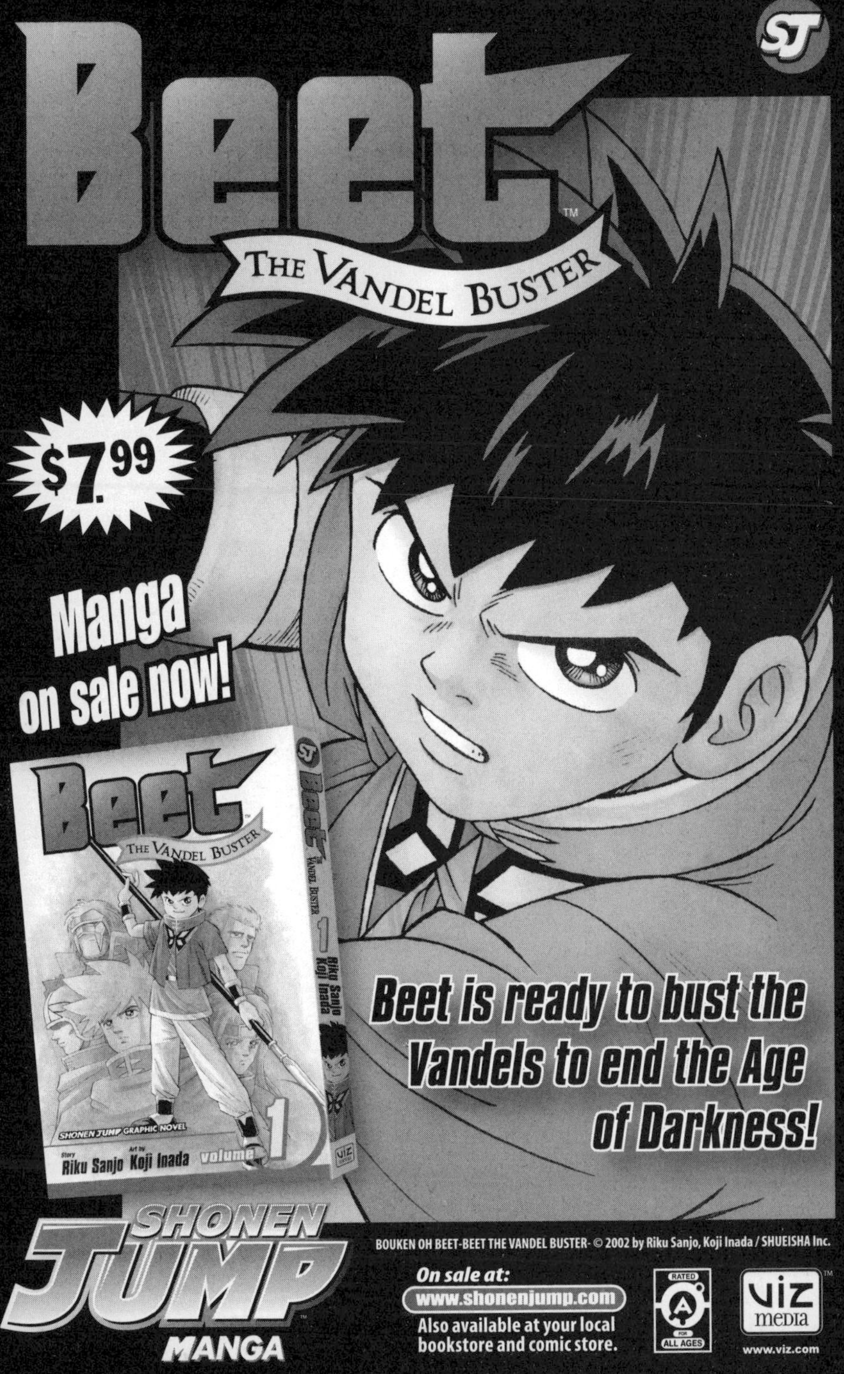
SJ
Beet™
THE VANDEL BUSTER
$7.99
Manga on sale now!
Beet THE VANDEL BUSTER
SHONEN JUMP GRAPHIC NOVEL
Story Riku Sanjo Art by Koji Inada
volume 1
Beet is ready to bust the Vandels to end the Age of Darkness!
SHONEN JUMP MANGA
BOUKEN OH BEET-BEET THE VANDEL BUSTER- © 2002 by Riku Sanjo, Koji Inada / SHUEISHA Inc.
On sale at:
www.shonenjump.com
Also available at your local bookstore and comic store.
RATED A FOR ALL AGES
viz media
www.viz.com

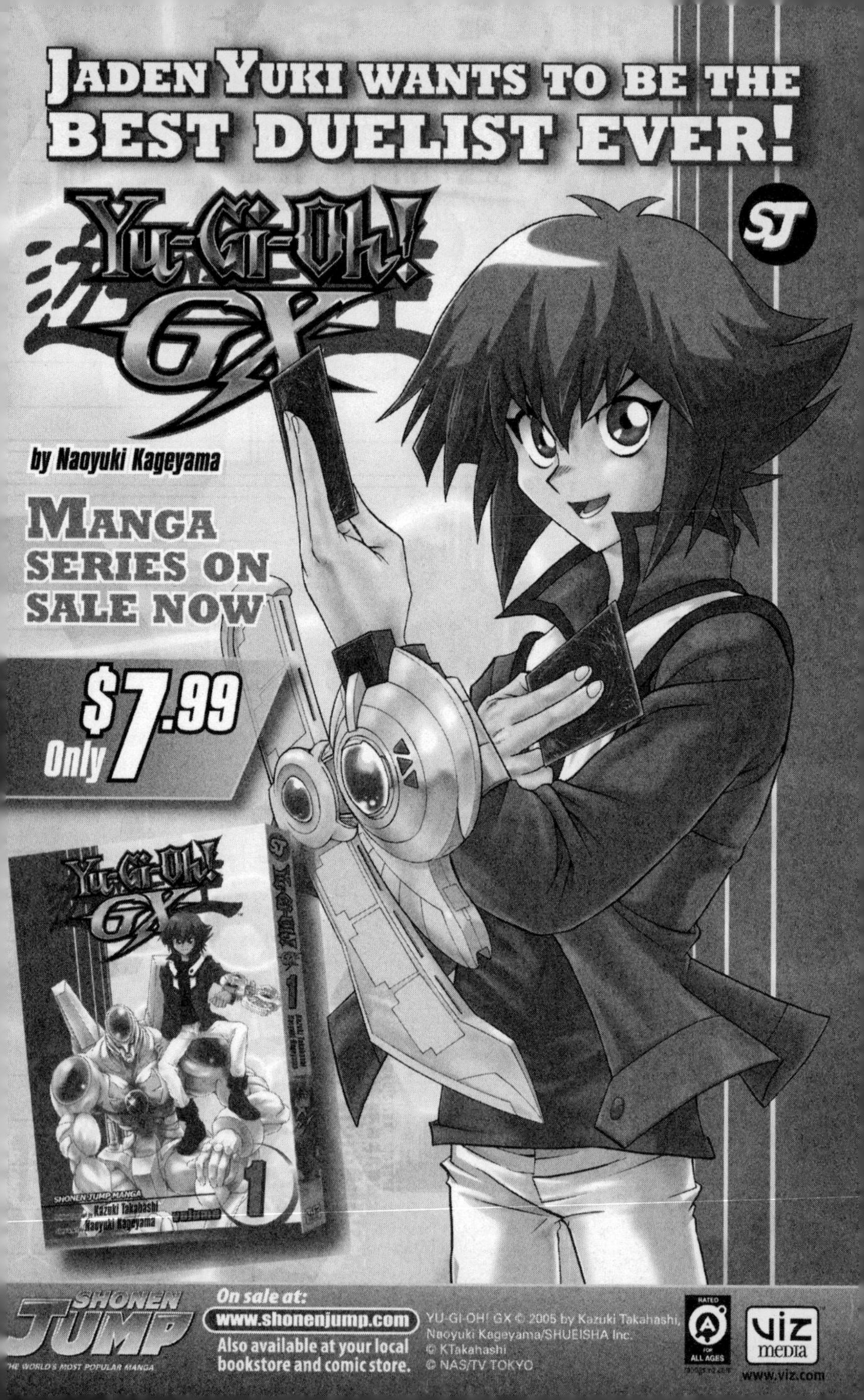

JADEN YUKI WANTS TO BE THE
BEST DUELIST EVER!
SJ
YU-GI-OH! GX
by Naoyuki Kageyama
MANGA
SERIES ON
SALE NOW
Only $7.99
YU-GI-OH! GX
1
SHONEN JUMP MANGA
Kazuki Takahashi
Naoyuki Kageyama
SHONEN JUMP
THE WORLD'S MOST POPULAR MANGA
On sale at:
www.shonenjump.com
Also available at your local
bookstore and comic store.
YU-GI-OH! GX © 2005 by Kazuki Takahashi,
Naoyuki Kageyama/SHUEISHA Inc.
© KTakahashi
© NAS/TV TOKYO
RATED A FOR ALL AGES
VIZ MEDIA
www.viz.com

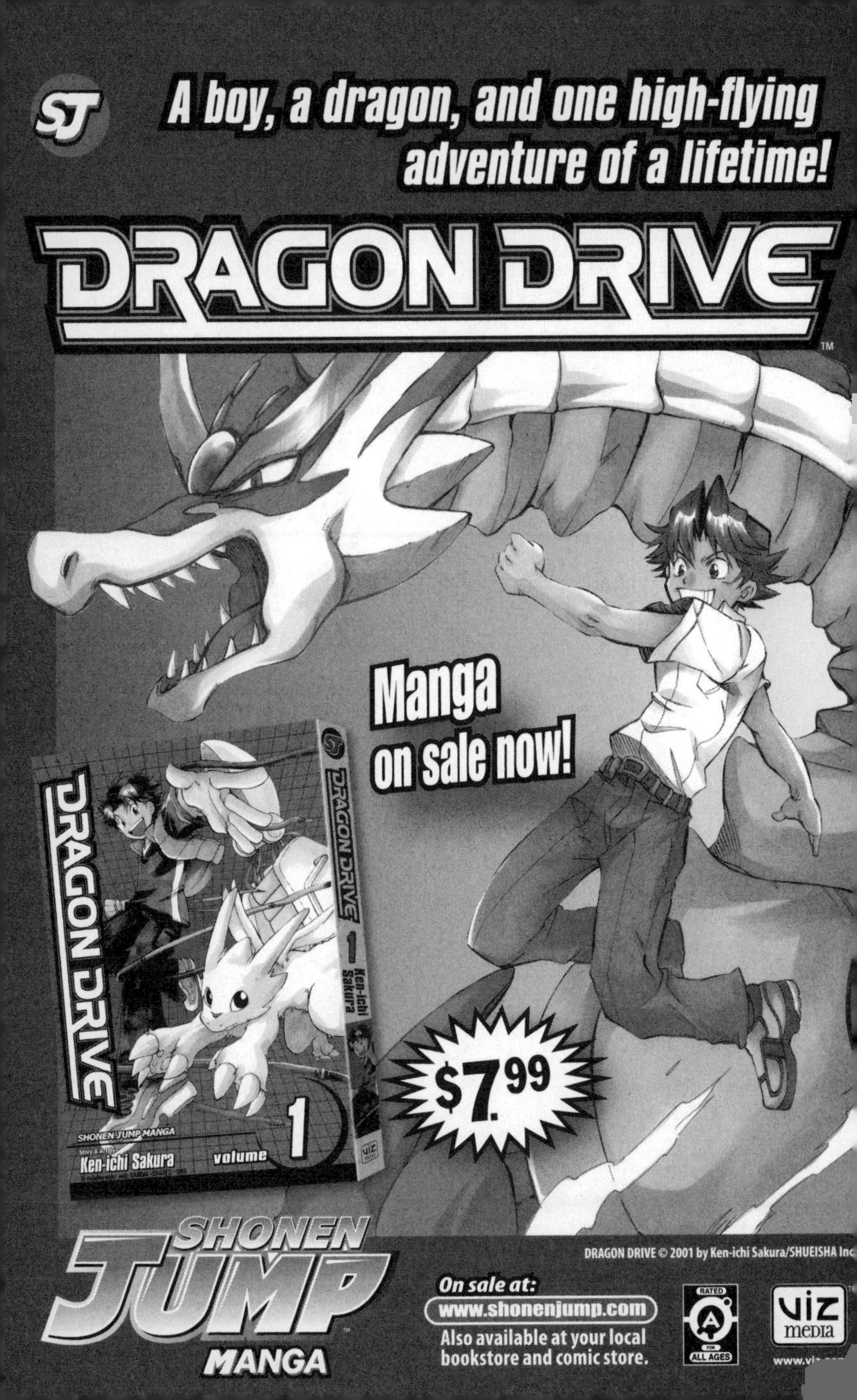
SJ
A boy, a dragon, and one high-flying adventure of a lifetime!
DRAGON DRIVE™
Manga on sale now!
DRAGON DRIVE
SJ
DRAGON DRIVE
1
Ken-ichi Sakura
SHONEN JUMP MANGA
Story & Art by
Ken-ichi Sakura
volume 1
$7.99
SHONEN JUMP™ MANGA
DRAGON DRIVE © 2001 by Ken-ichi Sakura/SHUEISHA Inc
On sale at:
www.shonenjump.com
Also available at your local bookstore and comic store.
RATED A FOR ALL AGES
viz media

Tell us what you think about SHONEN JUMP manga!

Our survey is now available online.
Go to: **www.SHONENJUMP.com/mangasurvey**

Help us make our product offering better!

THE REAL ACTION STARTS IN...

THE WORLD'S MOST POPULAR MANGA
www.shonenjump.com

ST ADVANCED

ST

VIZ MEDIA

BLEACH © 2001 by Tite Kubo/SHUEISHA Inc. NARUTO © 1999 by Masashi Kishimoto/SHUEISHA Inc.

Save 50% off the newsstand price!

WASHOE COUNTY LIBRARY

3 1235 03509 7240

JUMP
TM
THE WORLD'S MOST POPULAR MANGA

SUBSCRIBE TODAY and SAVE 50% OFF the cover price PLUS enjoy all the benefits of the SHONEN JUMP SUBSCRIBER CLUB, exclusive online content & special gifts ONLY AVAILABLE to SUBSCRIBERS!

☑ **YES!** Please enter my 1 year subscription (12 issues) to *SHONEN JUMP* at the INCREDIBLY LOW SUBSCRIPTION RATE of $29.95 and sign me up for the SHONEN JUMP Subscriber Club!

Only $29⁹⁵!

NAME

ADDRESS

CITY   STATE   ZIP

E-MAIL ADDRESS

☐ MY CHECK IS ENCLOSED   ☐ BILL ME LATER

CREDIT CARD: ☐ VISA   ☐ MASTERCARD

ACCOUNT #   EXP. DATE

SIGNATURE

CLIP AND MAIL TO →

SHONEN JUMP
Subscriptions Service Dept.
P.O. Box 515
Mount Morris, IL 61054-0515

Make checks payable to: **SHONEN JUMP.**
Canada add US $12. No foreign orders. Allow 6-8 weeks for delivery.

P6SJGN   YU-GI-OH! © 1996 by Kazuki Takahashi / SHUEISHA Inc.